Location Aware Apps for Tourism
Writing Smartphone Applications for the Tourism Market

by

Cathal Greaney

March 2011

Location Aware Apps for Tourism
by Cathal Greaney

Copyright © 2011 Cathal Greaney.
All rights reserved.
ISBN 978-1-291-08347-7

March 2011 First Edition

Acknowledgements

I would like to thank Dr. Martin Hayes of the University of Limerick for his patience and support during the course of this book. He gave freely of his time, often at short notice, and helped me greatly in deciding which areas to research and experiment.

About the Author

Cathal Greaney is a software engineer living in Galway, Ireland. He has worked as a Software Engineer/Developer for the past 10 years specializing in Smartphone Software Development since early 2007. He completed a Masters Degree in March 2011 and wrote this book as a result of the research he carried out into the suitability of modern smartphones to provide useful functionality to the tourist as an end user.

Cathal can be contacted at:

irishapps@gmail.com

www.irishapps.org
http://www.linkedin.com/pub/cathal-greaney/19/896/788

Preface

I wrote this book to investigate the usefulness of the modern smartphone for providing location aware applications to the tourist as an end user.

During the course of this book I've demonstrated that the modern smartphone has the accuracy and responsiveness required to provide excellent location aware functionality to the tourist end user. This book has proven that global navigation satellite systems such as GPS provide the resolution, accuracy and responsiveness required to cater for the tourism sector. It has been demonstrated that bluetooth and other technologies such as QR coding are effective at providing location aware functionality in situations where GNSS(GPS) is ineffective, such as in indoor environments.
It has also been demonstrated that the modern smartphone has the power and capacity to provide the internationalization features that are necessary when dealing with many different nationalities, as is typically the case in the tourism sector.

The results of the experiments give a clear indication of the maximum accuracy that is possible from modern smartphone hardware and operating systems up to March 2011. The experiments also demonstrate the minimum accuracy necessary for effective location aware functionality.
GPS accuracy, resolution and responsiveness has been measured and quantified.
Bluetooth discovery and pairing procedures have been examined in the environments used by tourists. QR Code scanning times have been recorded to measure their effectiveness to the tourism sector.

It can be concluded from this book that modern smartphones as of March 2011, have the necessary processing power, sensor hardware and operating system functionality, to differentiate between premises in densely packed shopping districts and other areas that tourists frequent.

Table of Contents

1.	**Introduction**	1
1.1	Objectives	1
1.2	Smartphones and Location Aware Applications	2
	1.2.1 What is a Smartphone	2
	1.2.2 What is a Location Aware Application	4
1.3	Physical Locations Referred to During the Project	4
	1.3.1 Shop St. Galway	5
	1.3.2 Galway Shopping Centre	5
	1.3.3 Caherconnell Folk Park	6
	1.3.4 Bunratty Castle and Folk Park	6
1.4	Existing Smartphone Applications for Tourism	7
	1.4.1 Existing Location Based Apps for Tourism	7
	1.4.2 Existing Translation Based Apps for Tourism	11
	1.4.3 Existing Bluetooth Apps for Tourism	11
1.5	Layout of Report	12
2.	**Software, Operating Systems and SDKs for Smartphones**	13
2.1	An Overview	13
2.2	Apple iOS	14
	2.2.1 iOS Software	15
	2.2.2 iOS SDK	15
	2.2.3 iOS Smartphones	16
2.3	Google Android OS	17
	2.3.1 Android Software	18
	2.3.2 Android SDK	19
	2.3.3 Android Smartphones	20
2.4	iOS and Android Comparison	23
	2.4.1 Worldwide Market Share	23
	2.4.2 SDK Differences and the Development Experience	24
	2.4.3 Location Aware Programming Techniques	28
	2.4.3.1 iOS Core Location	28
	2.4.3.2 Android Location Services	29
	2.4.4 Database Programming Techniques	29
	2.4.5 Bluetooth Programming Techniques	30
2.5	Nokia OS	31
	2.5.1 Nokia Software	32
	2.5.2 Maemo SDK	33
	2.5.3 Qt SDK	33
	2.5.4 Nokia Smartphones	34
2.6	RIM Blackberry OS	34
	2.6.1 Blackberry Software	34
	2.6.2 Blackberry SDK	34
	2.6.3 Blackberry Smartphones	35
2.7	Microsoft Mobile OS	35
	2.7.1 Microsoft Software for Mobiles	35
	2.7.2 Windows Mobile 6.5 SDK	36
	2.7.3 Windows Phone 7.0 SDK	36
	2.7.4 Microsoft Smartphones	37
2.8	HP Palm OS and WebOS	37
	2.8.1 Palm Software	37
	2.8.2 Palm WebOS SDK	38
	2.8.3 Palm WebOS Smartphones	38

Table of Contents

2.9	Other Mobile Software, OS and SDKs	38
	2.9.1 Java ME	38
	2.9.2 Flash Lite	39
	2.9.3 Lazarus/Python/Brew	39
2.10	Web Development vs SDK	40
	2.10.1 Comparing the Two Programming Styles	40
	2.10.2 Advantages and Disadvantages	40
	2.10.3 Web Development	41
	2.10.4 Web Development Models	41
	2.10.5 SDK Development	42
2.11	Smartphone Databases	42
	2.11.1 SQLite Mobile Database	42
	2.11.2 Microsoft SQL Server Compact Database	43
	2.11.3 Oracle DBLite Database	44
	2.11.4 IBM DB2 Everyplace Database	44
	2.11.5 Sybase SQL Anywhere Database	45
3.	**Technology Available for Building Tourism & Location Aware Applications**	**46**
3.1	Global Navigation Satellite Systems[GNSS]	47
	3.1.1 General Navigation	47
	3.1.2 GPS Predecessors	47
	3.1.3 Introduction to Galileo	48
	3.1.4 Satellite Based Augmentation System[SBAS]	48
	3.1.5 How GNSS Work	48
	3.1.6 Current GNSS	48
	3.1.6.1/2/3 GPS/GLONASS/Galileo	48
	3.1.7 Commercial Applications	48
	3.1.8 Tourism Market	49
	3.1.9 System Limitations and Vulnerabilities	49
	3.1.10 Dual Receivers	49
3.2	GNSS Experiments	49
	3.2.1 Establish Very Accurate(<=3m) Baseline GPS Coordinates for Locations in the Galway Area by Using a Calibrated GPS Recording Device.	50
	3.2.2 Test the Accuracy of the GPS Functionality on the Samsung GalaxyS Smartphone and the Apple iPhone 3GS while in a Stationary Position.	57
	3.2.3 Establish the Accuracy of Google and Yahoo Maps in the Galway and Limerick Area.	62
	3.2.4 Investigate the Possibility of Using GPS Technology for Indoor Use.	65
	3.2.5 Test the Accuracy of the GPS Functionality on the Samsung GalaxyS Smartphone and the Apple iPhone 3GS while Walking at 3 KPH.	67
	3.2.6 Test the Accuracy of GPS on the Android and iOS Operating Systems using the Latest Hardware (Samsung GalaxyS/Nexus S and Apple iPhone 3Gs/4).	83
3.3	WiFi	103
3.4	GSM Tower Triangulation	103
3.5	Bluetooth	103
	3.5.1 Basic Programming Essentials	104
	3.5.2 Important Bluetooth Concepts	109
	3.5.3 Limitations of Bluetooth	111
	3.5.4 Device Discovery	112
	3.5.5 Bluetooth Stacks	112

Table of Contents

3.6		Bluetooth Experiments	114
	3.6.1	Test the Ability of the Samsung Galaxy S to Discover Bluetooth Devices	114
	3.6.2	Examine the Characteristics of the Bluetooth RSSI Signal in an Open Unobstructed Static Environment	115
	3.6.3	Test the Ability of the Samsung Galaxy S to Detect Multiple Bluetooth Signals at Different Distances in an Unobstructed Space	119
	3.6.4	Examine the Characteristics of the Bluetooth RSSI Signal in an Open Unobstructed Space at Different Distances	122
	3.6.5	Determine the Drop in Bluetooth Discovery Performance Due to Different Obstructions and Materials	126
	3.6.6	Examine the Drop in Bluetooth RSSI Signal Strength Due to Different Materials Placed Between the Receiver and Transmitter	130
	3.6.7	Test Bluetooth Discovery Performance in an Indoor Shopping Ctr	135
	3.6.8	Measure the Time Required for Two Android Bluetooth Devices to Establish a Pairing Relationship and then Share Information	140
3.7		Hybrid Positioning Systems	142
3.8		Assisted GPS	142
3.9		2D Codes	142
	3.9.1	2D Code Reader Providers	143
	3.9.2	QR Codes	144
	3.9.3	Other 2D Code Types	149
	3.9.4	SPARQ Codes	151
3.10		2D Code Experiments	151
	3.10.1	Using 2D Codes to Provide Tourist Information	151
3.11		Near Field Communications[NFC]	159
3.12		Augmented Reality	159
4.		**Localisation and Internationalization for Tourism**	**161**
4.1		Manual Language Translation	161
4.2		Automatic Language Translation	162
4.3		Manual Translation using AndroidOS	162
4.4		Manual Translation using iOS	163
4.5		Bunratty Case Study	164
	4.5.1	The 'Bunratty Translate' Software App	165
	4.5.2	Translate Software App Results	166
	4.5.3	Manual vs Auto Translation Results	167
	4.5.4	Manually Translated Files	172
5.		**Discussion and Conclusions**	**177**
	5.1	Global Navigation Satellite Systems	177
	5.2	Bluetooth	177
	5.3	2D Codes	178
	5.4	Smartphones and Operating Systems	178
	5.5	Objectives	179
	5.6	Recommendations for Future Work	179
	5.7	Future Trends	180
	5.8	Final Comments	180
		Bibliography	**181**

Table of Contents

Appendix A

A1.	Visual Basic Source Code for Experiment 3.2.1	Appendix p1
A2.	Java Source Code for 'GPS Auto Log' Android Application for Experiment 3.2.2	Appendix p4
A3.	Java Source Code for 'GPS Galway' Android Application for Experiment 3.2.5 and 3.2.6	Appendix p15
A4.	Objective-C Source Code for 'GPS Galway' iOS Application for Experiment 3.2.5 and 3.2.6	Appendix p22
A5.	Java Source Code for 'Translate' Android Application for Chapter 4.	Appendix p27

Appendix B

B1.	Calibrated GPS Readings for Experiment 3.2.1	Appendix p31
B2.	Location Analysis for Experiment 3.2.1	Appendix p34
B3.	Raw GPS Data Overlaid onto Google/Yahoo Maps for Experiment 3.2.3	Appendix p38

Appendix C

C1.	Photos and Videos from the GPS Experiments	Appendix p42
C2.	Photos and Videos from the 2D Code Experiments	Appendix p42
C3.	Photos and Videos from the Bluetooth Experiments	Appendix p42

Appendix D

D1.	NFC Enabled Mobile Phones	Appendix p44

1. Introduction

While writing this book I've analysed the latest smartphone technology available up to March 2011. The smartphone industry is a rapidly evolving one and new technologies and innovations are appearing on a monthly basis. The evolution of the smartphone and the evolution of location aware services has gone hand in hand. Ever improving hardware has driven the demand for ever more sophisticated and accurate location aware functionality on handheld devices. This report aims to examine the hardware and software features available on the modern smartphone for providing useful functionality to the tourism industry, concentrating primarily on the location based functionality available to the developer of smartphone applications.

Location aware applications are allowing tourism operators and other commercial operators to more closely target the consumer and provide services and offers based on an individuals location in space and based on the preferences that the user has indicated by interacting with a smartphone application.
Future trends in this area are difficult to predict. It is reasonable to assume that personalised and customised content, being presented to an individual consumer based on their location in space and on other factors, will continue to expand rapidly. As more and more information about individuals enters the public domain through social media, and more accurate information about a persons location becomes available, it is inevitable that marketing and advertising companies will seize on the opportunity to provide ever more innovative methods of targeting these consumers using the above mentioned methods.

Clearly, the success of this approach to marketing and advertising is heavily dependent on the accuracy of the hardware and software being used by the end user. If the technology cannot provide an accurate location of the premises and of the customer, then location based targeting becomes impossible. It has been the focus of this book to determine if the technology available at the present time(March 2011) is good enough to begin to support this level of functionality.

During the experimental phase the focus has been to test devices to ascertain their ability to provide location information accurate enough to distinguish one premises from another adjacent premises in a densely packed tourist area such as a shopping district.

False positive situations, in which a device reports that it is closest to a promises, when in fact it is much closer to other premises is a major problem in the provisioning of location aware services and there has been a strong focus throughout the book in testing for this situation.

1.1 Objectives

The objectives have been achieved by carrying out:

1. Studies on the current market leaders in the smartphone industry.

2. Research on the leading smartphone handsets available as of March 2011.

3. Analysis of existing smartphone applications that target the tourism sector.

4. Studies into the different hardware technologies for providing location based functionality.

5. Experimentation and research on the different software options available to the smartphone developer/programmer.

6. Analysis and comparison of the different operating systems in use on modern smartphones.

7. Analysis and comparison of the different programming languages.

8. Development of custom applications so that experiments could be constructed and executed to ascertain the possibilities and limits of the leading smartphones.

9. An extensive array of hardware and software based experiments to prove/disprove the ability of the modern smartphone to provide useful location aware functionality to the tourism sector.

10. Exploration and experimentation with different techniques for internationalizing location aware smartphone applications, to allow different written languages to be used on the same application.

1.2 Smartphones and Location Aware Applications

1.2.1 What is a Smartphone

A **mobile phone** is any device that is wireless and can make a phone call.
A **feature phone** is a mini computer blended with a mobile phone which can run applications such as those supported by JavaME. Over 70% of the mobiles sold are feature phones[Gartner 2010-11-10].
A **smartphone** is powered by a complete operating system with a software platform that allows developers to develop and run advanced applications. The Apple iPhone and Android smartphones have become the industry standard for smartphones [Canalys Report 2011-02-01].
*Note: a **Nirvana phone** is considered to be the next step beyond smartphones. They are smartphone like devices that can be docked and used as full desktop computers.*

Smartphones are distinguished from feature phones by their powerful processors such as the iPhone 1 GHz ARMA8, memory up to 512Mb DRam, larger screens, and powerful operating systems.

The start of the smartphone era was 1992 when IBM launched the 'Simon' smartphone, featuring a touchscreen, address book, calendar, note pad, email, digital fax machine and many games. It operated by finger touch with an optional stylus.

Nokia produced it's first smartphone in 1996 with the Nokia Communicator 9000. It featured a hinged physical keyboard. The Nokia 9210 was the first colour smartphone and was the first to feature a truly open operating system. The Nokia 9500 was released soon after and featured a camera and WiFi. The Nokia 9300 was another advance in the smartphone world and featured a more streamlined design.

In 2007 Nokia launched the N95 which was another major step forward. It featured GPS, a 5 megapixel camera, 3G, WiFi, TV-out and other features that would become standard on future smartphones. However, it did not have a touchscreen.

The GS88 was introduced by Ericsson in 1997. It was the first phone to be marketed and branded as a smartphone. In 2000 they released the R380 which was the first use of the famous SymbianOS. They released the P800 in 2002 which was the first camera enabled smartphone.

Palm released the Treo smartphone in 2002 which featured wireless web browsing, email, calendar, and many 3rd party mobile apps that could be downloaded.

2002 saw the first Blackberry smartphone concentrating on SMS and email for the business community.

Later in 2007 Apple introduced the iPhone. It was one of the first mainstream smartphones to be controlled almost exclusively via it's touchscreen. The first generation iPhone failed to provide 3G functionality(unlike the N95) and it also didn't allow the use of any third party applications.

Google launched the Android platform in 2008 in partnership with some of the major phone manufacturers. They commissioned HTC to produce the first developer phone called the Nexus. However, HTC preceded this by introducing their own HTC Dream phone, this was the first Android phone to be commercially released.

Chapter 1

Progression of the Smartphone...

1992
IBM Simon

1996
Nokia 9000

1997
Ericsson GS88

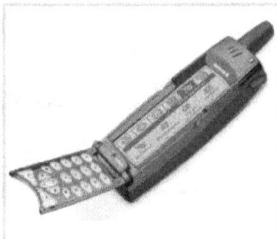
2000
Ericsson R380

2001
Nokia 9210

2002
Bberry 5810

2002
Ericsson P800

2002
Palm Treo 600

2007
Nokia N95

2007
iPhone

2008
Google Nexus

2008
HTC Dream

June 2009
iPhone 3Gs

March 2010
Samsung GalS

July 2010
iPhone4

Dec 2010
Google NexusS

The four smartphones used throughout this book

1.2.2 What is a Location Aware Application(LAA)

A Location Aware Application(LAA) is a smartphone application that is aware of it's precise geographic location and then uses this information to provide features and services to the end user.
LAAs can be used for industry, transport, parcel tracking, health and for tourism.
The first location aware application on a smartphone was the ZIP code positioning information system on the Palm VII in 1999. The first GPS based location aware applications began to emerge in 2002 after the first phones featuring built-in GPS were released in late 2001.

Examples of tourism based LAAs are shown in section 1.4.1. They include city walking tours, bus and train guides and other guides similar in format to traditional paper based tourism guides.

Many approaches are used in order to find the location of the phone user. These methods are discussed in detail throughout this report. They include WiFi, GSM, GPS and Bluetooth.

LAAs can selectively filter out the information being presented to the smartphone user based on their geographical position. Irrelevant information is relegated and the more relevant location based information can be brought to prominence on the screen.
LLAs can report the location of a shop or tourist attraction that is within walking distance of the user. Information that is geotagged(embedded with geographical coordinate metadata) can be streamed to the user in a developer defined manner. In the experimental applications written for this book, shop names and descriptions are stored in a database along with the metadata describing their location. When the user of a tourist application walks close to the shop in question, he/she can be prompted with marketing/advertising information about that shop. The less distance between the user and the target location, the more relevant the information is to that location, and the more screen space that information will occupy on the phone. When the user starts to move away from that location the information becomes less relevant and the phone presents new information to the user based on their proximity to a new location.

LAAs offer the tourist operator the opportunity to tailor the information being presented to a tourist(customer) based on their movements within a specified environment. Of course, the information in question must be overlaid with the necessary location metadata so that the application knows that it belongs to that particular location in space.

Users of modern smartphones expect data to be delivered in a seamless and speedy manner. They expect ever greater amounts of data regarding their surroundings. LAAs provide the means to superimpose a layer of data over the physical world that the tourist is occupying.

See section 1.4.1 for examples. 'Visit Dublin' Application by GeoGuides Ltd. is an example of an application superimposing location information to enhance the tourists experience while exploring a city[1.4.1].

1.3 Physical Locations Used During the Research for the Book

I've developed a number of Location Aware Applications for the purposes of testing the limits of modern smartphones. These LAAs were tested in Shop St., Galway and in the Galway Shopping Centre.

I've also developed a Language Translation Application for the purposes of testing the smartphones ability to provide internationalization features to smartphone applications. This feature was tested using tourist information from the Bunratty Folk Park in Co. Clare.

1.3.1 Shop St. Galway

Shop St. Galway is the main tourist and shopping area in Galway City. It has a wide range of shops, cafes and restaurants. There is also a wide variety of specialist and tourist oriented shops and premises.

The buildings on this street range in height from three to six storeys. The majority of the building are four storeys high.
There are 52 premises(locations) on the street counting both sides.
The west side of the street has 30 premises and the east side has 22.

The average distance between premises is 11.79m. The maximum distance from one location to the next adjacent location is 35.39m. The minimum distance from one location to the next adjacent location is 1.20m.

This is an ideal location for testing the GPS, Bluetooth, QR Coding etc.. abilities of the modern smartphone. It provides all the restrictions and problems that a software developer will have to consider when using Location Based Technologies in an outdoor environment.

1.3.2 Galway Shopping Centre

Galway Shopping Centre is the largest indoor shopping centre in Galway City. It contains a variety of shops, restaurants, services, hair stylists etc.

There are over 60 premises in the shopping centre, ranging from large clothing stores and supermarkets(Penneys/Tescos) to small boutique stores.

This is an ideal building for testing the indoor capabilities of the modern smartphone in relation to Bluetooth, GPS, Code scanning etc..

1.3.3 Caherconnell Folk Park

Caherconnell Stone Fort, situated in the Burren, contains example of the stone forts or stone ring forts, which are to be found in the Burren Ireland.
The fort at Caherconnell is in its original state.
For more information on Caherconnell see http://www.burrenforts.ie/

It is included here because it is sometimes referenced during the book.

1.3.4 Bunratty Castle and Folk Park

The 15th century Bunratty Castle and 19th century Bunratty Folk Park were used during this book to provide a case study for smartphone application localisation and internalization.
They were also referred to in various chapters to illustrate points regarding smartphone application design.

Bunratty Castle
The Castle is the most complete medieval fortress in Ireland. Built in 1425 it was restored in 1954 to its former state and now contains mainly 15th and 16th century furnishings, tapestries, and works of art.

Bunratty Folk Park
Within the grounds of Bunratty Castle is Bunratty Folk Park where 19th century life is recreated. Set on 26 acres, the park features over 30 buildings in a 'living' village and rural setting.

For more information on Bunratty see:
http://www.shannonheritage.com/Attractions/BunrattyCastleFolkPark/

1.4 Existing Smartphone Applications for Tourism

The number of applications, including tourism and location aware applications, available on the Apple Store and the Android Market App Store are growing at an exponential rate[Markets and Markets Report 2010-08-01]. Below is a snapshot of the most popular apps available for the tourism sector as of March 2011.

For section 1.4 the details regarding the applications discussed were found on the
Apple App Store/Google App Market/application company's own websites.... for example, the Update Date/Cost etc..

All applications are listed from the most expensive to the least expensive on the app store.

1.4.1 Existing Location Based Apps for Tourism

Most of the Tourism apps that employ GPS technology provide a service to find shops, restaurants and other specific businesses within a specified radius of the users current position.

Many also provide a navigation service to guide the user from their current location to the desired location.

While I carried out the research for this book, I noted that most of the existing smartphone applications that I found did not take full advantage of the phones accuracy and responsiveness with regard to GPS. Only the current applications that attempt to provide useful augmented reality functionality stretch the GPS capabilities of the modern smartphone.

Title: Zagat to Go By Handmark
For: iPhone, Android, Blackberry, Windows Mobile, PalmOS
Updated: 2011-01-27
Cost: 9.99eur

Used: GPS/GSM
Not Used: WiFi Triangulation
                  QR/DataMatrix Codes
                  Bluetooth
                  Augmented Reality

Description: Finds the shops and businesses nearest to the user based on the category of shop they are looking for. You can tap quick links to find nearby bars, restaurants, cafes etc. GPS location information is used in the normal way.

 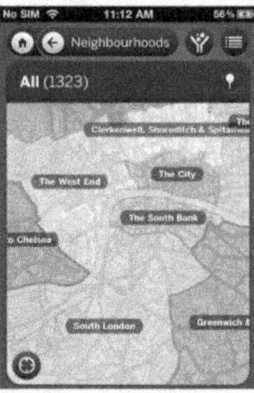

Title: Lonely Planet By Lonely Planet Pty Ltd
For: iPhone, Android, Blackberry
Updated: 2010-09-15
Cost: 4.99eur

Used: GPS/GSM
                  QR/DataMatrix Codes
Not Used: WiFi Triangulation
                  Bluetooth
                  Augmented Reality

Description: A typical City guide. There are both offline and online modes available. it uses basic GPS functionality to provide a route from point A to point B similar to most location based applications of this type. The Lonely Planet series of apps are one of the most popular iPhone and Android apps available under the heading of tourism apps. There are always two or three Lonely Planet apps in most top 10 listings in the various app stores.

Title:	Visit Dublin By GeoGuides Limited
For:	iPhone, Android
Updated:	2010-09-01
Cost:	2.99eur
Used:	GPS/GSM
Not Used:	WiFi Triangulation
	QR/DataMatrix Codes
	Bluetooth
	Augmented Reality

Description: Guide to Dublin. It provides online and offline directional searches for visitor attractions, restaurants, streets, landmarks, hotels and other areas of interest. There are audio files describing some of Dublin's historic monuments. Interestingly, this app uses GPS information to give the user an Augmented Reality* experience via the screen. There was no opportunity to test this app so it is unknown how accurate the GPS features are on this application.

see section 2.12 for a description of Augmented Reality as it applies to Smartphones

Title:	City Literary Walking Tours By GPSmycity.com
For:	iPhone
Updated:	2011-01-27
Cost:	2.39eur
Used:	GPS/GSM
Not Used:	WiFi Triangulation
	QR/DataMatrix Codes
	Bluetooth
	Augmented Reality

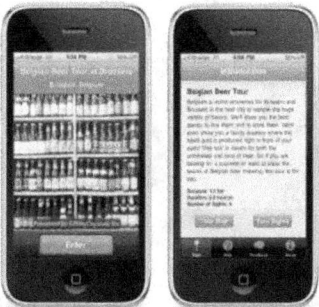

Description: GPSmyCity.com offers self-guided city walks and walking tours in different cities, including Dublin. Each walking tour offers turn-by-turn directions to the most famous attractions, monuments and interesting sights. It attempts to mimic a local guide. GPS location information is used in the normal way.

Title:	Dublin Rail By Toad Software Solutions Ltd
For:	iPhone
Updated:	2010-12-07
Cost:	1.99eur
Used:	GPS/GSM
Not Used:	WiFi Triangulation
	QR/DataMatrix Codes
	Bluetooth
	Augmented Reality

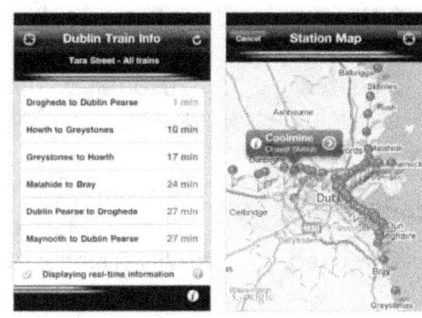

Description: This app provides live train information from Irish Rail and shows all incoming trains. Street maps are given to the user along with instructions on how to find the closest station.
Again, it uses basic GPS functionality to detect the nearest station to the users current location.

Chapter 1

Title: Metro Paris Subway By Presselite
For: iPhone
Updated: 2010-12-21
Cost: 0.79eur

Used: GPS/GSM
Not Used: WiFi Triangulation
QR/DataMatrix Codes
Bluetooth
Augmented Reality

Description: Metro Paris Subway is a location based app for getting around Paris, France.
Apple shortlisted this application for it's prestigious REWIND list in 2010.
It includes official subway maps and is compatible with Google Maps. The subway and bus stops are shown on the screen in the form of red dots or pins and the application indicates the current distance from the user to the stations. Updating is by GPS. When the users location changes by a few meters, the distances get updated. The app does not require a network connection to operate.
The app was originally available in French and has been subsequently translated into English, Spanish, German and Japanese.
It uses manual localisation. It does not use automated APIs to translate from French.

Title: Yelp By Yelp
For: iPhone, Android, Blackberry
Updated: 2010-12-23
Cost: Free

Used: GPS/GSM
Not Used: WiFi Triangulation
QR/DataMatrix Codes
Bluetooth
Augmented Reality

Description: Similar to Zagat.

Title: QR navi By Navius
For: iPhone
Updated: 2010-08-25
Cost: Free

Used: GPS/GSM
QR/DataMatrix Codes
Not Used: WiFi Triangulation
Bluetooth
Augmented Reality

Description: QR Navi lets the user scan a QR code that contains a detailed route from the users current location to the location that in encoded into the QR code. It uses the Google Maps API to achieve this. The QR code can be at any location or on a marketing or advertising leaflet. It will read the location of the shop being targeted and guide the user to that shop after they scan the QR code.

Title:	AudioBoo
For:	iPhone/Android
Updated:	Unknown
Cost:	Free
Used:	GPS
Not Used:	GSM
	QR/DataMatrix Codes
	WiFi Triangulation
	Bluetooth
	Augmented Reality

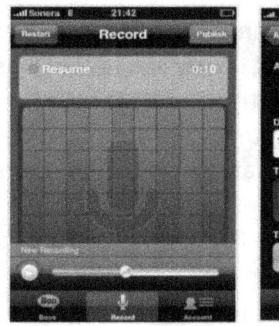 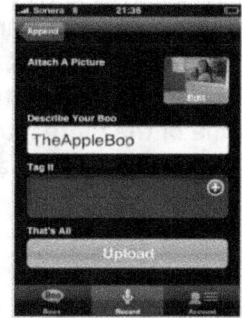

Description: Enables the user to record an audio message (with accompanying photo) and instantly publish to Twitter, Facebook and iTunes. It geo tags the audio message with location information to pinpoint the users position when they recorded the snippet.

Title:	Scavenger by Scvngr
For:	iPhone
Updated:	Unknown
Cost:	Free
Used:	GPS/GSM
	QR/DataMatrix Codes
Not Used:	WiFi Triangulation
	Bluetooth
	Augmented Reality

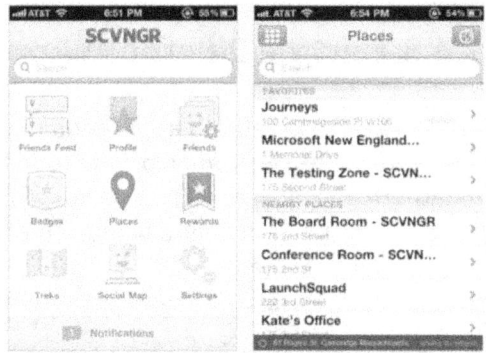

Description: SCVNGR offers apps for iPhone and Android, but they're also playable on more basic phones too using SMS. It is an app that allows the user to setup a treasure hunt that groups of people can engage it. It is primarily targeted at business team building and makes extensive use of GPS functionality. It's gaming engine has many potential uses in the tourism industry.

1.4.2 Existing Translation Based Apps for Tourism

Almost all of the translation apps that were found, used Google's Translation API to provide basic translation services.... very similar to the sample Localisation application that I've written for this book(see chapter on Localisation).
One of the more interesting apps attempted to also provide a voice translation. First using Google's API and then using a third party voice API to 'read' aloud the translation.

Title: Talk-a-Droid Pro Translator By Ideedle
For: Android
Updated: Unknown
Cost: 0.99eur

Description: This app will speak aloud the text that the user wishes to translate.

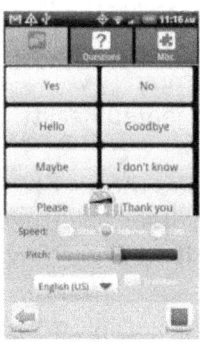 

1.4.3 Existing Bluetooth Apps for Tourism

There were no Bluetooth application that catered to the tourism sector available for download from the app stores.. The most popular(non tourism) apps were.
Bluetooth PhotoShare – File transfer of photos via bluetooth.
Wireless Chat – Chat over a bluetooth connection.
Bluetooth Chat – Same.
Bluetooth IM – Have IM conversations over a bluetooth connection.

However, bluetooth is used extensively using Bluetooth Content Zones that are often located in areas of high tourism footfall and in speciality locations associated with festivals and events that cater for the tourism sector.

When the mobile phone user comes within 10-20m of these areas, information can be pushed to their phone such as special offers and shopping coupons. Examples of some of these zones are the Dublin and Galway Irish Rail depots, Supermacs, Zhavigo Music Store, O'Briens Sandwiches, Galway Shopping Centre. All of these locations have used Bluetooth marketing techniques to push graphics based coupons to mobile phone users who pass into their content zone with bluetooth enabled mobile phones.

1.5 Layout of the Book

The contents and objectives of the remaining chapters are described here.

Chapter 2 reviews the different options available to the application designer/developer for developing applications on the most relevant operating systems and smartphones. Chapter 2 also makes a detailed comparison between the two leading operating systems, Android and iOS and compares web development to native SDK development.
We conclude this chapter with a brief review of the most relevant database options for the smartphone developer.

Chapter 3 describes the theory necessary to begin designing and developing location aware applications for smartphones.
Chapter 3 also includes the experiments that were carried out in some of the areas discussed. After the GPS theory section, the GPS experiments are listed, after the Bluetooth theory section, the Bluetooth experiments are listed and after the 2D Code theory section, the 2D Code experiments are listed.

Chapter 4 discusses localizing/internationalizing a tourism application.

Chapter 5 reviews the work done while writing the book with conclusions and recommendations for future work.

Additionally, there is an online resource available at http://www.irishapps.org/smartlla.html which contains additional information and data files relevant to the experimental sections of this report. These files contain detailed GPS data, video footage and photos of the experiments being carried out. They also contain some of the analysis carried out on the GPS data.

Appendix A lists all the relevant application source code from the experiments listed in Chapter 3 and Chapter 4.
Appendix B lists the GPS files used in the experiments.
Appendix C lists the photos and videos generated during the experiments.
Appendix D lists the NFC phones currently available(March 2011).

2. Software, Operating Systems and SDKs for Smartphones

There are a large number of operating systems, manufacturers and developers entering the smartphone arena at the moment. It is difficult to predict which technologies will prevail and which ones will disappear over the next 24 months. It is quite obvious from reading the popular media and from looking at sales figures, that Apple's iOS(iPhone) platform and Google's Android platform must be addressed and must be catered for when developing any mobile applications for the tourism industry. It is very likely that these two operating systems will be dominant in the smartphone marketplace for the next 2-3 years at least. After this, it becomes less clear which platforms will prevail. Ideally the developer should write his or her applications for all the major smartphone platforms, but of course this is not a practical route to take for any software writers, with the exception of the biggest multi-national software houses.

A common sense strategy for most software developers writing apps for the tourism industry will be to write his/her app for the iPhone and for the suite of Android devices and to leave it at that. However, the smartphone landscape can change very rapidly and it is a good idea to have some familiarity with the up and coming technologies that are trying to knock Apple and Google off their dominant positions.

Platforms such as the new Nokia Maemo platform or the new Microsoft Phone 7 platform may prevail. Currently, if a developer experiences great success with his/her app on the top two platforms, then it would be feasible to develop the app for more platforms such as the Microsoft platform which will soon power many of the new Nokia smartphones.

The beginning of this chapter presents a brief overview of the six most prominent players in the smartphone market. They are Apple, Google, Nokia, Microsoft, RIM(Blackberry) and HP(Palm).

The middle section of this chapter goes into greater detail regarding each of these companies software, OS and SDKs. This section will be useful to any developer trying to choose which platform to develop for. This section also lists the most popular smartphones available to the public. Most of the phones discussed in this section have widespread use and can be expected to be used by tourists from all countries.
Some of the models discussed are very new(Jan 2011) and some have not been fully released yet, but it is reasonable to assume that they will enjoy widespread use soon after their launch dates.
Rather than categorising the phones by manufacturer, they have been classified by operating system.

The latter section of this chapter deals with the databases that are available for developing mobile applications.

2.1 An Overview

The following is an outline of the major manufacturers, platforms and SDKs available to developers.

Apple(iPhone) iOS:
Powers the iPhone range. Support is provided via the iPhone Dev Centre. You must have a Mac OSX with the most recent Snow Leopard OS. The SDK costs 99eur. Native apps are written using Objective C or HTML and JavaScript. Apps are distributed through the Apple Corp App Store only.

Google Android:
Powers many HTC, Samsung, Motorola, LG and other smartphones. Support is provided via the developer section on the Android website. Android is an open source platform and can be installed on a Windows machine, an Apple Mac or Linux box. Native apps are written in Java or again using HTML and JavaScript. Apps can be distributed via any route including many app stores and by direct cable download. or simply from your own website.

Nokia Symbian and Maemo:
Symbian powers almost all current Nokia devices, Maemo powers the Nokia N900 and Nokia tablets and will power new Nokia smartphones.
Symbian dev support is provided on the Symbian Dev Site. Apps can be written using Symbian C++, WRT widgets and Qt(cross platform C++). Development can take place on PC, Linux and on Mac OSX for Symbian C++.

Maemo dev support is on the Maemo page on Nokia website. Maemo apps are written using Qt C++. Apps for Symbian and Maemo are distributed through many app stores. The official store is the Nokia Ovi Store. Microsoft and Nokia are in talks to establish a new app store.

Microsoft Phone 7:
Powers the newest Windows mobile devices. It replaces Mobile 6.5 OS and has been completely rewritten. App support is via MSDN. The development language is Silverlight and the apps are distributed through the Windows Marketplace for Mobile. It will soon power Nokia smartphones.

RIM Blackberry:
Powers all Blackberry devices and developer support is on the Blackberry website. Native applications are authored in Java. HTML and JavaScript can be used for newer devices. Development can take place on a PC, Mac or Linux machine. Again apps can be sold in a number of app stores. The official app store is Blackberry App World.

HP Palm:
Palm WebOS powers the Palm handsets. All apps are written using HTML, CSS and JavaScript. Developer support is via the Palm Developer Centre.

2.2 Apple iOS

The Apple iOS is the mobile operating system powering the iPhone.
As of Jan 2011, iOS powered smartphones hold 28% of the smartphone market so it is essential for any tourism developer to cater for iOS devices[Canaly's Report 2011-02-01].

Apple's iOS is loosely based on the Unix OS. It is derived from the Apple Macs operating system and Objective C is the shared programming language of the Mac and iPhone. There are four distinct layers. The core/service/media/cocoa touch layer.

Cocoa touch is the uppermost layer. Below this resides the Media layer and then the Services and OS layer. A more basic way to think of the OS is to visualise two layers, a C layer and a Cocoa layer.

The operating system is written in C. You use Unix style C functions to manipulate this layer. It handles all low level activity like file manipulation, network connections, threads and it handles the SQLite database. The media layer is also at t low level and contains many of the C APIs. The Cocoa layer brings things to a higher and simpler level and makes programming more manageable. For instance, rather than manipulating C strings, you use the Foundation framework string, NSString(you can see this later in the chapters listing the source code written for this book).

The OS presents the user with the same home screen every time the phone or tablet is turned on. This home screen is extended in the right direction by as many screens as is necessary to accommodate all the applications installed on the device. The GUI interface lets users move their app icons anywhere within these pages.
With iOS4, the user can create folders to hold a cluster of related applications.

iOS comes with a number of included applications such as Phone, Mail, Safari(web), iPod, Calendar, Camera and so on.

Before iOS4, multitasking was limited to some native Apple apps. Now multitasking is available to all developers to exploit. It is supported through a number of APIs such as VoIP, Push Notifications, Task Finding etc.

iOS is one of the most restrictive operating systems for smartphones. Apple limits developer access to some of the core iPhone functions, such as SMS and Phone Dialler.
There are a number of ways around this, but they are not available outside of the development environment. A JailBroken iPhone can run any of the restricted APIs and there is a large support forum available for distributing and using these APIs, however, Apple won't approve an app that uses there APIs so for the purposes of tourism application development, they are not an option.

2.2.1 iOS Software

iOS is a closed operating system and developers wishing to build applications must use Apples own programming language, Objective-C.

ObjectiveC
Apple's development language, Objective-C is an object-oriented programming language built on C. Objective-C is largely based on the Smalltalk language, one of the earliest mainstream object oriented languages. It's a full superset of C, allowing you to write any traditional C code. It adds object-oriented capabilities to the C language. Because of its origin in Smalltalk, Objective-C's messaging code look a little strange compared to traditional ANSI C code. Most of the C legacy coding conventions remain. The software developer is still required to have a header file and must therefore declare everything twice. Anyone used to working with a modern language will find working with pointers to be tedious and unfamiliar. The process of allocating and de-allocating memory also remains.

If the developer doesn't want to learn ObjectiveC, then there are some 3rd party development languages available that attempt to translate to ObjectiveC.

C and C++ with DragonFIre
Dragonfire provide a C++ solution for windows developers that want to develop iPhone applications using Visual C++, its debugger and its familiar C/C++ language.

JavaScript with Appcelerator and Nitobi
For web developers that want to avoid learning ObjectiveC, there are 3rd party APIs that will translate your code from JavaScript style coding to ObjectiveC.

2.2.2 iOS SDK

The iPhone SDK has been used extensively while writing the code for this book.
It is a comprehensive, all inclusive set of tools for developing applications for the iPhone and iPad(and iPod). You have to have an Apple Mac running OSX Snow Leopard or later in order to use it. It won't support Windows or Linux machines.(The default Android SDK works on Mac, Linux and Windows). The first hurdle for any non-Apple developer is obtaining a MacBook or an iMac running a recent version of the Mac operating system(Leopard OS).
The SDK comprises of three main components. Xcode, for writing the source code, Interface Builder for building the GUI interface, and the iPhone Simulator which acts as an iPhone/iPad/iPod emulator.

XCode and ObjectiveC
Xcode is the programming environment for writing ObjectiveC code(ObjectiveC is covered in detail in the previous page). It is an Apple only IDE and will run on Mac OSX. This is the only method approved by Apple for writing applications for the iPhone, or iPad. In addition, all of the applications written by any developer must be submitted to Apple for approval before they are allowed to be downloaded from the app store. The app store is the only distribution channel allowed for iPhone applications.

Of course there are ways around this and there are several companies offering a non-Apple approved way of getting apps onto an iPhone. But these are not mainstream and often require the user to invalidate the warranty on their device.
An enterprise licence can also allow the developer to distribute their application independent of the AppStore.
To write iPhone apps, existing C++ developers must upskill to the ObjectiveC language. There are syntax differences and other minor differences between C++ and Objective C. Of course there are many iPhone specific aspects to Objective C that must be learned. The debugger is integrated into the Apple IDE as is the emulator. Obviously, it's not cross-platform. The SDK is free but there is a fee for publishing to the AppStore and a bigger fee for independent distribution.

Developer resources are extensive, mostly via Apple website.

Interface Builder

Interface builder allows the developer to quickly build a GUI interface for an app.
2D and 3D support is integrated into the SDK and GUI builder. Speed is excellent due to it being a compiled language. Interface builder is very clearly/logically laid out and is intuitive to use, even for the beginner. However, some of the stock iPhone controls are not included in the set of widgets(controls). The developer has to construct them.

Most non-Apple developers will find XCode, InterfaceBuilder and ObjectiveC to be reasonably straight forward and intuitive after a few hours of coding.

One major drawback to developing for the iPhone is that there is no guarantee that your application will be accepted into the Apple AppStore. After months of development time, you may find that your app never gets approved. Currently there is no alternative to the app store.

SDK contains the following elements:
Cocoa Touch to control Multi-touch events, Accelerometer, Localization and the Camera.
Media Module to access OpenAL, audio, video and image files, Core Animation and OpenGL.
Core Services takes care of Networking, the SQLite database, Core Location(GPS).
OS X Kernel controls TCP/IP, Sockets, Power management, File system and Security

Tools	iPhone SDK
3rd Party SDKs	Ansca Corona, Appcelerator Titanium Mobile, Nitobi PhoneGap, Rhomobile Rhodes, iUI, DragonFireSDK, Unity
Languages	Objective-C, HTML, CSS and JavaScript
Cost	$99 per year for Apple iPhone Developer Program.
Devices	iPhone 3G, iPhone 4
Documentation	Apple Developer Program, gives full access to the iOS SDK and IDE and is free to download and includes the iPhone Reference Library and documentation
Developer Support	the Apple Developer Community provides extensive support for developers and designers.
App Delivery Mechanism	Apple Corp App Store or the enterprise license.

2.2.3 iOS Smartphones

Apple iPhone 3GS
Jun-09

Massively popular, and therefore, one of the most relevant phones for the current tourism demography.
This phone was used extensively during the experimental phase of this project.
Same as the iPhone 4 except:
No front mounted camera or flash
No HD video recording,
Lower resolution camera(but easily sufficient for 2D scanning),
No 802.11n, no three axis-gyroscope for gaming,
More standard 480 x 320 resolution screen.
Talk Time: 5 hours
Standby Time: 12.5 days
Platform: iOS 4
Wireless: 802.11b/g Wi-Fi, Bluetooth 2.1 +EDR
Network: GSM, HSPA 7.2 Storage: 8GB on-board

Apple iPhone 4
Jun-10

The latest in the iPhone line up.
This phone was used during some of the experiments conducted for this project.
High-resolution 'Retina Display' - 326 pixels per inch - 640 x 960 screen (2x no of pixels as the 3GS predecessor).
5-megapixel camera with LED flash and HD video capture
Front-facing camera for video conferencing (Wi-Fi only),
Three-axis gyroscope for gaming
Larger battery and faster A4 chip
New iOS 4 software (but the 3GS is upgradable and was using iOS4.2 during testing)
Talk Time: Up to 7 hours on 3G (14 on 2G)
Standby Time: 12.5 days
Platform: iOS 4
Wireless: 802.11b/g/n Wi-Fi, Bluetooth 2.1 + EDR
Network: GSM, HSPA 7.2
Storage: 16GB or 32GB on-board

iPhone 5
Slated for early/mid 2011 release.

Rumoured to support 4G networks wherever available.
Will run on the under development iOS 5.

2.3 Google Android OS

The Google Android OS is gaining more and more market share. Like the iOS, it cannot be ignored when dealing with the tourism industry. In the fourth quarter of 2010, Android powered smartphones overtook Nokia in smartphone sales. Up to this point Nokia were the global leader in smartphone sales [Reuters Report By Tarmo Virki and Sinead Carew Jan 31, 2011.... see 2.4.1]

Android is a Linux based OS. It is primarily used to power Android smartphones, but is also used to power Netbooks and tablets and some TV sets.

The OS is Linux based and the programming language Java based and both were developed from the ground up by Google. There is a Dalvik virtual machine(instead of the Java bytecode machine) which is specifically tailored for Android devices. Some apps are integrated into the OS such as a browser. The graphics engine is similar to Apples iOS in that it is based on OpenGL. Also, like the iOS there is built in support for the SQLite database format and most developers use this as their database.

The Android website provides the following graphic, which gives a good breakdown of the OS:

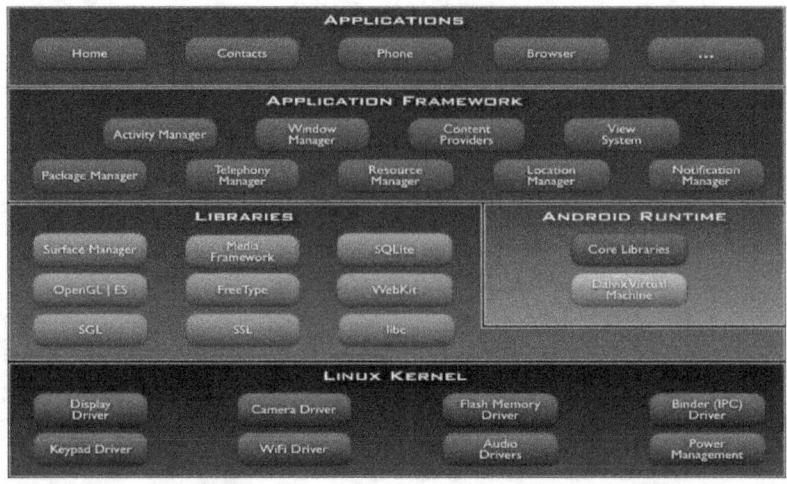

Android ships with a set of default applications including email clients, SMS, calendar, maps, browser etc. The operation is very similar to other smartphone GUIs. The user experience of the Android OS and the iOS is very similar.

With the Android model, there is absolutely no difference between any of the applications that ship with an android phone and those that the 3rd party developer makes with the supplied SDK. All the resources available to Google or manufacturer software developers are also available to the average 3rd party developer or software house. All the resources of the phone are at the developers disposal.
Additionally the OS itself is open source and is actually based on Linux(itself an open source platform). Other developers and developer communities can contribute to it and manufacturers can customise it as they see fit.

2.3.1 Android Software

The Android software bundle runs on the Dalvik virtual machine. It is a Java based framework and most of the applications written for Android are based on the Java programming language.
The GUI elements of Android apps are written using XML, which is then translated into Java code by the SDK.

Android Java
Anyone familiar with Java will be able to develop android apps in a very short time. Some of the java packages included in Android are:

```
java.lang;      //core Java language classes
java.io;        //input/output capabilities
java.net;       //network connections
java.util;      //utility classes. This package includes the
                //Log class used to write to the LogCat.
java.text;
java.math;
javax.net;
javax.security;
javax.xml;
```
etc...

For tourism based applications that use bluetooth, GPS and QR codes, then over 90% of the packages used will be the native Android packages such as:

```
android.app;         //Android application model access
android.content;     //accessing and publishing data in Android
android.net;         //contains the Uri class, used for
                     //accessing various content
android.graphics;    //graphics primitives
android.opengl;      //OpenGL classes
android.os;          //system level access to the
                     //Android environment
android.provider;    //Content Provider related classes
android.telepehony;  //Telephony capability access
android.text;        //Text layout
android.util;        //collection of utilities for text
                     //manipulation, including XML
android.view;        //User interface elements
android.webkit;      //Browser functionality
android.widget;      //more user interface elements
```

JavaScript with Appcelerator and Nitobi
For web developers that want to avoid using Java, there are 3rd party APIs that will translate your code from JavaScript style coding to Android Java.

Cloud Based Development
Companies such as rhomobile provide custom environments for developing Android apps that don't require much Java knowledge.

2.3.2 Android SDK

The Google Android SDK has also been used throughout the experimental phase of this book.
Google's approach to the SDK has been very different from Apple's. The Android development language is built around Java, and their approach to the SDK will be familiar to Java developers. Instead of providing an all inclusive closed SDK package, Google have provided a command-line set of tools and have then strongly recommended that the developer use a 3rd party development environment and integrate the command line tools into this development environment. Google recommends using Eclipse as your development environment. It is pretty obvious that the Android SDK was designed to use Eclipse from the outset and they have partnered with Eclipse to provide a solid, stable and user friendly development experience.

The SDK delivers a complete set of software tools to enable developers to create open applications. The developer can make calls, send SMS, use the camera etc from within the code. There is much more access to the phones functionality than is available with the iOS. As mentioned previously, the Dalvik machine is streamlined for optimum memory and hardware resource use.

Apart from the emulator, which can model almost any Android device and most common screen resolutions and sizes, there are a number of other very useful tools for development.

Android Development Tools Plugin (for the Eclipse IDE)
The ADT uses the existing and popular Eclipse IDE to allow developers to write applications. Google has partnered with Eclipse and has co-developed a suite of highly integrated tools. Most Java developers will be already familiar with Eclipse so moving to Android development will be a very smooth process. This is an indispensible tool for Android developers.
Android Emulator
As mentioned, it is versatile and can model any device necessary.
Android Virtual Devices (AVDs)
Associated with the emulator... it allows the uses to do a host of simulations, including providing dummy GPS coordinates, setting up fake SD cards, allocation memory etc.
Dalvik Debug Monitor Service (ddms)
Built into the Dalvik virtual machine, this tool greatly helps in the debugging process. You can add a trace to your applications, pick a thread to track, view heap information, take screen shots etc... a very handy tool.

Tools	Android SDK, Android Development Tools (ADT) plugin on Eclipse
3rd Party SDKs	Ansca Corona, Appcelerator Titanium Mobile, Nitobi PhoneGap, Rhomobile Rhodes, Unity
Languages	Java for native apps, Android Native Development Kit (NDK) for apps requiring C/C++ libraries
Cost	Free, open source; no upfront fees
Devices	Smartphones and PDAs from many different manufacturers, including HTC, LG, Motorola and Samsung
Documentation	SDK provides extensive developer documentation
Developer Support	Complete documentation online (with videos, official Android developer blog and an active Android development community)
App Delivery Mechanism	Google Android Market. Third-party app markets and publication channels

2.3.3 Android Smartphones

HTC G2(or Desire Z)
Oct-10

Slide-out QWERTY keyboard
800 MHz Qualcomm MSM7320 processor
5-megapixel camera
3.7-inch display
Android 2.2
4GB of internal memory
Supports HSPA+ 14.4 3G data services
Talk Time: Up to 6.5 hours
Standby Time: Up to 17.5 days
Platform: Android 2.2 "Froyo"
Wireless: 802.11b/g/n Wi-Fi, Bluetooth 2.1 +EDR
Network: GSM, HSPA 14.4
Storage: 4GB on-board; 8GB card included, 32GB supported via microSD

Motorola Droid 2
Aug-10

The original Droid from Motorola helped bring the Android platform to prominence.
The Droid 2 sports a faster processor
Mobile Wi-Fi hotspot feature
Adobe Flash
5-megapixel auto-focus camera with video capture
Wireless video output via DLNA.
Slide-out QWERTY keyboard
Large touch screen
GPS navigation with full turn-by-turn directions
Compass
3.5mm audio jack
40 GB of memory, and dual-mic noise reduction
Talk Time: Up to 9.6 hours
Standby Time: Up to 13.1 days
Platform: Android 2.2 "Froyo"
Wireless: 802.11b/g/n Wi-Fi, Bluetooth 2.1 +EDR
Network: CDMA, EV-DO Rev. A
Storage: 8GB on-board, 32GB supported via microSD

HTC Desire
Aug-10

1GHz Snapdragon processor,
1,400mAh battery,
3.7-inch 800 x 480 AMOLED screen,
5-megapixel autofocus camera and
512MB of ROM
Wi-Fi,
GPS,
Talk Time: Up to 5 hours
Standby Time: Up to 10.6 days
Platform: Android 2.1 "Eclair"
Wireless: 802.11b/g/n Wi-Fi, Bluetooth 2.1 +EDR
Network: CDMA, EV-DO Rev. A
Storage: 8GB card included, 32GB supported via microSD

2.3.3 Android Smartphones

Motorola Droid X
Jul-10

4.3-inch touch display
1GHz OMAP processor
24GB of storage capacity
multi-touch keyboard
8-megapixel camera with 720p video recording
HDMI output
Adobe Flash Player 10.1 support
Talk Time: Up to 8 hours
Standby Time: 9.2 days
Platform: Android 2.1
Wireless: 802.11b/g/n Wi-Fi, Bluetooth 2.1 + EDR
Network: CDMA, EV-DO Rev. A
Storage: 8GB on-board plus 16GB microSD card

Dell Streak
Jun-10

5-inch 800 x 480 capacitive touch screen
1GHz Snapdragon processor
5-megapixel camera with auto-focus and dual LED flash
front-facing camera
accelerometer
2GB on-board storage plus a pre-installed 16GB card.
Talk Time: 9.8 hours
Standby Time: 16.6 days
Platform: Android 1.6
Wireless: 802.11b/g Wi-Fi, Bluetooth 2.1 +EDR
Network: GSM, HSPA 7.2 Storage: 2GB built-in, 32GB supported via microSD

Samsung Galaxy S
Jun-10

4-inch AMOLED touch screen display,
1Ghz Cortex A8 Hummingbird processor,
5-megapixel camera with LED flash
720p video capture,
six-axis sensor for gaming,
16GB of internal storage,
GPS
Talk Time: Up to 6.5 hours
Standby Time: Up to 18 days
Platform: Android 2.1
Wireless: 802.11b/g/n Wi-Fi, Bluetooth 2.1 +EDR
Network: GSM, HSPA 7.2 Storage: Up to 16GB on-board

2.3.3 Android Smartphones

HTC EVO 4G
Jun-10
world's first 3G/4G Android handset
4.3-inch touch display,
1GHz Snapdragon processor,
512MB RAM,
8-megapixel camera
1.3 megapixel front-facing camera for video conferencing
GPS
digital compass
Talk Time: Up to 6 hours on 3G
Standby Time: 6 days
Platform: Android 2.1
Wireless: 802.11b/g Wi-Fi, Bluetooth 2.1 + EDR
Network: CDMA, EV-DO Rev. A, WiMAX
Storage: 1GB on-board, up to 32GB via microSD

HTC Droid Incredible
Apr-10
1GHz Snapdragon processor
8GB of internal storage
512MB ROM
512MB RAM
8-megapixel camera with dual LED flash and autofocus
3.7-inch (480 x 800) AMOLED capacitive touch screen
Talk Time: 5.2 hours
Standby Time: 6 days
Platform: Android 2.2
Wireless: 802.11b/g Wi-Fi, Bluetooth 2.1 + EDR
Network: CDMA, EV-DO Rev. A
Storage: 8GB on-board, up to 32GB via microSD

Chapter 2

2.4 iOS and Android Comparison

The Apple iOS(using iPhone 3Gs) and Google AndroidOS(using Samsung GalaxyS) have been used throughout this book.
The following section presents a comparison of these two operating systems in the following categories:

2.4.1 Worldwide Market Share
2.4.2 SDK Differences and the Development Experience
2.4.3 Location Aware Programming Techniques
2.4.4 Database Programming Techniques
2.4.5 Bluetooth Programming Techniques

2.4.1 Worldwide Market Share

Looking at the market share for each of the operating systems(devices) can guide the developer or tourism operator in deciding which platforms to support in order to reach the maximum number of end users for the minimum of effort. A brief look at the worldwide numbers makes it very clear that any tourism application must be written for the iPhone and for the Android series of devices.
If the tourism operator wishes to invest in developing applications for a third platform, then Nokia appears to be the best option. NOTE: On Feb 14th 2011 Nokia announced an alliance with Microsoft. Almost all future Nokia smartphones will run the Microsoft Phone 7 operating system, this further strengthens the argument for Nokia to be considered when developing new applications for the tourism sector.

World:
[Canalys Report, released on 1st Feb 2011]
Q4 2010: Android and Nokia both sold over 30 million handsets with Android just outselling Nokia. Apple and RIM (BlackBerry), each sold 15 million, followed by Microsoft with just 3.1 million.

Smartphone World Share Oct-10	
RIM Blackberry	14.40%
Apple iOS	16.00%
Android OS(incl OMS and Tapas)	**32.90%**
Microsoft Mobile	3.10%
Nokia OS	**30.60%**
Others	2.90%

Smartphone World Share(rounded to nearest whole number) From Q4 2009 to Q3 2010	Q4 2009	Q2 2010	Q3 2010	Q4 2010
RIM Blackberry	20.00%	18.00%	15.40%	14.40%
Apple iOS	16.30%	13.50%	17.40%	16.10%
Android OS(incl OMS and Tapas)	8.70%	17.10%	25.10%	32.90%
Microsoft Mobile	7.20%	4.90%	3.50%	3.10%
Nokia OS	44.40%	43.50%	36.50%	30.60%
Others	3.40%	3.00%	2.10%	2.90%

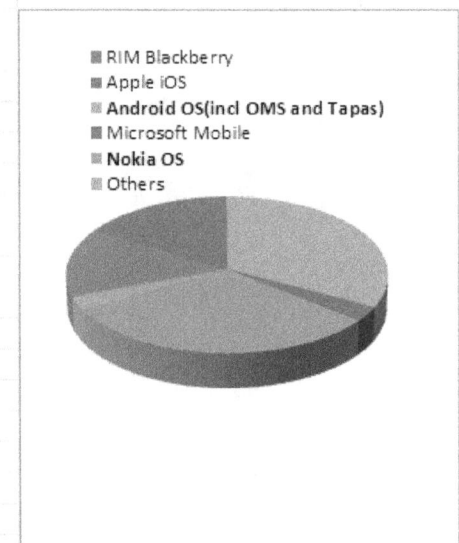

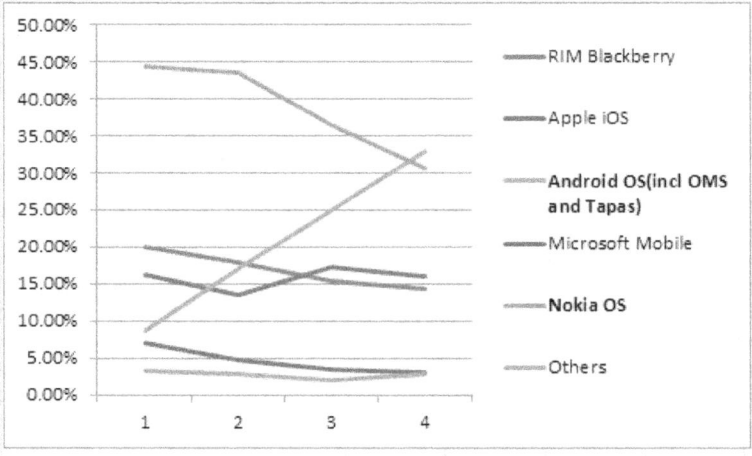

The last quarter of 2010 showed that over one hundred million smartphones had been purchased. This was almost double the amount sold in the same period in 2009.

Apple increased it's sales by almost the same margin. It's overall share of the market remained more or less static at sixteen percent.
Android grew by a huge six hundred percent... but it started out with a very small share. Half of all amdroid smartphones were manufactured by HTC and Samsung. LG and Acer also manufactured a significant amount of android devices.

These figures suggest that any developer working in the tourism industry should make certain to cater for Apple and Android handsets. Growth figures suggest they will be the dominant forces for the next few years.

US:
[Nielsen Report, released on 1st Dec 2010]
October 2010:

Total US Market Share
Oct-10

Feature Phones	70.30%
Smartphones	29.70%

Smartphone US Share
Oct-10

RIM Blackberry	27.40%
Apple iOS	27.90%
Android OS	22.70%
Microsoft Mobile	14.00%
Symbian OS	3.40%
Linux	3.30%
Palm OS	1.30%

Smartphone US Share(rounded to nearest whole number)

From Q4 2009 to Q3 2010	Q4 2009	Q1 2010	Q2 2010	Q3 2010
RIM Blackberry	37.00%	36.00%	34.00%	27.00%
Apple iOS	26.00%	27.00%	28.00%	28.00%
Android OS	4.00%	8.00%	13.00%	23.00%
Microsoft Mobile	20.00%	18.00%	15.00%	14.00%
Symbian OS	3.00%	3.00%	3.00%	3.00%
Linux/other	4.00%	4.00%	4.00%	4.00%
Palm OS	6.00%	4.00%	3.00%	1.00%

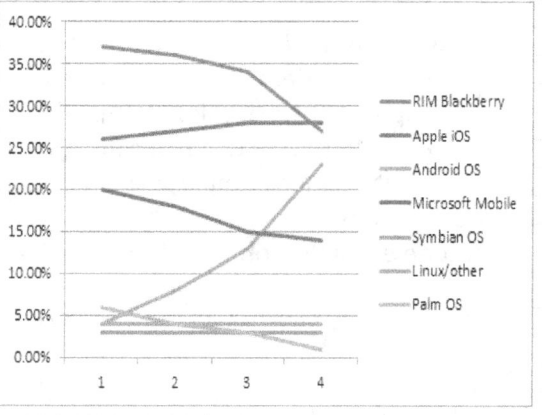

In the US, the Neilson market research group reported that Android is the largest growing mobile platform. Apple are showing a slight decline. But of course Apple are much more established than Android.
Again, these figures show that Apple and Android are the platforms to cater for.

2.4.2 SDK Differences and the Development Experience

Other areas to consider when working with the iOS(iPhone) and AndroidOS are as follows:

IDE:
Comparing IDEs can be very subjective and developers from both camps claim that their IDE is far superior. The Eclipse IDE has the advantage of being used far more extensively that the Xcode IDE. This is because the Eclipse IDE is used for general Java development as well as a host of other uses.
Because of this, Eclipse caters for a wide range of developers and has a more intuitive and free flowing feel to it than the Apple Xcode environment.
On the other hand, the closed environment of the iOS system is very well designed and very polished and can be a more inviting prospect for a beginner programmer.
Additionally, the Apple IDE works immediately after downloading, whereas the Google-Eclipse IDE requires the downloading of several separate components and then depends on the correct integration of these components, before the developer can start work.
A real advantage with eclipse is that the Java documentation is presented to the developer as he/she is in the process of writing source code. The correct class descriptions and help files appear automatically.

Programming Syntax: Android Java vs iOS ObjectiveC
ObjectiveC is the language of the iOS SDK. It is based on C with additional object oriented features such as classes, inheritance, messages.
Java is the language of the Android SDK. It was built from the beginning as an OO language.
The structure and syntax is very similar to C++.

Java development for Android is a lot easier than ObjectiveC development for the iPhone. There are many more java developers than AnsiC developers, and they can upskill to write android apps very quickly. Objective C was a very ground breaking language when it came out in the 1990's but it's memory management and syntax is unlike most other languages and it requires an update.
Most universities have switched from C to Java and therefore, new programmers will prefer Android to ObjectiveC.

Having said that, some of ObjectiveCs unique features can be quite useful. For example, message passing is used instead of calling methods. However, the traditional object oriented syntax of Java is superior to ObjectiveC.

Memory Management:
Another downside to ObjectiveC(similar to C and C++) is that the developer must always consider whether allocated memory objects are freed appropriately. Java uses its Garbage Collector to do this automatically. When programs become very large it can be difficult to find out if you have referenced a memory item that has been deallocated.

Header Files and Implementation Files:
The use of header files and separate implementation files, lead to a lot of source file swapping during development. The developer must declare everything in the header file and then jump to the implementation file to begin coding the variable of method just declared.
In Java, it's a much simpler experience. Usually, you just jump to the top of the file to look at your declarations.
A code example from one of the applications written for this book will illustrate this:

```objectivec
GPSProximityViewController.h

@class   LocationsTableCell;
#import <UIKit/UIKit.h>
#import <sqlite3.h>
#import <math.h>
#import <CoreLocation/CoreLocation.h>
#import "GPSProximityAppDelegate.h"

@interface GPSProximityViewController : UIViewController
    <CLLocationManagerDelegate, UIScrollViewDelegate> //
    UITableViewDataSource, UITableViewDelegate
    {
        CLLocationManager *locationManager;
        //..................
        //(20 ADDITIONAL LINES OF CODE(SEE APPENDIX FOR FULL LISTING)
        //..................
        IBOutlet UILabel *dist1
    }
    @property(nonatomic,retain) NSString    *userlatitude;
    @property(nonatomic,retain) NSString    *userlongitude;
    @property(nonatomic,retain) CLLocationManager *locationManager;
    @property(nonatomic,assign) CLLocationDegrees   userLat;
    @property(nonatomic,assign) CLLocationDegrees   userLongi;
    @property(nonatomic,assign) CLLocationDegrees   locationLat;
    @property(nonatomic,assign) CLLocationDegrees   locationLongi;
    @property(nonatomic, retain) NSMutableArray   *locationsArray;
    @property (nonatomic, retain) UIScrollView   *scrollbarView;
```

```
    @property(nonatomic, retain) IBOutlet UINavigationBar*navigationBar;
-(void) initializeTableData;
-(void)displayExistingLocationsData;
-(void) pingUserLocation:(NSTimer *)aTimer;
-(void)locationManager:(CLLocationManager *)manager
    didUpdateToLocation:(CLLocation *)newLocation
    fromLocation:(CLLocation *)oldLocation;
-(void)locationManager:(CLLocationManager *)manager
    didFailWithError:(NSError *)error;
-(double)
calculateDistance:(NSString*)current_latitud:(NSString*)current_longitud:
(NSString*)dest_latitud:(NSString*)dest_longitude;
@end
```

It should be noted that these are just declarations and all of this code is duplicated is the implementation file `GPSProximityViewController.m`

Imports:
Javas(with Eclipse) Imports and forward declarations are much easier to handle and are much quicker to implement that Objective-C's(with Xcode). There can be a lot of imports involved in a tourism based application that uses, the GPS, camera, QR Code APIs, Google Maps etc… so it can be time consuming not to have imports handled automatically. When you forget to import a package and an error occurs, it is a simple matter to get the Eclipse IDE to sort it out for you… this is not the case with Xcode and ObjectiveC.

Finding the Proper Functionality:
If you are very familiar with Android Java or ObjectiveC then finding functionality won't be an issue. However, if your are an experienced developer who is new to either the ObjectiveC or Android Java environments, then the ease with which you can find the functionality you need can be an important point to consider. On Android, the Java runtime libraries are easy to locate and the documentation points you in the right direction straight away. Finding the functionality using Xcode and ObjectiveC is not quite as straight forward. In practice, a developer will often forget about using the built in documentation and check the net for a solution to the problem. This is where the Java based open platform of Android holds a big advantage over the closed nature of Objective-C.

The developer has the luxury of having the full Android platform source code available in order to look for the functionality required. In this way the developer can examine the code use the examples and use the same methodology in his/her own code.

UI Programming:
With ObjectiveC, building a GUI is a simple task and this is where the Xcode/Interface Builder definitely outshine the Android XML approach to building a User Interface. On the iPhone, it is easy to have different screens sharing data.
Google have tried to match Apple's graphical method of building interfaces, but have not managed to equal Apple in this regard. Building the GUI for an Android application is a chore compared to building for the iPhone.
The Android UI builder is very limited and never displays things as they will appear at runtime. The Apple tools show the UI EXACTLY as it will appear at runtime. This is an extremely impressive and time saving aspect to the Xcode environment.
The iOS delegate model of TableViewController gives you great control and is much better than the AndroidOS adapter model of ListActivity.

Developer Help:
There is excellent documentation available for ObjectiveC developers using the iPhone. Additionally there are sample applications with source code and video tutorials provided on Apples website. There is extensive API documentation.
The same can be said for Google Android. Java developers have access to a host of online resources, which are also available offline when the SDK is installed. The Android sample applications are excellent.
Additionally, there are a large number of 3rd party open source applications available on Google's website. There apps are referenced extensively in later chapters.

Compiling and Running:
iOS XCode works really well when compiling your application. However, for the developer who is just starting out using Xcode and wants to debug onto a real device(not the emulator) then things are far more complicated with the iOS than with Android.
There is a plethora of downloads and permissions you have to go through in order to debug your app on a live device. First of all you have to create a device identification and download a separate device cert for debug and release. It is not practical to distribute an app by email, even to one person. First you have to get them to check their device for it's serial number and then you have to add it as on of your 99 developer devices and then you have to compile it especially for their device and then send it to them.

Bluetooth and SMS:
With the iOS direct Bluetooth API access and direct SMS access are blocked. With Android they are freely available.

QR Code Setup:
The Android camera code is overly complex compared with the code for the iOS. It's a lot easier to setup QRCode scanning on the iPhone than on the Android device..

Location Aware Apps:
Both operating systems make accessing location based services a very long winded experience. Both systems could easily simplify this process.

Maps:
Adding markers to maps is much more straight forward in iOS and requires 5 or 6 lines of code. In Android, to achieve the same things requires writing a separate inner class and requires 20 to 30 lines of code. The iOS is much simpler in this regard.
(see the next section for sample source code)

Menus:
Menus and navigation are superior on the iPhone. They look more polished and are easier to add and implement.
However, Android's XML layouts make it simpler to support multiple screen sizes and different orientations.

Debugging:
The Java debugger within Eclipse, when using the DDME view(Google Android view) is very useful for debugging. When projects become large and complex, the debugging process remains manageable.
Within Apple Xcode, the debugging process is more straight forward and easier and quicker to use for smaller applications. However, as the complexity grows, it becomes increasingly difficult to locate bugs in comparison to the Eclipse debugger. Another area where Xcode outshines Eclipse is in profiling and in heap analysis. The heap analysis tool allows the developer to make reports on objects and you can view the latest methods and memory used to call the methods.

With Android and iOS, developers often end up doing a lot of debugging by using Log messages. When this is the case, debugging on both systems is identical.

With the iPhone, it can be a real pain to locate a small bug soon after an application has been released and approved by the app store. The fixed version must go through the same process all over again.

App Store:
The Apple App Store is light years ahead of the Google App Market from the point of view of reaching the largest audience for your apps. Apart from the application acceptance process, the Apple App Store is better is every aspect.
However, getting your app approved can be a laborious process, and may requiring many changes to your code, most of which will have to be done on guess work, because Apple will rarely give a straight forward reason for rejecting an app.
The Google App Market will accept your application within minutes and your app will be visible and available straight away.

OS Features:
The big difference between Android and iOS until the recent introduction of iOS4 was Androids ability to multitask.
iOS have addressed this shortcoming in the iOS4 release.
But developers will have to develop applications for the older iOS which doesn't support multitasking because there are undoubtedly a large number of iPhone 3 users who will no bother to upgrade their handsets to iOS 4.2

2.4.3 Location Aware Programming Techniques

The following section outlines the main areas for the software developer to consider when designing and developing location aware apps for the iOS and for AndroidOS.
Both platforms have their advantages and disadvantages with regards to location aware features and implementation. The AndroidOS is easier to work with in this regard.

See section 1.4.1 for examples of Tourism Based Location Aware Applications.

2.4.3.1 iOS Core Location

Core Location is the OS module responsible for providing information about the phones location in space. It does this by using the GPS receiver and GSM triangulation.. older model iPhones have no GPS receiver and use GSM only.
Core Location lets you provide geotagged content or request local resources such as restaurant and events listings.

How Core Location Works
The iPhone uses four methods to locate you. These technologies depend on several providers including Skyhook Wireless(WiFi), Google Maps with GPS and GSM triangulation.

GPS Positioning
If you own a newer-model 3G iPhone, the on-board GPS system tracks your movement. Like any GPS system, this requires a clear path between you and the satellites,. GPS positioning is not available for the first generation 2.5G iPhone.

SkyHook WiFi Positioning
Core Location's preferred pseudo-GPS geopositioning method calls on SkyHook Wireless. SkyHook offers accurate WiFi placement. See the earlier chapter for details on SkyHook WiFi.

Cell Tower Positioning
Again, you can get more details on this from the Technology chapter earlier in this report. This mobile phone uses base station information to triangulate the position.

Hybridizing the Approaches
The iPhone approaches location in stages. First it depends on GPS, then it falls back to SkyHook WiFi and then it reverts to GSM triangulation. If that doesn't work, it finally fails. The latest releases of the SDK provide multiple success call-backs for each of these fall-back methods. You may receive three or four results at any time.

You can set your desired location accuracy to the highest possible settings using the **kCLLocationAccuracyBest** command. Each location request can take a long time… three separate checks can take up to 30 seconds, so the developer must choose the location method carefully.

Core Location Programming Steps:
The following steps are recommended for getting the phones latitude and longitude:

1. Add the Core Location framework.
2. Import both `CoreLocation.h` and `CLLocationManagerDelegate.h` files.
   ```
   #import <CoreLocation/CoreLocation.h>
   #import <CoreLocation/CLLocationManagerDelegate.h>
   ```

3. Allocate a location manager and request the best possible accuracy
   ```
   locmanager = [[CLLocationManager alloc] init];
   [locmanager setDelegate:self];
   [locmanager setDesiredAccuracy:kCLLocationAccuracyBest];
   ```
4. Start locating.
   Delegate call-backs will let you know when the location has been found. This can take many seconds or up to a minute:
   ```
   [locmanager startUpdatingLocation];
   ```
5. Handle the location events.

2.4.3.2 Android Location Services

Android uses the same hardware resources as iOS for getting location information. It uses GPS, WiFi and GSM triangulation as covered in the previous two pages. However, the programming steps are a little different for Android

Location Manager Programming Steps:
The starting point for Android location services is the **getSystemService( )** call. It returns a **LocationManager** class that is saved into a field for later use.

Call the method **dumpProviders( )**
This will give the developer a list of every location provider available.
Like the iOS example, there may be more than one provider. The developer must pick the provider, or request the best possible provider using the **getBestProvider( )** method.

Like the iOS example, it can take up to 30 seconds to pick a provider and give an initial location. There is an option to initially pick the last known location as the first location upon start-up. This will not always be accurate, especially if the phone has been moved a lot the location services were last used, but at least it will give the user something to look at when the phone is busy pinging the actual first location.

Updating the Location
Android will tell the developer when the location of the phone has changed. The `requestLocationUpdate()` method is used to do this.

2.4.4 Database Programming Techniques

Apple iOS and **Google AndroidOS** both provide extensive support for SQLite. It is the default database for both systems and is interchangeable across both systems.
(For more information on SQLite see the section later in this chapter)

For creating, changing and storing data with SQLite, the iOS and Android systems offer excellent functionality built-in. However, the Android platform makes it much easier and straight forward to create a database programmatically.

iPhone Database Techniques
The iOS offers full sqlite3 access. Compared to the android libraries, the iOS can seem very cumbersome. The routines are centred on C-based libsql calls, with little ObjectiveC feel to them.
For this reason, most programming guides recommend using a 3rd party package to handle SQLite access. The most popular one is from Gus Mueller and is available for free. He provides FMDB Cocoa wrappers for all the database needs. FMDB provides SQLite bindings that simplify iPhone database creation, access, and updates.

The steps are as follows:
1. Add a SQLite library to the project.
2. Expand the FMDB library and add it.
3. Create the database using a 3rd party SQLIte3 editing tool.
4. Create code to handle insert and select calls to the database.

Android Database Techniques
Unlike the iPhone, Android provides excellent resources to access it's inbuilt SQLite database tools. They are so good that there isn't even a need to create your database outside of Android. The developer can create the database within the Java code if they wish. This is technically true for iPhone as well, but it is so cumbersome that it is not really worth it.

The steps are as follows:
1. To make the database use `SQLiteOpenHelper` and use standard SQL commands to create the DB.
2. Use `getWritableDatabase()` and `getReadableDatabase()`, to access the DB after creation.
3. You use SQLite SQL commands, which are identical in most ways to regular SQL, to manipulate the database in any way you wish. Queries can be built and executed easily.

2.4.5 Bluetooth Programming Techniques

iPhone Bluetooth Programming Techniques.
Finding documentation and developer guides on using Bluetooth for the iPhone is very difficult. Apple seems to provide the minimum amount of support for this aspect of iPhone development.
As of iOS 3.0, there has been the introduction of a GameKit set of APIs which include support for Bluetooth. Using these APIs is the easiest way to access the Bluetooth hardware on the iPhone.
Even with this new API, the Bluetooth stack is still very limited. During the Bluetooth experiments for this report, it was not possible to do a simple Bluetooth task such as scan the vicinity and list all available bluetooth devices. The functionality is available, but if the developer uses it I an iOS application, then Apple will not allow it into the App Store, which means the developer can't distribute the application.
The steps for the GameKit are as follows:
1. Add the `GameKit` framework to the application(via the Xcode menu).
2. Declare a declare a `GKPeerPickerController` object. This class provides tools to allow discovery of other Bluetooth devices.
3. Implement the `btnConnect:` method to connect to another device.
4. After connection, then use the other methods in the class to communicate with the other device.
5. The `sendDataToAllPeers:` method looks after the transmission of data.
6. The `receiveData:fromPeer:inSession:context:` method will look after reception of data.

Android Bluetooth Programming Techniques.
Of course Android supports bluetooth as well. Almost all android devices come with bluetooth hardware preinstalled. Since Android 2.0, Google have provided a rich set of APIs. Before this there were 3rd party APIs available to enable bluetooth.
Android devices can do all the usual Bluetooth functions including pinging for devices, checking for paired and non-paired devices, generating RFCOMM channels, transferring data etc.
The steps are as follows:
1. Set the user permission in the AndroidManifest.xml file.
   `<uses-perm android:name="android.permission.BLUETOOTH"/>`
2. Create a function to switch on/off Bluetooth on the device.
   ```
   import android.bluetooth.BluetoothAdapter;
   public static void StartBluetooth(){
   BluetoothAdapter btAdapter = BluetoothAdapter.getDefaultAdapter();
   ```
   btAdapter.enable();
   Disabling Bluetooth is just as easy:
   ```
   public static void StopBluetooth(){
   BluetoothAdapter btAdapter = BluetoothAdapter.getDefaultAdapter();
   btAdapter.disable();
   ```
   Both methods (enable() and disable()) return a boolean value. 1 means success and 0 means failure.
3. Create functions for Discovering devices, services and transferring data in a similar fashion.

2.5 Nokia OS

Nokia are the largest manufacturer of mobile phones in the world, and have been making smartphones since 2006.
With the launch of the N95 in Sep 2006 Nokia introduced a phone model that could be considered the precursor to modern smartphones. The N95 had a host of new features and combined many features that were available on separate phone models including 3.5G, WiFi, quadGSM, bluetooth, miniUSB, camera, GPS, MicroSD. Nokia have been on the cutting edge of smartphone design despite their recent loss of the top-spot in worldwide smartphone sales. Outside of the US, Nokia have absolute dominance in the mobile marketplace.

Because of Nokia's legacy in the mobile space, they have a large number of operating system versions spread out over hundreds of mobile phone models. This section is limited to discussing only the most relevant operating system properties and SDKs that are of interest to the developer of modern tourism applications.

Symbian OS accounts for over 40% of worldwide smartphone sales.
It contains the following layers:
UI Layer, Java ME application layer, Services layer(comms, graphics, connectivity), Base Services layer and Kernel and HW Interface layer.

The latest Nokia smartphones use MeeGo/Maemo as their OS instead of Symbian.
MeeGo/Maemo is a Linux based open source OS. It provides support for Arm and x86 processors. The UI looks like the typical modern layout of the other smartphone operating systems.

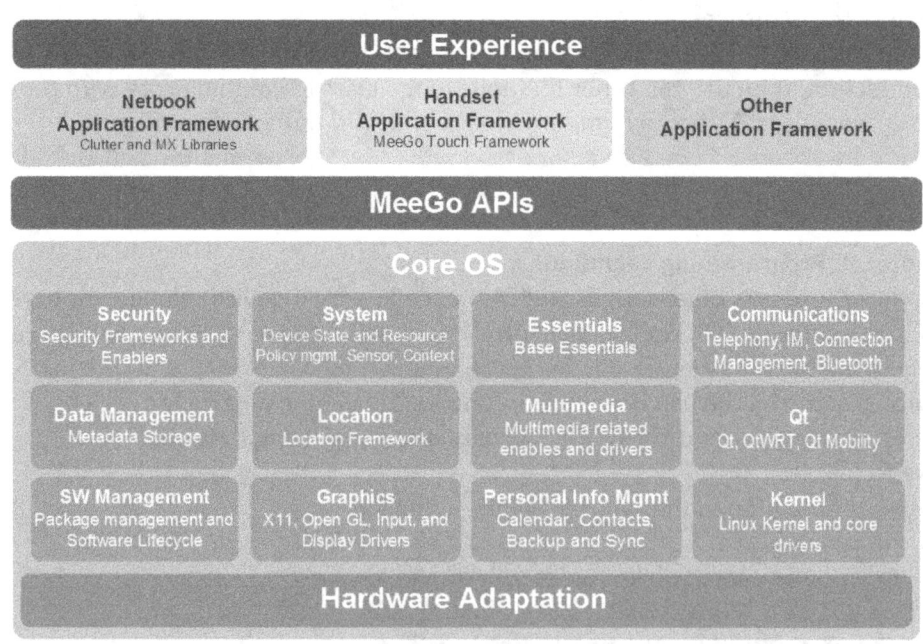

2.5.1 Nokia Software

Of all the mobile manufacturers, Nokia provide the most comprehensive and varied options for programming applications for their devices. Mostly because they've been making cutting edge phones for longer than most other companies.
With the rapid rise of touch screen smartphones, a lot of these technologies and approaches are becoming less useful, so we will not go into too much detail as they will probably have limited importance in the coming months/years.

Nokia Java Technology
Allows the developer to create applications for the Java ME environment, the most widely deployed mobile runtime environment(including non-smartphones).
The following setup is needed to develop JavaME applications on the S60 platform:
A Java SE (Standard Edition) Development Kit (JDK) with the Nokia SymbianOS/S60 SDK for Java, an IDE plus an add-on for Java ME development (Nokia supports Eclipse + EclipseME and NetBeans + Mobility Pack) documentation.

C++ on Nokia S60 with Symbian C++
The Nokia Smartphone S60 platform remains popular and Nokia recommends using Symbian C++ to develop applications for the S60 series of devices.
To access the full power of the S60 platform, Nokia recommends using Symbian.
Symbian C++ is the main language of Symbian OS. The S60 remains the most popular Nokia smartphone platform, although it will be discontinued after the Nokia N8(launched in 2010).
The other runtime environments available in the S60 platform, such as Java technology, Flash Lite from Adobe, Python, and Web Runtime may offer a more accessible development option for some developers, but Symbian C++ provides the richest application programming interfaces for the most powerful and sophisticated applications for the S60 platform. As a programming language optimised for mobile devices, Symbian C++ offers developers some different programming concepts compared to standard C++, which developers must master to make the most of this language.

Standard C/C++ on S60 with Open C/C++
For creating middleware and application engines, Open C can be used. This means less up skilling for the C or C++ developer.
Application engines and middleware for S60 3rd Edition devices and S60 5th Edition devices can be created using C/C++ PC-programming skills.
With the availability of Open C/C++, the S60 platform is open to a huge number of developers.
The APIs in Open C/C++ it's possible to port existing PC software to the S60 platform. The APIs also help developers who lack knowledge of the Symbian OS and S60 APIs.
It's important to note that using the Open C/C++ APIs doesn't put developers at a disadvantage: The performance characteristics closely match those of similar native S60 APIs.
Open C/C++ doesn't provide standard C/C++ APIs for the S60 UI or the S60 application engines, such as calendar, contacts, and messaging applications. To build applications with a standard S60 look and feel, developers will have to use S60 APIs or employ Python for S60. Similarly, to access the standard S60 application engines, Symbian OS and S60 APIs will be required.

Python
As mentioned in the Bluetooth section, python is used for prototyping or fully developed commercial applications that don't require cutting edge speed and don't require low level access to the devices hardware. Python provides more accessible development for S60 devices then Symbian C++.

Websites and web services on Nokia devices
Webpages can be created instead of creating local applications(see the Web vs SDK section).
Both the S60 Series 40 have web-browsing capabilities as well as all smartphones released by Nokia.
The S40 devices used Lite mobile browsing.
Nokia uses Web Runtime widgets on S60 devices to give the appearance of a native application. Programs look as if it were a native S60 or Java application.

2.5.2 Maemo SDK

Note: Nokia development is currently split between the old Symbian SDK and this new Maemo(and Meego) SDK. In practice, it's more practical to use the Nokia Qt SDK which integrates both the Symbian and the Maemo SDKs. All three are covered here.
[Additionally, Nokia have just announced(Feb11) an alliance with Microsoft and intend to adopt the Phone 7 platform for some of it's smartphones which puts Maemo into doubt]

Linux C for the Maemo Platform
Maemo is an open source Linux platform based on desktop Linux. Maemo, was first introduced in 2005 on Nokia's Internet Tablet concept. It stems from the ambition to bring PC-like user behaviour, including multitasking, browsing and communications to mobile devices. Maemo is based on global open source development and is today contributed by over large number of individuals, communities and companies. The Maemo home screen, navigation look and feel and general layout are similar to all of the latest smartphone operating systems. It has a sharper look and feel than most of the others.
The Maemo SDK provides the following subsystems:
Multimedia subsystem, Connectivity subsystem., Real time communications subsystem, Core subsystem, Application interfaces.

Tools	Maemo SDK
Languages	C, C++
Cost	free
Devices	All devices using Maemo are Nokia phones... currently just the Nokia N900
Documentation	Forum Nokia Knowledge Base.
Developer Support	Forum Nokia Knowledge Base
App Delivery Mechanism	Nokia's apps store, Ovi Store

2.5.3 Qt SDK

The Qt SDK was introduced to integrate many of the various platforms under the Nokia family. It allows developers to amalgamate a lot of the older SDKs and the newer ones available and combine them in a uniform development environment. So it is a tool for writing applications for most of the popular Symbian and Maemo devices. It is unknown at this stage whether Qt will be integrated into Microsoft's SDL of if they will keep the application development within the Phone 7 SDK only.
Qt is a C++ based framework. Once the developer knows C++ then using Qt becomes intuitive and straight forward.
Qt Development:
Qt Creator is a cross-platform Qt IDE. You can download it as a standalone application or separately as a set of different libraries. It comes packaged with a very comprehensive source code editor.
Qt Designer is the GUI creator and layout editor for Qt. It is similar to the apple Interface Builder in that it is very much point an click based. The views and window layouts created using Qt Designer are similar to the finished product.
Qt Emulator allows emulation of the N97 and the N900. Lots of options available to configure different setups and screen sizes etc.
Qt Linguist is a formal setup for localising and internationalizing an application. It adopts the usual approach used by most SDKs... different resource files for different languages.

Tools	Nokia QT SDK
Languages	C++
Cost	free
Devices	Large number of Nokia devices – Symbian and Maemo devices
Documentation	Forum Nokia Knowledge Base.
Developer Support	Forum Nokia Knowledge Base
App Delivery Mechanism	Nokia's apps store, Ovi Store

2.5.4 Nokia Smartphones

Nokia N8
Oct-10

12-megapixel camera and Xenon flash
720p HD video recording,
Dolby surround sound
3.5-inch AMOLED screen with a 640 x 360 pixel resolution,
16GB of internal storage
Symbian^3 operating system
(last N-series phone based on this platform).
Talk Time: 5.8 hours
Platform: Symbian^3
Wireless: 802.11b/g/n Wi-Fi, Bluetooth 3.0
Network: quad-band GSM, penta-band WCDMA
Storage: 16GB built-in, 32GB supported via microSD

Nokia N900
Oct-10

Wi-Fi and 3.5G
Full AJAX support
1GB of application memory
3.5" WVGA touch display (800 x 480 pixels).
Maemo 5 software on Linux
Wide screen video capture
48GB of storage
Mozilla Technology
Adobe Flash 9.4

2.6 RIM Blackberry OS

Research in Motion(RIM) produce the BlackBerry line of smartphones. Blackberry historically provide superior messaging and email services than other smartphone operating systems. Most Blackberrys use a physical qwerty keyboard, rather than the soft on-screen keyboards preferred by most of the other smartphones on the market. Although all the major smartphone OS support physical qwerty.
The OS is a closed multitasking system developed in-house by RIM. It features a Web kit browser(like Nokia) and supports tabbed browsing. It supports a number of services including, location services(GPS) and maps service to allow mapping within applications. The Blackberry push service is a strong feature of the OS, allowing applications to run in the background and give users instant information.
It supports all the features one expects from modern smartphones. Some of the features more unique to the Blackberry OS are push email, faxing, devices often feature a built-in physical keyboard.

2.6.1 Blackberry Software

The Blackberry is Java based and the learning curve for existing Java developers is minimal. The Blackberry debugger is integrated into the Java development environment and the emulator is free. Obviously it's not cross-platform. Programs written for the Blackberry are specific to that device.
2D graphics. Functionality is via APIs only and is therefore limited, but there is full file access. Again the speeds are compromised because it uses bytecode. Blackberry are one of the largest smartphone players. There is very good developer support.

2.6.2 Blackberry SDK

There are a few options available to the developer when it comes to the Blackberry. But the vast majority choose the Java based SDK plug-in for Eclipse.
For tourism apps that require location based services such as GPS, then the Java SDK and Java Eclipse plug-in are the best options.
Using the BlackBerry Java Plug-in for Eclipse, incorporates all the necessary APIs and allows the developer to start out in a familiar environment. Anyone coming from a Java or Android development background will very likely be familiar with this environment.
A large collection of BlackBerry APIs are available to allow the developer to use all the tools necessary for developing tourism and locations based applications.

2.6.3 Blackberry Smartphones

BlackBerry Torch 9800
Aug-10
Optical trackpad
Vertical slide-out keyboard
360x480 resolution touch screen,
OS 6.0.
Talk Time: Up to 5.8 hours
Standby Time: 13 days
Platform: BlackBerry OS 6
Wireless: 802.11b/g/n Wi-Fi, Bluetooth 2.1 +EDR
Network: GSM, HSPA 7.2
Storage: 4GB built-in, 4GB microSD

2.7 Microsoft Mobile OS

Windows CE based Windows Mobile 6 has been discontinued since the introduction of Windows Phone 7. We will cover it briefly because there are some handsets still in use. It was meant to look similar to Vistas look and feel. It supported a 320x320 screen resolution, supported Office Mobile, provided extensive bluetooth functionality. Microsoft SQL Compact edition was integrated into the OS.
Windows Mobile never captured much of the market and was in steady decline until it was discontinued in 2010.

Windows Phone 7 is it's successor and represents a complete redesign. This new operating system bears little relationship to the outgoing Mobile 6.5 operating system.
Phone 7 OS was launched in October 2010.
The Home screen looks a little different than other smartphones. It uses multi-touch functionality and supports on-screen virtual keyboards. The web browser is based on IE Mobile.
Win Phone 7 handsets are instantly recognisable because there is a requirement for each one to have a physical search button prominently visible with the Windows logo on it. Microsoft Office Mobile is integrated into the OS.
Microsoft has been ahead of the curve in the display of advertising on the phone, it has integrated an advert display system into the OS ahead of Apple and Google. Adverts can be pushed to the device using this system. Apple and Google have since implemented similar functionality on their OS.

2.7.1 Microsoft Software for Mobiles

.NET Compact Framework:
For deployment on Pocket PC / Windows Mobile devices. Based on C sharp, and VB.Net. Applications are developed within Visual Studio and the platforms it targets are Windows mobile, CE, Symbian devices. Supports 2D and 3D graphics and many widgets. Uses a visual form based GUI builder. There is full mobile access to the file system. Runtime speeds are average to poor.
There is extensive developer support via MSDN.

Pocket PC and Microsoft Smartphone:
Not relevant for use in the tourism industry due to it's limited audience. It is only used on Microsoft devices and it is not cross-platform.
Based on Basic4App. It is easy to learn to program and development is via the Basic4App IDE.
Supports 2D and 3D graphics, many widgets and has a limited GUI builder. There are no restrictions to functionality and full file system access. It's a compiled language so the speeds are good.
MSDN give excellent developer support.

Visual C++:
Native code for MS Mobile 6.5 can be written using Visual C++.

Silverlight C#:
Applications for Phone 7 must be written in Silverlight C# (or in Visual Basic).
C sharp looks very similar to C++ and Java and it has mimicked many of the attributes of these two languages and has improved on some of the features. It is a user-friendly, powerful programming language. C sharp source code can contain higher level managed code and lower level unmanaged code. The managed code is administered by the system which runs it. This makes sure that it is hard to crash your smartphone running managed code. However, this level of oversight causes your programs to run more slowly.
To get better running speeds and memory optimization, the C sharp system allows the developer to manipulate some areas of the OS… this code is marked as unmanaged and it is therefore, possible to crash the OS if the developer leaves a bug in the code…. Apple and Google don't allow this level of access (to the app developer).

2.7.2 Windows Mobile 6.5 SDK

Windows Phone 7 has completely replaced 6.5 with a completely new suite of tools that have little or no relation to the 6.5 SDK. But there are a lot of 6.5 devices in use and it may be necessary to cater for them in certain tourism markets. However, development will become increasingly difficult on this platform because windows have completely cut off all developer support and all the Microsoft forums and discussion boards are being redirected to the Phone 7 sites.

Developers using this platform have a few options open to them. They can use Visual C++ to write the operating system managed code or write server code and distribute it thru Internet Explorer for Mobile. Microsoft released SDKs that integrated with the Visual Studio development environment. These SDKs included the Mobile 6.5 emulators for testing.

Tools	Microsoft Visual Studio 2008 Professional Edition or better, but not Visual Studio 2010
Languages	Native C++ or supported .NET languages C# or Visual Basic .NET
Cost	Free SDK, Visual Studio 2008 Professional - $1200, Application marketplace subscription - $99/year
Devices	Smartphones and PDAs from many different manufacturers, including HTC, LG and Samsung
Documentation	Microsoft Developer Network and related sites, Large amount of community content
Developer Support	Microsoft Professional support, Free community support
App Delivery Mechanism	Through a memory card, network or an ActiveSync connection, Microsoft Windows Marketplace for Mobile

2.7.3 Windows Phone 7.0 SDK

Windows Phone 7 was received by the mobile development community very enthusiastically. Initial reports suggested that it was very developer friendly and quite easy to develop for. It uses the Silverlight platform and allows for very fast up skilling. It is generally thought of as an easier SDK to learn than the Android Java SDK or the Apple Xcode SDK.

Silverlight is one of Microsoft's latest development environments. It was used extensively before it started to support the Windows Phone 7 operating system. Version four of Silverlight was the first version to support mobile development and was released in mid 2010. It supports Windows Phone 7 and Symbian for the series 60 set of Nokia phones.

All of the development can be done within Silverlight, but Microsoft provides an alternative set of tools for dedicated UI design for the Phone 7 platform.

The Windows Phone Emulator
As with all modern SDKs and IDEs, Microsoft supplies a feature rich emulator to allow off-line testing of applications. Uniquely, Microsoft allows the emulation of multi-touch screen input with the emulator. This is not the case with the Apple and Google emulators. Of course the emulator is limited when it comes to checking accelerometer, GPS and other hardware specific functions… but this is the same case with all mobile emulators.

Nokia and Microsoft:
It is worth mentioned here again that Nokia and Microsoft have teamed up on the mobile front and most of Nokia's new smartphones will feature the Microsoft operating system... this will greatly increase the importance of the Windows Phone 7 operating system... it will become the number three player in the smartphone field after Google and Apple.

Tools	Microsoft Visual Studio 2010 Express for Windows Phone, Expression Blend 4 for Windows Phone
Languages	.NET; C# only, Silverlight, XNA
Cost	Free SDK, Windows Marketplace for Mobile developer subscription - $99/year
Devices	Smartphones and PDAs from many different manufacturers, including HTC, LG and Samsung
Documentation	Electronic on MSDN and on the SDK
Developer Support	Microsoft developer support, Broad community support
App Delivery Mechanism	Via Windows Marketplace for Mobile

2.7.4 Microsoft Smartphones

HTC Mondrian
Scheduled for October 2011

1.3GHz Snapdragon processor,
4.3-inch screen with a WVGA resolution, and a camera with HD capabilities and at least 5 megapixels.

LG Optimus 7
LG's flagship Windows Phone

1.3GHz Qualcomm Snapdragon processor,
3.5-inch capacitive touch screen display and
5-megapixel camera.

2.8 HP Palm OS and WebOS

Palm OS should always be considered because a lot of US tourists use Palm devices.
The Palm OS provides a simple, single tasking system with a simple GUI.
It includes all the basic systems that you would expect on a mobile OS. In addition it supports handwriting recognition, hot sync technology for comms with the desktop.
The following applications are built into PalmOS: Address program, date book, expense tracker, hot sync tool, memo pad, to do list.

HP WebOS is the successor to PalmOS. It is Linux based.
The webOS uses what Palm refer to as a card management system to handle multitasking. Each applications runs on a card(basically a thread. The user toggles from one application to the next by changing which card he is on... the UI lets the user shuffle between cards or apps.
The webOS uses a feature called Synergy to integrate a users information into a synced format. It attempts to integrate Gmail, Yahoo, Facebook etc.. into a single source. The web browser uses Web kit similar to Nokia.
The following default apps are built into the operating system: phone, email, web, music player. Also included are messaging, calendar, camera, photos, video, Google maps, memos, doc view, PDF view and contacts.

Under the GUI, the software stack is similar to Linux desktop systems.

2.8.1 Palm Software

PalmOS is based on C, C++ and Pascal.
WebOS is based on JavaScript, HTML and CSS.

2.8.2 Palm WebOS SDK

The Palm WebOS SDK is available for Mac OSX, Ubuntu and Windows

HP webOS SDK uses simple technologies familiar to anyone who writes web applications: HTML, CSS, and JavaScript. A set of standard APIs gives the developer access to the webOS.
This approach makes it very easy for a desktop web developer to start writing applications for Palm devices. The Palm applications that come pre-installed on Palm devices are written using the same method.

The web approach to programming for the Palm has not limited the access to any of the devices underlying features. The developer can still run multiple apps in the background and respond to events on the phone in the same was as other platforms allow.
PalmSource provide a free emulator and development is via the PalmOS Development System.
Supports 2D and 3D graphics, many widgets and has a good GUI builder. There are no restrictions to functionality and full file system access. Again it's a compiled language so the speeds are good.
There is extensive developer support.
(see table on next page)

Tools	Palm webOS SDK, The Mojo framework, Palm Developer Tools (PDT)
Languages	Applications typically written in JavaScript, HTML, AJAX, and other common Web technologies, as well as in C and C++
Cost	$99 annual fee for developer account(sometimes fee is suspended/waived)
Devices	Palm Pre, Palm Pixi, Palm Plus
Documentation	Documentation at developer.palm.com
Developer Support	At developer.palm.com
App Delivery Mechanism	The Palm App Store

2.8.3 Palm WebOS Smartphones

Palm Pre Plus	
Jan-10	
3.1-inch (320 x 480) display,	
3-megapixel camera with LED flash and geo-tagging support,	
600MHz processor and 16GB of storage.	
Talk Time: 5.5 hours	
Standby Time: 14.6 days	
Platform: webOS	
Wireless: 802.11b/g Wi-Fi, Bluetooth 2.1 + EDR	
Network: CDMA, EV-DO Rev. A on Verizon; GSM, HSPA 7.2 on AT&T	
Storage: 16GB built-in	

2.9 Other Mobile Software, OS and SDKs

2.9.1 Java ME

Java ME can be a good choice of programming language for mobile development so long as the functionality that the developer requires is contained within the ME platform. There are many libraries written by the different manufacturers to allow apps to me developed and run on their mobile devices. Java ME has been traditionally used to write graphics heavy applications for mobile devices. It must be considered that any apps requiring more than 1Mb will not run very well on many of the older generation of feature phones. Obviously, if you know Java then learning how to program in Java ME is straight forward. The learning curve is minimal. If you're not familiar with programming in java or in another similar language, then the learning curve is very steep ! There are many debuggers available and they are all very good.

Sun provide a good Java ME emulator and provide a good Java Wireless Toolkit. Like Symbian, Java ME should be cross platform, especially considering Javas ethos of being a cross-platform development environment, but in order to avoid device specific bugs, a separate implementation must be written for each device. Java ME programs are packaged inside a JAR/JAD file and almost all the development tools for Java ME are free.
Java ME supports 2D and 3D graphics, many widgets and Visual Formbased GUI builder.
There are some restrictions to its functionality such as limited file access. It provides full phone data access. Runtime speeds are average because of the Java bytecode.
There is excellent support available from the development community and it has been deployed on a large number of devices.
Because Java is the most widely used programming language, it is necessary to be familiar with it, even if most of the applications you write are not written in Java.

Java ME has the following restrictions over standard Java:
For security reasons, there is additional user interaction required when networking or sending SMSs.
There are no Swing classes... each manufacturer provides GUI classes of their own.
The APIs can vary from manufacturer to manufacturer so you have to familiarise yourself with each one as you move from one device to another.

2.9.2 Flash Lite

Macromedia originally developed Flash in the 1990s. Adobe took them over and continued intensive development of the Flash set of tools. It has always been Adobes aim to keep the simplicity of the language so that up-skilling for developers is minimal. Developing applications in Flash is extremely fast and the time from idea to market is short.
Flash Lite is the mobile version of Flash, like Java ME, it has been paired down to the essentials required for mobile development, with the emphasis on providing good effects in a resource light environment such as the mobile phone environment. This has been done by sacrificing the detail that would not be normally visible on a small screen anyway. Resource heavy graphics processing has been minimized as much as possible. Other functionality has been added to Flash Lite such as mobile keypad support, soft keyboards and other mobile specific requirements.
Like regular Flash on a desktop, Flash Lite is good for Graphics-heavy options with a market that can support the Flash Lite player. If you plan to develop applications with a lot of graphics, perhaps targeting kids, then Flash Lite is worth investigating.
Flash Lite is based on Action Script and it's emulator is bundled with the Macromedia Flash Integrated Development Kit. The top five mobile manufacturers support Flash Lite without any need to download add ins on all new phones. The cost of the development tools varies, but most are free.
Flash supports 2D graphics and many widgets. It supports partial functionality, again via the APIs. There is NO phone data access and runtime speeds are below average because like Python, it is an interpreted language.
There is an extensive development community using Flash Lite and as a result there is a lot of support for this technology. It is expected to grow rapidly through 2010 and beyond.
A major drawback with Flash Lite is that Apple don't currently support it, citing performance issues and claiming that it crashes the OS... even though many 3rd party developers have released iPhone apps that do support Flash Lite.

2.9.3 Lazarus/Python/Brew

Lazarus is good for prototyping and quickly developing database powered applications. Lazarus is based on Object Pascal and the time to upskill is dependent on your familiarity with Pascal, but developers tend to agree that up skilling is easy compared to other platforms. Lazarus can debug on ActiveSync for Windows CE. The Lazarus IDE includes an integrated GUI designer and debugger. It has been used to develop for Windows 6 devices and for Nokia Symbian devices. Development tools are free.
Lazarus supports 2D graphics, many widgets and Visual Formbased GUI builder.
There are no restrictions to its functionality. It provides full phone data access. Runtime speeds are good because it's a compiled language. There is decent support available although it has not achieved widespread usage.

Python:
Nokia always recommends using Python when writing rapid prototypes and when you require functionality that is not available in the Nokia version of Java ME.
Python is not based on any base programming language and it is easy to learn(by intention). The development tools are available for free from Nokia. Mainly used for use on Nokia series 60 devices.

Python supports 2D graphics and some simple widgets.
There is partial functionality via the APIs. It provides some phone data access to calendars, contacts.
Runtime speeds are poor because it's an interpreted language.
There is decent support available. The development community is growing. Like Lazerus, it has not achieved widespread usage yet.

BREW:
Brew has had very little use in Europe. It is used to write applications that will run on CDMA based networks.
Brew is based on C with C++ style syntax. Many developers claim that it is a very difficult language to learn. Applications are developed within Visual Studio. There is no emulator available.

Supports 2D and 3D graphics and a limited set of widgets. There is no visual form based GUI builder. There is powerful API functionality and full access to the file systems. Runtime speeds are excellent and are comparable to Symbian and Lazarus.

There is very poor support at present, for developers. Just one website at Qualcomm.
It's used extensively in Japan and Korea. There is growing uptake in North and South America and in China.

2.10 Web Development vs SDK

The modern smartphone is in many ways a rival to the traditional laptop and is increasingly providing many of the features of a laptop. Like the desktop/laptop, there is an alternative to native software development. The feature rich internet browsers on modern smartphones allow the developer to consider writing web based applications for the smartphone using HTML, JavaScript and CSS.

2.10.1 Comparing the Two Programming Styles

Surprisingly, a web based smartphone application can provide a similar look an feel to a natively developed application and can provide much of the same features and functionality.
A traditional web developer can get up and running almost immediately by choosing the web development path instead of the SDK path. There are only very specific circumstances when the functionality required will not be available to the web developer.

Of course a compiled programming language differs from PHP, Perl, or Ruby on Rails. If your C/Java skills are rusty or non-existent then the learning curve to go from web development to SDK development can be very steep. When the developer wants to make extensive use of the smartphones GPS, its accelerometers, and its unique input devices then the SDK is an attractive choice.

2.10.2 Advantages and Disadvantages
The advantages and disadvantages are listed below:

Web development advantages	SDK advantages
Ease of development	Sophisticated development environment
Ease of first-time user access	Improved language depth
Rapid deployment	Integration with smartphone libraries
Automated updating	Improved graphics libraries
Access to dynamic data	Ease of continued user access
Access to existing web content	No downloading
Offline server access	Native speed
Integration with external web content	Improved privacy
Access to other users	Built-in economic model

2.10.3 Web Development

Simplicity.
Web based development is generally simpler then SDK programming, both from the perspective of the developer and the end user.
The developer can use a dynamic language rather than the traditional object oriented languages like Java and objective C. Dynamic languages can be quite complex in their own right but generally speaking they are easier to learn and easier to use than native languages.
The uses also enjoys a simpler experience when using the app or program for the first time. They are more likely to take the time to access a program through the browser rather than having to download it from an app store. However, with the massive increase in popularity and the increased acceptance of downloading apps, this is becoming less of an issue.
Dynamism.
You can update your web based application at any time. When the developer wants to update or enhance their existing application, then they have to re-release it and get it onto the app stores and prompt any existing users about the new version. With web development, the developer simply updates the web program on their server and the next time a user accesses it, they will instantly have the updated version. The developer can easily give users access to their newest data with web development. With SDK development any data that is stored within the app such as a SQLite database, is static and will only be updated upon a reissue or if the developer specifically designs the app to update online at regular intervals. For tourism apps this isn't critical... it is unlikely that the developer would have to update the information too often after the app has been written and even if they do, the users change all the time... regular visits from the same users are unlikely.
Globalization.
In some cases the web programmer can create one app that can be used on desktops and mobile phones. In many cases, customization for mobiles will not be necessary. The smartphone app can be integrated into the overall website for the location that you are programming for... for example, the Bunratty or Caherconnell websites can simply have a section for the smartphone app and the app can be later used on the tourists desktop when they arrive home.

2.10.4 Web Development Models

We classify web pages into three types:
- Those that haven't received any special development work for the smartphone
- Those that have received normal development work
- Those that have received development work using specific smartphone web development tools

Non-Developed Web Pages
Non-developed web pages are pages that haven't been designed for use on a smartphone, but which are viewed by smartphone users anyway. For example, existing Bunratty and Caherconnell websites can possibly be viewed on a mobile device without alteration.

Non-developed webpages usually fall into two categories:
1. Smartphone Incompatible: If a web page has tiny font sizes that require the used to zoom in a lot, if it depends heavily on unsupported smartphone features like Flash or if the tables within the page do not display well on a small screen then this type of website is an incompatible non-developed website.
2. Smartphone Compatible: If the website works well on a smartphone, despite the fact that the developer of the website has not made efforts to make it compatible with smartphones, then this can be considered a smartphone compatible non-developed webpage.

Developed Web Pages
Web pages that are developed with the smartphone user in mind are considered developed web pages.

This can be an existing website that has been retooled to look good and be useful to the smartphone user or it can be a webpage that was developed from the beginning to be used by smartphone users. Good design of tables and style sheets, non-use of incompatible tools like Flash and the use of commands that deal with smartphone specific features all provide a better experience for the end user.

2.10.5 SDK Development

Sophistication.
Web applications may be a lot easier to develop and deploy, but SDK programs allow for improved depth and sophistication. This offers some important advantages.
Dynamic web languages are quickly catching up to the traditional native programming languages, but they have not reached a level where they can be considered direct replacements.
For the developer to access all the hardware features of a smartphone, then the SDK object oriented languages are the only option.
Many of the experiments undertaken for this book could not have been done using a web based development approach. Accessing and reading the detailed information and feedback provided by the bluetooth stack, the GPS stack and the other hardware functionality could not have been achieved using a dynamic web language.
Accessibility.
Looking up webpages is very handy, but once the uses has gone to the bother of downloading a native application, it sits on their screen and can be accessed very easily after the initial installation process. It is always there on the screen and the user is reminded that the functionality is available to them without the bother of opening a browser and clicking on a bookmark.
There will also be times when the internet is not available and when this happens the native SDK developed app is still available to the user whereas the web app is not.
Also, a lot of users have an inherent mistrust of sending data over the net and value the additional perceived security of using a native application.
Monetization.
This is a major consideration when designing apps for the tourism sector. It is easier to commercialise a native application than a web application. The native app can have a cost to initially download which the web app cannot... unless they charge a subscription for first accessing the app.
In circumstances where your application must handle sophisticated user interaction and must handle complex actions then the SDK model is better.
If your program must make extensive use of the GPS receiver, Bluetooth communications, the accelerometer then SDK programming is the way to go.
If you want to access the address book or the phones dialler and SMS functionality then SDK is again superior.

2.11 Smartphone Databases

There are a large number of smartphone database options available to the smartphone developer. There are five database types that have been used more often than most, and they are discussed in this section. SQLite was chosen as the most suitable database to use while writing apps for the book. The reasons are listed on the next page.
The choice of database is an easy one if your application is small and self contained. However, when integration with a server based information store is required, then the solutions on offer become harder to choose. The most complete, feature rich and expensive options are the IBM and Oracle databases. For most tourist type applications a free or open-source database will have to be used.

2.11.1 SQLite Mobile Database

SQLite has become very popular amongst most of the smartphone manufacturers. In particular Apple and Google. It is a self-contained SQL database engine that resides inside a single file that can easily be copied from one phone to another and from one operating system to another. A SQLite database on Google Android is identical to one on Apple iOS.
For these reasons, SQLite was used throughout the experimental phase. During the experimental phase of the project, the same SQLite database was used on the Android device and on both iPhone devices. In some instances, the database was created on Microsoft Windows(using a Mozilla Firefox plug-in), fully populated and then copied directly to the iPhone 3Gs and 4 and to the Android powered Samsung GalaxyS. In other cases, the database was created and populated on the Android device and then copied directly to the iPhone devices.
SQLite3 was used in all experiments that necessitated the use of a database.

Chapter 2

Apple iOS and **Google AndroidOS** both provide extensive support for SQLite.

Unfortunately, the new **Windows Phone 7 does not come with a SQLite** database component. Microsoft prefers developers to use cloud-based services for database storage. It is highly likely that 3rd party developers will provide a solution to this drawback.

Newer versions of **Nokia's Symbian OS** have SQLite built in. The new **Nokia/Intel MeeGo OS** supports SQLite.

Tools	TCL (Tool Command Language), C/C++ interface to SQLite, Management Tools, Converter Tools, SQLite Wrappers, SQLite Reporting
Features	Zero-Configuration, Serverless, Single Database File, Stable Cross-Platform Database file
Max Size	1 terabyte
Language Supported	SQL-92
Connection Protocols	N/A
Footprint	<275K
Operating Systems Support	Cross-platform, 32-bit and 64-bit systems
Synchronization/Integration	N/A
Security	Support for reading and writing encrypted databases using these algorithms RC4, AES-128 in OFB mode, AES-128 in CCM mode, and AES-256 in OFB mode
Documentation/Developer	Documentation, Wiki, Sample code, Upgrade guidance, API references
Cost	Public domain

2.11.2 Microsoft SQL Server Compact Database

SQL Server Compact was released by Microsoft to allow developers to use a low impact database on performance restrained desktops and on mobile phones. It runs on all of the Windows platforms including the PocketPC.

Strangely, Microsoft's Windows Phone 7 does not support SQL Server Compact without 3rd party tools.

Tools	Microsoft SQL Server Management Studio, Microsoft Visual Studio
Features	Can be deployed on smart devices and computers. SQL Server Compact Edition Tools for Visual Studio 2005 SP1. SQL Server Compact Edition Developer SDK. SQL Server Compact Edition Server Tools
Max Size	4Gb
Language Supported	T-SQL
Connection Protocols	ADO.NET, ODBC, OLE DB, LINQ
Footprint	<2MB disk space, 5MB memory
Operating Systems Support	Windows Embedded, Windows Mobile, Windows Desktop, Windows Server
Synchronization/Integration	Remote Data Access (RDA), Merge replication, Requires a Client Access License (CAL) to the host SQL Server
Deployment Options	ClickOnce, Microsoft Installer Package (MSI), Xcopy
Security	Data transfer - 128-bit data encryption, Authentication and authorization for RDA handled by Internet Information Services (IIS), Encryption via Secure Sockets Layer (SSL), DB file secured using RSA 128-bit data file encryption and can be password protected
Documentation/Developer	Microsoft Support, Books Online, Blogs, Videos, Community Forums, Newsgroups
Cost	Free

2.11.3 Oracle DBLite Database

Suitable for enterprise type mobile applications and not relevant to small-medium tourism applications. However, it is an option available and because it integrates with SQLite, it can be used on most mobile platforms, including iPhone and Android.
It provides a mechanism to access server side data on a mobile device without requiring a network connection. It accomplishes this by having a limited data mirroring capability. It keeps some data on a small client database and synchronizes with the server database whenever there is a connection available.

Tools	Mobile database offering consists of Database Lite Client and middle tier, Oracle Database Lite Mobile Server. User interface into Mobile Server is Mobile Manager. Mobile Database Workbench (MDW). Mobile Development Kit (MDK). Packaging Wizard
Features	Synchronization support for SQLite databases. Windows Mobile 5 and 6/CE Standard SDK 5.0 support. Android and Blackberry device support. JDK 1.5 compatibility. C++/.NET stored procedures support
Max Size	4GB of relational data. 16TB of BLOB data
Language Supported	SQL-92, Java, C++, .NET stored procedures and triggers
Connection Protocols	ODBC, JDBC, ADO.NET
Footprint	Starting around 1MB
Operating Systems Support	Windows (2003, XP, Vista), Windows Mobile (5, 6), Linux (RedHat), Linux Embedded, Symbian (7, 8, 9)
Synchronization/Integration	Mobile Server provides bi-directional data synchronization to an enterprise instance of an Oracle database.
Deployment Options	Packaging Wizard, Mobile Server, Mobile Server integration with the WebLogic Server 11g and Oracle, Application Server (OAS)
Security	FIPS-140 compliance, SSL, 128-bit AES encryption
Documentation/Developer	Code samples, and tutorials provided with MDK.
Cost	60eur per user, Mobile Server - $23,000 per processor

2.11.4 IBM DB2 Everyplace Database

IBM DB2 is big blues answer for small footprint relational database.
The developer can create a secure embedded mobile database and use industry standard SQL to control it. It is intended for small/medium sized organizations but is not suitable for tourism or consumer end users because of its cost per application. Unless your application uses huge numbers of records then it has no advantage over one of the cheaper or fee options. Enterprise applications for the Palm WebOS have made extensive use of the DB2 database.

Tools	Mobile Devices Administration Centre. XML Scripting Tool
Features	Optimized for SAP. Transaction support. Failure recovery. Allows for indexing for performance tuning. Stored procedures only supported as remote calls via the Remote Query and Stored Procedure Adapter
Max Size	2GB is max size of a single table... overall max size refer to IBMs website.
Language Supported	C/C++, Java, .NET, VB, Subset of standard SQL
Connection Protocols	DB2 Call Level Interface (CLI), ODBC, JDBC, ADO.NET
Footprint	350KB
Operating Systems Support	Windows (2000, 2003, XP, Vista, CE), Linux, Linux Embedded, Symbian, QNX, Palm OS
Synchronization/Integration	DB2 Everyplace Sync Server, DB2 Everyplace Sync Client - secure, bi-directional synchronizing - Runs on Windows (32-bit), Linux (32-bit), Solaris (64-bit), and AIX (64-bit), servlet is provided for simple, low-volume scenarios
Deployment Options	WebSphere Application Server Network Deployment
Security	Local data encryption provided by plugins based on individual platforms, DSYEncrypt utility encrypts passwords
Documentation/Developer	SDK, including tutorials and code samples, IBM website - documentation, support, community forums
Cost	166eur per user; includes license, software subscription and 12 months of support

2.11.5 Sybase SQL Anywhere Database

Again, designed with the light footprint user in mind. It is used on smartphones, tablets, desktop and laptops. Like the Oracle and IBM products on the previous pages, it is intended for the enterprise developer and is not very suitable for the tourism industry.

Tools	Visual Studio, Eclipse, PowerBuilder
Features	20,000 transactions per minute. Veritas Cluster Server (VCS) agent. UltraLiteJ for use on BlackBerry devices and with J2SE. Support for spatial data, language extensions, performance improvements, support for iPhone, and morev.12
Max Size	Hundreds of GB of data
Language Supported	C#, VB.NET, C/C++, ASP, XML, Java, Special drivers for PERL and PHP
Connection Protocols	ODBC, JDBC, ADO.NET, OLE DB, Open Client
Footprint	10MB hard disk, 4MB of memory, UltraLite version 75KB
Operating Systems Support	Windows, Windows Mobile, Linux, Linux Embedded, Mac OSX on Intel, Sun Solaris, IBM AIX, HP-UX MobiLink Windows, Linux, Mac OS X, Sun Solaris, IBM AIX, HP-UX
Synchronization/Integration	Bi-directional replication is accomplished using MobiLink
Deployment Options	Deployment Wizard
Security	Optional purchases RSA and ECC encryption protocols
Documentation/Developer	Documentation, Community forums, Webcasts
Cost	Variable depending on user profile and platform(not free)

3. Technology Available for Building Tourism & Location Aware Applications

This chapter discusses the hardware, software, standards and specifications available for building successful location based smartphone applications for the tourism sector.
It contains all of the 15 experiments carried out for this book.

The first section deals with space-based satellite systems, the most popular being the US GPS system. This section also considers other competing systems that will become relevant in the near future.

The second and third sections deal briefly with WiFi and GSM Tower Triangulation, which are technologies that have failed to gain widespread use in Europe.

The fourth section deals with Bluetooth technology, which is important for providing location aware capabilities in areas not covered by GPS. We deal with Bluetooth extensively throughout this book, so there is a detailed section outlining it's specification relating to smartphones and the tourism industry. In this section we have tested the bluetooth discovery cycle, the strength of the bluetooth signal with reference to distance from the device, the materials the signal passes through, air/glass/concrete, the time required to pair two devices and the effectiveness of a smartphone in finding multiple bluetooth devices during one discovery cycle.

The fifth and sixth sections briefly discuss Hybrid Positioning Systems and Assisted GPS.

The seventh section deals with the rapidly expanding area of 2D codes as it relates to the tourism sector.

The eighth and ninth section briefly discuss Near Field Communications and Augmented Reality.

This book deals extensively with GPS, Bluetooth and QR 2D Coding and these three areas are discussed in detail throughout this chapter.

These are the major technical areas to consider when dealing with location aware services on modern smartphones. However, there are many areas that are not covered by this book and which are worthy of future work.

Technology Available That is Not Covered in This Report:
The area of personalised information on each consumer, and how to harvest this information is an important consideration for future applications. There is an increasing amount of personal data available through Facebook and other social media. Much of this information can be analysed in an automated manner to provide business owners with information about individual consumers purchasing or potential purchasing preferences.

The area of cloud based mobile tourism applications is discussed in section 2.10(Web Development vs SDK). However, experimentation in this area is warranted and further study is recommended. As connection speeds increase and as the availability of 4G mobile internet connections become available, more and more cloud based applications will appear.

3.1 Global Navigation Satellite Systems[GNSS]

Global Navigation Satellite Systems are by far the most accurate way of determining a smartphone users position in space. Currently, the American GPS system is the dominant GNSS system in use today. The Russian GLONASS system is also used extensively and is very useful for improving the accuracy of GPS, but because of the increased cost of including a separate GLONASS detector in mobile phones, it is not used in most smartphones. The GLONASS satellites are also suffering from orbital degeneration due to lack of investment so it is unknown how long they will continue to be accurate. The European GALILEO system is due to come into operation soon and will greatly increase the choice and accuracy available. It is anticipated that by 2012, the Galileo system will be available[Mendizabel 2008].

3.1.1 General Navigation

Navigation is the act of reading, planning and controlling a persons or vehicles route from one position in space to another position in space by making references to known landmarks and structures. Clocks, odometers and radio beacons are all considered to be navigational aids.
GNSS systems are some of the most sophisticated navigational aids ever developed and provide the modern smartphone with a means to accurately determine its position, velocity and altitude.

3.1.2 GPS Predecessors

As mentioned, GPS was developed in the US. During the 1960s, several US military agencies began developing satellite based navigation systems. Global, all weather and accurate systems were required to serve the military. The first system was called TRANSIT and began operations in 1964. It used Doppler Shift technology to calculate a users position and was used primarily for shipboard navigation. It was too slow for high speed uses. The Russians developed the TSIKADA system which was in competition with the Transit system. Both of these systems were important predecessors to the GPS and GLONASS systems.

TIMATION satellites were designed and launched in the 1970s to increase the accuracy of the previous satellite systems. They used on-board atomic clocks to calculate time shifts between signals.

In 1969 the US government consolidate all of their satellite navigation teams into one joint team and this eventually led to the development of the modern GPS system.

The ORG4472, made by OriginGPS.
One of the worlds smallest GPS chips, complete with ARM CPU and firmware. Its power draw is *58 milliwatts*.
(Mobile Conference in Barcelona on 14th Feb 2011)

3.1.3 Introduction to Galileo

In 2002 the European Space Agency announced a European alternative to GPS called GALILEO. It is scheduled for launch in 2012. It is reasonable to expect smartphones to adopt this technology within 1-2 years of it going live. (The first Galileo satellite was put into orbit in 2005). Galileo has been designed from the outset to be very compatible with GPS so it is expected that the same receiver will be able to communicate with GPS and Galileo. This will greatly increase the accuracy of mobile phone location services as there will be double the amount of satellites to calculate the position of the phone.
The US is cooperating with Europe in ensuring that both systems are interoperable. The objective is that everyone will be able to use both systems with a single receiver. Negotiations with the Russian GLONASS team are also in progress [http://www.gsa.europa.eu/].

Racelogic Ltd(UK), the manufacturers of the GPS calibration hardware used during the experimental phase of this book, have demonstrated that using the GLONASS system in conjunction with the GPS system increases the accuracy from a diameter of 3m to a diameter of 30cm. With the addition of the Galileo system, the accuracy should improve even more.

3.1.4 Satellite Based Augmentation System[SBAS]

SBAS augments GPS by providing additional information about the GPS signal. Assisted GPS is an example of an SBAS system. Ground stations take readings from GPS or Galileo and SBAS information is generated and shared with the smartphones that are equipped to use the information. This increases the response time and accuracy of the location based applications on the phone.

Many of the mobile carriers provide Assisted GPS along with the ground stations operated by: the US Federal Aviation Administration, European Space Agency, US DOD, Japan's Ministry of Land, Infrastructure and Transport, the StarFire navigation system owned by John Deere, the Starfix System owned by Fugro.

3.1.5 How GNSS Work

Global Navigation Satellite System(GNSS) work by finding the position of fixed and dynamic objects anywhere in the world by using the information provided by satellites that orbit the earth twice every 24 hours. The orbits are established so that there are always four or more satellites within range of a GNSS receiver placed anywhere on earth. The receiver uses a system called TRILATERATION in three-dimensions to find it's own location. With trilateration, the receiver needs to know the position of three or more satellites and it must know the distance to each satellite. If finds this by reading the high frequency radio signals from the satellites in orbit and in sight of the receiver. In this way it calculates the distance by timing the signals path from the satellite to the receiver[Mendizabel 2008].

3.1.6 Current GNSS

At present there are two operational GNSS systems. The US GPS and the Russian GLONASS systems. Both systems are operated by the military and provide a downgraded accuracy level to non-military users. The Russian system is undergoing some financial difficulty at the moment and the orbits of it's satellites are in decay. The European Galileo system is almost complete and is due for launch in 2012. It is intended to be interoperable with GPS and Glonass[http://www.gsa.europa.eu/].

3.1.7 Commercial Applications

The commercial application of satellite navigation systems are well established. Over the past twenty years many commercial organisation have made use of satellite navigation to some extent, from enabling it's road vehicles to equipping planes, ships and people with navigation receivers.
As mentioned, the Galileo system will have a much greater commercial focus that GPS or Glonass. However, the US is currently in a race to upgrade it's existing system with commercially friendly satellites, which will augment and replace the existing GPS systems. It will incorporate a new dedicated civilian channel which will result in increased accuracy and reliability.

3.1.8 Tourism Market

Engineers are beginning to exploit the recreational possibilities offered by GNSS. Experts predict that more than 40 million potential users in Europe[Mendizabel 2008] will use GNSS for recreational purposes such as sport fishing, sea navigation, hiking and of course navigating tourism hotspots. Nowadays a basic receiver costs around €50-100, yet consumers will soon demand retail prices of less than half that cost. GNSS manufacturers will have to respond to this by reducing cost of manufacture and the cost to the end user. Mandatory services such as the European E112 and American E911 will force more and more smartphone providers to pinpoint the location of their users from any call down to a 100m radius. Thus, every mobile phone will have to include a GNSS receiver. Taking into account the prediction of over 2 billion mobile phone users by 2020, sales for GNSS mobile phone receivers alone will be exceptional[Jacobson 2007].

3.1.9 System Limitations and Vulnerabilities

Despite the capabilities of GNSS systems, there are some limitations and drawbacks within these systems. The major drawback from a tourism perspective is the degradation of the signal in an urban setting. Tall buildings and trees tend to interfere with the accuracy. Poor weather conditions and heavy cloud also lower the accuracy due to interference with the speed of the signal from the satellite to the received. Another major drawback is the inability of current GNSS systems to operate indoors.

3.1.10 Dual Receivers

Dual and triple receivers will have to be developed to allow a single low cost component to be fitted to smartphones that will be capable of receiving signals from all three global satellite positioning systems. Because Galileo is being designed and built to be compatible with the other two systems, it is likely that Galileo receivers will be designed from the outset to pick up all three satellite systems [http://www.gsa.europa.eu/].

3.2 GNSS Experiments

The following section contains all the GNSS – GPS based experiments carried out for this report.

All of the GNSS testing centred around the measurement of false positives. If a device reported it was closest to a particular location out of a data set of multiple locations when in fact it was closer to one of the other locations, then this was registered as a failure to operate and was considered to be a false positive result.

The first experiment established a set of baseline GPS locations in as accurate a manner as was possible. These location coordinates were then used extensively to calculate the accuracy of different smartphones, and technologies.

The second experiment used the locations to measure the accuracy of smartphones in determining their exact position while stationary.

The third experiment was conducted to find out the accuracy of the different online mapping services, to determine if they could be relied upon to provide very accurate location information.

The fourth experiment was a short experiment to find out if there was any merit to using GPS in an indoor environment.

All of the above experiments were conducted in part to provide enough information and knowledge to allow the fifth and sixth experiments to take place.

The fifth and sixth experiments tested the accuracy of the modern smartphone in using GPS information to provide useful functionality to the tourism end user.

3.2.1 Establishment of Very Accurate(<=3m) Baseline GPS Coordinates for Locations in the Galway Area Through the Use of a Calibrated GPS Recording Device

Aim/Goals:
Choose a number of suitable locations in the Galway area (65+ locations), and establish their latitude and longitude to within a diameter of 3meters. This experiment is a benchmarking exercise for all of the later GPS based experiments.

Data from Previous Experiments:
None.

Follow On Experiments:
This experiment will establish all the locations necessary to carry out all further GPS based experiments.

Methodology/Preparation/Planning:
Locations recorded as follows:
1. Place an accurate, calibrated GPS recording device in the location and record the output.
2. If option one is not possible due to physical constraints or due to poor GPS signal, then place the GPS recording device in a location as near as possible to the desired location, record that position and then physically measure the offset distance and bearing to the desired location. Using this information, calculate the exact position of the desired location.
3. In the event that option one and option two are not available because of the inaccessibility of the location or poor GPS satellite line of sight, then take location measurements of nearby landmarks and verify their accuracy on Google Maps and apply an offset if necessary. Then find the desired location on Google Maps and apply this same offset to ascertain the exact latitude and longitude.

Using the most accurate GPS measurement device commercially available, the Racelogic Vbox VB2SX10[1]. Choose many different outdoor locations starting 5Km east of Galway city centre and proceed through the city and on to 5km west of the city. Choose locations based on the following criteria in order of importance:
1. Locations that are useful for later experiments and which are typical of locations visited by tourists.
2. Choose locations that are suitable for testing the limits of current GPS smartphones. Locations that are surrounded by trees, tall buildings, and are predominately in a built up urban environment.
3. Choose a minority of locations in suburban areas that are less built up, in order to get a good cross section of locations and in order to provide a comparison to the more built up city centre locations.

Implementation/Execution:
Each of the 65+ locations were located and marked. Photographs were taken. The Racelogic Vbox receiver was placed in the position and the GPS location information generated by the Vbox was recorded. The device was given as much time as was required to establish the best GPS lock possible. A minimum of 100 readings for each location were recorded.
The following information for each location was recorded:
1. Latitude
2. Longitude
3. Altitude
4. Accuracy(number of satellites being tracked).
5. Time
6. Weather.

This exercise was repeated several times and on different days and in varying weather conditions.

Retesting:
The experiment was designed to allow easy retesting and verification. The photos, combined with the GPS coordinates will allow easy retesting. Locations which were likely to change in the near future were avoided, such as temporary structures/outdoor markets etc.

1: The most accurate GPS device on the market is the Racelogic VBOX 3i R2G2 / VBOX 3i R10G10. This device is capable of tracking Glonass as well as GPS satellites and is accurate to 2cm 95% CEP positional accuracy. However, this item is not available. A good alternative is the Racelogic Vbox VB2SX10 which is accurate to 3m 95% CEP. See the 'Hardware Used' section on the next page for specs.

Hardware Used:
Racelogic Vbox VB2SX10 GPS Recording Device.
(see next page for the cert of calibration).

Absolute Positioning :	Accuracy:	3m 95% CEP[2]
	Update Rate:	10 Hz
	Resolution:	1cm
	Height Acc:	6 m 95% CEP[2]

Software Used:
Software was designed and written to do the following: calculate distances and bearings from one location to another, calculate average locations based on a large collection of coordinates(max 300), segregate the data into categories ranging from category 5(best accuracy) to category 0(unusable).
The Vbox software was used to export the data into usable text files and XML files.

Results/Analysis:
The following rating system was used to categorise the accuracy of the data recorded.
5 is the maximum rating and 0 is the minimum rating.
Category 5: represents the best possible signal from the device used(Vbox VB2SX10). It means that the device has a line of site to 10 or more GPS satellites.
Category 4: represents an excellent signal and can be considered very reliable. It means the device is tracking at least 8 GPS satellites.
Category 3: represent a good signal and can be considered reliable, it means the device is using 6 or more satellites to establish a set of coordinates. But it is advisable to verify the accuracy of the location by comparing it to the nearest other locations that are already established as accurate and by verifying the location using existing maps and online GPS resources that have been established as accurate.
Category 2: represents a signal using 4-5 satellites and acceptable enough to be used to establish a location, but only with verification from other sources, such as Google and Yahoo street maps where high quality locations(in categories 5 and 4) are positioned on the map and the desired location is verified by measuring the offset from these locations.
Category 1: represent signals from less than 4 satellites and cannot be considered reliable. Any category 1 data that is recorded should not be used in any calculations... Except to report on the quality of a location.
Category 0: means that no satellites can be tracked. No location data can be recorded.

Note: Experiments 3.2.5 and 3.2.6 use an alternative 5 point scale to classify their signals. It is important to note that this is not the same as the 5 point scale used in this experiment. This experiment did not use and smartphone devices.

Weather(observed 2010-10-31 13:05):
Lightly overcast, dry with light winds, temperature 9degC.

Weather Report(Met Eireann 2010-10-31 11:00):
Wind = SSE 6.7Knots   Cloud = Cloudy   Temp = 8.3degC
Humidity = 69%   Rain = 3.6mm   Pressure = 1013 hPa.

Changes to Plan During Testing:
None

Validation/Evaluation:
The goal of establishing usable locations for future experiments was achieved. In most cases, location coordinates that were accurate to within 3m were established. Greater accuracy would have been desirable, but this level of accuracy is sufficient for the scope of this book.

2: CEP = (Circle Error Probable) means 95% of the time the position readings will fall within a circle of the stated diameter.

Vbox Cert of Calibration:

CERTIFICATE OF CALIBRATION

RACELOGIC

Customer		Equipment	VBOX IISX 10Hz GPS Datalogger
Location	Ireland	Model	VB2SX10
Customer ID #		Serial Number	014436
In tolerance as received (Y/N)	N/A (New Unit)	Calibration date	09-07-10
Certificate No	007021	Calibration due	08-07-11
Temperature	24.5°C	Engineer	Kate Foskett
Humidity	43%		

Calibration Procedure

The unit under test was subjected to the standard production test procedure. This procedure covers measured velocity by the VBOX over a simulated test course. Simulation data is provided via a calibrated GPS simulator. Analogue output voltage and Digital output frequency are checked for calibration against simulated Longitudinal Acceleration and Speed respectively. Voltage Output range is configured to 0 volts at 0 Km/h, and +5 volts at 400 Km/h. Frequency output is configured to 25Hz per Km/h. VBOX indicated values are taken from MMC data stored by the unit.

Equipment Used

Equipment	Serial Number	CAL Cert No	CAL Due
Simulation of GPS	C001-Spirent 1234	HC43203001	20-01-11
Analogue Voltage measurement	TTI-1906 178199	2264	23-10-10
Frequency Measurement	TTI-1604 170679	2265	23-10-10

Results

Accuracy of analogue and digital output signals

Applied Longitudinal Acceleration	Analogue Output 1			Analogue Output 2		
	Expected	As received	As returned	Expected	As received	As returned
-5G	-5.000 V ± 5.0mV	-	-4.9958 V	-5.000 V ± 5.0mV	-	-5.0010 V
-4G	-4.000 V ± 5.0mV	-	-3.9965 V	-4.000 V ± 5.0mV	-	-4.0007 V
-3G	-3.000 V ± 5.0mV	-	-2.9971 V	-3.000 V ± 5.0mV	-	-3.0002 V
-2G	-2.000 V ± 5.0mV	-	-1.9978 V	-2.000 V ± 5.0mV	-	-1.9999 V
-1G	-1.000 V ± 5.0mV	-	-0.9984 V	-1.000 V ± 5.0mV	-	-0.9994 V
0G	0.000 V ± 5.0mV	-	0.0007 V	0.000 V ± 5.0mV	-	0.0007 V
1G	1.000 V ± 5.0mV	-	1.0001 V	1.000 V ± 5.0mV	-	1.0011 V
2G	2.000 V ± 5.0mV	-	1.9994 V	2.000 V ± 5.0mV	-	2.0015 V
3G	3.000 V ± 5.0mV	-	2.9988 V	3.000 V ± 5.0mV	-	3.0020 V
4G	4.000 V ± 5.0mV	-	3.9981 V	4.000 V ± 5.0mV	-	4.0023 V
5G	5.000 V ± 5.0mV	-	4.9976 V	5.000 V ± 5.0mV	-	5.0027 V

Applied Speed	Frequency Output 1			Frequency Output 2		
	Expected	As received	As returned	Expected	As received	As returned
30 Km/h	750 Hz ± 2.5Hz	-	750 Hz	750 Hz ± 2.5Hz	-	750 Hz
60 Km/h	1,500 Hz ± 2.5Hz	-	1,500 Hz	1,500 Hz ± 2.5Hz	-	1,500 Hz
100 Km/h	2,500 Hz ± 2.5Hz	-	2,501 Hz	2,500 Hz ± 2.5Hz	-	2,501 Hz
400 Km/h	10,000 Hz ± 2.5Hz	-	10,000 Hz	10,000 Hz ± 2.5Hz	-	10,000 Hz

Simulation of constant speed by GPS simulator

Applied simulated value	VBOX indicated speed		
	Criteria	As received	As returned
30 Km/h	±0.1 Km/h	-	30.00 Km/h
60 Km/h	±0.1 Km/h	-	59.99 Km/h
100 Km/h	±0.1 Km/h	-	99.99 Km/h
400 Km/h	±0.1 Km/h	-	399.96 Km/h

Simulation of constant heading by GPS simulator

Applied simulated value	VBOX indicated heading		
	Criteria	As received	As returned
0°	±0.1°	-	0.00°
90°	±0.1°	-	89.97°
180°	±0.1°	-	179.98°
270°	±0.1°	-	269.94°

Summary

The unit (VB2SX10 Serial Number 014436) passed all standard production tests and was found to be fully compliant with the product specification. Racelogic certifies the above instrument meets or exceeds published specifications, and has been calibrated using instruments and standards of known accuracies, which are traceable to "UKAS" United Kingdom Accreditation Service.

Calibration Engineer _____

Racelogic Ltd. Unit 10 Swan Business Centre, Osier Way,
Buckingham, Bucks MK18 1TB.
Tel +44 (0) 1280 823803 Fax +44 (0) 1280 823595

Chapter 3

Results/Analysis(CONTINUED):
With all data, even high quality Category 4 and 5, a large set of latitude and longitude coordinates were gathered (100+ samples) and the average used to establish the location.

NOTE1: In the following results pages, when reference is made to ALL the data or an average of all the data.... It is capped at 300 samples.. So even if more than 300 samples were originally recorded, the additional samples beyond 300 were discarded and the average results were taken from the first 300 samples.

NOTE2: In the photos taken from Google Street View, and in the map snippets that were taken from Google Maps, ignore the RED markers with the letter 'A' in them...
This is a little icon which is auto-generated by Google Maps to indicate local businesses or places of interest. It has no relationship with the data or locations used in the experiment. However, the RED symbol with NO letters present should not be ignored, this represents the experiments locations(as interpreted by Google Street View). Also, the GREEN arrow in Google Maps represents the experiments locations.

Calculations and Formulae Used:
The following formula was used to calculate the distance between two sets of coordinates:

```
1603.9     * sqrt(x * x + y * y)
x = 69.1 *   (lat2 - lat1)
y = 69.1 * -(lon2 - lon1) * cos( lat1 /57.3).
```

This formula is very accurate, and is sufficient for this experiment.
However, there is a more accurate formula available called the Haversine Formula(which is used in the custom software written for this book).

A comparison of the established Haversine formula and the formula used in this experiment are as follows:
Sample point A and B:
Location A: 53.273904, -9.051244
Location B: 53.273914, -9.051221
Distance calculated with the first formula: 1.90541 m
Distance calculated with the Haversine formula: 1.90581m
99.97901% accurate.

The following formula was used to calculate the bearing between two sets of coordinates:
Convert the Latitude and Longitude into Radians and use the following calculations.

```
Bearing = Mod(ArcTan(x, y),2*3.14)
c = COS(lat1)*SIN(lat2)
d = SIN(lat1)*COS(lat2)
e = COS(lon2-lon1)
a = SIN(lon2-lon1)
b = COS(lat2)
x = (c)-(d*e)
y = a*b
```
Convert the result back into degrees.

Locations:
Locations were spread out over a 10Km distance, with the majority within the city centre.

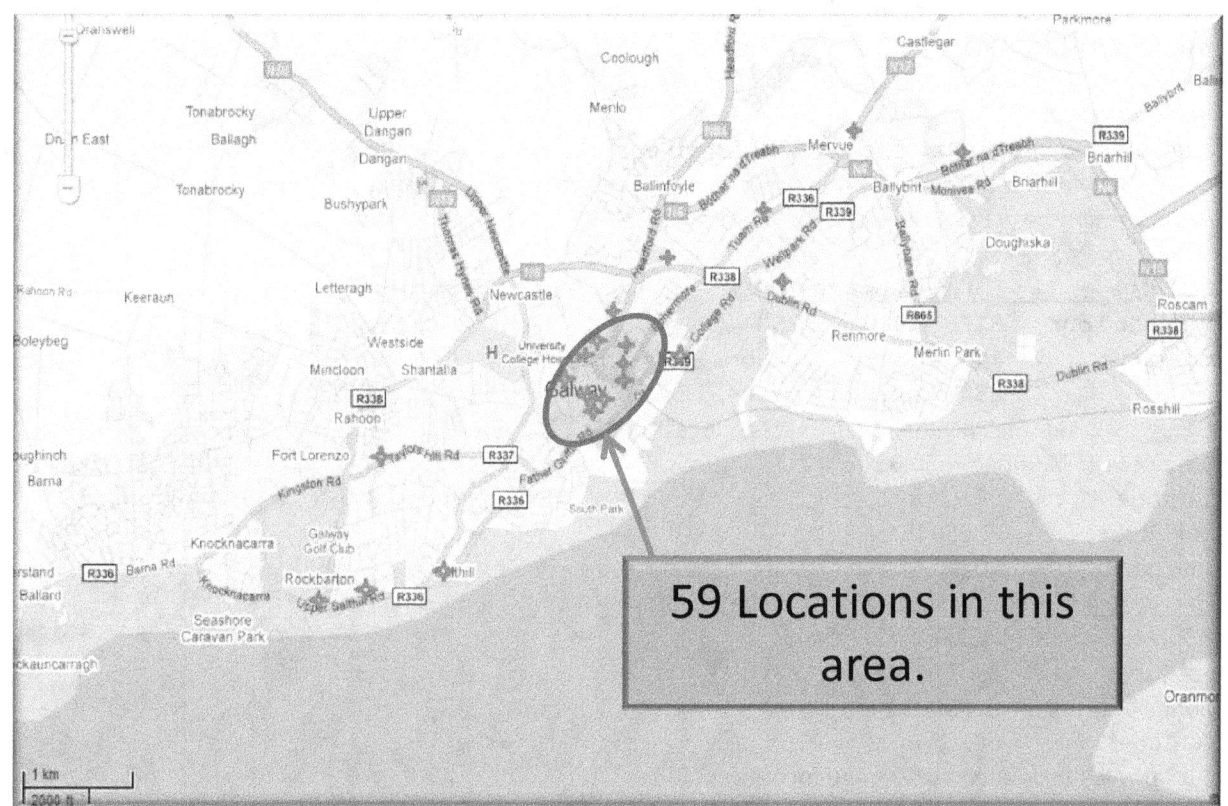

59 Locations in this area.

No	Name	Description	No	Name	Description	No	Name	Description
1	Location 1	O2 Shop	25	Location 25	Brennans	49	Location 49	Fallers
2	Location 2	Logues	26	Location 26	Elles Cafe	50	Location 50	Hanleys
3	Location 3	GBC	27	Location 27	Tommy	51	Location 51	Hollands
4	Location 4	EyreSq SC	28	Location 28	River	52	Location 52	Vodafone
5	Location 5	Monsoon	29	Location 29	Anthony	53	Location 53	Block 6
6	Location 6	Whelans	30	Location 30	Taaffes	54	Location 54	Monaghans
7	Location 7	Monsoon	31	Location 31	Zatsuna	55	Location 55	Liosban
8	Location 8	Galway	32	Location 32	Cafe Express	56	Location 56	Dunnes
9	Location 9	Foot Locker	33	Location 33	Flanagans	57	Location 57	Omniplex
10	Location 10	Hartmann	34	Location 34	Eason	58	Location 58	Webworks
11	Location 11	Treasure	35	Location 35	Sasha	59	Location 59	Supermacs
12	Location 12	Corner Shp	36	Location 36	McDonalds	60	Location 60	BOI
13	Location 13	Meteor	37	Location 37	Carphone	61	Location 61	St Nicks
14	Location 14	Tribes	38	Location 38	McCambridges	62	Location 62	Town Hall
15	Location 15	Hsamuel	39	Location 39	AIB Main	63	Location 63	Courthouse
16	Location 16	Vision Exp	40	Location 40	Zerep	64	Location 64	Cathedral
17	Location 17	Powells	41	Location 41	Garavans	65	Location 65	Seapoint
18	Location 18	O2	42	Location 42	Harts	66	Location 66	Salthill Htl
19	Location 19	Lifestyle	43	Location 43	Butler Chocs	67	Location 67	GalwayGC
20	Location 20	Dubray	44	Location 44	The Body Shop	68	Location 68	Joyces SC
21	Location 21	Zhivago	45	Location 45	Carpenters	69	Location 69	Sailin
22	Location 22	3 Store	46	Location 46	Lazlo	70	Location 70	Eyre House
23	Location 23	McCarthys	47	Location 47	Brown Thomas			
24	Location 24	Schuh	48	Location 48	maxwell			

Chapter 3

Conclusion:

The aim of this experiment was to gather latitude and longitude coordinates for a large number of outdoor points. The experiment was a success because accurate information was gathered for 70 locations, spread out over a large urban geographical area and comprising of a good mixture of different environments. The results of this experiment will allow further experimentation and simulation of typical environments in which tourists frequent.

Results:
Below is an extract from Appendix B2. The Latitude and Longitude for each of the 70 locations were found using this method. All detailed Analysis and extrapolation of the Latitude and Longitude for each of the 70 locations can be viewed in Appendix B2.

Results File: O2 Williamsgate.VBO
Recorded on: 31/10/2010 @ 20:50
Contains: 140 category 3 locations - USABLE
                    65 category 4 locations - USABLE
Category 3 samples produced an average location of:
53.274347, -9.050454, 70.33
Latitude: 53.274343
Longitude: -9.050454
Altitude: 70.33
Category 4 samples produced an average location of:
53.274344, -9.050452, 68.72
Latitude: 53.274344
Longitude: -9.050452
Altitude: 68.72
All samples produced an average location of:
53.274343, -9.050453, 69.84
Latitude: 53.274343
Longitude: -9.050453
Altitude: 69.84

Exact Location

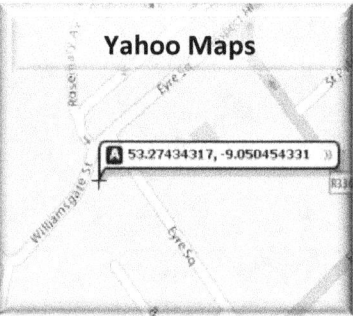

Yahoo Maps

Analysis:
Distance from Category 4 to Category 3 result:
$1603.9 * \sqrt{x*x + y*y}$
$x = 69.1 * (53.274344 - 53.274343)$
$y = 69.1 * -(9.050452 - 9.050454) * \cos(53.274343 / 57.3)$
Distance(calculated):   0.2168 m
There are less that 100 category 4 GPS points,
but they are verified by the category 3 information.
However, all the mapping tools show this location
to be over 15m ESE from it's expected
position on the maps. Therefore, the Google maps
location was used rather than the Vbox location.
Maps: 53.274350,-9.050687

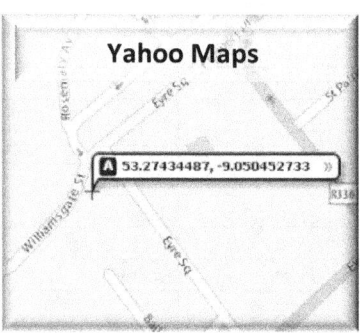

Yahoo Maps

Conclusion:
There are not enough category 4 samples to
Google, Bing and Yahoo Maps, they are also
verified by Google Street View photos.

Use the Maps result.
53.274350, - 9.050687
Latitude: 53.274350
Longitude: - 9.050687

Google Street View

The online resource at http://www.irishapps.org/smartlla.html
contains all 70 PDF files which contain the data and analysis for this test.

Results:

List of all the locations measured. The latitude and longitude were recorded and the most accurate readings available were used. Minimum accuracy was observed when 4-5 satellites were in range. Maximum accuracy was observed when over 10 satellites were in range.

> See the online resource for this book at http://www.irishapps.org/smartlla.html .
>
> There were over 30,000 readings taken across the 70 different locations. All the samples are spread across 133 text files which are available here for download.

Name		Latitude	Longitude	Accuracy	No of Satellites
O2Shop	Location 1	53.274350	-9.050687	3	6 satellites
Logues	Location 2	53.274197	-9.050716	2	4-5 satellites
GBCRes	Location 3	53.274182	-9.050888	3	6 satellites
EyreSC	Location 4	53.274072	-9.051042	4	8 satellites
MonNth	Location 5	53.273994	-9.051117	4	8 satellites
Whelan	Location 6	53.273923	-9.051182	3	6 satellites
MonSth	Location 7	53.273904	-9.051244	2	4-5 satellites
GalCam	Location 8	53.273798	-9.051195	3	6 satellites
FotLoc	Location 9	53.273769	-9.051229	3	6 satellites
Hartma	Location 10	53.273699	-9.051312	3	6 satellites
TrChes	Location 11	53.273566	-9.051454	3	6 satellites
CorShp	Location 12	53.273564	-9.051471	3	6 satellites
Meteor	Location 13	53.273511	-9.051542	2	4-5 satellites
Tribes	Location 14	53.273484	-9.051544	2	4-5 satellites
Samuel	Location 15	53.273285	-9.051793	3	6 satellites
VisExp	Location 16	53.273256	-9.051834	3	6 satellites
Powell	Location 17	53.273156	-9.052020	4	8 satellites
O2Shop	Location 18	53.273122	-9.052089	4	8 satellites
Lifest	Location 19	53.273032	-9.052140	4	8 satellites
Dubrey	Location 20	53.272980	-9.052262	4	8 satellites
Zhivgo	Location 21	53.272935	-9.052316	3	6 satellites
3Store	Location 22	53.272900	-9.052402	3	6 satellites
McCarth	Location 23	53.272863	-9.052424	2	4-5 satellites
Schuh	Location 24	53.272889	-9.052488	2	4-5 satellites
Brenns	Location 25	53.272871	-9.052619	2	4-5 satellites
EllesC	Location 26	53.272711	-9.052589	2	4-5 satellites
TommyH	Location 27	53.272701	-9.052655	2	4-5 satellites
RiverI	Location 28	53.272659	-9.052823	2	4-5 satellites
Anthny	Location 29	53.272683	-9.052961	4	8 satellites
Taaffs	Location 30	53.272420	-9.053261	2	4-5 satellites
Zatsna	Location 31	53.272471	-9.053240	4	8 satellites
CafExp	Location 32	53.272524	-9.053218	2	4-5 satellites
Flanag	Location 33	53.272588	-9.053070	2	4-5 satellites
Eason	Location 34	53.272709	-9.052828	2	4-5 satellites
Sasha	Location 35	53.272786	-9.052665	3	6 satellites
McDona	Location 36	53.272909	-9.052492	3	6 satellites
Carpho	Location 37	53.272964	-9.052449	2	4-5 satellites
McCam	Location 38	53.273012	-9.052246	3	6 satellites
AIB	Location 39	53.273079	-9.052052	3	6 satellites
Zerep	Location 40	53.273199	-9.051934	3	6 satellites
Garava	Location 41	53.273293	-9.051946	3	6 satellites
Harts	Location 42	53.273343	-9.051731	4	8 satellites
Butler	Location 43	53.273379	-9.051692	2	4-5 satellites
BodySh	Location 44	53.273431	-9.051668	3	6 satellites
Carpen	Location 45	53.273573	-9.051558	2	4-5 satellites
Lazlo	Location 46	53.273717	-9.051430	3	6 satellites
BrownT	Location 47	53.273970	-9.051318	3	6 satellites
Maxwel	Location 48	53.274044	-9.051235	3	6 satellites
Faller	Location 49	53.274181	-9.051074	3	6 satellites
Hanley	Location 50	53.274229	-9.050964	2	4-5 satellites
Hollan	Location 51	53.274279	-9.050830	3	6 satellites
Vodafo	Location 52	53.274323	-9.050727	3	6 satellites
Block6	Location 53	53.290752	-9.003176	4	8 satellites
Monagh	Location 54	53.292286	-9.018995	3	6 satellites
Liosba	Location 55	53.285665	-9.033417	4	8 satellites
Dunnes	Location 56	53.284144	-9.045492	4	8 satellites
Omnipl	Location 57	53.279768	-9.050499	2	4-5 satellites
Webwor	Location 58	53.274863	-9.045795	3	6 satellites
Superm	Location 59	53.274683	-9.050708	3	6 satellites
BOI	Location 60	53.274962	-9.050146	3	6 satellites
StNics	Location 61	53.272641	-9.054344	4	8 satellites
TownHl	Location 62	53.276074	-9.054293	3	6 satellites
Court	Location 63	53.275943	-9.054498	2	4-5 satellites
Catdrl	Location 64	53.275281	-9.057131	3	6 satellites
Seapoi	Location 65	53.259579	-9.075986	3	6 satellites
SaltHtl	Location 66	53.258558	-9.086876	2	4-5 satellites
GalGC	Location 67	53.258368	-9.096081	4	8 satellites
Joyces	Location 68	53.262431	-9.104460	5	>10 satellites
Sailin	Location 69	53.282376	-9.028960	4	8 satellites
EyreHs	Location 70	53.274523	-9.047072	3	6 satellites

3.2.2 Test the Accuracy of the GPS Functionality on the Samsung GalaxyS Smartphone and the Apple iPhone 3GS while in a Stationary Position

Aim/Goals:
To establish the accuracy of the above mentioned smartphones with regard to their GPS functionality while in a stationary position.

Data from Previous Experiments:
Location data from Exp001 was used.

Follow On Experiments:
More experiments comparing some of the technical differences between the two phones, such as GPS functionality while moving at a 3Kph.

Methodology/Preparation/Planning:
A subset of 20 locations were chosen from Exp001. These locations started 5Km east of Galway city centre and proceeded through the city and on to 5km west of the city.

The accuracy was established under three conditions.
1. (At 10 sec) During the initialization phase, when a GPS application is first launched and starts to query the hardware for GPS location coordinates.
2. (At 30 sec) After the initialization phase, when a regular stream of GPS data becomes available to the application.
3. (At 60 sec) This represents the normal operation of a location based application. In almost all cases the user of a location based application has their application running for 60 sec or more before they begin to actually use it in any meaningful way... In most cases the user is continually operating the application. It is this information that is of most interest and of most use when comparing both phones.

Information gathered after 60 seconds of operation is the most relevant information to use when comparing the accuracy of both phones. The accuracy of the phones before 60 seconds of operation is interesting to note, but should not be used as a primary source of comparison.

NOTE: When recording each set of results, the 10sec/30sec/60sec... the experiments occurred on separate days(the 26th, 27th Oct and 7th-9th ,12th Nov 2010). The results for the 10/30/60 sec were not recorded immediately after each other.
Bear this in mind when reading the Analysis section, as it may appear misleading, and the reader could easily assume(incorrectly) that all results were gathered at the same time.

A clipboard was used to rest each phone on, the GPS application was started on each phone simultaneously. This ensured that both phones are receiving the same strength and quality GPS signal.

Implementation/Execution:
Measurements were recorded at each location as follows:
The position was established using the photos from Exp001. Both phones were placed on the clipboard. The location based applications were started on each phone. The location was recorded after a specified time had elapsed (10sec, 30sec or 60sec). One reading was taken from the Samsung phone and then one reading was taken from the Apple phone.
At each location, the application was shut down completely and restarted.
The following information was recorded for each location:
1. Latitude
2. Longitude
3. Accuracy.
4. Time
5. Weather.
This exercise was repeated five times, once to record the 10sec/30sec/and three times to record the 60sec information.

Chapter 3

Retesting:
The test was designed to allow easy retesting. Established locations were used from Exp001.

Hardware Used:
Apple iPhone 3GS
Samsung GalaxyS(GT-I9000)

Software Used:
A custom Android application, written for this experiment, to report Latitude and Longitude.
A 3rd party iPhone application to view the Latitude and Longitude reported by the iPhone.
MS Excel to calculate averages, maximums and minimums.

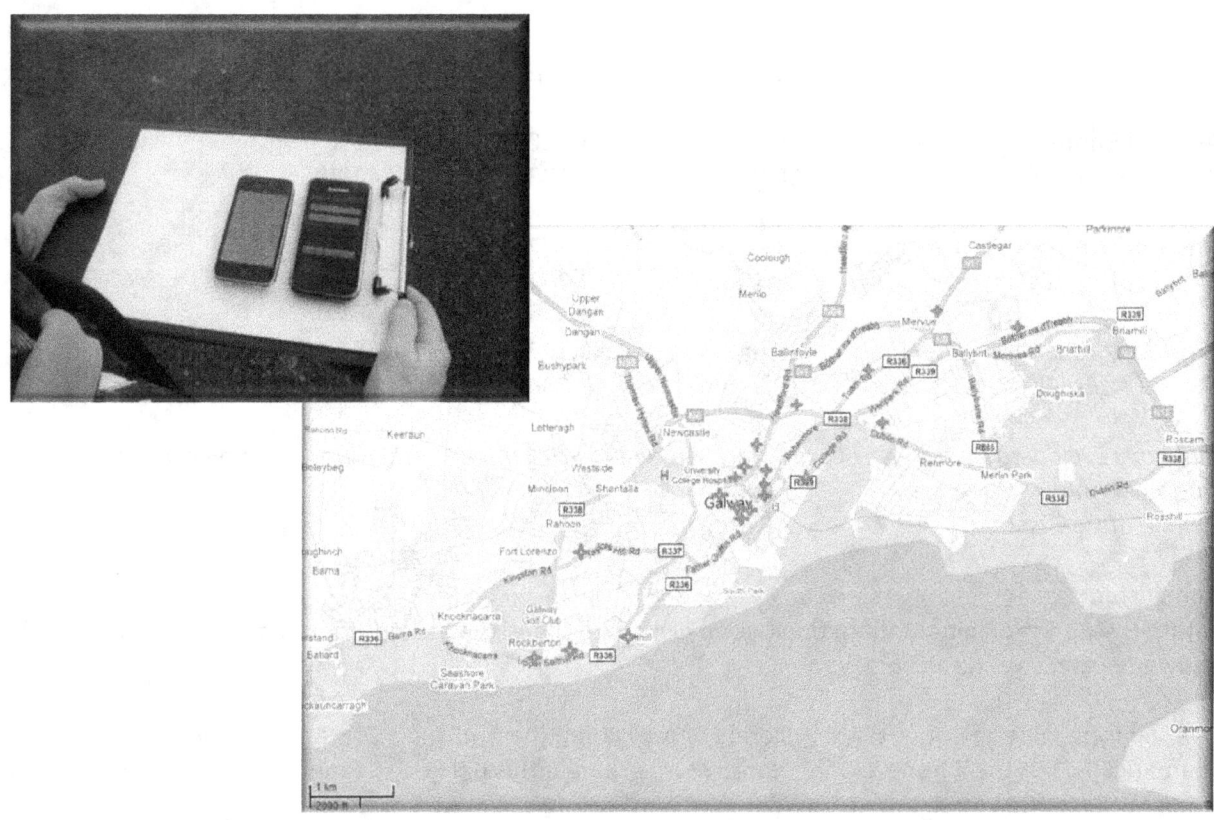

Weather(observed 2010-11-11 19:25):
Weather during this experiment was generally, wet and lightly overcast. On the final day of testing, the weather was extremely bad with heavy rain and stormy conditions.

Weather Report(Met Eireann 2010-11-11 09:00):
Wind = SE 8.2Knots   Cloud = Cloudy   Temp = 9.0degC
Humidity = 57%   Rain = 4.1mm   Pressure = 1019 hPa.

Changes to Plan During Testing:
During the final day, some location information was not recorded due to stormy weather. These locations were marked in red on the following pages, and were NOT included in any calculations.
The location labelled 'Sailin' was not included in any 60sec calculations, due to lack of data.

Validation/Evaluation:
The goal of establishing a basic knowledge of how accurate and responsive smartphones are at reporting location based information while in a stationary position has been achieved.

Calculations and Formulae Used:
None.

Locations:
Locations were spread out over a 10Km distance, with the majority within the city centre.

Analysis:
20 locations were chosen, with results recorded after 10 seconds, 30 sec and 60 sec after launching the location based applications. GPS coordinated were then recorded from each phone.

NOTE: For the 10 sec records, the application was launched, 10 sec elapsed and the coordinates were recorded.
This exercise was repeated for the 30 sec records and the 60 sec period.
The 10/30/60 sec records were not recorded immediately after one another… because there was not enough time to take note of the 10 sec information before the 30 sec information appears etc..

The Average/Min/Max accuracy in meters were as follows(over all 20 locations):

	Average Accuracy	Best(Min) Accuracy	Worst(Max) Accuracy
Android Phone after 10sec:	35.877m	1.620m	92.197m
iPhone after 10sec:	16.905m	1.133m	44.286m
Android Phone after 30sec:	13.009m	3.357m	42.832m
iPhone after 30sec:	38.100m	4.247m	106.22m
Android Phone after 60sec:	10.941m	0.472m	45.610m
iPhone after 60sec:	10.970m	0.834m	31.408m

Accuracy Excluding Locations with Interference Due to Structures Nearby(marked in blue in results):
Android Phone after 60sec: 5.958m
iPhone after 60sec: 7.929m

Conclusion:
After 10 seconds of initialization, the iPhone picked up GPS signals faster than the Android phone and showed better average accuracy rates.

In a separate experiment, after 30 seconds of operation, the Android's average accuracy improved dramatically, but the iPhone's didn't improve at all and in this particular experiment, the average iPhone accuracy became worse.
The Android device was more accurate than the iPhone after 30 seconds of operation.

In a separate experiment, after 60 seconds of operation, taking three readings per phone, the accuracy of both phones improved from the 30 to 60 seconds time span, and both phones showed essentially the same level of accuracy.

In conclusion, during real world operations, the iPhone and Android devices show an almost identical accuracy rate while in a stationary position.

Results:

The columns are as follows:
Latitude, Longitude and Altitude: The raw data returned by the phones GPS hardware. Accuracy: The accuracy as reported by the operating system of each phone. It should be noted that this is an arbitrary figure and the figures returned by different operating systems cannot be used for comparison.
Accuracy(M): This is the distance calculated in meters from the position the phones reported and the actual positions of the phones during measurement.

No	NAME		BASELINE FROM EXPERIMENT 1 BASELINE	Initial Fix(after 10 sec) Android 26/10/2010	Initial Fix(after 10 sec) iPhone 26/10/2010	Best Fix(after 30 sec) Android 27/10/2010	Best Fix(after 30 sec) iPhone 27/10/2010	Best Fix(after 60 sec) Android 07/11/2010	Best Fix(after 60 sec) iPhone 07/11/2010	Best Fix(after 60 sec) Android 12/11/2010(A)	Best Fix(after 60 sec) iPhone 12/11/2010(A)	Best Fix(after 60 sec) Android 12/11/2010(B)	Best Fix(after 60 sec) iPhone 12/11/2010(B)
65	Seapoint	Latitude	53.25957914	53.2596675	53.259831	53.25953097	53.259362	53.25952524	53.25954	53.25954667	53.259487	53.25955754	53.259507
		longitude	-9.075986005	-9.0758156	-9.075772	-9.076140852	-9.076314	-9.076204023	-9.0762	-9.076215436	-9.076311	-9.076113701	-9.076265
		Altitude		65	77	112	104	82		83		82	
		Accuracy		30	47	10	47		17	5	17	5	17
		Lat/Long											
		Accuracy(M)		15.00208533	31.41833618	11.61070948	32.54509244	15.69380231	14.88681185	15.68460951	23.92577198	8.828150834	20.22001859
66	Salthill Htl	Latitude	53.25855826	53.2581366	53.258626	53.25837382	53.258314	53.25853074	53.258551	53.2574552	53.258488	53.25768508	53.258458
		longitude	-9.08687606	-9.08627935	-9.087087	-9.086310859	-9.086407	-9.086911472	-9.086763	-9.085191993	-9.08698	-9.085420737	-9.086991
		Altitude		110	68	112	93	63		199		171	
		Accuracy		30	17	5	76	10	9	10	17	5	17
		Lat/Long											
		Accuracy(M)		61.43754548	15.92737276	42.83182133	41.37132112	3.86186331	7.564865513	106.1288707	10.43363269	137.1224856	13.51949254
67	GalwayGC	Latitude	53.25836809	53.25837582	53.258322	53.25828441	53.25823	53.25836436	53.258366	53.25836584	53.258335	53.25835907	53.258346
		longitude	-9.096081034	-9.096045788	-9.096090	-9.096047123	-9.095133	-9.096104124	-9.096069	-9.096087053	-9.096091	-9.096116375	-9.09607
		Altitude		75	68	68	57	63		63		63	
		Accuracy		10	17	5	17	5	17	5	17	5	17
		Lat/Long											
		Accuracy(M)		2.497452089	5.159922845	9.574791804	64.91359635	1.591189271	0.833654589	0.472279348	3.738950805	2.556313582	2.563803843
68	Joyces SC	Latitude	53.26243088	53.2624369	53.262351	53.26254386	53.26253	53.26240759	53.262419	53.26242614	53.262391	53.2624351	53.262393
		longitude	-9.10445968	-9.104321	-9.103955	-9.104601557	-9.104072	-9.104481409	-9.104489	-9.104484445	-9.104493	-9.104479655	-9.1045
		Altitude		52	100	70	28	63		64		64	
		Accuracy		50	47	5	47	5	9	5	17	10	17
		Lat/Long											
		Accuracy(M)		9.249533548	34.72761814	15.71408318	28.0460251	2.966346508	2.355723599	1.729839507	4.957826111	1.409217836	4.993792959
69	Sailin	Latitude	53.28237584	53.282581008	53.282350	53.2822245	53.282234						
		longitude	-9.02895986	-9.02901377	-9.029061	-9.029273756	-9.02919						
		Altitude		133	80	54	69						
		Accuracy		30	163	10	17						
		Lat/Long											
		Accuracy(M)		23.09508991	7.313081589	26.81116063	21.97602225						
70	Eyre House	Latitude	53.27452306	53.27495366	53.274164	53.27468723	53.274155	53.27451096	53.274519	53.2745418	53.274562	53.27455202	53.274556
		longitude	-9.047071945	-9.04783033	-9.047360	-9.047177083	-9.046707	-9.047165248	-9.047149	-9.047122703	-9.04713	-9.047123202	-9.047161
		Altitude		0	133	68	109	54		55		57	
		Accuracy		50	47	5	47	10	17	10	9	10	17
		Lat/Long											
		Accuracy(M)		69.54536562	44.28603958	19.54882071	47.58399559	6.349249619	5.144256815	3.967287948	5.801467064	4.689313909	6.963693971
50	Hanleys	Latitude	53.2742292	53.27363	53.274148	53.27423135	53.274214	53.27425335	53.274221	53.27459205	53.274116	53.27451412	53.274118
		longitude	-9.050963557	-9.0500054	-9.050976	-9.050864339	-9.050415	-9.050919887	-9.05111	-9.050718623	-9.05081	-9.050470211	-9.05081
		Altitude		25	67	66	68	70		197		193	
		Accuracy		50	47	5	47	5	47	10	17	10	17
		Accuracy(M)		92.19689829	9.067491854	6.602720739	36.52020053	3.955275693	9.781595189	43.51401825	16.20951378	45.61047435	16.0374083
34	Eason	Latitude	53.272709	53.2723118	53.272595	53.27263963	53.273664	53.27266855	53.272601	53.27291514	53.272842	53.27237548	53.272847
		longitude	-9.052828	-9.0521831	-9.052657	-9.052778795	-9.052862	-9.052751475	-9.05275	-9.052545058	-9.053028	-9.052755758	-9.052857
		Altitude		16	59	58	29	69		289		286	
		Accuracy		10	17	5	47	5	17	10	47	10	47
		Lat/Long										1.28959E+12	
		Accuracy(M)		61.56697148	17.03066093	8.379091008	106.222582	6.792434523	13.08232324	29.65749935	15.89132514	37.39777612	15.46668574

Chapter 3

Results:

No	NAME		BASELINE FROM EXPERIMENT 1 BASELINE	Initial Fix (after 10 sec)		Best Fix (after 30 sec)		Best Fix (after 60 sec)		Best Fix (after 60 sec)		Best Fix (after 60 sec)	
				Android 26/10/2010	iPhone 26/10/2010	Android 27/10/2010	iPhone 27/10/2010	Android 07/11/2010	iPhone 07/11/2010	Android 12/11/2010(A)	iPhone 12/11/2010(A)	Android 12/11/2010(B)	iPhone 12/11/2010(B)
53	Block 6	Latitude	53.29075153	53.290892	53.290563	53.29075814	53.290588	53.29074523	53.290674	53.29067715	53.290714	53.29069464	53.290744
		longitude	-9.003176237	-9.003197	-9.002981	-9.003225503	-9.003133	-9.003165523	-9.003178	-9.003045313	-9.003193	-9.003107168	-9.003214
		Altitude		77	91	100	69	101		113		113	
		Accuracy		10	47	5	17	5	47	5	17	5	17
		Lat/Long											
		Accuracy(M)		15.68149765	24.65737273	3.35648271	18.41072084	0.999338107	8.622336476	12.00663807	4.31965031	7.817411997	2.646377532
54	Monaghans	Latitude	53.29228599	53.29246605	53.292239	53.29227691	53.292179	53.29223512	53.292334	53.29227164	53.292223	53.29231054	53.292246
		longitude	-9.018995318	-9.0189809	-9.019133	-9.018729371	-9.018756	-9.018919711	-9.019005	-9.018877459	-9.019078	-9.018778499	-9.018971
		Altitude		93	67	85		125		96		93	
		Accuracy		30	47	10	47	5	47	30	47	10	17
		Lat/Long											
		Accuracy(M)		20.04607132	10.53912055	17.70777262	19.86560621	7.566766717	5.377493519	7.995563784	8.903644007	14.66956153	4.73170095
55	Liosban	Latitude	53.28566477	53.2856122	53.285738	53.28569831	53.285661	53.28566504	53.285631	53.28563917	53.285609	53.28565693	53.285591
		longitude	-9.033417103	-9.0332917	-9.033265	-9.033402114	-9.033093	-9.033391957	-9.033401	-9.033408311	-9.033389	-9.033406845	-9.033386
		Altitude		99	85	70	66	67		65		65	
		Accuracy		30	47	5	47	5	17	10	17	5	47
		Lat/Long											
		Accuracy(M)		10.18279111	12.98388426	3.860954111	21.55235737	1.672105779	3.904946446	2.905930113	6.477119499	1.106727008	8.460042717
56	Dunnes	Latitude	53.28414436	53.2842329	53.284077	53.28415887	53.284512	53.28410227	53.284144	53.28415743	53.2841	53.2841104	53.284147
		longitude	-9.045491993	-9.045415	-9.045404	-9.045279751	-9.044328	-9.045424501	-9.04537	-9.045494853	-9.04536	-9.045508762	-9.045336
		Altitude		74	69	91	62	66		57		55	
		Accuracy		30	47	5	47	5	17	5	17	10	17
		Lat/Long											
		Accuracy(M)		11.09715603	9.504609298	14.20358751	87.52647575	6.483767512	8.111201688	1.465948042	10.06736832	3.937719831	10.37585794
57	Omniplex	Latitude	53.27976823	53.28002359	53.279746	53.27992322	53.279814	53.27974667	53.279713	53.27972285	53.279845	53.27973939	53.279668
		longitude	-9.050498737	-9.04979277	-9.050505	-9.050363849	-9.05034	-9.05050168	-9.050402	-9.050579589	-9.050189	-9.050582899	-9.050482
		Altitude		65	39	90		66		57		57	
		Accuracy		30	47	5	47	10	17	5	47	30	17
		Lat/Long											
		Accuracy(M)		54.86391066	2.506869002	19.42991773	11.71829091	2.405178333	8.893718632	7.373840546	22.29518728	6.45023723	11.20126552
58	Webworks	Latitude	53.27486259	53.275086	53.274732	53.27479916	53.274675	53.27496287	53.274962	53.27496237	53.2748	53.27491752	53.274708
		longitude	-9.04579468	-9.0465735	-9.046088	-9.04593281	-9.046413	-9.04557128	-9.045603	-9.04560356	-9.046235	-9.045964872	-9.046164
		Altitude		118	92	59	85	92		91		85	47
		Accuracy		30	47	5	47	10	17	10	17	30	
		Lat/Long											
		Accuracy(M)		57.44383354	24.31858253	11.58150676	46.10868579	18.5763327	16.87297963	16.87182038	30.09828996	12.86118246	29.97925836
59	Supermacs	Latitude	53.27468278	53.2745958	53.274612	53.27473985	53.274411	53.27474823	53.274741	53.2747502	53.274623	53.27415475	53.274318
		longitude	-9.05070764	-9.0502276	-9.050685	-9.050756017	-9.050296	-9.050765732	-9.050762	-9.050769008	-9.050629	-9.049099886	-9.050124
		Altitude		105	63	69	0	69		66		206	
		Accuracy		50	17	5	47	5	47	5	47	10	17
		Lat/Long											
		Accuracy(M)		33.35720382	8.013633992	7.115502297	40.77762865	8.240380776	7.41515008	8.535949277	8.458284469	121.9827751	42.92177745
60	BOI	Latitude	53.27496152	53.2747794	53.275121	53.27503805	53.274889	53.27492678	53.274986	53.27499744	53.274979	53.27492678	53.274986
		longitude	-9.05014564	-9.04984818	-9.050152	-9.050139242	-9.049884	-9.050101261	-9.050148	-9.050172376	-9.050127	-9.050301261	-9.050148
		Altitude		95	104	72	64	92		0		116	
		Accuracy		30	47	5	47	10	17	5	47	10	17
		Lat/Long											
		Accuracy(M)		28.3103171	17.7396383	8.520964083	19.17772879	4.861971616	2.726760853	4.372075417	2.305443699	11.04688864	2.726760853
61	St Nicks	Latitude	53.27264095	53.272643	53.272752	53.27262394	53.272653	53.272688	53.27272	53.272688	53.272745	53.27262739	53.272761
		longitude	-9.054343577	-9.0543677	-9.054372	-9.054432555	-9.054283	-9.054204162	-9.05421	-9.054204162	-9.054349	-9.054257311	-9.054333
		Altitude		48	85	61	79	0		0		1	
		Accuracy		30	47	5	47	30	17	30	9	10	17
		Lat/Long											
		Accuracy(M)		1.620443377	12.4928915	6.212438228	4.245745208	10.64623411	12.4977633	10.64623411	11.57625332	5.932135097	13.36839571
62	Town Hall	Latitude	53.27607404	53.2755749	53.275985	53.2760122	53.276045	53.27605152	53.27605	53.2760616	53.276051	53.27601628	53.276043
		longitude	-9.054292909	-9.05533578	-9.054278	-9.054476374	-9.054451	-9.054294104	-9.054276	-9.054284702	-9.054388	-9.054431059	-9.054447
		Altitude		83	83	55	62	61		61		80	
		Accuracy		30	17	5	47	5	17	5	17	5	17
		Lat/Long											
		Accuracy(M)		88.82876394	9.950997115	14.00526566	10.99797747	2.505983392	2.900173867	1.487581484	6.822953054	11.20968034	10.81291296
63	Courthouse	Latitude	53.27594259	53.27580919	53.275772	53.27593375	53.275984	53.27595227	53.276123	53.27611226	53.276195	53.27610675	53.27583
		longitude	-9.05449804	-9.0537489	-9.053980	-9.05444546	-9.05451	-9.054810973	-9.054432	-9.054198136	-9.054374	-9.054430262	-9.054542
		Altitude		98	10	61	74	56		131		143	
		Accuracy		50	76	5	17	5	47	10	17	10	47
		Lat/Long											
		Accuracy(M)		51.98029326	39.32783538	3.632141631	4.673082233	20.83817889	20.53713179	27.45456173	29.25563067	18.80376269	12.85706789
64	Cathedral	Latitude	53.27528133	53.2753200	53.275280	53.27535859	53.274893	53.27528114	53.275272	53.27556453	53.275175	53.27555364	53.275166
		longitude	-9.05713111	-9.057259	-9.057148	-9.057191091	-9.055812	-9.057072288	-9.057091	-9.0566815	-9.056751	-9.056656922	-9.0567
		Altitude		74	65	67	131	70		94		95	
		Accuracy		50	47	5	47	5	17	10	47	30	47
		Lat/Long											
		Accuracy(M)		9.530262264	1.132915109	9.472303533	97.77635226	3.911819044	2.862072177	43.42551051	27.90686666	43.71923259	31.40751937

3.2.3 Establish the Accuracy of Google and Yahoo Maps in the Galway and Limerick Area

Aim/Goals:
Find the accuracy of the online mapping tools. If the mapping tools prove to be accurate, they can be used in future experiments to ascertain or to verify other GPS locations.

Data from Previous Experiments:
None.

Follow On Experiments:
Results will be used in Experiment 001.

Methodology/Preparation/Planning:
A number of locations were chosen in the Galway and Limerick area and their GPS coordinates were measured in a way that permitted comparison with Google/Yahoo and Bing maps.

The most accurate GPS measurement device available was used, the Racelogic Vbox VB2SX10.
(see Experiment 001 for technical information/calibration/accuracy regarding this device).

Implementation/Execution:
The GPS device was attached to a vehicle and driven at a speed ranging from 30Kph to 100Kph on roads, roundabouts, intersections etc. that were well marked on the online mapping tools. The locations were recorded at a rate of 10Hz and this information was saved to text files for later analysis.

Measurements were taken at each point as follows:
The position was located and the GPS location information generated by the Vbox was recorded. The device was allowed as much time as was required to establish the best GPS lock possible.
The following information was recorded for each location:
1. Latitude
2. Longitude
3. Altitude
4. Accuracy(number of satellites being tracked).
5. Time
6. Weather.

This exercise was repeated several times on different days and in varying weather conditions.

Retesting:
The experiment was designed and executed to allow east retesting, so long as the infrastructure does not change(roads, intersections).

Hardware Used:
Racelogic Vbox VB2SX10 GPS Recording Device.
(see Exp001 for the cert of calibration).
Absolute Positioning :   Accuracy: 3m 95% CEP[3]
                              Update Rate: 10 Hz
                              Resolution: 1cm
                              Height Acc: 6 m 95% CEP

Software Used:
Vbox application, MS Excel/Paint etc.

Weather(observed 2010-11-20 15:41):
Lightly overcast, dry with light winds, temperature 14degC.

Weather Report(Met Eireann 2010-11-20 09:00):
Wind = light winds   Cloud = Cloudy   Temp = 8.2degC
Humidity =48%   Rain = nil   Pressure = 1021 hPa.

[3]: CEP = (Circle Error Probable) means 95% of the time the position readings will fall within a circle of the stated diameter.

Changes to Plan During Testing:
none

Validation/Evaluation:
By completing this experiment, the accuracy of the online mapping tools was established.

Locations:
The locations were spread out over a 70Km distance.

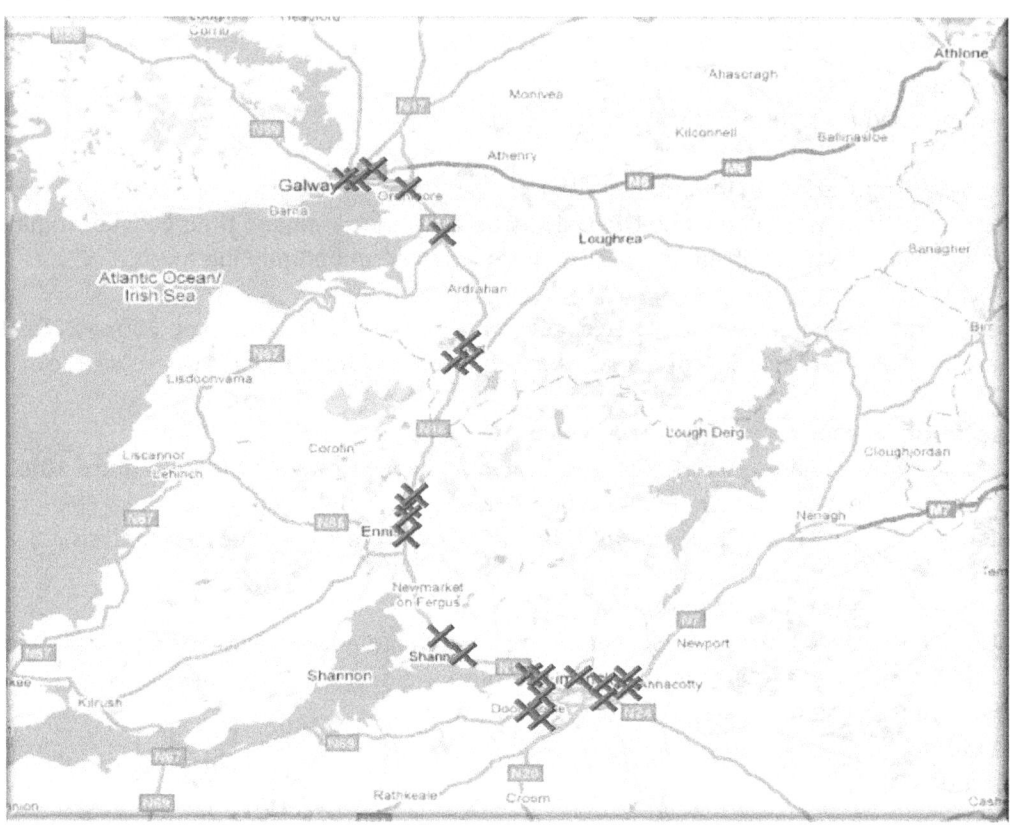

Overall Results/Analysis/Conclusion:

There were 56 locations sampled over two days.

Google Maps:
Of these 56 locations, there were 2 Google locations that were slightly inaccurate(<=3m).

The other 54 locations were accurate.

Yahoo Maps:
Of these 56 locations, there were 12 Yahoo locations that were out of date(missing).

Out of the remaining 44 locations, there was also 1 location that was slightly inaccurate(<=3m).

Bing Maps:
I could not load a file into Bing in the same way as Yahoo and Google allow. I checked all the Bing locations against the Google locations and they correlated very closely.

Conclusion:
Google and Yahoo maps can be used to verify and/or increase the accuracy of the locations gathered by other means.
In all cases, the location should be confirmed as up to date by visual examination.

There were two false positives reported by Google and one false positive reported by Yahoo out of a total of 56 locations.

Overall Results/Analysis/Conclusion:

See Appendix B3(Raw GPS Data Overlaid onto Google/Yahoo Maps for Experiment 3.2.3)

Accurate:
Areas are marked as accurate if the raw GPS data gathered by the calibrated GPS device matches up with the relevant mapping software when it is overlaid onto it.
Missing:
Areas are marked as missing if the particular landmark or structure that was measured does not exist within the mapping software.
InAccurate:
Areas are marked as InAccurate if the raw GPS data does not match the GPS data for that landmark/road or structure within the mapping software.

Title	Description	Google	Yahoo	Title	Description	Google	Yahoo
Route 001	Galway: Ballybrit - Briarhill - Carn			Route 008	Co Clare: Crusheen - Barefield		
Location 1	Lynch Roundabout	Accurate	Accurate	Location 30	Bypass1	Accurate	Missing
Location 2	M6	Accurate	Missing	Location 31	Bypass1	Accurate	Missing
Location 3	Morris Roundabout	InAccurate	InAccurate	Location 32	Bypass2	Accurate	Missing
Route 002	Galway: Ballybrit - Tuam Rd - Merv			Route 009	Co Clare: Barefield		
Location 4	Ballybane Industrial Estate	Accurate	Accurate	Location 33	Barefield Round1	Accurate	Accurate
Location 5	Monaghans Garage	Accurate	Accurate	Location 34	Barefield Round2	Accurate	Accurate
Location 6	Font Roundabout	Accurate	Accurate	Location 35	Barefield Combined	Accurate	Accurate
Location 7	Wellpark Rd	Accurate	Accurate	Route 010	Co Clare: Ennis to Limerick		
Location 8	Mervue	Accurate	Accurate	Location 36	Big Roundabout	Accurate	Accurate
Route 003	Galway: Kingston - Headford Rd			Location 37	Slip Road	Accurate	Missing
Location 9	Threadkneedle Rd	Accurate	Accurate	Route 011	Limerick: Limerick Tunnel		
Location 10	Deane Roundabout	InAccurate	Accurate	Location 38	Slip Road Tunnel	Accurate	Missing
Location 11	Browne Roundabout	Accurate	Accurate	Location 39	Double Roundabout	Accurate	Accurate
Location 12	Bodkin Roundabout	Accurate	Accurate	Route 012	Limerick: Dooradoyle		
Route 004	Galway: Headford Rd - Dublin Rd			Location 40	Dooradoyle Roundabout1	Accurate	Accurate
Location 13	Bodkin Roundabout	Accurate	Accurate	Location 41	Dooradoyle Roundabout2	Accurate	Accurate
Location 14	Moneenageisha	Accurate	Accurate	Location 42	Dooradoyle Roundabout3	Accurate	Accurate
Location 15	Sailin	Accurate	Missing	Location 43	Dooradoyle Roundabout4	Accurate	Accurate
Route 005	Galway: Dublin Rd - Ballybrit			Location 44	Dooradoyle Roundabout5	Accurate	Accurate
Location 16	Wellpark Rd	Accurate	Missing	Route 013	Limerick: Tunnel to Castletr		
Location 17	Morris Roundabout	Accurate	Accurate	Location 45	Double Roundabout1	Accurate	Missing
Location 18	City East Business Park	Accurate	Accurate	Location 46	Slip Road	Accurate	Missing
Route 006	Co Galway: Galway - Clarinbridge			Location 47	T Turn	Accurate	Accurate
Location 19	Morris Roundabout	Accurate	Accurate	Location 48	Castletroy Round1	Accurate	Accurate
Location 20	N20 Roundabout	Accurate	Accurate	Location 49	Castletroy Round2	Accurate	Accurate
Location 21	Oranmore Roundabout	Accurate	Accurate	Route 014	Limerick: Plassey		
Location 22	Oranmore2 Roundabout	Accurate	Accurate	Location 50	UL Entrance	Accurate	Accurate
Location 23	Oranmore Roundabout	Accurate	Accurate	Location 51	UL Campus	Accurate	Accurate
Location 24	Galway Rd	Accurate	Missing	Location 52	UL Foundation	Accurate	Missing
Location 25	Bypass	Accurate	Missing	Route 015	Limerick: Parkway		
Route 007	Co Galway: Gort			Location 53	Plassey Roundabout	Accurate	Accurate
Location 26	Gort Turn1	Accurate	Accurate	Location 54	Parkway Roundabout	Accurate	Accurate
Location 27	Gort Turn2	Accurate	Accurate	Location 55	Absolute Roundabout	Accurate	Accurate
Location 28	Gort Turn1	Accurate	Accurate	Route 016	Co Limerick: Limerick to Bunr		
Location 29	Gort Turn2	Accurate	Accurate	Location 56	Coonagh Roundabout	Accurate	Accurate

The online resource at http://www.irishapps.org/smartlla.html contains the 16 PDF files which contain the data and analysis for the above table.

3.2.4 Investigate the Possibility of Using GPS Technology for Indoor Use

Aim/Goals:
Choose a number of suitable indoor locations in the Galway area and test the strength and accuracy of the GPS signal.

Data from Previous Experiments:
None.

Follow On Experiments:
More experiments will be conducted if the GPS signal is found to be usable in an indoor environment.

Methodology/Preparation/Planning:
Locations recorded as follows:
Place a GPS enabled smartphone in the location and record GPS data.

Implementation/Execution:
Proceed to each point and take measurements as follows:
Find and mark the position. Place the smartphone in the position and began recording the GPS data.
Record the following information for each location:
1. Latitude
2. Longitude
3. Altitude
4. Accuracy(number of satellites being tracked).
5. Time
6. Outside Weather.

Repeat this exercise several times on different days and in varying weather conditions.

Retesting:
Construct the tests in such a manner as to allow retesting. List the name of the premises and the location within the premises where the GPS data was recorded.

Hardware Used:
Samsung GalaxyS Phone and Apple iPhone 3Gs

Software Use:
Custom GPS software to report GPS data and record to a SQLite database on each phone.

Weather(observed 2010-10-31 13:05):
Lightly overcast, dry with light winds, temperature 9degC.

Changes to Plan During Testing:
After the first six locations it became obvious that GPS data could not be accurately recorded indoors, so the experiment was terminated.

Validation/Evaluation:
By completing this experiment, the goal of investigating the usefulness of using GPS data derived during indoor roaming has been achieved.

Sample of Indoor Location Photos:

Chapter 3

Summary of Results:
The numbers in the table represent the accuracy as reported by the operating system in use. These figures are a measurement in meters. Location 1 for the Samsung Galaxy S had an estimated accuracy rating of 50 meters diameter.

Notes:
'x' indicates that no testing was done. This is because no signal could be picked up.

Conclusion:
The Samsung Galaxy S managed an average accuracy of 82m diameter and the Apple iPhone managed an average accuracy of 134m(excl location 15). These experiments showed that neither phone produces any accurate GPS data when used in an indoor environment.

Results:
The columns are as follows:
Latitude, Longitude and Altitude: The raw data returned by the phones GPS hardware. Accuracy: The accuracy as reported by the operating system of each phone. It should be noted that this is an arbitrary figure and the figures returned by different operating systems cannot be used for comparison.

	Samsung Galaxy S	Apple iPhone
Location 1	50	47
Location 2	200	163
Location 3	x	253
Location 4	30	17
Location 5	x	111
Location 6	x	106
Location 7	100	50
Location 8	x	147
Location 9	x	x
Location 10	x	170
Location 11	x	x
Location 12	x	x
Location 13	x	x
Location 14	x	x
Location 15	x	1438
Location 16	x	133
Location 17	x	x
Location 18	x	x
Location 19	x	x
Location 20	30	161
Location 21	x	253
Average Accuracy(m)	82	234.5384615
Excluding Location 15	82	134.25

NAME		Android GPS 2010-10-25	Android GPS 2010-10-25	iPhone GPS 2010-10-25
In1 Block 6 My desk	Latitude	53.2906288	53.290731	53.29083
	longitude	-9.004088756	-9.003409	-9.003647
	Altitude	32	40	45
	Accuracy	50	50	47
	Date/Time	2010-10-24 18:04	2010-10-24 18:04	2010-10-24 18:06
In2 Monaghans DeliCounter	Latitude	53.2922738	53.2922738	53.292061
	longitude	-9.0195162	-9.0195162	-9.01923
	Altitude	92	92	65
	Accuracy	200	200	163
	Date/Time	2010-10-25 11:04	2010-10-25 11:04	2010-10-25 11:05
In3 Foodland	Latitude	0	0	53.286232
	longitude			-9.033641
	Altitude			0
	Accuracy			253
	Date/Time	2010-10-25 11:19	2010-10-25 11:19	2010-10-25 11:21
In4 Dunnes Centre	Latitude	53.284052	53.284052	53.279746
	longitude	-9.0451697	-9.04516979	-9.045622
	Altitude	148	148	80
	Accuracy	30	30	17
	Date/Time	2010-10-25 11:38	2010-10-25 11:38	2010-10-25 11:40
In5 Smyths Toys	Latitude	0	0	53.280024
	longitude			-9.050741
	Altitude			0
	Accuracy			111.5
	Date/Time	2010-10-25 11:53	2010-10-25 11:53	2010-10-25 11:53
In6 Webworks Centre	Latitude	0	0	53.274725
	longitude			-9.046494
	Altitude			0
	Accuracy			106
	Date/Time	2010-10-25 12:22	2010-10-25 12:22	2010-10-25 12:21
In7 Supermacs Centre	Latitude	53.27455778	53.27455778	53.274737
	longitude	-9.0506626	-9.0506626	-9.049407
	Altitude	126	126	0
	Accuracy	100	100	50
	Date/Time	2010-10-25 12:32	2010-10-25 12:32	2010-10-25 12:31
In8 BOI Centre	Latitude	0	0	53.274774
	longitude			-9.04921
	Altitude			0
	Accuracy			147
	Date/Time	2010-10-25 12:35	2010-10-25 12:35	2010-10-25 12:36
In9 Hanleys Centre	Latitude	0	0	0
	longitude			
	Altitude			
	Accuracy			
	Date/Time	2010-10-25 12:45	2010-10-25 12:45	2010-10-25 12:44
In10 Boots Centre	Latitude	0	0	53.273534
	longitude			-9.051835
	Altitude			0
	Accuracy			170
	Date/Time	2010-10-25 12:47	2010-10-25 12:47	2010-10-25 12:47

NAME	Android GPS 2010-10-25	Android GPS 2010-10-25	iPhone GPS 2010-10-25
In11 Eason Centre	0	0	0
	2010-10-25 12:54	2010-10-25 12:54	2010-10-25 12:54
In12 StNicholas Church Centre	0	0	0
	2010-10-25 12:57	2010-10-25 12:57	2010-10-25 12:57
In13 TownHall Lobby	0	0	0
	2010-10-25 13:10	2010-10-25 13:10	2010-10-25 13:10
In14 CourtHouse Lobby	0	0	0
	2010-10-25 13:06	2010-10-25 13:06	2010-10-25 13:06
In15 Cathedral Centre	0	0	53.27991 / -9.055074 / 0 / 1438
	2010-10-25 13:13	2010-10-25 13:13	2010-10-25 13:13
In16 Seapoint Centre	0	0	53.259989 / -9.076101 / 0 / 133
	2010-10-25 14:52	2010-10-25 14:52	2010-10-25 14:52
In17 Salthill Htl Reception	0	0	0
	2010-10-25 15:05	2010-10-25 15:05	2010-10-25 15:05
In18 GalwayCG Bar	0	0	0
	2010-10-25 15:13	2010-10-25 15:13	2010-10-25 15:14
In19 Joyces SC Centre	0	0	0
	2010-10-25 15:18	2010-10-25 15:18	2010-10-25 15:18
In20 Home69 SittingRoom	53.28228205 / -9.028408 / 35 / 30	53.282282 / -9.028408 / 35 / 30	53.282833 / -9.029086 / 0 / 161
	2010-10-25 10:30	2010-10-25 10:30	2010-10-25 10:31
In21 Eyre House	0	0	53.274468 / -9.04696 / 0 / 253
	2010-10-25 12:07	2010-10-25 12:07	2010-10-25 12:05

Chapter 3

3.2.5 Test the Accuracy of the GPS Functionality on the Samsung GalaxyS Smartphone and the Apple iPhone 3GS while Walking at >3 kPH

Aim/Goals:
To establish the accuracy of the above mentioned smartphones with regard to their GPS functionality while walking at >3 kPH(typical walking speed during tourist activity).

Data from Previous Experiments:
This experiment used the location data from Exp001.

Follow On Experiments:
Other GPS and Bluetooth experiments are planned using both of these phones.

Methodology/Preparation/Planning:
30 locations were chosen from a busy shopping district in Galway city.

An aluminium harness was constructed to house both smartphones and to allow video recording of their performance while roaming the street and passing the locations(shops) at typical walking pace(3kPH).

This ensured that both phones were receiving identical GPS signals and it also ensured that a good quality video image was captured to allow later analysis of the results.

The following photos illustrate the method used:

Extract from test 2011-01-25 iPhone v Samsung GPS4-Exp5.

27	Tommy	53.272701	-9.052655	01:14	1	1	13.276	15.342
28	River	53.272659	-9.052823	01:03	2	1	22.491	13.572
29	Anthony	53.272683	-9.052961	00:55	1	0	34.337	18.108

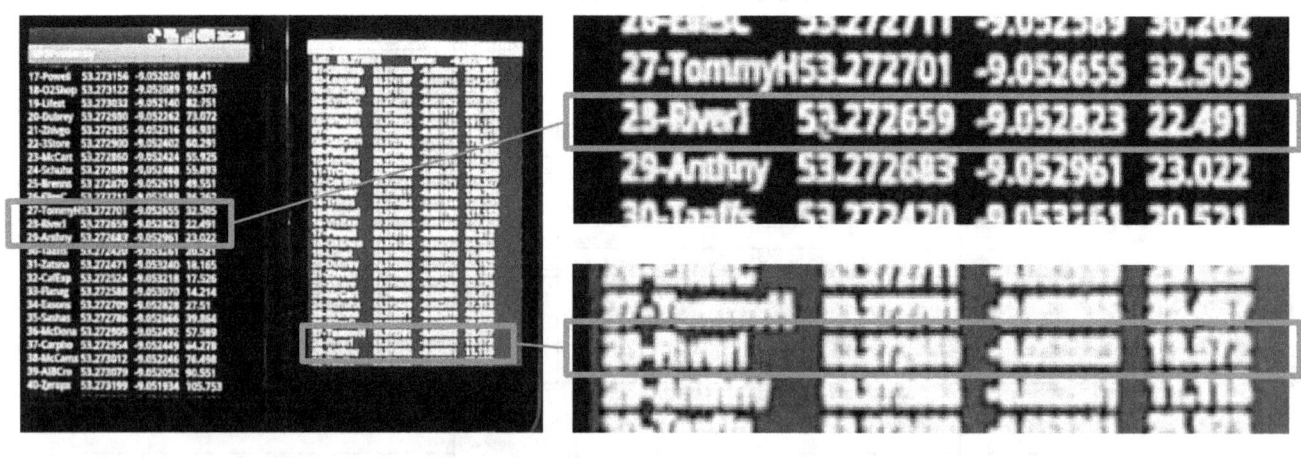

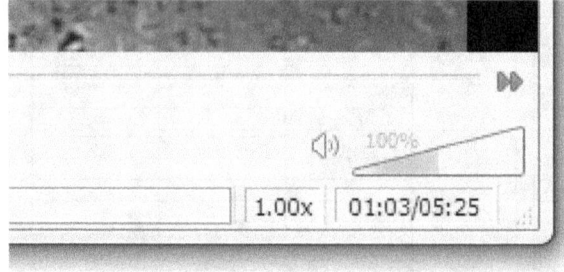

Screenshot captured at 1m03s into recording

Implementation/Execution:
1. Proceed to a position 20m from the first location.
2. Find the position using the photos from Exp001.
3. Hold a specially constructed clipboard and place both phones on the clipboard.
4. Place a video camera onto the clipboard and record the output from each phone simultaneously.
5. Start the location based applications on each phone.
6. Begin walking down the street and call(by voice) a set of 30 locations, passing a new location every 5-10 seconds.
7. Allow the camera to record the screen output from both phones.
8. Shut down both GPS applications and stop and save the recorded video.

Retesting:
The experiment can be retested easily, as only one street is being used.

Hardware Used:
Apple iPhone 3GS
Samsung GalaxyS(GT-I9000)
Panasonic HD Camcorder(DMC-FS30).

Software Used:
iPhone operating system iOS 4.2.1 used throughout.
Samsung GalaxyS operating system Android 2.1-update1 used throughout.
A custom Android(java) application to report current and stored GPS locations on the GalaxyS.
A custom Apple(objectiveC) application to report current and stored GPS locations on the iPhone.

Both software applications were written specifically for this experiment so as to ensure that the same programming methodology, algorithms and software design were used.

All classes were written according to the manufacturers recommendations for writing location based applications. The relevant source code is listed in the appendix.

It was necessary to rewrite the iPhone application because the phone did not have the necessary processing power to calculate the distances and to use the UITableview widget at the same time. The application was recoded to use ordinary UILabel widgets instead... housed in a simple Scrollview widget.

Both applications were coded to update every 1 second and to update every time a change in location occurred.
The same formula was used to calculate the distances on both phones.

Weather(observed 2011-01-20 09:35):
Weather during this experiment was generally, dry and lightly overcast. Temperature of 5degC.

Weather(observed 2011-01-25 20:05):
Weather during this experiment was generally, wet and heavily overcast. Temperature of 7degC.

Weather Report(Met Eireann 2011-01-20 11:00):
Wind = N 7.1Knots   Cloud = Cloudy   Temp = 5.6degC
Humidity = 92%   Rain = 3.1mm   Pressure = 1021 hPa.

Weather Report(Met Eireann 2011-01-25 11:00):
Wind = N 9.2Knots   Cloud = Cloudy   Temp = 4.1degC
Humidity = 78%   Rain = 1.6mm   Pressure = 1024 hPa.

Changes to Plan During Testing:
iPhone custom application was modified after the first two tests and before the last four tests.

Validation/Evaluation:
By completing this experiment, the goal has been achieved of establishing a basic knowledge of how accurate and responsive smartphones are at reporting location based information while walking.

Calculations and Formulae Used:
As listed in the source code.

Locations:
All locations were on Williamsgate St. and Shop St., Galway(city centre)..

There were 52 locations in all, 30 of which were used for this experiment.
The average distance between locations was **11.79m**.
The maximum distance from one location to the next adjacent location was **35.39m**.
The minimum distance from one location to the next adjacent location was **1.20m**.

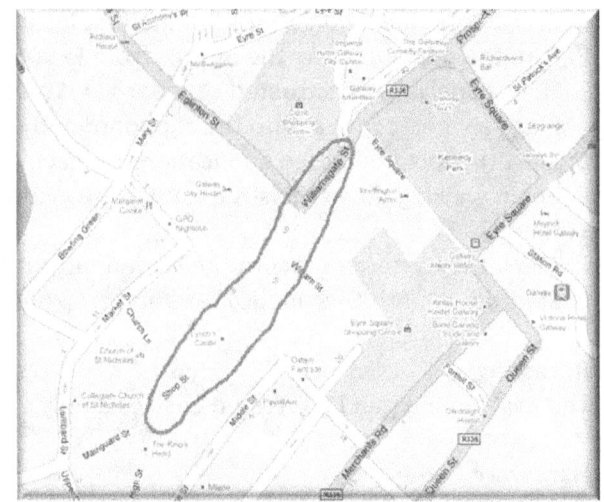

Locations:

The 'Dist' column indicates the distance from one location to the next.

	Name	Latitude	Longitude	Dist		Name	Latitude	Longitude	Dist
1	Location 1	53.274350	-9.050687		27	Location 27	53.272701	-9.052655	4.56
2	Location 2	53.274197	-9.050716	17.15	28	Location 28	53.272659	-9.052823	12.12
3	Location 3	53.274182	-9.050888	11.52	29	Location 29	53.272683	-9.052961	9.55
4	Location 4	53.274072	-9.051042	15.97	30	Location 30	53.272420	-9.053261	35.39
5	Location 5	53.273994	-9.051117	9.99	31	Location 31	53.272471	-9.053240	
6	Location 6	53.273923	-9.051182	8.99	32	Location 32	53.272524	-9.053218	6.07
7	Location 7	53.273904	-9.051244	4.64	33	Location 33	53.272588	-9.053070	12.12
8	Location 8	53.273798	-9.051195	12.24	34	Location 34	53.272709	-9.052828	20.96
9	Location 9	53.273769	-9.051229	3.94	35	Location 35	53.272786	-9.052665	13.77
10	Location 10	53.273699	-9.051312	9.52	36	Location 36	53.272909	-9.052492	17.97
11	Location 11	53.273566	-9.051454	17.60	37	Location 37	53.272964	-9.052449	6.72
12	Location 12	53.273564	-9.051471	1.20	38	Location 38	53.273012	-9.052246	14.54
13	Location 13	53.273511	-9.051542	7.50	39	Location 39	53.273079	-9.052052	14.94
14	Location 14	53.273484	-9.051544	3.02	40	Location 40	53.273199	-9.051934	15.43
15	Location 15	53.273285	-9.051793	27.64	41	Location 41	53.273293	-9.051946	10.49
16	Location 16	53.273256	-9.051834	4.25	42	Location 42	53.273343	-9.051731	15.34
17	Location 17	53.273156	-9.052020	16.57	43	Location 43	53.273379	-9.051692	4.73
18	Location 18	53.273122	-9.052089	5.99	44	Location 44	53.273431	-9.051668	5.98
19	Location 19	53.273032	-9.052140	10.55	45	Location 45	53.273573	-9.051558	17.42
20	Location 20	53.272980	-9.052262	9.96	46	Location 46	53.273717	-9.051430	18.12
21	Location 21	53.272935	-9.052316	6.16	47	Location 47	53.273970	-9.051318	29.14
22	Location 22	53.272900	-9.052402	6.92	48	Location 48	53.274044	-9.051235	9.88
23	Location 23	53.272863	-9.052424	4.33	49	Location 49	53.274181	-9.051074	18.65
24	Location 24	53.272889	-9.052488	5.15	50	Location 50	53.274229	-9.050964	9.09
25	Location 25	53.272871	-9.052619	8.94	51	Location 51	53.274279	-9.050830	10.48
26	Location 26	53.272711	-9.052589	17.82	52	Location 52	53.274323	-9.050727	8.44

Smartphone Adequacy for Location Aware Use Benchmark:

There was a rating system devised to allow easy interpretation of the results of the experiment. This rating system is explained in the next two pages. However, it was also necessary to establish an overall benchmark to determine if a smartphones overall performance was good enough to consider it suitable for location aware applications.
Observations of the different phones performance indicated that if a phone maintained GPS satellite coverage for over 80% of the duration of the tests then it was deemed suitable for locations aware applications.

Rating System:

It was necessary to devise a suitable rating system to categorise the quality of the data being generated by each phone during testing and analysis. It was decided to use a 5 point rating system, 5 being the highest accuracy/responsiveness GPS information generated and 1 being the lowest. 0 represented a loss of GPS information.
This scale may appear somewhat similar to the Likert scale which is a psychometric scale commonly used in questionnaires, and is the most widely used scale in survey research. However, the 5 point scale used in this experiment is objective in nature and does not depend on any user bias or opinion. It is merely a means to present the GPS data in a more user friendly and intuitive format.. instead of using a distance measurement.
Note: This rating system is different to the rating system used in experiment 3.2.1. Experiment 3.2.1 did not use any smartphones.

Accuracy/responsiveness of the data recorded. 5 is the maximum rating and 0 is the minimum rating.
Category 5: represents the best possible outcome from the device. It means that the device has reported that it is at the correct location. In other words, the device is reporting that it is closer to this location than to any other location within its dataset.
Category 4: represents an excellent outcome and can be considered very usable. It means the device has reported that it is one location away from the actual location.
Category 3: represent a good outcome and can be considered usable. It means the device has reported that it is two locations away from the actual location.
Category 2: represent a fair to poor outcome and can be considered unusable in the most straight forward sense. It means the device has reported that it is three locations away from the actual location. In future smartphones with larger screens, or on tablets, this information is usable. Also, with some ingenuity practiced by the software designer/developer this information could be considered usable. But for the purposes of this experiment it is considered unusable.
Category 1: represent a poor outcome and can be considered totally unusable. It means the device has reported that it is four or more locations away from the actual location. This information represents a failure to function accurately at a walking pace of 3kPH or more.
Category 0: means that no satellites can be tracked. No location data can be recorded. Completely useless.

Example Scenarios:
The following is an example scenario of the above categorisations:
In this example the software developer has programmed the phone to display the closest location in the middle of the screen….
Remember the phones ACTUAL location in all these examples is at Location 10.

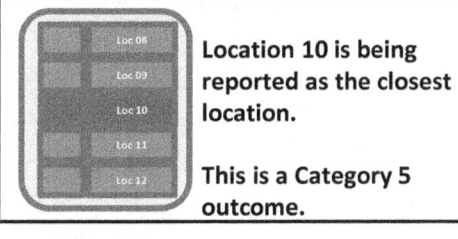
Location 10 is being reported as the closest location.

This is a Category 5 outcome.

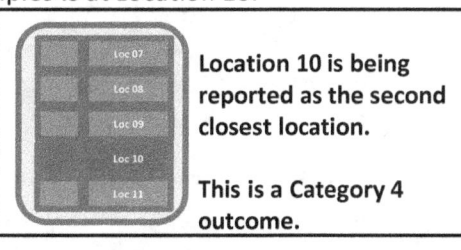
Location 10 is being reported as the second closest location.

This is a Category 4 outcome.

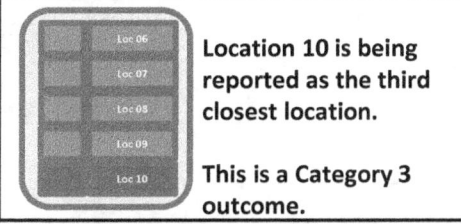
Location 10 is being reported as the third closest location.

This is a Category 3 outcome.

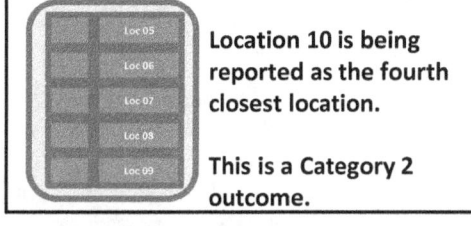
Location 10 is being reported as the fourth closest location.

This is a Category 2 outcome.

Chapter 3

Analysis:
The smartphones being tested had to report the correct location information quickly enough to allow the user to easily locate the premises(or destination) that the smartphone was attempting to provide information about.

The typical modern smartphone is capable of showing up to five photos and descriptions on its screen at any one time, so the smartphones had to be accurate and responsive enough to make sure that at least one of the photos/descriptions being shown was the location that the user was passing by at that time. Ideally, the smartphone should be able to tell exactly which premises the user is passing by and to centre that premises photo/description on the screen of the phone.
However, if this level of accuracy/responsiveness is not reached then the phone must be capable of reporting the location as being a maximum of two steps in front or back of the current actual location.

To illustrate this, see the screen grabs below. The Samsung screen easily shows 2 photos above and below the main photo.

Source Code Written to Calculate Distances:

The methodology and formulae used to calculate the distances were identical for the iPhone and Samsung GalaxyS:

Method provided by Objective-C(not used):
```
{
userLat = [userLatitude.text   doubleValue];
userLongi = [userLongitude.text   doubleValue];
CLLocation *userLocation = [[CLLocation   alloc] initWithLatitude:userLat
longitude:userLongi];
CLLocation *tableLocation = [[CLLocation alloc]
initWithLatitude:locationLat   longitude:locationLongi];
distance = [userLocation   distanceFromLocation:tableLocation] / 1000;
cell.dist.text = [[NSString   alloc]   initWithFormat:@"%.6f", distance];
}
```

iPhone Algorithm Written for Experiment:
```
-(double)
calculateDistance:(NSString*)current_latitud:(NSString*)current_longitud:
(NSString*)dest_latitud:(NSString*)dest_longitude   {
    if (current_latitud == @"" || current_longitud == @"")
    {
        double   value = 0.000;
        return   value;
    }
    double  cgLat1 = [current_latitud   doubleValue];
    double  cgLon1 = [current_longitud  doubleValue];
    double  cgLat2 = [dest_latitud      doubleValue];
    double  cgLon2 = [dest_longitude    doubleValue];
    double  cgX = 69.1 * (cgLat2 - cgLat1);
    double  cgY = 69.1 * -(cgLon2 - cgLon1) * cos(cgLat1/57.3);
    double  cgDist = 1603.9 * sqrt(cgX * cgX + cgY * cgY);
    double  cgFinal = 1609.3 * (sqrt(((69.1 * (cgLat1 - cgLat2)) *
        (69.1 * (cgLat1 - cgLat2))) + ((69.1 * (cgLon1 - cgLon2) *
        cos(cgLat2/57.3)) * (69.1 * (cgLon1 - cgLon2) *
cos(cgLat2/57.3)))));
    return (cgFinal / 1000);
}
```

Samsung GalaxyS Algorithm Written for Experiment:
```
public double calculateDistance(String current_latitud, String
current_longitud, String dest_latitud, String dest_longitude) {

    if (current_latitud == null || current_longitud == null ){
        double value = 0.000;
        return value;
    }
    double cgLat1 = Double.valueOf(current_latitud);
    double cgLon1 = Double.valueOf(current_longitud);
    double cgLat2 = Double.valueOf(dest_latitud);
    double cgLon2 = Double.valueOf(dest_longitude);
    double cgX = 69.1 * (cgLat2 - cgLat1);
    double cgY = 69.1 * -(cgLon2 - cgLon1) * Math.cos(cgLat1/57.3);
    double cgDist = 1603.9 * Math.sqrt(cgX * cgX + cgY * cgY);
    double cgFinal = 1609.3 * (Math.sqrt(((69.1 * (cgLat1 - cgLat2)) *
    (69.1 * (cgLat1 - cgLat2))) + ((69.1 * (cgLon1 - cgLon2) *
    Math.cos(cgLat2/57.3)) * (69.1 * (cgLon1 - cgLon2) *
Math.cos(cgLat2/57.3)))));

    return cgFinal;
}
```

Source Code Written to Ping for Locations and to Set for GPS Use:

iPhone Rev 1.0:
(essentially same as below)

iPhone Rev 2.8:
```
- (void)loadView {
  [super loadView];

  [self.view  addSubview:scrollbarView];
  [scrollbarView setContentSize:CGSizeMake(320, 300)];
  [scrollbarView setScrollEnabled:YES];
  [scrollbarView setClipsToBounds:YES];    // default is NO, we want to restrict drawing                                              within our scrollview

  [NSTimer  scheduledTimerWithTimeInterval:1.0
        target:self
        selector:@selector(pingUserLocation:)
        userInfo:nil  repeats:YES];
}

-(void)pingUserLocation:(NSTimer *)aTimer
{
  locationManager = [[CLLocationManager  alloc] init];
  locationManager.delegate = self;
  locationManager.desiredAccuracy = kCLLocationAccuracyBest;
  [locationManager  startUpdatingLocation];
}
```

Samsung GalaxyS:
```
try{
   cgGPSEnabled=cglocationManager.isProviderEnabled(LocationManager.GPS_P
ROVIDER);
   }catch(Exception ex){}
if(!cgGPSEnabled ){
}
try{
   locationListener = new GPSLocationListener();
   Criteria criteria = new Criteria();
   criteria.setAccuracy(Criteria.ACCURACY_FINE);
   cglocationManager = (LocationManager)
   getBaseContext().getSystemService(Context.LOCATION_SERVICE);
   String bestProvider = cglocationManager.getBestProvider(criteria,
true);
   cglocationManager.requestLocationUpdates(bestProvider, 1000, 0,
locationListener);


android:name="android.permission.ACCESS_COARSE_LOCATION">
android:name="android.permission.ACCESS_FINE_LOCATION">
```

Analysis of Results:
Total across all four tests conducted.

	Samsung	iPhone
Usable:	109	71
Unusable	3	41
Category 5(best)	54	14
Category 4(very good)	47	32
Category 3(good)	8	25
Category 2(bad)	1	15
Category 1(unusable)	2	11
Category 0(no GPS signal)	0	15
Samsung vs iPhone	96	16
No GPS Signal (sec)	0	153
No GPS Signal (%)	0	

Test Duration	19m13s
Test Distance	1098.120
Avg Speed	3.429
Total Locations	112

Analysis of all four tests carried out:
<u>Samsung GalaxyS vs iPhone:</u>
The Samsung detected 109 of the 112 locations successfully producing a hit rate of 97.32%
The iPhone detected 71 of the 112 locations successfully producing a hit rate of 63.39%
[Category 5, 4, 3: represents a hit, Category 2, 1, 0: represents a miss]

The Samsung detected 54 of the 112 locations at cat5 accuracy, equivalent to 48.21%
The iPhone detected 14 of the 112 locations at cat5 accuracy, equivalent to 12.50%
[Category 5: represents the best possible outcome from the device]

The Samsung detected 47 of the 112 locations at cat5 accuracy, equivalent to 41.96%
The iPhone detected 32 of the 112 locations at cat5 accuracy, equivalent to 28.57%
[Category 4: represents an excellent outcome and can be considered very usable]

The Samsung detected 8 of the 112 locations at cat5 accuracy, equivalent to 7.14%
The iPhone detected 25 of the 112 locations at cat5 accuracy, equivalent to 22.32%
[Category 3: represent a good outcome and can be considered usable]

The Samsung detected 1 of the 112 locations at cat5 accuracy, equivalent to 0.89%
The iPhone detected 15 of the 112 locations at cat5 accuracy, equivalent to 13.39%
[Category 2: represent a fair to poor outcome and can be considered unusable in the most cases]

The Samsung detected 2 of the 112 locations at cat5 accuracy, equivalent to 1.79%
The iPhone detected 11 of the 112 locations at cat5 accuracy, equivalent to 9.82%
[Category 1: represent a poor outcome and can be considered totally unusable]

The Samsung detected 0 of the 112 locations at cat5 accuracy, equivalent to 0.00%
The iPhone detected 15 of the 112 locations at cat5 accuracy, equivalent to 13.39%
[Category 0: means that no satellites can be tracked. No location data can be recorded]

Conclusion:

During the four tests where both phones were put head to head, the Samsung produced consistently better results.
However, both phones showed their ability to perform adequately under these very difficult environmental conditions.
Either phone is suitable for hosting location based GPS applications for the tourism industry.

Results:

The following 8 pages contain the detailed results from this experiment.
Note on STRIKE THROUGH entries:
During the two Jan 20th tests the iPhone showed some lag in updating the screen. It was subsequently discovered that the use of the UITableview widget was producing an unacceptable load on the CPU so a new version of the software was written for the Jan 25th tests. For this reason, ignore the iPhone information for this test(2011-01-20 GPS1-Exp5) and for the next test(2011-01-20 GPS2-Exp5). However, the Samsung information is valid in all tests.

The UITableview widget was replaced with simple Label widgets housed inside a basic UIScrollview widget and this fixed the problem and allowed iPhone testing to resume in the four tests conducted on the 25th Jan 2010.

The online resource at http://www.irishapps.org/smartlla.html
contains the 8 video files which capture the information shown in the following 8 pages.

GPS Test 1(2011-01-20 GPS1-Exp5)
Results:

2011-01-20 iPhone v Samsung GPS1-Exp5
2011-01-20 GPS1-Exp5

Test Duration	min:sec	05m:07s
Test Distance	meters	274.53
Avg Speed	KPH	3.21924

	Samsung	~~iPhone~~
Usable:	28	~~3~~
Unusable	0	~~25~~
Category 5(best)	13	~~1~~
Category 4(very good)	12	~~1~~
Category 3(good)	3	~~1~~
Category 2(bad)	0	~~4~~
Category 1(unusable)	0	~~21~~
Category 0(no GPS signal)	0	~~0~~
Samsung vs iPhone	28	~~0~~
No GPS Signal (sec)	0.000	~~0.000~~
No GPS Signal (%)	0.000	~~0.000~~

No	Name	Latitude	Longitude	Time	Samsung Positions Away from Ctr	~~iPhone Positions Away from Ctr~~	Samsung Dist Away	~~iPhone Dist Away~~	Samsung Category	~~iPhone Category~~
1	Location 1	53.274350	-9.050687	01:20	0	~~0~~	18.730	~~50.056~~	5	~~5~~
2	Location 2	53.274197	-9.050716	01:38	1	~~1~~	11.814	~~45.886~~	4	~~4~~
3	Location 3	53.274182	-9.050888	01:47	0	~~2~~	7.111	~~54.220~~	5	~~3~~
4	Location 4	53.274072	-9.051042	01:57	1	~~3~~	11.835	~~50.736~~	4	~~2~~
5	Location 5	53.273994	-9.051117	02:04	1	~~4~~	15.818	~~55.704~~	4	~~1~~
6	Location 6	53.273923	-9.051182	02:09	2	~~5~~	21.170	~~64.583~~	3	~~1~~
7	Location 7	53.273904	-9.051244	02:15	2	~~6~~	20.565	~~64.545~~	3	~~1~~
8	Location 8	53.273798	-9.051195	02:25	1	~~5~~	25.449	~~63.205~~	4	~~1~~
9	Location 9	53.273769	-9.051229	02:30	2	~~6~~	19.491	~~64.944~~	3	~~1~~
10	Location 10	53.273699	-9.051312	02:40	1	~~7~~	13.346	~~67.773~~	4	~~1~~
11	Location 11	53.273566	-9.051454	02:53	1	~~7~~	16.428	~~72.482~~	4	~~1~~
12	Location 12	53.273564	-9.051471	03:05	0	~~7~~	3.928	~~63.377~~	5	~~1~~
13	Location 13	53.273511	-9.051542	03:12	0	~~8~~	1.657	~~69.823~~	5	~~1~~
14	Location 14	53.273484	-9.051544	03:20	0	~~7~~	2.682	~~54.316~~	5	~~1~~
15	Location 15	53.273285	-9.051793	03:37	0	~~6~~	14.016	~~79.898~~	5	~~1~~
16	Location 16	53.273256	-9.051834	03:58	1	~~4~~	13.250	~~49.773~~	4	~~1~~
17	Location 17	53.273156	-9.052020	04:13	0	~~4~~	14.662	~~50.163~~	5	~~1~~
18	Location 18	53.273122	-9.052089	04:20	0	~~5~~	10.394	~~48.510~~	5	~~1~~
19	Location 19	53.273032	-9.052140	04:31	1	~~4~~	11.949	~~50.156~~	4	~~1~~
20	Location 20	53.272980	-9.052262	04:38	0	~~5~~	9.893	~~45.185~~	5	~~1~~
21	Location 21	53.272935	-9.052316	04:53	0	~~3~~	9.620	~~27.319~~	5	~~2~~
22	Location 22	53.272900	-9.052402	05:01	0	~~4~~	8.340	~~33.900~~	5	~~1~~
23	Location 23	53.272863	-9.052424	05:07	1	~~4~~	10.316	~~23.732~~	4	~~1~~
24	Location 24	53.272889	-9.052488	05:17	1	~~3~~	6.564	~~13.695~~	4	~~2~~
25	Location 25	53.272871	-9.052619	05:24	0	~~4~~	3.259	~~19.545~~	5	~~1~~
26	Location 26	53.272711	-9.052589	05:30	1	~~5~~	17.710	~~29.444~~	4	~~1~~
27	Location 27	53.272701	-9.052655	05:36	0	~~5~~	15.293	~~29.986~~	5	~~1~~
28	Location 28	53.272659	-9.052823	05:49	1	~~3~~	11.091	~~30.348~~	4	~~2~~
29	Location 29	53.272683	-9.052961	05:56	0	~~0~~	6.906	~~15.288~~	5	~~5~~
30	Location 30	53.272420	-9.053261	06:27	0	~~0~~	18.620	~~13.105~~	5	~~5~~

Observations:

Samsung GalaxyS:
This was the first test conducted for GPS accuracy/response while moving at a walking pace(>= 3kPH). At an average speed of 3.22 kPH the Samsung detected all 28 locations successfully. The GPS signal was consistent and was maintained throughout the test.
On three occasions the Samsung experienced enough lag to cause its reporting of the locations to fall behind by two places, but these locations were updated quickly enough to be still visible in a scenario where a maximum of 5 locations are displayed on the screen.

iPhone:
See note on previous page

GPS Test 2(2011-01-20 GPS2-Exp5)

Results:

2011-01-20 iPhone v Samsung GPS2-Exp5
2011-01-20 GPS2-Exp5

Test Duration	min:sec	04m:49s
Test Distance	meters	274.53
Avg Speed	KPH	3.41975

	Samsung	~~iPhone~~
Usable:	28	~~2~~
Unusable	0	~~26~~
Category 5(best)	12	~~0~~
Category 4(very good)	15	~~1~~
Category 3(good)	1	~~1~~
Category 2(bad)	0	~~2~~
Category 1(unusable)	0	~~24~~
Category 0(no GPS signal)	0	~~0~~
Samsung vs iPhone	28	~~0~~
No GPS Signal (sec)	0.000	~~0.000~~
No GPS Signal (%)	0.000	~~0.000~~

No	Name	Latitude	Longitude	Time	Samsung Positions Away from Ctr	~~iPhone Positions Away from Ctr~~	Samsung Dist Away	~~iPhone Dist Away~~	Samsung Category	~~iPhone Category~~
1	Location 1	53.274350	-9.050687	05:26	0	~~3~~	2.659	~~39.106~~	5	~~2~~
2	Location 2	53.274197	-9.050716	05:09	1	~~4~~	12.047	~~42.154~~	4	~~1~~
3	Location 3	53.274182	-9.050888	04:59	0	~~6~~	7.009	~~48.704~~	5	~~1~~
4	Location 4	53.274072	-9.051042	04:47	0	~~8~~	6.963	~~62.509~~	5	~~1~~
5	Location 5	53.273994	-9.051117	04:37	0	~~7~~	13.115	~~52.529~~	5	~~1~~
6	Location 6	53.273923	-9.051182	04:30	1	~~6~~	12.797	~~43.546~~	4	~~1~~
7	Location 7	53.273904	-9.051244	04:18	0	~~8~~	8.448	~~69.473~~	5	~~1~~
8	Location 8	53.273798	-9.051195	04:08	1	~~7~~	18.490	~~61.491~~	4	~~1~~
9	Location 9	53.273769	-9.051229	04:03	0	~~6~~	18.219	~~57.564~~	5	~~1~~
10	Location 10	53.273699	-9.051312	03:56	0	~~5~~	18.496	~~48.050~~	5	~~1~~
11	Location 11	53.273566	-9.051454	03:39	1	~~5~~	14.166	~~43.536~~	4	~~1~~
12	Location 12	53.273564	-9.051471	03:31	0	~~4~~	12.197	~~42.612~~	5	~~1~~
13	Location 13	53.273511	-9.051542	03:23	0	~~4~~	11.852	~~45.570~~	5	~~1~~
14	Location 14	53.273484	-9.051544	03:18	0	~~3~~	12.527	~~43.237~~	5	~~2~~
15	Location 15	53.273285	-9.051793	03:10	0	~~4~~	14.007	~~31.405~~	5	~~1~~
16	Location 16	53.273256	-9.051834	02:51	1	~~4~~	10.421	~~41.203~~	4	~~1~~
17	Location 17	53.273156	-9.052020	02:33	1	~~5~~	7.553	~~37.010~~	4	~~1~~
18	Location 18	53.273122	-9.052089	02:26	0	~~5~~	11.056	~~39.274~~	5	~~1~~
19	Location 19	53.273032	-9.052140	02:17	1	~~4~~	15.064	~~29.581~~	4	~~1~~
20	Location 20	53.272980	-9.052262	02:08	0	~~6~~	10.668	~~33.858~~	5	~~1~~
21	Location 21	53.272935	-9.052316	02:01	1	~~6~~	9.367	~~32.708~~	4	~~1~~
22	Location 22	53.272900	-9.052402	01:56	2	~~5~~	5.295	~~34.822~~	3	~~1~~
23	Location 23	53.272863	-9.052424	01:51	1	~~5~~	5.259	~~41.932~~	4	~~1~~
24	Location 24	53.272889	-9.052488	01:41	1	~~5~~	12.921	~~52.979~~	4	~~1~~
25	Location 25	53.272871	-9.052619	01:35	1	~~5~~	11.366	~~54.840~~	4	~~1~~
26	Location 26	53.272711	-9.052589	01:29	1	~~4~~	12.380	~~48.618~~	4	~~1~~
27	Location 27	53.272701	-9.052655	01:23	1	~~3~~	13.262	~~65.878~~	4	~~2~~
28	Location 28	53.272659	-9.052823	01:11	1	~~2~~	12.272	~~54.728~~	4	~~3~~
29	Location 29	53.272683	-9.052961	01:04	1	~~1~~	21.809	~~54.321~~	4	~~4~~
30	Location 30	53.272420	-9.053261	00:37	0	~~0~~	13.959	~~21.825~~	5	~~5~~

Observations:

Samsung GalaxyS:
This was the second test conducted for GPS accuracy/response while moving at a walking pace(>= 3kPH). Again the Samsung performed well. At an average speed of 3.42 kPH the Samsung detected all 28 locations successfully. The GPS signal was consistent and was maintained throughout the test.
On one occasions the Samsung experienced enough lag to cause its reporting of the location to fall behind by two places, but this location was updated quickly enough to be still visible in a scenario where a maximum of 5 locations are displayed on the screen.

iPhone:
See note two pages previous.

GPS Test 3(2011-01-25 GPS1-Exp5)
Results:

2011-01-25 iPhone v Samsung GPS1-Exp5
2011-01-25 GPS1-Exp5

Test Duration	min:sec	04m:47s
Test Distance	meters	274.53
Avg Speed	KPH	3.44358

	Samsung	iPhone
Usable:	26	15
Unusable	2	13
Category 5(best)	12	4
Category 4(very good)	11	8
Category 3(good)	3	3
Category 2(bad)	1	1
Category 1(unusable)	1	2
Category 0(no GPS signal)	0	10
Samsung vs iPhone	26	2
No GPS Signal (sec)	0.000	106.000
No GPS Signal (%)	0.000	36.930

No	Name	Latitude	Longitude	Time	Samsung Positions Away from Ctr	iPhone Positions Away from Ctr	Samsung Dist Away	iPhone Dist Away	Samsung Category	iPhone Category
1	Location 1	53.274350	-9.050687	00:43	0	0	17.368	92.779	5	5
2	Location 2	53.274197	-9.050716	01:05	1	1	14.681	100.540	4	4
3	Location 3	53.274182	-9.050888	01:15	0	26	10.569	215.813	5	0
4	Location 4	53.274072	-9.051042	01:30	0	25	8.684	199.871	5	0
5	Location 5	53.273994	-9.051117	01:42	1	24	7.501	190.104	4	0
6	Location 6	53.273923	-9.051182	01:55	1	23	9.073	181.386	4	0
7	Location 7	53.273904	-9.051244	02:03	0	22	9.230	177.023	5	0
8	Location 8	53.273798	-9.051195	02:11	1	5	13.993	53.753	4	1
9	Location 9	53.273769	-9.051229	02:15	2	5	12.673	42.907	3	1
10	Location 10	53.273699	-9.051312	02:28	3	19	17.175	157.733	2	0
11	Location 11	53.273566	-9.051454	02:37	4	1	29.604	25.433	1	4
12	Location 12	53.273564	-9.051471	02:45	2	2	22.101	25.767	3	3
13	Location 13	53.273511	-9.051542	02:54	1	3	12.787	22.948	4	2
14	Location 14	53.273484	-9.051544	02:57	1	15	13.762	130.380	4	0
15	Location 15	53.273285	-9.051793	03:05	2	2	27.888	31.462	3	3
16	Location 16	53.273256	-9.051834	03:21	1	1	21.872	20.359	4	4
17	Location 17	53.273156	-9.052020	03:43	0	1	13.280	8.195	5	4
18	Location 18	53.273122	-9.052089	03:48	0	11	11.684	77.246	5	0
19	Location 19	53.273032	-9.052140	04:01	0	10	11.140	68.202	5	0
20	Location 20	53.272980	-9.052262	04:09	0	0	9.117	9.940	5	5
21	Location 21	53.272935	-9.052316	04:16	0	1	9.218	11.470	5	4
22	Location 22	53.272900	-9.052402	04:22	0	7	6.785	47.158	5	0
23	Location 23	53.272863	-9.052424	04:26	1	1	8.639	8.867	4	4
24	Location 24	53.272889	-9.052488	04:33	1	0	5.545	3.739	4	5
25	Location 25	53.272871	-9.052619	04:39	0	0	3.617	2.861	5	5
26	Location 26	53.272711	-9.052589	04:44	1	1	13.426	14.825	4	4
27	Location 27	53.272701	-9.052655	04:49	0	2	11.596	14.544	5	3
28	Location 28	53.272659	-9.052823	04:59	1	1	9.516	11.588	4	4
29	Location 29	53.272683	-9.052961	05:07	0	0	3.498	8.965	5	5
30	Location 30	53.272420	-9.053261	05:30	0	0	9.827	86.785	5	5

Observations:

Samsung GalaxyS:
At an average speed of 3.44 kPH the Samsung detected 26 of the 28 locations successfully.
The GPS signal was consistent and was maintained throughout the test.

The Samsung's resolution dropped just below the threshold established for this test at 2m28s into the test and recovered again at 2m45s. During this time it reported one location as being three positions away from it's actual location and reported the next location as being four steps away from it actual location. It then recovered back to normal operations and reported all the following locations accurately enough to allow then to appear on the screen of a smartphone showing a maximum of five locations at once.

iPhone:
Of all the tests conducted, this was the iPhone's worst performance compared to the Samsung.
At an average speed of 3.44 kPH the iPhone detected only 15 of the 28 locations successfully.
The GPS signal was inconsistent and was maintained for just 63.09% of the test duration.

This was a poor performance from the iPhone considering that the Samsung device maintained GPS signal reception during the same time and under the exact same conditions. Had the phones been tested separately, it would have been easy to assume that it was a general lack of GPS satellite coverage that caused this outage and not the phones capabilities of lack thereof.

At 1m15s into the test the iPhone lost GPS reception for 56seconds resulting in it's failure to report any data for five locations. It again lost reception at 2m28s into the test for 9seconds and on two more occasions, it briefly lost GPS reception at 4m01s and at 4m22s.

During the time that the iPhone did detect GPS information, it reported three locations as being outside of the threshold for this test. In all, the iPhone failed to pick up on 13 locations.

However, the iPhone did perform adequately for more than 60% of the time(uptime vs downtime in seconds). It was accurate enough and for long enough to give adequate levels of performance to keep the user engaged. When the phone did lose GPS reception, it would have been easy for a developer/designer to provide the user with a message indicating that the signal had been temporarily lost and to wait a few seconds for it's return.
The following three tests showed improved performance from the iPhone.

Samsung: 100.00% GPS Signal Uptime
iPhone: 63.07% GPS Signal Uptime

The iPhone fell below the benchmark of 80% and was not adequate during this particular test for Location Aware application use.

GPS Test 4(2011-01-25 GPS2-Exp5)
Results:

2011-01-25 iPhone v Samsung GPS2-Exp5
2011-01-25 GPS2-Exp5

Test Duration	min:sec	04m:40s
Test Distance	meters	274.53
Avg Speed	KPH	3.52967

	Samsung	iPhone
Usable:	27	13
Unusable	1	15
Category 5(best)	15	2
Category 4(very good)	11	4
Category 3(good)	1	7
Category 2(bad)	0	5
Category 1(unusable)	1	5
Category 0(no GPS signal)	0	5
Samsung vs iPhone	24	4
No GPS Signal (sec)	0.000	47.000
No GPS Signal (%)	0.000	16.786

No	Name	Latitude	Longitude	Time	Samsung Positions Away from Ctr	iPhone Positions Away from Ctr	Samsung Dist Away	iPhone Dist Away	Samsung Category	iPhone Category
1	Location 1	53.274350	-9.050687	05:15	0	0	9.430	3.140	5	5
2	Location 2	53.274197	-9.050716	04:54	0	2	5.990	17.646	5	3
3	Location 3	53.274182	-9.050888	04:46	1	2	15.823	30.440	4	3
4	Location 4	53.274072	-9.051042	04:32	1	25	14.627	199.871	4	0
5	Location 5	53.273994	-9.051117	04:23	1	24	10.362	190.164	4	0
6	Location 6	53.273923	-9.051182	04:15	1	4	6.754	25.659	4	1
7	Location 7	53.273904	-9.051244	04:10	1	3	8.601	28.740	4	2
8	Location 8	53.273798	-9.051195	03:58	2	4	15.143	28.714	3	1
9	Location 9	53.273769	-9.051229	03:54	1	3	14.549	30.908	4	2
10	Location 10	53.273699	-9.051312	03:44	1	4	12.750	32.252	4	1
11	Location 11	53.273566	-9.051454	03:34	1	3	6.231	14.954	4	2
12	Location 12	53.273564	-9.051471	03:18	0	0	9.447	8.285	5	5
13	Location 13	53.273511	-9.051542	03:10	0	16	10.223	132.419	5	0
14	Location 14	53.273484	-9.051544	03:06	1	1	11.781	18.952	4	4
15	Location 15	53.273285	-9.051793	02:59	1	0	20.829	4.453	4	5
16	Location 16	53.273256	-9.051834	02:44	0	2	9.590	20.133	5	3
17	Location 17	53.273156	-9.052020	02:26	0	2	3.460	12.896	5	3
18	Location 18	53.273122	-9.052089	02:20	0	11	3.480	77.246	5	0
19	Location 19	53.273032	-9.052140	02:11	0	1	10.357	12.788	5	4
20	Location 20	53.272980	-9.052262	01:56	0	9	8.228	53.338	5	0
21	Location 21	53.272935	-9.052316	01:50	0	2	8.466	10.351	5	3
22	Location 22	53.272900	-9.052402	01:43	0	3	7.045	13.517	5	2
23	Location 23	53.272863	-9.052424	01:41	1	1	9.743	8.555	4	4
24	Location 24	53.272889	-9.052488	01:31	0	5	4.128	41.418	5	1
25	Location 25	53.272871	-9.052619	01:27	0	4	5.041	32.878	5	1
26	Location 26	53.272711	-9.052589	01:23	0	3	8.959	23.378	5	2
27	Location 27	53.272701	-9.052655	01:16	0	2	5.200	27.133	5	3
28	Location 28	53.272659	-9.052823	01:05	0	2	11.721	125.555	5	3
29	Location 29	53.272683	-9.052961	00:57	4	1	23.749	33.845	1	4
30	Location 30	53.272420	-9.053261	00:35	0	0	15.769	19.947	5	5

Observations:

Samsung GalaxyS:
At an average speed of 3.53 kPH the Samsung detected all 27 of the 28 locations successfully.
The GPS signal was consistent and was maintained throughout the test.
The Samsung's resolution dropped well below the threshold established for this test at 57s into the test and recovered 8seconds later. During this time it reported one location as being four positions away from it's actual location. It then recovered back to normal operations and reported all the following locations accurately enough to allow then to appear on the screen of a smartphone showing a maximum of five locations at once.

iPhone:
At an average speed of 3.53 kPH the iPhone detected 13 of the 28 locations successfully.
The GPS signal was somewhat inconsistent and was maintained for just 83.21% of the test duration.
This was an improvement over the first test. It lost GPS reception on four separate occasions for 15s, 6s, 8s and 23s.

While this loss of performance was not ideal, each loss was for a brief period of time. The average separate downtime was just 13seconds which is acceptable to most users.

Even though the iPhone only managed to report 15 of the 28 locations correctly, closer inspection of the figures show that five of the locations lost were just outside the threshold for this test, and with some ingenuity and creativity, a software designer/developer could overcome this slight lack of accuracy and incorporate these five locations into usable data.

From this test, it must be concluded that the iPhone did perform adequately enough to be used as a device for GPS based roaming in shopping and tourist districts.

Samsung: 100.00% GPS Signal Uptime
iPhone: 83.21% GPS Signal Uptime

Both phones performed adequately enough for Location Based usage.

GPS Test 5(2011-01-25 GPS3-Exp5)
Results:

2011-01-25 iPhone v Samsung GPS3-Exp5
2011-01-25 GPS3-Exp5

Test Duration	min:sec	04m:56s
Test Distance	meters	274.53
Avg Speed	KPH	3.33888

	Samsung	iPhone
Usable:	28	23
Unusable	0	5
Category 5(best)	15	6
Category 4(very good)	11	12
Category 3(good)	2	5
Category 2(bad)	0	3
Category 1(unusable)	0	2
Category 0(no GPS signal)	0	0
Samsung vs iPhone	20	8
No GPS Signal (sec)	0.000	0.000
No GPS Signal (%)	0.000	0.000

No	Name	Latitude	Longitude	Time	Samsung Positions Away from Ctr	iPhone Positions Away from Ctr	Samsung Dist Away	iPhone Dist Away	Samsung Category	iPhone Category
1	Location 1	53.274350	-9.050687	00:43	0	0	14.251	20.133	5	5
2	Location 2	53.274197	-9.050716	01:04	0	1	5.564	23.696	5	4
3	Location 3	53.274182	-9.050888	01:12	0	2	4.530	23.989	5	3
4	Location 4	53.274072	-9.051042	01:26	0	1	9.096	22.529	5	4
5	Location 5	53.273994	-9.051117	01:34	1	2	11.914	29.277	4	3
6	Location 6	53.273923	-9.051182	01:42	2	2	17.990	27.640	3	3
7	Location 7	53.273904	-9.051244	01:47	2	3	18.165	28.825	3	2
8	Location 8	53.273798	-9.051195	02:00	1	3	17.420	26.411	4	2
9	Location 9	53.273769	-9.051229	02:07	0	4	13.937	28.234	5	1
10	Location 10	53.273699	-9.051312	02:17	0	3	12.886	23.612	5	2
11	Location 11	53.273566	-9.051454	02:27	1	4	18.790	38.365	4	1
12	Location 12	53.273564	-9.051471	02:39	0	2	7.977	18.339	5	3
13	Location 13	53.273511	-9.051542	02:47	0	1	7.025	13.979	5	4
14	Location 14	53.273484	-9.051544	02:52	0	2	9.871	15.860	5	3
15	Location 15	53.273285	-9.051793	02:59	1	1	19.113	25.543	4	4
16	Location 16	53.273256	-9.051834	03:26	1	1	15.333	10.804	4	4
17	Location 17	53.273156	-9.052020	03:41	1	0	15.737	10.545	4	5
18	Location 18	53.273122	-9.052089	03:47	1	1	10.575	6.297	4	4
19	Location 19	53.273032	-9.052140	04:02	0	1	9.301	9.787	5	4
20	Location 20	53.272980	-9.052262	04:09	0	1	7.382	7.608	5	4
21	Location 21	53.272935	-9.052316	04:16	0	1	7.728	11.471	5	4
22	Location 22	53.272900	-9.052402	04:22	0	1	6.670	6.144	5	4
23	Location 23	53.272863	-9.052424	04:26	1	1	8.800	5.548	4	4
24	Location 24	53.272889	-9.052488	04:34	1	0	6.546	4.411	4	5
25	Location 25	53.272871	-9.052619	04:40	0	0	4.339	7.976	5	5
26	Location 26	53.272711	-9.052589	04:45	1	0	12.229	8.675	4	5
27	Location 27	53.272701	-9.052655	04:51	0	0	10.384	7.787	5	5
28	Location 28	53.272659	-9.052823	05:03	1	1	9.854	7.986	4	4
29	Location 29	53.272683	-9.052961	05:17	0	0	0.220	8.684	5	5
30	Location 30	53.272420	-9.053261	05:39	0	0	6.722	14.910	5	5

Chapter 3

Observations:

<u>Samsung GalaxyS:</u>
At an average speed of 3.34 kPH the Samsung detected all of the 28 locations successfully.
The GPS signal was consistent and was maintained throughout the test.

<u>iPhone:</u>
At an average speed of 3.34 kPH the iPhone detected 23 of the 28 locations successfully.
The GPS signal was consistent and was maintained throughout the test.
Again, this was an improvement over the previous two tests. The iPhone matched the Samsung in maintaining GPS reception throughout the test.
Of the five locations that were outside the threshold, three of the locations were just outside the threshold for this test.

Samsung: 100.00% GPS Signal Uptime
iPhone: 100.00% GPS Signal Uptime
Both phones performed adequately enough for Location Based usage.

GPS Test 6(2011-01-25 GPS4-Exp5)

Results:

2011-01-25 iPhone v Samsung GPS4-Exp5
2011-01-25 GPS4-Exp5

Test Duration	min:sec	04m:50s
Test Distance	meters	274.53
Avg Speed	KPH	3.40796

	Samsung	iPhone
Usable:	28	20
Unusable	0	8
Category 5(best)	12	2
Category 4(very good)	14	8
Category 3(good)	2	10
Category 2(bad)	0	6
Category 1(unusable)	0	2
Category 0(no GPS signal)	0	0
Samsung vs iPhone	26	2
No GPS Signal (sec)	0.000	0.000
No GPS Signal (%)	0.000	0.000

No	Name	Latitude	Longitude	Time	Samsung Positions Away from Ctr	iPhone Positions Away from Ctr	Samsung Dist Away	iPhone Dist Away	Samsung Category	iPhone Category
1	Location 1	53.274350	-9.050687	05:22	0	0	8.891	8.638	5	5
2	Location 2	53.274197	-9.050716	05:03	1	2	9.971	21.235	4	3
3	Location 3	53.274182	-9.050888	04:54	1	3	15.497	33.004	4	2
4	Location 4	53.274072	-9.051042	04:41	1	3	11.142	19.951	4	2
5	Location 5	53.273994	-9.051117	04:32	1	4	6.955	24.427	4	1
6	Location 6	53.273923	-9.051182	04:24	1	3	4.081	15.581	4	2
7	Location 7	53.273904	-9.051244	04:17	0	3	7.029	17.674	5	2
8	Location 8	53.273798	-9.051195	04:06	1	3	12.925	29.354	4	2
9	Location 9	53.273769	-9.051229	04:01	1	3	10.316	25.425	4	2
10	Location 10	53.273699	-9.051312	03:53	0	4	8.352	28.449	5	1
11	Location 11	53.273566	-9.051454	03:40	1	1	4.822	9.080	4	4
12	Location 12	53.273564	-9.051471	03:26	0	2	2.523	17.731	5	3
13	Location 13	53.273511	-9.051542	03:17	0	1	3.216	11.301	5	4
14	Location 14	53.273484	-9.051544	03:11	0	1	8.810	19.030	5	4
15	Location 15	53.273285	-9.051793	03:04	0	0	12.444	6.688	5	5
16	Location 16	53.273256	-9.051834	02:47	0	1	6.311	13.155	5	4
17	Location 17	53.273156	-9.052020	02:31	1	2	4.022	15.900	4	3
18	Location 18	53.273122	-9.052089	02:24	0	2	4.418	16.848	5	3
19	Location 19	53.273032	-9.052140	02:17	0	1	4.479	12.319	5	4
20	Location 20	53.272980	-9.052262	02:07	0	2	2.203	12.959	5	3
21	Location 21	53.272935	-9.052316	02:00	0	1	3.499	8.481	5	4
22	Location 22	53.272900	-9.052402	01:52	1	2	4.804	6.460	4	3
23	Location 23	53.272863	-9.052424	01:46	0	2	5.958	8.363	5	3
24	Location 24	53.272889	-9.052488	01:38	2	2	15.566	18.684	3	3
25	Location 25	53.272871	-9.052619	01:33	1	2	15.090	14.615	4	3
26	Location 26	53.272711	-9.052589	01:20	1	2	6.396	12.023	4	3
27	Location 27	53.272701	-9.052655	01:14	1	1	13.276	15.342	4	4
28	Location 28	53.272659	-9.052823	01:03	2	1	22.491	13.572	3	4
29	Location 29	53.272683	-9.052961	00:55	1	0	34.337	18.108	4	5
30	Location 30	53.272420	-9.053261	00:32	0	0	17.158	11.484	5	5

Observations:

Samsung GalaxyS:
At an average speed of 3.41 kPH the Samsung detected all of the 28 locations successfully.
The GPS signal was consistent and was maintained throughout the test.

iPhone:
At an average speed of 3.41 kPH the iPhone detected 20 of the 28 locations successfully.
The GPS signal was consistent and was maintained throughout the test.
A slight drop in performance from the previous test in the sense that 8 of the locations were outside of the threshold compared to only 5 in the previous test.
However, 6 of the 8 locations that were categorised as failures were just one location away from making the cut. As mentioned before, crafty software development could incorporate these six results and make them usable.

In any case the iPhone performed adequately enough to prove it's suitability for location based applications in built up urban areas where tourists are likely to frequent.

Samsung: 100.00% GPS Signal Uptime
iPhone: 100.00% GPS Signal Uptime

Both phones performed adequately enough for Location Based usage.

3.2.6 Test the Accuracy of GPS on the Android and iOS Operating Systems using the Latest Hardware(Samsung GalaxyS/Nexus S and Apple iPhone 3Gs/4)

Aim/Goals:
To establish the accuracy of the above mentioned smartphones with regard to their GPS functionality while walking at 3 kPH(typical walking speed during tourist activity).
This experiment is very similar to Experiment 005, except that we have included the latest smartphones available. The iPhone 4 and the Samsung Nexus S.

Data from Previous Experiments:
This experiment used the location data from Exp001 and follows the methodology from Exp005.

Follow On Experiments:
Other GPS and Bluetooth experiments are planned using both of these phones.

Methodology/Preparation/Planning:
30 locations were chosen from a busy shopping district in Galway city.
The aluminium harness from Exp005 was used to house all smartphones and to allow video recording of their performance while roaming the street and passing the locations(shops) at typical walking pace(3kPH). This ensured that all phones were receiving identical GPS signals and it also ensured that a good quality video image was captured to allow later analysis of the results.
The following photos illustrate the method used:

Extract from test 2011-01-25 iPhone v Samsung GPS4-Exp5.

27	Tommy	53.272701	-9.052655	01:14	1	1	13.276	15.342
28	River	53.272659	-9.052823	01:03	2	1	22.491	13.572
29	Anthony	53.272683	-9.052961	00:55	1	0	34.337	18.108

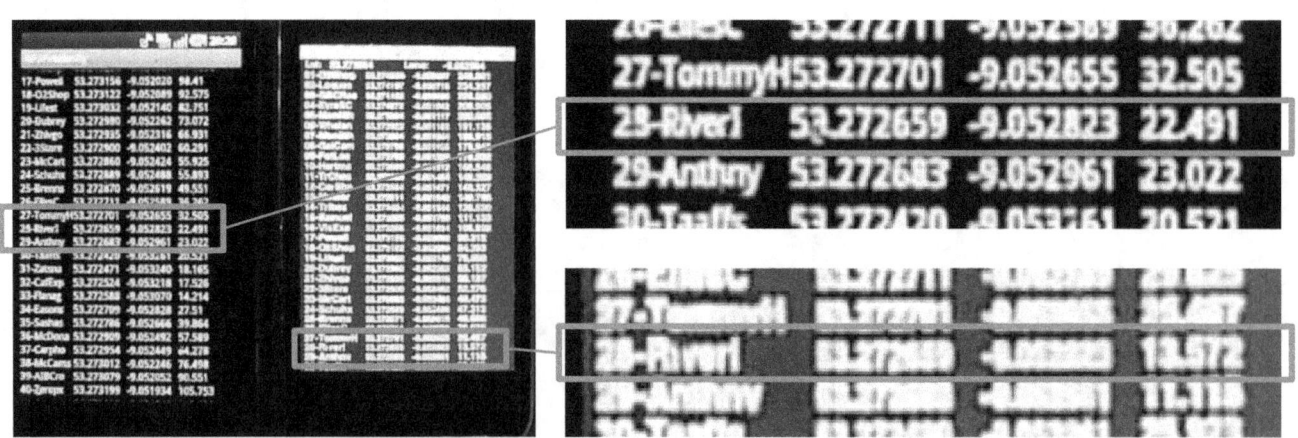

Screenshot captured at 1m03s into recording

Implementation/Execution:
1. Proceed to a position 20m from the first location.
2. Find the position using the photos from Exp001.
3. Hold a specially constructed clipboard and place all phones on the clipboard.
4. Place a video camera onto the clipboard and record the output from each phone simultaneously.
5. Start the location based applications on each phone.
6. Begin walking down the street and call(by voice) a set of 30 locations, passing a new location every 5-10 seconds.
7. Allow the camera to record the screen output from all four phones.
8. Stop and save the recorded video.

Retesting:
The experiment can be retested easily, as only one street is being used.

Hardware Used:
Apple iPhone 3GS
Samsung GalaxyS(GT-I9000)
Apple iPhone 4
Samsung Nexus S Development phone.
Panasonic HD Camcorder(DMC-FS30).

Software Used:
iPhone operating system iOS 4.2.1 used throughout.
Samsung GalaxyS operating system Android 2.1-update1.
Samsung Nexus S operating system Android 2.3 Gingerbread.
A custom Android(java) application to report current and stored GPS locations on the GalaxyS/Nexus S
A custom Apple(objective-C) application to report current and stored GPS locations on the iPhone 3Gs/4.

Both software applications were written specifically for this experiment and for Exp005 so as to ensure that the same programming methodology and software design were used.

All classes were written according to the manufacturers recommendations for writing location based applications. The relevant source code is listed in the appendix of Exp005.

Both applications were coded to update every 1 second and to update every time a change in location occurred.

The same formula was used to calculate the distances on both phones.

Weather(observed 2011-03-07 18:05):
Weather during this experiment was generally, dry and lightly overcast. Temperature of 10degC.

Weather Report(Met Eireann 2011-03-07 11:00):
Wind = E 3.4Knots   Cloud = S. Cloudy Temp = 9.3degC
Humidity = 48%   Rain = 0.6mm   Pressure = 1017 hPa.

Changes to Plan During Testing:
None.

Validation/Evaluation:
By completing this experiment, I have achieved by goal of establishing a basic knowledge of how accurate and responsive the latest smartphones are at reporting location based information while walking.

Calculations and Formulae Used:
As listed in the source code.

Locations:

All locations were on Williamsgate St. and Shop St., Galway(city centre)..

There were 52 locations in all, 30 of which were used for this experiment.
The average distance between locations was **11.79m**.
The maximum distance from one location to the next adjacent location was **35.39m**.
The minimum distance from one location to the next adjacent location was **1.20m**.

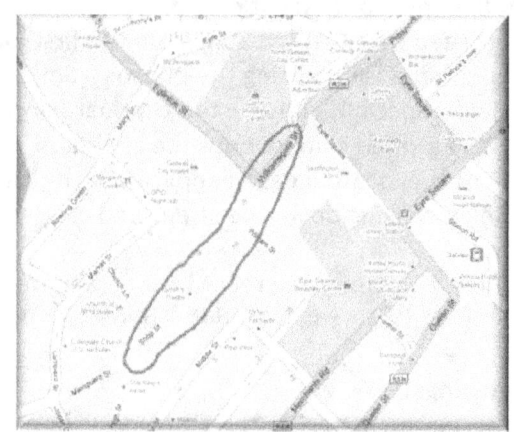

Locations:

The 'Dist' column indicates the distance from one location to the next.

	Name	Latitude	Longitude	Dist		Name	Latitude	Longitude	Dist
1	Location 1	53.274350	-9.050687		27	Location 27	53.272701	-9.052655	4.56
2	Location 2	53.274197	-9.050716	17.15	28	Location 28	53.272659	-9.052823	12.12
3	Location 3	53.274182	-9.050888	11.52	29	Location 29	53.272683	-9.052961	9.55
4	Location 4	53.274072	-9.051042	15.97	30	Location 30	53.272420	-9.053261	35.39
5	Location 5	53.273994	-9.051117	9.99	31	Location 31	53.272471	-9.053240	
6	Location 6	53.273923	-9.051182	8.99	32	Location 32	53.272524	-9.053218	6.07
7	Location 7	53.273904	-9.051244	4.64	33	Location 33	53.272588	-9.053070	12.12
8	Location 8	53.273798	-9.051195	12.24	34	Location 34	53.272709	-9.052828	20.96
9	Location 9	53.273769	-9.051229	3.94	35	Location 35	53.272786	-9.052665	13.77
10	Location 10	53.273699	-9.051312	9.52	36	Location 36	53.272909	-9.052492	17.97
11	Location 11	53.273566	-9.051454	17.60	37	Location 37	53.272964	-9.052449	6.72
12	Location 12	53.273564	-9.051471	1.20	38	Location 38	53.273012	-9.052246	14.54
13	Location 13	53.273511	-9.051542	7.50	39	Location 39	53.273079	-9.052052	14.94
14	Location 14	53.273484	-9.051544	3.02	40	Location 40	53.273199	-9.051934	15.43
15	Location 15	53.273285	-9.051793	27.64	41	Location 41	53.273293	-9.051946	10.49
16	Location 16	53.273256	-9.051834	4.25	42	Location 42	53.273343	-9.051731	15.34
17	Location 17	53.273156	-9.052020	16.57	43	Location 43	53.273379	-9.051692	4.73
18	Location 18	53.273122	-9.052089	5.99	44	Location 44	53.273431	-9.051668	5.98
19	Location 19	53.273032	-9.052140	10.55	45	Location 45	53.273573	-9.051558	17.42
20	Location 20	53.272980	-9.052262	9.96	46	Location 46	53.273717	-9.051430	18.12
21	Location 21	53.272935	-9.052316	6.16	47	Location 47	53.273970	-9.051318	29.14
22	Location 22	53.272900	-9.052402	6.92	48	Location 48	53.274044	-9.051235	9.88
23	Location 23	53.272863	-9.052424	4.33	49	Location 49	53.274181	-9.051074	18.65
24	Location 24	53.272889	-9.052488	5.15	50	Location 50	53.274229	-9.050964	9.09
25	Location 25	53.272871	-9.052619	8.94	51	Location 51	53.274279	-9.050830	10.48
26	Location 26	53.272711	-9.052589	17.82	52	Location 52	53.274323	-9.050727	8.44

Smartphone Adequacy for Location Aware Use Benchmark:

There was a rating system devised to allow easy interpretation of the results of the experiment. This rating system is explained in the next two pages. However, it was also necessary to establish an overall benchmark to determine if a smartphones overall performance was good enough to consider it suitable for location aware applications.
Observations of the different phones performance indicated that if a phone maintained GPS satellite coverage for over 80% of the duration of the tests then it was deemed suitable for locations aware applications.

Rating System:

It was necessary to devise a suitable rating system to categorise the quality of the data being generated by each phone during testing and analysis. It was decided to use a 5 point rating system, 5 being the highest accuracy/responsiveness GPS information generated and 1 being the lowest. 0 represented a loss of GPS information.
This scale may appear somewhat similar to the Likert scale which is a psychometric scale commonly used in questionnaires, and is the most widely used scale in survey research. However, the 5 point scale used in this experiment is objective in nature and does not depend on any user bias or opinion. It is merely a means to present the GPS data in a more user friendly and intuitive format.. instead of using a distance measurement.
Note: This rating system is different to the rating system used in experiment 3.2.1. Experiment 3.2.1 did not use any smartphones.

Accuracy/responsiveness of the data recorded. 5 is the maximum rating and 0 is the minimum rating.
Category 5: represents the best possible outcome from the device. It means that the device has reported that it is at the correct location. In other words, the device is reporting that it is closer to this location than to any other location within its dataset.
Category 4: represents an excellent outcome and can be considered very usable. It means the device has reported that it is one location away from the actual location.
Category 3: represent a good outcome and can be considered usable. It means the device has reported that it is two locations away from the actual location.
Category 2: represent a fair to poor outcome and can be considered unusable in the most straight forward sense. It means the device has reported that it is three locations away from the actual location. In future smartphones with larger screens, or on tablets, this information is usable. Also, with some ingenuity practiced by the software designer/developer this information could be considered usable. But for the purposes of this experiment it is considered unusable.
Category 1: represent a poor outcome and can be considered totally unusable. It means the device has reported that it is four or more locations away from the actual location. This information represents a failure to function accurately at a walking pace of 3kPH or more.
Category 0: means that no satellites can be tracked. No location data can be recorded. Completely useless.

Example Scenarios:
The following is an example scenario of the above categorisations:
In this example the software developer has programmed the phone to display the closest location in the middle of the screen....
Remember the phones ACTUAL location in all these examples is at Location 10.

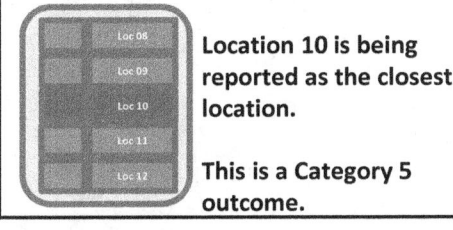
Location 10 is being reported as the closest location.

This is a Category 5 outcome.

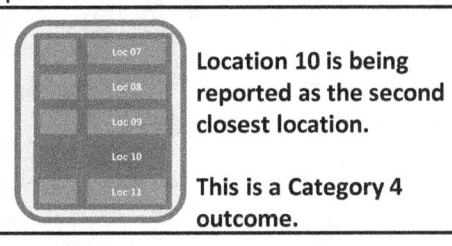
Location 10 is being reported as the second closest location.

This is a Category 4 outcome.

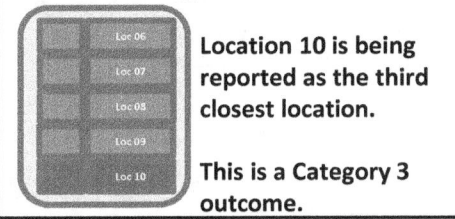
Location 10 is being reported as the third closest location.

This is a Category 3 outcome.

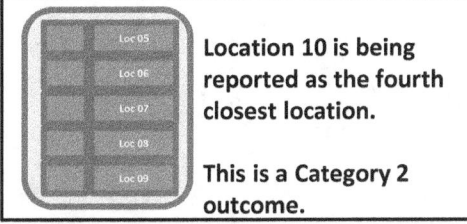
Location 10 is being reported as the fourth closest location.

This is a Category 2 outcome.

Analysis:
The smartphones being tested had to report the correct location information quickly enough to allow the user to easily locate the premises(or destination) that the smartphone was attempting to provide information about.

The typical modern smartphone is capable of showing up to five photos and descriptions on its screen at any one time, so the smartphones had to be accurate and responsive enough to make sure that at least one of the photos/descriptions being shown was the location that the user was passing by at that time. Ideally, the smartphone should be able to tell exactly which premises the user is passing by and to centre that premises photo/description on the screen of the phone.
However, if this level of accuracy/responsiveness is not reached then the phone must be capable of reporting the location as being a maximum of two steps in front or back of the current actual location.

To illustrate this, see the screen grabs below. The Samsung screen easily shows 2 photos above and below the main photo.

Source Code Written to Calculate Distances:

The methodology and formulae used to calculate the distances were identical for the iPhone and Samsung GalaxyS:

Method provided by Objective-C(not used):
```
{
userLat = [userLatitude.text   doubleValue];
userLongi = [userLongitude.text   doubleValue];
CLLocation *userLocation = [[CLLocation   alloc] initWithLatitude:userLat longitude:userLongi];
CLLocation *tableLocation = [[CLLocation alloc] initWithLatitude:locationLat   longitude:locationLongi];
distance = [userLocation   distanceFromLocation:tableLocation] / 1000;
cell.dist.text = [[NSString    alloc]    initWithFormat:@"%.6f", distance];
}
```

iPhone Algorithm Written for Experiment:
```
-(double)
calculateDistance:(NSString*)current_latitud:(NSString*)current_longitud:
(NSString*)dest_latitud:(NSString*)dest_longitude   {
    if (current_latitud == @"" || current_longitud == @"")
    {
        double    value = 0.000;
        return   value;
    }
    double   cgLat1 = [current_latitud   doubleValue];
    double   cgLon1 = [current_longitud  doubleValue];
    double   cgLat2 = [dest_latitud      doubleValue];
    double   cgLon2 = [dest_longitude    doubleValue];
    double   cgX = 69.1 * (cgLat2 - cgLat1);
    double   cgY = 69.1 * -(cgLon2 - cgLon1) * cos(cgLat1/57.3);
    double   cgDist = 1603.9 * sqrt(cgX * cgX + cgY * cgY);
    double   cgFinal = 1609.3 * (sqrt(((69.1 * (cgLat1 - cgLat2)) *
        (69.1 * (cgLat1 - cgLat2))) + ((69.1 * (cgLon1 - cgLon2) *
        cos(cgLat2/57.3)) * (69.1 * (cgLon1 - cgLon2) *
cos(cgLat2/57.3)))));
    return (cgFinal / 1000);
}
```

Samsung GalaxyS Algorithm Written for Experiment:
```
public double calculateDistance(String current_latitud, String
current_longitud, String dest_latitud, String dest_longitude) {

    if (current_latitud == null || current_longitud == null ){
        double value = 0.000;
        return value;
    }
    double cgLat1 = Double.valueOf(current_latitud);
    double cgLon1 = Double.valueOf(current_longitud);
    double cgLat2 = Double.valueOf(dest_latitud);
    double cgLon2 = Double.valueOf(dest_longitude);
    double cgX = 69.1 * (cgLat2 - cgLat1);
    double cgY = 69.1 * -(cgLon2 - cgLon1) * Math.cos(cgLat1/57.3);
    double cgDist = 1603.9 * Math.sqrt(cgX * cgX + cgY * cgY);
    double cgFinal = 1609.3 * (Math.sqrt(((69.1 * (cgLat1 - cgLat2)) *
       (69.1 * cgLat1 - cgLat2))) + ((69.1 * (cgLon1 - cgLon2) *
    Math.cos(cgLat2/57.3)) * (69.1 * (cgLon1 - cgLon2) *
Math.cos(cgLat2/57.3)))));

    return cgFinal;
}
```

Source Code Written to Ping for Locations and to Set for GPS Use:

iPhone Rev 1.0:
(essentially same as below)

iPhone Rev 2.8:
```
- (void)loadView {
  [super loadView];

  [self.view   addSubview:scrollbarView];
  [scrollbarView setContentSize:CGSizeMake(320, 300)];
  [scrollbarView setScrollEnabled:YES];
  [scrollbarView setClipsToBounds:YES];   // default is NO, we want to
restrict drawing                                             within our
scrollview

  [NSTimer   scheduledTimerWithTimeInterval:1.0
         target:self
         selector:@selector(pingUserLocation:)
         userInfo:nil   repeats:YES];
}

-(void)pingUserLocation:(NSTimer *)aTimer
{
  locationManager = [[CLLocationManager  alloc] init];
  locationManager.delegate = self;
  locationManager.desiredAccuracy = kCLLocationAccuracyBest;
  [locationManager   startUpdatingLocation];
}
```

Samsung GalaxyS:
```
try{
   cgGPSEnabled=cglocationManager.isProviderEnabled(LocationManager.GPS_P
ROVIDER);
   }catch(Exception ex){}
if(!cgGPSEnabled ){
}
try{
   locationListener = new GPSLocationListener();
   Criteria criteria = new Criteria();
   criteria.setAccuracy(Criteria.ACCURACY_FINE);
   cglocationManager = (LocationManager)
   getBaseContext().getSystemService(Context.LOCATION_SERVICE);
   String bestProvider = cglocationManager.getBestProvider(criteria,
true);
   cglocationManager.requestLocationUpdates(bestProvider, 1000, 0,
locationListener);


android:name="android.permission.ACCESS_COARSE_LOCATION">
android:name="android.permission.ACCESS_FINE_LOCATION">
```

Analysis of Results:
Total across all six tests conducted.

	iPhone4	GalaxyS	NexusS	iPhone3Gs	Android	iOS
Usable:	64	156	158	114	314	178
Unusable	96	4	2	46	6	142
Category 5(best)	11	73	78	39	151	50
Category 4(very good)	29	67	63	48	130	77
Category 3(good)	24	16	17	27	33	51
Category 2(bad-unusable)	20	4	2	11	6	31
Category 1(unusable)	76	0	0	14	0	90
Category 0(no GPS signal)	0	0	0	21	0	21
Best Phone per sample	5	60	58	37	118	42

Analysis of all six tests carried out:

The Samsung Galaxy S proved to be the best performer when it comes to providing the user with good raw GPS data. It proved to be superior in 60 of the 160 locations checked over the six tests.
The Google Nexus S was the second best and performed almost as well as the Samsung.
The iPhone 3Gs was third and the iPhone 4 was fourth, recoding the best signal in only 5 of the 160 test locations.
On pure accuracy, the Google Nexus S came out on top. It recorded 78 category 5 locations which is the highest possible accuracy.
The Galaxy S recorded 73, the iPhone 3Gs 39 and the iPhone 4 recorded just 11 out of 160.

Loss of Satellite Signal:
Both Android devices maintained full satellite coverage during the entire test.
The iPhone 3Gs lost satellite signal for 211sec(11.814%) over all the tests.
The iPhone 4 failed to recognise movement(effectively losing satellite signal) for 429sec(24.580%).
Despite the iPhone 3Gs loss of satellite signal for 11.8%, it still maintained good performance throughout all tests.
The iPhone 4 displayed a more degraded performance and effectively lost satellite signal for 25.6% of the testing time. This loss of signal noticeably affected the performance of the phone.
It is unknown why the iPhone 4 performed so poorly in comparison to the iPhone 3Gs(and the Android phones).
It is important to note that both iOS devices were using the same iOS version and running identical software. The software was downloaded to both phones 60mins before the test began. Both phones had fully charged batteries and both phones were in identical positions during the testing.

Conclusion:

In conclusion, both Android phones performed excellently and are accurate enough to be used in the tourism industry.
The iPhone 3Gs was not as accurate or responsive as the two Android phones, but it is more than adequate for use in the tourism sector.
The iPhone 4 performed poorly, although it still maintained enough signal accuracy to keep the used informed of their general location.

In a comparison between the Google Android system and the Apple iOS system, the Android phones clearly outperformed the iOS phones. All four phones were chosen because they are an accurate representation of what's available on both platforms. As of the time of writing, the iPhone 4 is the best iOS phone available and the Google Nexus S is the most advanced Android phone available and is recommended by Google for development of the latest Android apps.

All four phones are suitable for hosting location based GPS applications for the tourism industry.

GPS Test 1(2011-03-07 GPS1-Exp7)
Results:

No	Name	Latitude	Longitude	Time	iPhone4 Positions Away from Ctr	GalaxyS Positions Away from Ctr	NexusS Positions Away from Ctr	iPhone3Gs Positions Away from Ctr	iPhone4 Dist Away	GalaxyS Dist Away	NexusS Dist Away	iPhone3Gs Dist Away
1	Location 1	53.274350	-9.050687	00:50	0	0	0	0	142.798	19.180	17.334	160.342
2	Location 2	53.274197	-9.050716	01:10	1	0	0	1	69.096	4.856	6.324	22.638
3	Location 3	53.274182	-9.050888	01:18	0	1	1	2	4.306	8.301	8.199	40.816
4	Location 4	53.274072	-9.051042	01:32	1	0	0	no sig	20.194	6.086	4.938	no sig
5	Location 5	53.273994	-9.051117	01:41	0	0	1	1	9.391	4.997	5.382	10.453
6	Location 6	53.273923	-9.051182	01:47	1	0	1	2	12.083	3.503	8.502	18.851
7	Location 7	53.273904	-9.051244	01:53	2	1	1	3	13.348	3.685	7.451	22.136
8	Location 8	53.273798	-9.051195	02:05	2	1	1	4	15.462	9.703	17.826	32.663
9	Location 9	53.273769	-9.051229	02:10	1	2	2	5	12.980	10.574	22.528	36.274
10	Location 10	53.273699	-9.051312	02:24	0	1	3	0	11.182	7.316	27.218	8.745
11	Location 11	53.273566	-9.051454	02:34	1	1	1	1	23.216	12.462	18.921	21.927
12	Location 12	53.273564	-9.051471	02:46	2	1	1	2	23.561	2.294	2.108	22.374
13	Location 13	53.273511	-9.051542	02:55	3	1	0	2	30.281	5.618	2.967	18.591
14	Location 14	53.273484	-9.051544	03:02	2	0	0	3	33.222	7.280	3.199	19.668
15	Location 15	53.273285	-9.051793	03:18	5	0	1	4	59.659	10.058	16.980	45.631
16	Location 16	53.273256	-9.051834	03:32	6	0	1	6	63.731	5.122	5.964	54.582
17	Location 17	53.273156	-9.052020	03:51	7	1	0	1	79.335	6.152	4.925	18.130
18	Location 18	53.273122	-9.052089	03:58	8	1	0	0	84.928	6.427	1.669	5.643
19	Location 19	53.273032	-9.052140	04:13	9	0	0	no sig	95.267	3.126	3.327	no sig
20	Location 20	53.272980	-9.052262	04:24	10	0	0	no sig	104.413	3.910	2.023	no sig
21	Location 21	53.272935	-9.052316	04:32	1	0	1	0	6.114	6.045	4.323	2.919
22	Location 22	53.272900	-9.052402	04:40	2	0	0	no sig	13.000	6.671	3.261	no sig
23	Location 23	53.272863	-9.052424	04:46	3	1	1	1	16.850	11.687	4.325	9.899
24	Location 24	53.272889	-9.052488	05:00	4	1	1	3	18.438	7.713	9.360	16.081
25	Location 25	53.272871	-9.052619	05:06	5	0	0	2	27.110	3.498	6.799	9.875
26	Location 26	53.272711	-9.052589	05:13	6	1	1	1	36.823	19.198	9.644	9.358
27	Location 27	53.272701	-9.052655	05:19	7	2	0	2	40.507	16.060	8.047	10.938
28	Location 28	53.272659	-9.052823	05:33	8	1	0	3	51.709	9.876	3.726	18.635
29	Location 29	53.272683	-9.052961	05:42	1	0	0	2	11.681	3.950	8.763	15.800
30	Location 30	53.272420	-9.053261	06:03	1	0	0	2	45.408	3.254	3.046	36.837

No	Name	Latitude	Longitude	iPhone4 Category	GalaxyS Category	NexusS Category	iPhone3Gs Category	Best Phone	Best OS
1	Location 1	53.274350	-9.050687	5	5	5	5	NexusS	Android
2	Location 2	53.274197	-9.050716	4	5	5	4	GalaxyS	Android
3	Location 3	53.274182	-9.050888	5	4	4	3	iPhone4	iOS
4	Location 4	53.274072	-9.051042	4	5	5	0	NexusS	Android
5	Location 5	53.273994	-9.051117	5	5	4	4	GalaxyS	Android
6	Location 6	53.273923	-9.051182	4	5	4	3	GalaxyS	Android
7	Location 7	53.273904	-9.051244	3	4	4	2	GalaxyS	Android
8	Location 8	53.273798	-9.051195	3	4	4	1	GalaxyS	Android
9	Location 9	53.273769	-9.051229	4	3	3	1	iPhone4	iOS
10	Location 10	53.273699	-9.051312	5	4	2	5	iPhone4	iOS
11	Location 11	53.273566	-9.051454	4	4	4	4	GalaxyS	Android
12	Location 12	53.273564	-9.051471	3	4	4	3	NexusS	Android
13	Location 13	53.273511	-9.051542	2	4	5	3	NexusS	Android
14	Location 14	53.273484	-9.051544	3	5	5	2	NexusS	Android
15	Location 15	53.273285	-9.051793	1	5	4	1	GalaxyS	Android
16	Location 16	53.273256	-9.051834	1	5	4	1	GalaxyS	Android
17	Location 17	53.273156	-9.052020	1	4	5	4	NexusS	Android
18	Location 18	53.273122	-9.052089	1	4	5	5	NexusS	Android
19	Location 19	53.273032	-9.052140	1	5	5	0	GalaxyS	Android
20	Location 20	53.272980	-9.052262	1	5	5	0	NexusS	Android
21	Location 21	53.272935	-9.052316	4	5	4	5	iPhone3Gs	iOS
22	Location 22	53.272900	-9.052402	3	5	5	0	NexusS	Android
23	Location 23	53.272863	-9.052424	2	4	4	4	NexusS	Android
24	Location 24	53.272889	-9.052488	1	4	4	2	GalaxyS	Android
25	Location 25	53.272871	-9.052619	1	5	5	3	GalaxyS	Android
26	Location 26	53.272711	-9.052589	1	4	4	4	iPhone3Gs	iOS
27	Location 27	53.272701	-9.052655	1	3	5	3	NexusS	Android
28	Location 28	53.272659	-9.052823	1	4	5	2	NexusS	Android
29	Location 29	53.272683	-9.052961	4	5	5	3	GalaxyS	Android
30	Location 30	53.272420	-9.053261	4	5	5	3	NexusS	Android

Summary of Results:

Test Duration	min:sec	05m:13s
Test Distance	meters	274.53
Avg Speed	KPH	3.15753

Usable results are from Category 5/4/3
Unusable results are from Category 2/1/0

	iPhone4	GalaxyS	NexusS	iPhone3Gs	Android	iOS
Usable:	15	28	27	16	55	31
Unusable	13	0	1	12	1	25
Category 5(best)	3	13	13	3	26	6
Category 4(very good)	7	13	13	6	26	13
Category 3(good)	5	2	1	7	3	12
Category 2(bad-unusable)	2	0	1	4	1	6
Category 1(unusable)	11	0	0	4	0	15
Category 0(no GPS signal)	0	0	0	4	0	4
Best Phone per sample	3	12	11	2	23	5
No GPS Signal (sec)	0.000	0.000	0.000	48.000		
No GPS Signal (%)	0.000	0.000	0.000	15.335		

Observations:

The Samsung Galaxy S and the Google Nexus S(manufactured under license by Samsung) both performed well. The GalaxyS maintained consistent satellite coverage throughout the entire test. The Nexus S also maintained coverage during the test, however, at 2m24s is experienced enough of a lag to momentarily produce an unusable result.

The iPhone 3Gs and iPhone 4 performed poorly in comparison to the two Android phones.

The iPhone 3Gs lost satellite signal for 48sec(15.3%).
The iPhone 4 did not register a loss of satellite signal, but did fail to recognise the movement of the user from 03:18 to 04:24 and again from 05:06 to 05:33 which effectively means that it did not read the satellites for 93sec(29.7%).

Both iOS devices performed poorly in comparison to the Android devices, however, all phones performed well enough to keep the user engaged. A designer/developer could build in a feature into any software program to inform the user that the satellite signal was temporarily unavailable.

Out of a total of 28 locations:
iPhone 3Gs	16 USABLE	12 UNUSABLE	57%
iPhone 4	15 USABLE	13 UNUSABLE	54%
Galaxy S	28 USABLE	00 UNUSABLE	100%
Nexus S	27 USABLE	01 UNUSABLE	96%

Google Android OS vs Apple iOS Head to Head Accuracy:
Android Performance:	23/28	82.143 %
Apple iOS Performance	05/28	17.857%

Best GPS Performance: Samsung Galaxy S

GPS Test 2(2011-03-07 GPS2-Exp7)
Results:

No	Name	Latitude	Longitude	Time	iPhone4 Positions Away from Ctr	GalaxyS Positions Away from Ctr	NexusS Positions Away from Ctr	iPhone3Gs Positions Away from Ctr	iPhone4 Dist Away	GalaxyS Dist Away	NexusS Dist Away	iPhone3Gs Dist Away
1	Location 1	53.274350	-9.050687	05:35	0	0	0	0	76.103	13.961	13.413	8.271
2	Location 2	53.274197	-9.050716	05:16	11	0	0	3	91.646	4.117	4.197	37.805
3	Location 3	53.274182	-9.050888	05:06	10	0	0	2	83.582	12.087	4.179	25.828
4	Location 4	53.274072	-9.051042	04:52	9	2	1	2	67.740	16.695	13.416	25.474
5	Location 5	53.273994	-9.051117	04:44	8	3	1	2	57.741	17.398	12.787	14.872
6	Location 6	53.273923	-9.051182	04:36	7	3	2	1	48.758	15.652	12.299	11.578
7	Location 7	53.273904	-9.051244	04:29	6	2	2	2	44.813	17.504	16.652	14.751
8	Location 8	53.273798	-9.051195	04:16	5	1	2	1	37.216	7.767	12.591	9.882
9	Location 9	53.273769	-9.051229	04:13	4	1	1	no sig	33.322	6.852	10.001	no sig
10	Location 10	53.273699	-9.051312	04:03	3	0	0	1	23.936	8.658	7.934	10.198
11	Location 11	53.273566	-9.051454	03:51	2	1	1	0	8.354	2.237	2.932	13.947
12	Location 12	53.273564	-9.051471	03:40	1	1	2	1	7.202	5.142	13.321	15.044
13	Location 13	53.273511	-9.051542	03:31	1	0	2	no sig	8.348	5.435	17.837	no sig
14	Location 14	53.273484	-9.051544	03:26	1	0	1	no sig	8.106	8.050	18.801	no sig
15	Location 15	53.273285	-9.051793	03:18	2	1	0	4	33.155	18.371	6.068	45.670
16	Location 16	53.273256	-9.051834	03:03	5	1	1	2	46.386	10.020	11.067	22.086
17	Location 17	53.273156	-9.052020	02:44	4	0	2	2	29.783	8.361	22.374	16.519
18	Location 18	53.273122	-9.052089	02:37	3	0	1	1	23.812	9.117	26.976	12.384
19	Location 19	53.273032	-9.052140	02:26	2	1	1	6	15.447	12.904	14.238	45.255
20	Location 20	53.272980	-9.052262	02:06	9	0	0	5	59.160	11.594	2.184	35.293
21	Location 21	53.272935	-9.052316	01:59	8	1	0	4	53.151	13.082	3.414	29.645
22	Location 22	53.272900	-9.052402	01:51	7	1	0	3	46.287	10.478	3.339	22.769
23	Location 23	53.272863	-9.052424	01:46	6	1	1	2	42.501	10.730	6.417	19.825
24	Location 24	53.272889	-9.052488	01:36	5	0	0	1	41.316	4.016	4.568	17.104
25	Location 25	53.272871	-9.052619	01:29	4	1	0	0	34.168	9.621	5.418	3.643
26	Location 26	53.272711	-9.052589	01:22	3	0	1	2	24.136	4.922	9.650	20.633
27	Location 27	53.272701	-9.052655	01:15	2	0	0	0	19.092	2.894	6.128	16.127
28	Location 28	53.272659	-9.052823	01:00	1	0	0	0	7.652	7.203	4.360	4.049
29	Location 29	53.272683	-9.052961	00:52	0	0	0	1	7.311	15.571	10.308	6.409
30	Location 30	53.272420	-9.053261	00:29	0	0	0	0	30.173	10.199	0.598	168.146

No	Name	Latitude	Longitude	iPhone4 Category	GalaxyS Category	NexusS Category	iPhone3Gs Category	Best Phone	Best OS
1	Location 1	53.274350	-9.050687	5	5	5	5	iPhone3Gs	iOS
2	Location 2	53.274197	-9.050716	1	5	5	2	GalaxyS	Android
3	Location 3	53.274182	-9.050888	1	5	5	3	NexusS	Android
4	Location 4	53.274072	-9.051042	1	3	4	3	NexusS	Android
5	Location 5	53.273994	-9.051117	1	2	4	3	NexusS	Android
6	Location 6	53.273923	-9.051182	1	2	3	4	iPhone3Gs	iOS
7	Location 7	53.273904	-9.051244	1	3	3	3	iPhone3Gs	iOS
8	Location 8	53.273798	-9.051195	1	4	3	4	GalaxyS	Android
9	Location 9	53.273769	-9.051229	1	4	4	0	GalaxyS	Android
10	Location 10	53.273699	-9.051312	2	5	5	4	NexusS	Android
11	Location 11	53.273566	-9.051454	3	4	4	5	iPhone3Gs	iOS
12	Location 12	53.273564	-9.051471	4	4	3	4	GalaxyS	Android
13	Location 13	53.273511	-9.051542	4	5	3	0	GalaxyS	Android
14	Location 14	53.273484	-9.051544	4	5	4	0	GalaxyS	Android
15	Location 15	53.273285	-9.051793	3	4	5	1	NexusS	Android
16	Location 16	53.273256	-9.051834	1	4	4	3	GalaxyS	Android
17	Location 17	53.273156	-9.052020	1	5	3	3	GalaxyS	Android
18	Location 18	53.273122	-9.052089	2	5	4	4	GalaxyS	Android
19	Location 19	53.273032	-9.052140	3	4	4	1	GalaxyS	Android
20	Location 20	53.272980	-9.052262	1	5	5	1	NexusS	Android
21	Location 21	53.272935	-9.052316	1	4	5	1	NexusS	Android
22	Location 22	53.272900	-9.052402	1	4	5	2	NexusS	Android
23	Location 23	53.272863	-9.052424	1	4	4	3	NexusS	Android
24	Location 24	53.272889	-9.052488	1	5	5	4	GalaxyS	Android
25	Location 25	53.272871	-9.052619	1	4	5	5	iPhone3Gs	iOS
26	Location 26	53.272711	-9.052589	2	5	4	3	GalaxyS	Android
27	Location 27	53.272701	-9.052655	3	5	5	5	GalaxyS	Android
28	Location 28	53.272659	-9.052823	4	5	5	5	iPhone3Gs	iOS
29	Location 29	53.272683	-9.052961	5	5	5	4	iPhone4	iOS
30	Location 30	53.272420	-9.053261	5	5	5	5	NexusS	Android

Summary of Results:

Test Duration	min:sec	05m:06s
Test Distance	meters	274.53
Avg Speed	KPH	3.22976

Usable results are from Category 5/4/3
Unusable results are from Category 2/1/0

	iPhone4	GalaxyS	NexusS	iPhone3Gs	Android	iOS
Usable:	9	26	28	19	54	28
Unusable	19	2	0	9	2	28
Category 5(best)	1	13	12	4	25	5
Category 4(very good)	4	11	10	7	21	11
Category 3(good)	4	2	6	8	8	12
Category 2(bad-unusable)	3	2	0	2	2	5
Category 1(unusable)	16	0	0	4	0	20
Category 0(no GPS signal)	0	0	0	3	0	3
Best Phone per sample	1	13	9	5	22	6
No GPS Signal (sec)	0.000	0.000	0.000	23.000		
No GPS Signal (%)	0.000	0.000	0.000	7.516		

Observations:
The Galaxy S and Nexus S both performed consistently again. They reported relevant and accurate information for almost the entire test.

The iPhone 3Gs performed better during this second test, but the iPhone 4 performed poorly. It was inferior to the Android phones and inferior to the older iPhone 3Gs even though both phones were running the exact same operating system and both phones were running identical GPS software.

Again the iOS devices performed poorly in comparison to the Android devices. The iPhone 3Gs performed well enough to keep the user engaged and was adequate for tourism purposes. The iPhone 4 failed to adequately update it's location for much of the test, and most users would abandon it's use after such poor response.

The iPhone 3Gs lost satellite signal for 23sec(7.5%).
The iPhone 4 failed to recognise movement for 60sec(19.3%).

Out of a total of 28 locations:
iPhone 3Gs   19 USABLE   9 UNUSABLE   68%
iPhone 4   9 USABLE   19 UNUSABLE   32%
Galaxy S   26 USABLE   02 UNUSABLE   93%
Nexus S   28 USABLE   00 UNUSABLE   100%

Google Android OS vs Apple iOS Head to Head Accuracy:
Android Performance: 22/28   78.571 %
Apple iOS Performance: 06/28   21.429%

Best GPS Performance: Samsung Galaxy S

GPS Test 3(2011-03-07 GPS3-Exp7)
Results:

No	Name	Latitude	Longitude	Time	iPhone4 Positions Away from Ctr	GalaxyS Positions Away from Ctr	NexusS Positions Away from Ctr	iPhone3Gs Positions Away from Ctr	iPhone4 Dist Away	GalaxyS Dist Away	NexusS Dist Away	iPhone3Gs Dist Away
1	Location 1	53.274350	-9.050687	00:25	0	0	0	0	83.901	16.985	14.783	150.142
2	Location 2	53.274197	-9.050716	00:44	1	0	0	1	97.560	1.761	0.865	110.329
3	Location 3	53.274182	-9.050888	00:53	2	0	0	2	108.519	8.097	5.722	121.229
4	Location 4	53.274072	-9.051042	01:08	1	0	0	3	8.831	5.881	5.468	136.047
5	Location 5	53.273994	-9.051117	01:16	0	0	0	1	5.736	4.592	5.135	10.779
6	Location 6	53.273923	-9.051182	01:23	1	0	0	0	12.857	3.066	3.460	10.456
7	Location 7	53.273904	-9.051244	01:29	2	0	1	2	15.868	3.672	6.939	9.196
8	Location 8	53.273798	-9.051195	01:44	3	1	2	no sig	26.779	9.163	19.998	no sig
9	Location 9	53.273769	-9.051229	01:49	4	2	3	no sig	30.244	13.165	21.371	no sig
10	Location 10	53.273699	-9.051312	01:58	5	1	2	0	38.995	12.567	15.958	11.223
11	Location 11	53.273566	-9.051454	02:11	6	1	1	1	55.945	12.583	10.399	24.214
12	Location 12	53.273564	-9.051471	02:22	7	1	1	2	58.574	4.560	5.218	13.928
13	Location 13	53.273511	-9.051542	02:32	8	1	1	3	63.821	5.459	9.813	21.195
14	Location 14	53.273484	-9.051544	02:44	9	0	0	4	68.639	11.635	12.211	23.206
15	Location 15	53.273285	-9.051793	02:52	10	0	0	5	93.663	13.013	10.150	50.770
16	Location 16	53.273256	-9.051834	03:10	3	0	0	6	30.941	2.438	2.570	54.903
17	Location 17	53.273156	-9.052020	03:26	4	0	0	7	48.418	3.719	2.653	71.526
18	Location 18	53.273122	-9.052089	03:32	5	0	0	8	52.046	0.817	1.265	77.419
19	Location 19	53.273032	-9.052140	03:44	6	0	0	no sig	62.348	2.802	3.549	no sig
20	Location 20	53.272980	-9.052262	03:53	2	0	0	0	10.228	0.333	2.386	4.098
21	Location 21	53.272935	-9.052316	04:01	1	0	0	no sig	6.635	5.218	5.418	no sig
22	Location 22	53.272900	-9.052402	04:08	0	0	0	no sig	6.139	6.648	4.844	no sig
23	Location 23	53.272863	-9.052424	04:13	1	1	1	1	10.273	9.475	5.787	4.475
24	Location 24	53.272889	-9.052488	04:23	2	1	1	no sig	8.983	7.172	7.569	no sig
25	Location 25	53.272871	-9.052619	04:30	3	0	0	0	16.747	1.776	6.784	6.536
26	Location 26	53.272711	-9.052589	04:40	1	1	0	1	13.146	15.868	7.470	11.940
27	Location 27	53.272701	-9.052655	04:49	2	0	0	no sig	12.302	12.822	5.595	no sig
28	Location 28	53.272659	-9.052823	05:02	3	1	1	no sig	18.420	7.478	2.305	no sig
29	Location 29	53.272683	-9.052961	05:25	1	0	1	no sig	7.069	4.545	12.844	no sig
30	Location 30	53.272420	-9.053261	05:45	2	0	0	1	37.306	5.425	4.637	39.297

No	Name	Latitude	Longitude	iPhone4 Category	GalaxyS Category	NexusS Category	iPhone3Gs Category	Best Phone	Best OS
1	Location 1	53.274350	-9.050687	5	5	5	5	NexusS	Android
2	Location 2	53.274197	-9.050716	4	5	5	4	NexusS	Android
3	Location 3	53.274182	-9.050888	3	5	5	3	NexusS	Android
4	Location 4	53.274072	-9.051042	4	5	5	2	NexusS	Android
5	Location 5	53.273994	-9.051117	5	5	5	4	GalaxyS	Android
6	Location 6	53.273923	-9.051182	4	5	5	5	GalaxyS	Android
7	Location 7	53.273904	-9.051244	3	5	4	3	GalaxyS	Android
8	Location 8	53.273798	-9.051195	2	4	3	0	GalaxyS	Android
9	Location 9	53.273769	-9.051229	1	3	2	0	GalaxyS	Android
10	Location 10	53.273699	-9.051312	1	4	3	5	iPhone3Gs	iOS
11	Location 11	53.273566	-9.051454	1	4	4	4	NexusS	Android
12	Location 12	53.273564	-9.051471	1	4	4	3	GalaxyS	Android
13	Location 13	53.273511	-9.051542	1	4	4	2	GalaxyS	Android
14	Location 14	53.273484	-9.051544	1	5	5	1	GalaxyS	Android
15	Location 15	53.273285	-9.051793	1	5	5	1	NexusS	Android
16	Location 16	53.273256	-9.051834	2	5	5	1	GalaxyS	Android
17	Location 17	53.273156	-9.052020	1	5	5	1	NexusS	Android
18	Location 18	53.273122	-9.052089	1	5	5	1	GalaxyS	Android
19	Location 19	53.273032	-9.052140	1	5	5	0	GalaxyS	Android
20	Location 20	53.272980	-9.052262	3	5	5	5	GalaxyS	Android
21	Location 21	53.272935	-9.052316	4	5	5	0	GalaxyS	Android
22	Location 22	53.272900	-9.052402	5	5	5	0	NexusS	Android
23	Location 23	53.272863	-9.052424	4	4	4	4	iPhone3Gs	iOS
24	Location 24	53.272889	-9.052488	3	4	4	0	GalaxyS	Android
25	Location 25	53.272871	-9.052619	2	5	5	5	GalaxyS	Android
26	Location 26	53.272711	-9.052589	4	4	5	4	NexusS	Android
27	Location 27	53.272701	-9.052655	3	5	5	0	NexusS	Android
28	Location 28	53.272659	-9.052823	2	4	4	0	NexusS	Android
29	Location 29	53.272683	-9.052961	4	5	4	0	GalaxyS	Android
30	Location 30	53.272420	-9.053261	3	5	5	4	NexusS	Android

Summary of Results:

Test Duration	min:sec	05m20s
Test Distance	meters	274.53
Avg Speed	KPH	3.08846

Usable results are from Category 5/4/3
Unusable results are from Category 2/1/0

	iPhone4	GalaxyS	NexusS	iPhone3Gs	Android	iOS
Usable:	14	28	27	12	55	26
Unusable	14	0	1	16	1	30
Category 5(best)	2	18	17	4	35	6
Category 4(very good)	7	9	8	5	17	12
Category 3(good)	5	1	2	3	3	8
Category 2(bad-unusable)	4	0	1	2	1	6
Category 1(unusable)	10	0	0	5	0	15
Category 0(no GPS signal)	0	0	0	9	0	9
Best Phone per sample	0	16	10	2	26	2
No GPS Signal (sec)	0.000	0.000	0.000	99.000		
No GPS Signal (%)	0.000	0.000	0.000	30.938		

Observations:
Both Android phones performed consistently during this third test and maintained a similar performance.

The iPhone 3Gs performance dropped and the iPhone 4 performance improved from the previous test. Both of the iOS phones performed adequately enough to keep the user's attention, they performed equally well, despite the iPhone 3Gs losing signal reception for 30 % of the test.

Again the iPhone 4 failed to outperform the older generation iPhone 3Gs despite the fact that they are using identical software and operation system versions.

The iPhone 3Gs lost satellite signal for 99sec(30.9%).
The iPhone 4 failed to recognise movement for 54sec(16.9%).

Out of a total of 28 locations:
iPhone 3Gs	12 USABLE	16 UNUSABLE	43%
iPhone 4	14 USABLE	14 UNUSABLE	50%
Galaxy S	28 USABLE	00 UNUSABLE	100%
Nexus S	27 USABLE	01 UNUSABLE	100%

Google Android OS vs Apple iOS Head to Head Accuracy:
Android Performance:	26/28	92.857 %
Apple iOS Performance	02/28	07.143%

Best GPS Performance: Samsung Galaxy S

GPS Test 4(2011-03-07 GPS4-Exp7)
Results:

No	Name	Latitude	Longitude	Time	iPhone4 Positions Away from Ctr	GalaxyS Positions Away from Ctr	NexusS Positions Away from Ctr	iPhone3Gs Positions Away from Ctr	iPhone4 Dist Away	GalaxyS Dist Away	NexusS Dist Away	iPhone3Gs Dist Away
1	Location 1	53.274350	-9.050687	05:47	10	0	0	0	99.171	14.811	16.732	22.490
2	Location 2	53.274197	-9.050716	05:27	9	0	0	1	83.922	3.857	4.682	10.390
3	Location 3	53.274182	-9.050888	05:15	8	0	0	0	76.288	10.205	9.859	2.883
4	Location 4	53.274072	-9.051042	04:59	7	2	1	1	60.645	16.286	12.624	5.289
5	Location 5	53.273994	-9.051117	04:47	6	2	1	1	50.653	15.913	13.241	7.931
6	Location 6	53.273923	-9.051182	04:40	5	3	2	1	41.659	15.241	10.230	6.154
7	Location 7	53.273904	-9.051244	04:30	4	3	2	1	38.041	23.185	16.967	9.745
8	Location 8	53.273798	-9.051195	04:16	3	2	2	no sig	29.305	15.189	11.928	no sig
9	Location 9	53.273769	-9.051229	04:10	2	1	1	1	25.369	14.931	9.007	12.101
10	Location 10	53.273699	-9.051312	04:00	1	1	1	1	15.833	13.627	12.996	10.796
11	Location 11	53.273566	-9.051454	03:47	0	1	2	0	2.359	3.626	7.009	4.565
12	Location 12	53.273564	-9.051471	03:37	1	2	2	0	2.679	8.581	17.274	1.024
13	Location 13	53.273511	-9.051542	03:27	2	1	1	0	15.980	5.080	15.732	3.311
14	Location 14	53.273484	-9.051544	03:22	3	0	1	0	18.914	8.754	16.817	6.153
15	Location 15	53.273285	-9.051793	03:10	3	0	0	1	30.067	15.215	4.228	13.029
16	Location 16	53.273256	-9.051834	02:56	2	1	0	0	25.862	9.354	5.972	3.828
17	Location 17	53.273156	-9.052020	02:40	1	0	1	no sig	9.252	4.856	9.231	no sig
18	Location 18	53.273122	-9.052089	02:31	0	0	1	no sig	3.499	4.588	9.008	no sig
19	Location 19	53.273032	-9.052140	02:19	1	0	1	0	7.125	6.611	6.692	5.660
20	Location 20	53.272980	-9.052262	02:10	5	0	1	0	28.011	4.480	7.480	6.177
21	Location 21	53.272935	-9.052316	01:52	4	1	1	1	28.973	4.544	6.636	6.858
22	Location 22	53.272900	-9.052402	01:45	3	0	1	no sig	20.207	2.596	9.903	no sig
23	Location 23	53.272863	-9.052424	01:39	2	1	0	no sig	17.278	3.653	7.386	no sig
24	Location 24	53.272889	-9.052488	01:31	1	1	2	0	14.443	7.626	12.661	1.570
25	Location 25	53.272871	-9.052619	01:24	4	1	1	0	39.108	9.586	13.714	5.219
26	Location 26	53.272711	-9.052589	01:18	3	1	1	1	29.000	6.314	4.522	11.213
27	Location 27	53.272701	-9.052655	01:11	2	0	0	0	24.607	4.657	3.768	7.838
28	Location 28	53.272659	-9.052823	00:58	1	0	0	0	12.665	5.484	4.590	2.479
29	Location 29	53.272683	-9.052961	00:49	0	0	0	1	10.175	12.565	12.906	223.376
30	Location 30	53.272420	-9.053261	00:28	0	0	0	0	37.290	7.622	5.440	183.149

No	Name	Latitude	Longitude	iPhone4 Category	GalaxyS Category	NexusS Category	iPhone3Gs Category	Best Phone	Best OS
1	Location 1	53.274350	-9.050687	1	5	5	5	GalaxyS	Android
2	Location 2	53.274197	-9.050716	1	5	5	4	GalaxyS	Android
3	Location 3	53.274182	-9.050888	1	5	5	5	iPhone3Gs	iOS
4	Location 4	53.274072	-9.051042	1	3	4	4	iPhone3Gs	iOS
5	Location 5	53.273994	-9.051117	1	3	4	4	iPhone3Gs	iOS
6	Location 6	53.273923	-9.051182	1	2	3	4	iPhone3Gs	iOS
7	Location 7	53.273904	-9.051244	1	1	2	4	iPhone3Gs	iOS
8	Location 8	53.273798	-9.051195	2	3	3	0	NexusS	Android
9	Location 9	53.273769	-9.051229	3	4	4	4	NexusS	Android
10	Location 10	53.273699	-9.051312	4	4	4	4	iPhone3Gs	iOS
11	Location 11	53.273566	-9.051454	5	4	3	5	iPhone4	Android
12	Location 12	53.273564	-9.051471	4	3	3	5	iPhone3Gs	iOS
13	Location 13	53.273511	-9.051542	3	4	4	5	iPhone3Gs	iOS
14	Location 14	53.273484	-9.051544	2	5	4	5	iPhone3Gs	iOS
15	Location 15	53.273285	-9.051793	2	5	5	4	NexusS	Android
16	Location 16	53.273256	-9.051834	3	4	5	5	iPhone3Gs	iOS
17	Location 17	53.273156	-9.052020	4	5	4	0	GalaxyS	Android
18	Location 18	53.273122	-9.052089	5	5	4	0	GalaxyS	Android
19	Location 19	53.273032	-9.052140	4	5	4	5	iPhone3Gs	iOS
20	Location 20	53.272980	-9.052262	1	5	4	5	GalaxyS	Android
21	Location 21	53.272935	-9.052316	1	4	4	4	GalaxyS	Android
22	Location 22	53.272900	-9.052402	2	5	4	0	GalaxyS	Android
23	Location 23	53.272863	-9.052424	3	4	5	0	NexusS	Android
24	Location 24	53.272889	-9.052488	4	4	3	5	iPhone3Gs	iOS
25	Location 25	53.272871	-9.052619	1	4	4	5	iPhone3Gs	iOS
26	Location 26	53.272711	-9.052589	2	4	4	4	NexusS	Android
27	Location 27	53.272701	-9.052655	3	5	5	5	NexusS	Android
28	Location 28	53.272659	-9.052823	4	5	5	5	iPhone3Gs	iOS
29	Location 29	53.272683	-9.052961	5	5	5	4	GalaxyS	Android
30	Location 30	53.272420	-9.053261	5	5	5	5	NexusS	Android

Summary of Results:

			05m19s
Test Duration	min:sec		05m19s
Test Distance	meters		274.53
Avg Speed	KPH		3.09814

Usable results are from Category 5/4/3
Unusable results are from Category 2/1/0

	iPhone4	GalaxyS	NexusS	iPhone3Gs	Android	iOS
Usable:	14	26	28	23	54	37
Unusable	14	2	0	5	2	19
Category 5(best)	3	12	8	12	20	15
Category 4(very good)	6	10	14	11	24	17
Category 3(good)	5	4	6	0	10	5
Category 2(bad-unusable)	5	2	0	0	2	5
Category 1(unusable)	9	0	0	0	0	9
Category 0(no GPS signal)	0	0	0	5	0	5
Best Phone per sample	1	7	6	14	13	15
No GPS Signal (sec)	0.000	0.000	0.000	41.000		
No GPS Signal (%)	0.000	0.000	0.000	12.853		

Observations:

The Android phones maintained their GPS operating performance.

The iPhone 4 failed to recognise that the user was in motion during the beginning of the test(even though the phone and GPS application were left running well before the test begun). This failure to recognise user movement greatly affected the overall performance score for the iPhone 4 during this test.

The iPhone 3Gs in contrast, performed consistently during most of the test. It lost satellite signal for 12.9% of the duration of the test but it crucially maintained an excellent accuracy level for the time that it did maintain GPS signal. The iOS devices almost matched the Android devices during this test… mainly due to the iPhone 3Gs. And in aggregate, the iOS devices maintained a slightly higher accuracy level.

The iPhone 3Gs lost satellite signal for 41sec(12.9%).
The iPhone 4 failed to recognise movement for 47sec(14.7%).

Out of a total of 28 locations:
iPhone 3Gs   23 USABLE   05 UNUSABLE   82%
iPhone 4   14 USABLE   14 UNUSABLE   50%
Galaxy S   26 USABLE   02 UNUSABLE   93%
Nexus S   28 USABLE   00 UNUSABLE   100%

Google Android OS vs Apple iOS Head to Head Accuracy:
Android Performance: 13/28   46.429 %
Apple iOS Performance   15/28   53.571%

Best GPS Performance: iPhone 3Gs

GPS Test 5(2011-03-07 GPS5-Exp7)
Results:

No	Name	Latitude	Longitude	Time	iPhone4 Positions Away from Ctr	GalaxyS Positions Away from Ctr	NexusS Positions Away from Ctr	iPhone3Gs Positions Away from Ctr	iPhone4 Dist Away	GalaxyS Dist Away	NexusS Dist Away	iPhone3Gs Dist Away
1	Location 1	53.274350	-9.050687	00:25	0	0	0	0	97.787	11.871	16.902	31.905
2	Location 2	53.274197	-9.050716	00:45	1	0	0	1	19.714	2.450	3.005	10.537
3	Location 3	53.274182	-9.050888	00:54	2	0	0	1	16.535	4.047	5.145	8.753
4	Location 4	53.274072	-9.051042	01:08	3	0	0	1	29.965	4.899	3.128	11.547
5	Location 5	53.273994	-9.051117	01:19	4	1	0	1	39.774	7.233	4.506	11.899
6	Location 6	53.273923	-9.051182	01:26	5	1	1	2	48.961	14.047	9.476	16.911
7	Location 7	53.273904	-9.051244	01:35	6	2	1	2	52.265	10.156	8.536	14.902
8	Location 8	53.273798	-9.051195	01:48	7	1	2	2	62.081	14.372	16.902	22.656
9	Location 9	53.273769	-9.051229	01:56	8	2	2	3	65.851	14.182	15.586	25.437
10	Location 10	53.273699	-9.051312	02:06	9	1	1	3	75.042	14.955	12.788	20.047
11	Location 11	53.273566	-9.051454	02:19	10	1	1	1	92.289	17.348	12.804	27.735
12	Location 12	53.273564	-9.051471	02:30	8	1	0	1	85.185	8.674	4.262	4.890
13	Location 13	53.273511	-9.051542	00:15	7	1	1	2	77.699	7.300	5.341	12.979
14	Location 14	53.273484	-9.051544	00:21	6	0	0	2	75.569	8.128	8.730	11.719
15	Location 15	53.273285	-9.051793	00:29	5	0	0	2	48.780	11.245	8.419	30.965
16	Location 16	53.273256	-9.051834	00:46	4	1	0	1	44.702	4.904	5.416	14.149
17	Location 17	53.273156	-9.052020	01:04	3	0	0	0	28.320	4.559	4.794	9.259
18	Location 18	53.273122	-9.052089	01:12	2	1	0	1	22.490	4.009	1.668	10.391
19	Location 19	53.273032	-9.052140	01:23	1	0	0	1	16.893	4.367	5.601	12.908
20	Location 20	53.272980	-9.052262	01:33	0	1	0	1	10.284	6.488	3.081	11.563
21	Location 21	53.272935	-9.052316	01:40	1	1	0	1	11.783	5.895	2.816	10.593
22	Location 22	53.272900	-9.052402	01:47	2	1	0	2	14.586	8.660	2.240	12.485
23	Location 23	53.272863	-9.052424	01:52	3	2	1	3	18.811	9.762	3.322	15.195
24	Location 24	53.272889	-9.052488	02:01	4	0	0	4	17.058	3.380	5.893	14.083
25	Location 25	53.272871	-9.052619	02:07	5	1	0	1	23.377	6.917	6.877	12.499
26	Location 26	53.272711	-9.052589	02:14	6	1	1	2	37.943	12.913	8.893	24.272
27	Location 27	53.272701	-9.052655	02:29	7	2	0	2	40.681	9.693	7.201	14.819
28	Location 28	53.272659	-9.052823	02:41	8	0	0	1	50.366	7.107	4.511	12.953
29	Location 29	53.272683	-9.052961	02:50	9	0	0	0	54.172	2.394	4.749	4.824
30	Location 30	53.272420	-9.053261	03:12	10	0	0	0	89.243	10.413	3.203	15.354

No	Name	Latitude	Longitude	iPhone4 Category	GalaxyS Category	NexusS Category	iPhone3Gs Category	Best Phone	Best OS
1	Location 1	53.274350	-9.050687	5	5	5	5	GalaxyS	Android
2	Location 2	53.274197	-9.050716	4	5	5	4	GalaxyS	Android
3	Location 3	53.274182	-9.050888	3	5	5	4	GalaxyS	Android
4	Location 4	53.274072	-9.051042	2	5	5	4	NexusS	Android
5	Location 5	53.273994	-9.051117	1	4	5	4	NexusS	Android
6	Location 6	53.273923	-9.051182	1	4	4	3	NexusS	Android
7	Location 7	53.273904	-9.051244	1	3	4	3	NexusS	Android
8	Location 8	53.273798	-9.051195	1	4	3	3	GalaxyS	Android
9	Location 9	53.273769	-9.051229	1	3	3	2	GalaxyS	Android
10	Location 10	53.273699	-9.051312	1	4	4	2	NexusS	Android
11	Location 11	53.273566	-9.051454	1	4	4	4	NexusS	Android
12	Location 12	53.273564	-9.051471	1	4	5	4	NexusS	Android
13	Location 13	53.273511	-9.051542	1	4	4	3	NexusS	Android
14	Location 14	53.273484	-9.051544	1	5	5	3	GalaxyS	Android
15	Location 15	53.273285	-9.051793	1	5	5	3	NexusS	Android
16	Location 16	53.273256	-9.051834	1	4	5	4	NexusS	Android
17	Location 17	53.273156	-9.052020	2	5	5	5	GalaxyS	Android
18	Location 18	53.273122	-9.052089	3	4	5	4	NexusS	Android
19	Location 19	53.273032	-9.052140	4	5	5	4	GalaxyS	Android
20	Location 20	53.272980	-9.052262	5	4	5	4	NexusS	Android
21	Location 21	53.272935	-9.052316	4	4	5	4	NexusS	Android
22	Location 22	53.272900	-9.052402	3	4	5	3	NexusS	Android
23	Location 23	53.272863	-9.052424	2	3	4	2	NexusS	Android
24	Location 24	53.272889	-9.052488	1	5	5	1	GalaxyS	Android
25	Location 25	53.272871	-9.052619	1	4	5	4	NexusS	Android
26	Location 26	53.272711	-9.052589	1	4	4	3	NexusS	Android
27	Location 27	53.272701	-9.052655	1	3	5	3	NexusS	Android
28	Location 28	53.272659	-9.052823	1	5	5	4	NexusS	Android
29	Location 29	53.272683	-9.052961	1	5	5	5	GalaxyS	Android
30	Location 30	53.272420	-9.053261	1	5	5	5	NexusS	Android

Summary of Results:

Test Duration	min:sec	05m18s
Test Distance	meters	274.53
Avg Speed	KPH	3.11769

Usable results are from Category 5/4/3
Unusable results are from Category 2/1/0

	iPhone4	GalaxyS	NexusS	iPhone3Gs	Android	iOS
Usable:	7	28	28	24	56	31
Unusable	21	0	0	4	0	25
Category 5(best)	1	10	19	2	29	3
Category 4(very good)	3	14	7	13	21	16
Category 3(good)	3	4	2	9	6	12
Category 2(bad-unusable)	3	0	0	3	0	6
Category 1(unusable)	18	0	0	1	0	19
Category 0(no GPS signal)	0	0	0	0	0	0
Best Phone per sample	0	9	19	0	28	0
No GPS Signal (sec)	0.000	0.000	0.000	0.000		
No GPS Signal (%)	0.000	0.000	0.000	0.000		

Observations:
Both the Nexus S and Galaxy S recorded accurate readings for 100% of the locations during this test. The Nexus S performed particularly well, recording 19 category 5 location measurements. The Galaxy S recorded 10 category 5 location measurements.

The iPhone 3Gs performed well. It did not record as many high level category five locations, but kept a consistent and accurate fix on the users location throughout the entire test... there was no downtime whatsoever for the iPhone 3Gs.

The iPhone 4 recorded it's worst performance of all the tests. It again failed to match the iPhone 3Gs performance level and resulted in the Android phones outperforming both iOS phones in ALL of the 28 recorded locations. The iPhone 4 failed to update the users location for much of the test. It updated at the beginning of the test and again at 2m30s into the test and again towards the end of the test. The Android phones in comparison, were updating their locations continuously as was the iPhone 3Gs.

The iPhone 3Gs maintained consistent satellite signal.
The iPhone 4 failed to recognise movement for 93sec(29.2%).

Out of a total of 28 locations:
iPhone 3Gs   24 USABLE   04 UNUSABLE   82%
iPhone 4   07 USABLE   21 UNUSABLE   50%
Galaxy S   28 USABLE   00 UNUSABLE   100%
Nexus S   28 USABLE   00 UNUSABLE   100%

Google Android OS vs Apple iOS Head to Head Accuracy:
Android Performance: 28/28   100.0 %
Apple iOS Performance   00/28   0%

Best GPS Performance: Google Nexus S

GPS Test 6(2011-03-07 GPS6-Exp7)
Results:

No	Name	Latitude	Longitude	Time	iPhone4 Positions Away from Ctr	GalaxyS Positions Away from Ctr	NexusS Positions Away from Ctr	iPhone3Gs Positions Away from Ctr	iPhone4 Dist Away	GalaxyS Dist Away	NexusS Dist Away	iPhone3Gs Dist Away
10	Location 10	53.273699	-9.051312	03:56	0	0	0	1	5.289	8.668	8.156	11.569
11	Location 11	53.273566	-9.051454	03:45	1	1	0	0	13.942	5.846	3.440	1.772
12	Location 12	53.273564	-9.051471	03:33	2	1	1	1	14.544	8.617	6.897	3.848
13	Location 13	53.273511	-9.051542	03:25	3	1	1	0	21.893	8.416	4.885	1.491
14	Location 14	53.273484	-9.051544	03:19	4	0	0	0	24.642	12.791	6.827	4.334
15	Location 15	53.273285	-9.051793	03:11	3	0	0	0	38.360	9.105	14.569	13.171
16	Location 16	53.273256	-9.051834	02:56	14	0	0	0	129.061	5.164	2.721	0.518
17	Location 17	53.273156	-9.052020	02:28	13	1	1	1	112.453	5.428	7.707	5.443
18	Location 18	53.273122	-9.052089	02:20	12	1	1	0	106.539	8.658	7.946	5.589
19	Location 19	53.273032	-9.052140	02:10	11	1	1	1	97.129	11.861	7.318	6.925
20	Location 20	53.272980	-9.052262	02:00	10	2	1	0	87.251	10.375	6.526	3.130
21	Location 21	53.272935	-9.052316	01:52	9	2	1	0	81.283	10.941	6.800	4.273
22	Location 22	53.272900	-9.052402	01:44	8	1	1	0	74.373	10.579	5.382	4.560
23	Location 23	53.272863	-9.052424	01:40	7	1	0	1	70.496	9.629	3.768	7.587
24	Location 24	53.272889	-9.052488	01:30	6	2	1	0	69.467	15.004	10.725	2.073
25	Location 25	53.272871	-9.052619	01:24	5	1	1	0	62.200	12.780	10.922	4.000
26	Location 26	53.272711	-9.052589	01:18	4	1	1	1	51.270	7.765	5.718	15.403
27	Location 27	53.272701	-9.052655	01:09	3	0	0	0	47.110	5.134	4.185	9.466
28	Location 28	53.272659	-9.052823	00:57	2	0	0	0	35.616	4.609	5.767	4.064
29	Location 29	53.272683	-9.052961	00:49	1	0	0	0	31.943	10.578	11.130	8.544
30	Location 30	53.272420	-9.053261	00:26	1	0	0	0	89.243	2.029	3.633	5.349

No	Name	Latitude	Longitude	iPhone4 Category	GalaxyS Category	NexusS Category	iPhone3Gs Category	Best Phone	Best OS
10	Location 10	53.273699	-9.051312	5	5	5	4	NexusS	Android
11	Location 11	53.273566	-9.051454	4	4	5	5	iPhone3Gs	iOS
12	Location 12	53.273564	-9.051471	3	4	4	4	iPhone3Gs	iOS
13	Location 13	53.273511	-9.051542	2	4	4	5	iPhone3Gs	iOS
14	Location 14	53.273484	-9.051544	1	5	5	5	iPhone3Gs	iOS
15	Location 15	53.273285	-9.051793	2	5	5	5	GalaxyS	Android
16	Location 16	53.273256	-9.051834	1	5	5	5	iPhone3Gs	iOS
17	Location 17	53.273156	-9.052020	1	4	4	4	GalaxyS	Android
18	Location 18	53.273122	-9.052089	1	4	4	5	iPhone3Gs	iOS
19	Location 19	53.273032	-9.052140	1	4	4	4	iPhone3Gs	iOS
20	Location 20	53.272980	-9.052262	1	3	4	5	iPhone3Gs	iOS
21	Location 21	53.272935	-9.052316	1	3	4	5	iPhone3Gs	iOS
22	Location 22	53.272900	-9.052402	1	4	4	5	iPhone3Gs	iOS
23	Location 23	53.272863	-9.052424	1	4	5	4	NexusS	Android
24	Location 24	53.272889	-9.052488	1	3	4	5	iPhone3Gs	iOS
25	Location 25	53.272871	-9.052619	1	4	4	5	iPhone3Gs	iOS
26	Location 26	53.272711	-9.052589	1	4	4	4	NexusS	Android
27	Location 27	53.272701	-9.052655	2	5	5	5	NexusS	Android
28	Location 28	53.272659	-9.052823	3	5	5	5	iPhone3Gs	iOS
29	Location 29	53.272683	-9.052961	4	5	5	5	iPhone3Gs	iOS
30	Location 30	53.272420	-9.053261	4	5	5	5	GalaxyS	Android

Summary of Results:

Test Duration	min:sec	03m30s
Test Distance	meters	193.21
Avg Speed	KPH	3.31217

Usable results are from Category 5/4/3
Unusable results are from Category 2/1/0

	iPhone4	GalaxyS	NexusS	iPhone3Gs	Android	iOS
Usable:	5	20	20	20	40	25
Unusable	15	0	0	0	0	15
Category 5(best)	1	7	9	14	16	15
Category 4(very good)	2	10	11	6	21	8
Category 3(good)	2	3	0	0	3	2
Category 2(bad-unusable)	3	0	0	0	0	3
Category 1(unusable)	12	0	0	0	0	12
Category 0(no GPS signal)	0	0	0	0	0	0
Best Phone per sample	0	3	3	14	6	14
No GPS Signal (sec)	0.000	0.000	0.000	0.000		
No GPS Signal (%)	0.000	0.000	0.000	0.000		

Observations:

Another consistent performance from the Android phones produced 100% usable information... although the level of outright accuracy was down slightly from the previous test. The Nexus S slightly out performed the older designed Galaxy S.

The iPhone 3Gs performed the best of all four phones during this test. It was the most accurate. This was the first test from this experiment or from Exp005, in which the iPhone 3Gs outperformed all it's rivals. It produced 14 maximum accuracy results, and the remaining results were all superior category 4 results.

This iPhone 4 again failed to match it's older designed counterpart and was the worst performing phone of the test.

The iPhone 3Gs maintained consistent satellite signal.
The iPhone 4 failed to recognise movement for 92sec(43.8%).

Out of a total of 28 locations:
iPhone 3Gs   20 USABLE   00 UNUSABLE   100%
iPhone 4   05 USABLE   15 UNUSABLE   33.3%
Galaxy S   20 USABLE   00 UNUSABLE   100%
Nexus S   20 USABLE   00 UNUSABLE   100%

Google Android OS vs Apple iOS Head to Head Accuracy:
Android Performance: 06/20   30.0%
Apple iOS Performance   14/20   70.0%

Best GPS Performance: iPhone 3Gs

The online resource at http://www.irishapps.org/smartlla.html
contains the 7 video files which capture the information shown in the previous 11 pages.

3.3 WiFi

Wi-Fi Positioning is a method used by feature phones and smartphones to pinpoint their position in space. It was pioneered by Skyhook Systems. Smartphones use their inbuilt WiFi detectors(as used by Bluetooth and WiFi networks) to sense the different WiFi routers within range of the phone and it reads the address of these routers and then references the Skyhook database to find the exact location of each router detected. It then triangulates its exact position based on this information.

Of course the accuracy of the location calculated depends on the accuracy of the referenced database. Skyhook must maintain an accurate database of wireless routers in order for the system to be effective.

WiFi positioning is usually accurate to 10-20 meters depending on the amount of registered wireless routers within range of the smartphone.

Skyhook gather their WiFi information by driving through cities and locating as many wireless routers as they can and then recording the MAC address of these routers and attaching accurate GPS coordinates to each of the routers. Obviously, any area that skyhook have not surveyed will not have accurate WiFi positioning information available.

Also, movement of a WiFi router after Skyhook have scanned it will render the positional information within the database ineffective.

Most of the Skyhook information has been generated in the major US cities and coverage in Ireland is limited.

3.4 GSM Tower Triangulation

Cell Tower Triangulation in Ireland is very poor but it can provide a fall back when other systems are unavailable such as GPS. Testing for this book has shown GSM triangulation to be accurate to within 1Km which is effectively useless. In other territories, particularly in the US, GSM triangulation can be accurate to within 10m when there is a high density of GSM towers in the area.

GSM measures the power and pattern of signal originating from a mobile phone in order to estimate it's distance from each GSM tower and to triangulate it's position. Advanced algorithms read these signals and also take into account which base station the mobile phone is closest to, the interpolation of signals between different base stations etc.. to calculate the position of the phone as accurately as possible.

3.5 Bluetooth

Introduction
Bluetooth allows two devices to communicate with each other over distances ranging from 0.1m to 100m, but typically within distances of 0.5 to 10m.
Bluetooth is different from most other forms of wireless communications in that it specialises in short distance communication... usually less than 10m.
Both the hardware and software is designed for this range of communication.

Bluetooth is a simple but very broad ranging set of protocols. There is a vast amount of detail within the basic specification, however, only a small amount of this detail is essential for 99% of applications.

The word Bluetooth encompasses a wide range of subjects and protocols. Bluetooth describes how to modulate and demodulate radio signals, how to transmit audio between devices etc.. For this book we are interested in how to discover devices and how to determine the signal strength and possibly how to automatically transmit data between them.

3.5.1 Basic Programming Essentials

Bluetooth programming is similar to any of the other networking programming methods. Like all networks, we are basically just connecting two devices and exchanging data between them.
The most popular network programming is TCP/IP programming, and Bluetooth programming is not all that different from TCP/IP. The major difference between Bluetooth programming and TCP/IP programming is that Bluetooth concentrates on short distance communication whereas TCP/IP has no consideration for distance. Once this difference has been addressed, then both programming methods are similar.
So the initial process of two devices finding each other is greatly different, but once communication is established, things become quite familiar for the general network programmer.

The procedure involved in establishing a reliable connection depends on what device is the client and what device is the server. The client refers to the device which sends the first packet and the server refers to the device that receives the first packet. In Bluetooth(unlike some protocols) it is normal for the client to act as a server and vice-versa.

Outgoing connection devices will choose a target and a protocol and will then begin transferring data. Incoming connections on the other hand, will choose a transport protocol and subsequently listen before accepting a connection.

Once the outgoing connection is established, Bluetooth and TCP/IP behave similarly.
Outgoing Connection Process:
General Network Programming:
Choose a target device.
Pick a transport protocol/port number.
Establish a connection.
Transfer data.
Disconnect.
TCP/IP Network Programming:
1a.	Connect to DNS server.
1b.	Lookup the IP address of the DNS name.
2a.	Hard-code the protocol.
2b.	Choose a port number.
3.	Establish a connection.
4.	Transfer data
5.	Disconnect.

Bluetooth Network Programming:
1a.	Search for nearby devices(Device enquiry).
1b.	Query device for its human friendly name.
1c.	Choose device with user-specified name.
2a.	Hard-code the protocol.
2b.	Search device for records matching a UUID name.
2c.	Choose port number of matching record.
3.	Establish a connection(socket(), connect()).
4.	Transfer date(send(), receive()).
5.	Disconnect(close()).

Once an incoming connection is established, they are also similar, except that Bluetooth has added support for dynamically assigned port numbers.
Incoming Connection Process:
General Network Programming:
Choose a protocol/port number.
Book the resources/enter listening mode.
Establish the incoming connection.
Transfer data.
Disconnect.

TCP/IP Network Programming:
1a.   Hard-code the desired protocol.
1b.   Choose a port number.
2.   Book resources/enter listening mode.
3.   Wait for incoming connection.
4.   Transfer data.
5.   Disconnect.

Bluetooth Network Programming:
1a.   Choose the protocol.
1b.   Choose the port number.
2.   Start listening.
3.   Listen and accept the connection.
4.   Transfer data(Send(), Receive()).
5. Disconnect(Close()).

Of course, some of these steps aren't always relevant and in some situations there are steps that are left out or are not followed in the order listed. If the address of the server is hardcoded than you don't need to refer to the DNS table etc...

Choosing a Target Device
Every Bluetooth chip manufactured is supposed to be imprinted with a globally unique 48-bit address called the Bluetooth address or device address. Similar to the MAC address for Ethernet cards.
The IEEE Registration Authority administers both sets of addresses.
These addresses should be unique and last the lifetime of the chip. It serves as the basic addressing unit in all Bluetooth communications.
Note: some of the devices tested during the experimental phase had no MAC address imprinted !! So the programmer should consider this when debugging an application.
This address is used extensively from the lowest to the highest layers in the Bluetooth framework. It is used in the lower radio transmission protocols and in the higher application protocols. TCP/IP in contrast, discards the MAC address and switches to using IP addresses at higher protocols. In both cases the unique identifier must be known to program and communicate.
The client application does not always have advance knowledge of these target addresses. In Bluetooth the user will use a human friendly name and the client translates this into a numerical address by searching for nearby devices with this human friendly name.

Bluetooth Human Friendly Device Name
Bluetooth devices will always have a human-friendly name. This name is shown to the user to identify the device. Usually the name is configurable and chosen by the end user. There is no requirement to choose a unique name, and there must be provision made for this while programming. Bluetooth differs from internet programming in this respect. In Bluetooth the lookup process is opposite to TCP/IP. First a device searches for nearby Bluetooth ready devices and compiles a list of their addresses. Then it contacts each device individually and queries it for its name.

Searching for Devices(Device Enquiry or Discovery)
The client broadcasts a discovery message and waits for replies. Each reply contains the 48-bit address and an integer which identifies the kind of device. More detailed information is then obtained by contacting each device individually.
[Latest Bluetooth protocol 2.1, uses Extended Enquiry Response, whereby the most commonly used information such as the name, is transmitted directly in the inquiry response, which saves time].

This process is simple in theory, but programming using this technique often proves very difficult if the SDK you are using doesn't provide higher level mechanisms for doing it. This is because of the large amount of time required to detect nearby devices. It can sometimes take up to 15 seconds to detect a device. During the discovery process, the device is changing frequencies faster than 1000 times a second and there are only 79 different frequencies to choose from, so this process should be completed in a few mS. The reasons for the delay have to do with the search algorithm used by Bluetooth... newer iterations of the Bluetooth specification will very likely address this issue.
NOTE: Bluetooth devices do not announce their presence upon entering an area... it is always up to the client to query the surrounding space and detect devices.

Discover and Connect
There are two options in Bluetooth that determine if a device is discovered and connected.
Inquiry Scan, controls whether the device responds to inquiries or not.
Page Scan, controls how the device responds to connection attempts.

When BOTH Inquiry and Page Scan are ON, the device is detectable by others and will accept incoming connection requests.
When Inquiry Scan is OFF and Page Scan is ON, the device will not be detectable but it will still allow communication by devices that already have its address.
When Inquiry Scan is ON and Page Scan is OFF, the device will be detectable but it will not allow communication – basically useless and effectively same as both being OFF.
When BOTH Inquiry and Page Scan are OFF, the device will not be detectable and it will not allow communication.

Picking a Transport Protocol
The different Bluetooth transport protocols are described using the terminology used to describe general networking protocols.
Different applications use different transport protocols based on their requirements and uses.
We will discuss how hard a protocol tries to deliver information(its Guarantee) and whether is uses packets or streams to deliver the information(Semantics). These are the two primary factors that define a Bluetooth transport protocol.

Reliable protocols like TCP take a deliver or die approach. All sent packets are delivered or die trying.
Best-effort protocols like UDP make a reasonable attempt at delivering packets but ignore when the packets do not arrive.

Protocols can be packet based or stream based... but in Bluetooth a packet based protocol can be massaged into a stream based protocol and vice-versa.. so it's not as critical.
Packet based protocols like UDP send data in datagrams of fixed length.
Stream based protocols like TCP send data in streams and is not worried about where one packet ends and another begins.
The most common Bluetooth transport protocols are RFCOMM, L2CAP, ACL, SCO.

Of the four major protocols RFCOMM is usually the best/only choice, L2CAP can be used when the streaming nature of RFCOMM is not required. ACL is used to carry L2CAP and RFCOMM and is rarely/never used directly by the programmer. SCO is highly specialised and is only used to communicate where voice quality audio is required(no good for CD quality audio).
Two Bluetooth devices can have a maximum of one SCO and one ACL connection.
L2CAPP(and RFCOMM) are only limited by the number of available ports(discussed later).

Radio Frequency Communications Protocol
RFCOMM is a reliable streams based protocol(similar service and reliability to TCP).
It was originally designed to emulate RS232 serial ports.
The biggest difference between RFCOMM and TCP is that RFCOMM allows a maximum of 30 ports whereas TCP allows 65535 open ports on a single machine. This greatly impacts on the way to choose port numbers for server applications.
Windows XP and Nokia Series 60 will only work with the RFCOMM transport protocol. For most applications this effectively means that RFCOMM is the only option when choosing a transport protocol.

Logical Link Control and Adaption Protocol
L2CAP is a packet based protocol that can be programmed for varying levels of reliability. The maximum packet size is 672bytes and this maximum can be raised to 65535 after a connection has been established.

L2CAP is similar enough to UDP in that it is a best effort packet based protocol. There are many differences however. L2CAP has a much broader scope than UDP. In L2CAP, the order of arriving packets must be maintained. In UDP the second transmitted packet can arrive before the first. UDP is never set to anything but best-effort guarantee. L2CAP on the other hand can be configured for several levels of reliability.
Reliability is achieved by using a transmit/acknowledge system. Unacknowledged packets are usually

retransmitted until they are acknowledged but this is not always the case. There are three possible options:
never retransmit
always retransmit until success or failure(usually default)
drop a packet and move onto queued data if a packet hasn't been acknowledged after a set time period(0-1279mS).
Adjusting the delivery method affects ALL L2CAP connections to the device. L2CAP serves as the transport protocol for RFCOMM, so that is affected by changes to L2CAP as well. ie RFCOMM is encapsulated inside L2CAP.
If no other Bluetooth applications are running on the device then the retransmit policy can be useful.

Asynchronous Connection-oriented Logical Transport Protocol
Chances are that as a programmer you will never use ACL transport protocol. But all L2CAP(and therefore all RFCOMM), are encapsulated inside ACL. ACL is used to transport all L2CAP(and RFCOMM) traffic. Two devices can have only one ACL connection between them. ACL is a base protocol that is not used to directly transport data(usually) but is almost always used to encapsulate higher level protocols. It is very much like Internet Protocol in this respect.

Synchronous Connection Oriented Logical Transport Protocol
SCO is a best-effort packet based protocol that is primarily used to transmit voice quality audio at 64kb/s. This is not high enough to transmit CD quality audio, but is sufficient for voice communications. Bluetooth headsets generally use SCO. Bluetooth headphones for listening to MP3 use L2CAPP.

SCO packets are not reliable and are never retransmitted. But the connection is always guaranteed to have 64kb/s transmission rate. If other programs are competing for radio time, then the SCO connection has priority. To ensure this priority and transmission rate, any Bluetooth device can have only three SCO connections. Two devices can have a maximum of one SCO connection. In practice, a device never has more than one SCO connection.
Applications transmitting data should always have an L2CAPP connection.
SCO primary interest is in headsets... it's not used outside of this. If you're not involved in using headsets then you will never come across SCO.

Protocol Service Multiplexers/Port Numbers
Ports are used to allow several applications on the same device to utilize the same transport protocol.
In L2CAP ports are called 'PSMs – Protocol Service Multiplexers' and they have odd numbered values between 1 and 32767.
In RFCOMM channels 1 to 30 are used.

Reserved Ports on Bluetooth
Bluetooth uses reserved(well-known) ports for specific tasks.. similar to most network protocols.
TCP/IP: port 80 is for web traffic   port 23 is for email etc...
Bluetooth: L2CAP reserves ports 1 to 1023 for general usage.
   Service Discovery Protocol, uses L2CAP port 1.
   RFCOMM connections on L2CAP port 3.
   RFCOMM itself does not have any reserved ports, because it has none to spare !!

Service Discovery Protocol
Every Bluetooth device has an SDP server listening on a reserved port number. When a server application is started on a device it registers a description of itself and a new port number with the SDP(on it's own local device).

Service Record
The Service Record simply refers to the description that the server application provides to the SDP. The SDP then transmits this description to the inquiring client applications.
This is also referred to as the SDP Record.
It contains a list of attribute and value pairs. The attribute is an integer and the value an integer or a string. The most vital element in a service record is the port number and after this the next most important attributes are the Service Identification and the Service Class Ident List. These are both used to identify a required service.

Service Unique Identifier

Every service has a unique identifier. The client must know the unique ID of the (type of)service it is looking for.

In practice, this means that the developer assigns a unique ID at design time instead of assigning a port number.

This is similar to the approach that's used when using the 128bit UUID in internet programming.

When the application runs, it registers a record with its Service Identifier with the SDP. The client application queries the SDP to see if the device offers any services with the same Service ID(= UUID).

Service Class Identifier List

Service IDs are intended for use by custom applications which are written by large organisations or design teams.

Two development houses might design an application to provide audio services over Bluetooth. Provided the two teams agree… they can both use the same Service Class ID to identify the type of service on offer.

This is basically just another UUID.

Also, an application can have multiple uses and provide different services. In this case, it will have one Service ID and multiple Service Class IDs.

Reserved UUIDs for Service Classes

Bluetooth has reserved UUIDs. These are used to identify pre-defined service classes.

The lower 96bits of all reserved UUIDs are the same, so usually only the upper 16 or 32 bit portion is referred to… then to reconstruct the UUID you add on the base 96bit number again !!

Example of Reserved UUIDs are:

SDP	0x0001
RFCOMM	0x0003
L2CAP	0x0100
SDP ServerServiceClass	0x1000
SerialPortServiceClass	0x1101
HeadsetServiceClass	0x1108

To obtain the full 128bit UUID from the reserved UUID, simply shift it left by 96bits and add the Bluetooth Base UUID.

Common SDP Attributes

The Bluetooth Specification reserves some unique attribute IDs… the rest are arbitrary.

The most common reserved attributes are…

Service Class ID List:	List of Service class UUIDs that the application provides. This is a mandatory attribute, and it must appear in the service record.
Service Description:	Text string describing the service.
Protocol Descriptor List:	A list of Bluetooth profile descriptors that the service complies with. Each descriptor contains a UUID and a version number.
Service Record Handle:	An integer that identifies the record.
Service ID:	A UUID identifying the specific service.
Service Name:	A text string describing the service on offer.

SDP Record Structure

The SDP is contained within a data element. A data element contains a type, size and value. Types are basic like an integer or string or they can be a series of data elements. Size indicates how much space in bytes the value will take up. Value is the actual data that is to be sent.

Communicating via Sockets

Bluetooth takes a similar approach to internet network programming in that it uses sockets. A socket represents either end of a data link. The client and the server use two distinct sockets.

First a program creates a socket(same for Client and Server). In Bluetooth programming we will normally only create a RFCOMM or an L2CAP socket.

The second step is different for clients and servers.

Client Sockets: When the socket has been created we issue a connect command, in which we outline the address/port of the server device. The OS then looks after the lower level detail. Once the socket is connected, it is used for data transfer.

Server Sockets: (Or Listening Sockets) Three steps follow the create command. Firstly the socket is bound to a local Bluetooth adaptor(usually only one to choose from because most machines have only one Bluetooth engine) in which we outline the port number to use. The socket is placed into listening mode using the appropriate command. This causes the OS to accept incoming connections that are using that port number. Then we ACCEPT the link and the socket can be used for data transfer.

The main difference between a server and client socket is that the server socket is never actually involved in transferring data. When the server socket accepts a new incoming connection, it creates a new socket that represents that connection... after which it returns to listening for devices. The application uses the new socket to transfer data.

Communicating Using a Connected Socket

After connecting a socket, the send and receive commands are used to communicate. Send pushes the bytes from the application address space to the OS buffer(they may/may not have left the device). A receive returns when some data has arrived. The receive will return a 0 when the connection is broken. This frees up the port.

Non-Blocking Sockets

Sockets can be switched into non-blocking mode so that all operations that would normally be blocked can return immediately instead. A Bluetooth socket is by default blocked so the select command must be used to unblock it.

In the basic communications routines within Bluetooth, there is a waiting period involved. The first thread blocks and cannot do other tasks. This is OK for simple applications but is not acceptable for complex programs which must do lots of tasks simultaneously. This is the usual pitfall of synchronous programming and to avoid it we can use multiple threads.. as used by later generation programming languages... but this gets complicated and an alternative is to use asynchronous programming techniques.

Asynchronous programming uses an event loop to wait for everything to happen at once. If any events occur that are relevant then the app executes the event and continues to loop. In order for the event loop to work well, processes must happen quickly and without delay and this is why the select command is used.

3.5.2 Important Bluetooth Concepts

When dealing with Bluetooth file transfer to and from mobile devices, some important concepts need to be considered. The practical constraints of file size/type(video vs SMS for example) and the seamless initiation of the process are influenced by these concepts.

Communications Range

There are three power classes within Bluetooth.
Class 1 operates at 100mW with an advertised range of 100m.
Class 2 operates at 2.5mW and has an advertised range of 10m.
Class 3 operates at 1mW with an advertised range of 1m.

Almost all mobile devices are class 2 devices. Class 3 devices are also widely available. During the duration of this book, no Class 1 devices were encountered.

The actual range can vary. Walls, trees, furniture etc.. all greatly affect the signal. WiFi and cordless(not GSM!!!) phones also degrade the signal. Microwave ovens can completely block the signal. People also block the signal because they absorb the radio signal at the Bluetooth range of frequencies.

Communications Speed

Theoretically, one device transmitting uses a data rate of 723.2kb/s and two devices transmitting have a data rate of 433.9kb/s.

In practice the rates are less due to packet overheads and noise in the wireless environment.

The signal strength decreases with increasing distance from the source. This has been demonstrated during the test phase of this book. The communications speed is therefore strongly linked to the devices proximity to each other. Obviously, you must design your application for lower communication speeds and noisy environments.

Bluetooth devices designed around the Bluetooth 2.0 specification have triple the speed of the older devices... 2178.1kb/s asymmetric and 1306.9kb/s symmetric. Obviously, when an older and newer device are communicating, the older device governs the maximum speed.

Radio Freq and Channel Hop

As mentioned before, all Bluetooth devices operate in the 2.4GHz frequency band, similarly to WiFi and cellular phones(and wireless cameras etc..). (Similar to microwaves and 802.11 wireless).
Bluetooth however, is different in that it divides the 2.4GHz into 79 separate channels and employs channel hopping so that devices are always changing frequencies when transmitting and receiving. Therefore, interference on one channel does not matter as much. There should not be any interference after hopping to a new channel.
WiFi, for example, is divided into 14 channels that are 5MHz wide. Upon setup, one channel is chosen and all devices on the network will use the radio frequency for that channel. When other networks in the region are present(eg. small offices or apt block), then it's likely that some of these networks will collide and overall performance will suffer.
Bluetooth also divides into channels, but into 79 instead of 14. Each channel is 1MHz wide. Bluetooth signals never stay on the same channel. Every 625uS a bluetooth phone will switch channels.

It does this in as random an order as possible so that no single channel is over utilised. Two devices communicating must both hop to the same channel to ensure continued communication... ie they must remain on the same frequencies. This approach of channel hopping is intended to make Bluetooth more robust and better able to avoid interference from nearby signals in the wireless environment(including other Bluetooth devices). AFH - Adaptive frequency hopping is used on the 1.2 Bluetooth specification and later. This is where devices avoid noisy channels with severe interference. This makes Bluetooth a lot more complicated. For most operating systems this complexity is hidden from the developer.

Piconets, Scatternets, Masters, Slaves

This is a very brief rundown of Piconets and Scatternets. They are of limited importance when programming for bluetooth.
To support channel hopping, two devices communicating with each other form a piconet. Eight devices are the total allowed for piconets. Each piconet has one device that takes on the role of the master device. This device is responsible for telling the other devices which frequencies to use and the master must ensure that the slaves communicate in a coordinated fashion.
In WiFi communication there is no such thing as an orderly transmission method. A device wishing to send a packet first listens for a gap and then transmits it's data. The recipient replies with an acknowledge. When there are a great many handsets trying to communicate simultaneously, then things can get chaotic.
Bluetooth uses an alternative, turn based system. The master handset tells the other phones when it is appropriate to stay idle and when is the right window in which to send data. Data rates are therefore more predictable.
Most devices don't support this ability to participate in more than one piconet. But when this does happen, then the two piconets are collectively called a scatternet. The operating system and drivers handle most of this.

Security

The default Bluetooth security model provides light to moderate secure transmissions. It is strong enough to stop other casual Bluetooth devices from snooping on the data being transferred.

Two devices can perform an authentication procedure to verify their identities. This can be done with or without encryption. This authentication procedure relies on the 'shared secret' method. The two devices share a common Pin number that no other device knows and they use this Pin to leverage a secure communications channel. The shared secret is a maximum 16 character alphanumeric sequence.
The first time two devices go through the authentication process is known as the pairing procedure. A common pin is given to both devices by hard-coding or more commonly by the users entering the same Pin into both machines(this will be familiar to anyone who syncs their phone with a computer or a car hands-free kit).
After this, a link key is created by the handset. This Link Key is used to encrypt data being transferred. During this process, the Pin is never transmitted.
After the devices have been paired, applications can request authentication and encryption as required. Encryption takes effect at the lower Physical Link Level so packets for all connections between the devices are encrypted even if it's requested for just one connection. Therefore, authentication and encryption are handled by the operating system directly.

Bluetooth Profiles and RFCs
The Bluetooth specification goes further than merely defining transport protocols and methods of communication. It also specifies methods and specifications to accomplish higher level tasks. This is referred to as Bluetooth Profiles. It defines standardised ways to transfer files, play music, use printers etc. Bluetooth is designed for short distance communications and because of this it is assumed that handsets are in close range to each other.

The most common Bluetooth Profiles are:
OBjectEXchange Object Push: Permits devices to send and receive arbitrary data files such as documents, images, sounds or business cards. Both push and pull are supported.
File Transfer: Sending and receiving of files is permitted. Unlike OBEX, this allows full access to upload, download, rename, copy etc.
Dial-Up Networking: Allows handsets to tether to desktops to allow access to the internet.
Hands-Free Audio: Allows connection from the bluetooth handset to a bluetooth headset to allow hands free operation. It uses SCO connections.
Advanced Audio Distribution: Allows high quality audio transmission(ie higher than phone call quality). Uses L2CAP connections.
Personal Area Network: Permits devices to form IP networks and to share one device's Internet connection with another device.
Human Interface Device: For using devices such as wireless keyboards and mice.
Serial Port Profile: Permits RFCOMM connections between two device to be treated as a serial cable connection.

There are many more Bluetooth Profiles but these are the most popular ones.
NOTE: Bluetooth Profiles are similar to RFCs managed my the Internet Engineering Task Force, which detail standardised ways of sending email, browsing the web, routing data packets etc.

Host Controller Interface
HCI defines at a low level, how the host(computer) interacts with the Controller(local Bluetooth adaptor). All communications between the two are encapsulated within HCI packets.
HCI applies only to a computer and its local Bluetooth adaptors. It is not possible for two Bluetooth devices to have a HCI connection.

There are four types of packets:

1. Command Packet: Packet is sent from the host computer to the Bluetooth adaptor and is used to control the adaptor. These are used to initiate a handset inquiry, connect to a remote handset, adjust connection parameters etc.
2. Event Packet: Packet is generated by the Bluetooth adaptor to inform the host whenever an item of interest has occurred such as a detected device, a connection established, other info about the local Bluetooth adaptor.
3. ACL Data Packet: These Packets encapsulate data destined for or received from a remote Bluetooth device. HCI is the protocol used for all ACL, L2CAP, RFCOMM. Once the HCI packet passes through the Bluetooth adaptor, the HCI headers are stripped away and the pare ACL packet is transmitted over the air and rewrapped after being received.
4. Synchronous Data Packet: These are also encapsulated within HCI. The HCI headers are stripped away when it's transmitted over the air and are rewrapped after being received.
To perform most low level operations, applications need access to the HCI layer. Most high level languages don't give direct control to the programmer and instead provide easier to use wrappers that are a bit more restrictive.

3.5.3 Limitations of Bluetooth

Bluetooth is similar to many other wireless communications technologies, but it has it's limitations. Other specifications can accomplish the following tasks whereas Bluetooth cannot:
Bluetooth cannot announce its presence. It can only inquire for local devices within range.
When an inquiry message is received there is no bluetooth event that is triggered within the bluetooth stack. The Bluetooth adaptor will detect this event, but it won't pass that information onto the host computer(but custom hardware devices have been built to allow this).

A Bluetooth handset never transmits information about itself when it is scanning for other devices. Therefore, it's not possible for software to identify the device.

There is no distance calculation for bluetooth devices communicating with each other. In this book we have used the signal strength to estimate the relative distance between several different bluetooth handsets.

Bluetooth handsets cannot broadcast a message to all listening handsets. In order to send information from one handset to another, they must be paired together, which requires user interaction in order to authorise the pairing.

3.5.4 Device Discovery

As mentioned earlier, Bluetooth splits the 2.4GHz band into 79 channels. Each device on a piconet uses one of these channels at a time
Thirty two of the channels are used for finding handsets and for making a connection. Inquiry messages are sent from the device doing the pinging. The hidden bluetooth devices are listening for these pings and then send a reply to the inquiry message to show their existence to the inquiring handset.

3.5.5 Bluetooth Stacks

A stack refers to a Bluetooth software environment. It comprises all the USB drivers and other hardware drives, all the APIs and libraries and the user development environments that are necessary to make a bluetooth application. There are many specific stacks discussed later in Chapter 2 when dealing with specific operation systems.
In most operating systems there is usually one dominant bluetooth stack.
Both Python and the Java ME language usually have wrappers in order to convert the lower level bluetooth functionality into user friendly higher level commands. Technically these type of environments should be called Wrappers instead of Stacks, but I will refer to all the environments as stacks/SDKs or IDEs in the remainder of this report.

Bluetooth programming is closely related to internet programming. Both share common techniques. The primary difference is that Bluetooth devices can be assumed to have close proximity.

Python Programming.
Python, as a general programming language is not as widely used as C or Java. However, it is a higher level language and is ideal for use in creating simpler Bluetooth applications that don't require much direct control of the lower levels of Bluetooth protocol. The code is short and readable and looks almost like pseudo-code. Because of this, Python may be a suitable choice for the programmer who wishes to construct a working rapid prototype which will later be developed more fully in another language after approval is received, based on the prototype. With Python, the programmer can focus more on the functionality and algorithms without worrying about memory leaks or matching braces. Also, there is no need to consider compiling object files, linking against libraries or setting the correct class paths.

C and GNU/Linux
C is a suitable language to choose when an application needs a large degree of control over the lower level protocols or when the application is running on a very restrictive set of hardware with limited processor and memory reserves. C allows the programmer to squeeze functionality into the smallest possible size while maintaining maximum speed and minimum memory usage. The project may also require the creation of a shared library for other applications to link into instead of a stand-alone application.
Developing Bluetooth applications in C is definitely more troublesome and tedious, but it does afford greater control over the behaviour and performance of the applications.

C and Windows
Microsoft began supporting bluetooth with the introduction of Windows XP and they have continued this support with Vista and Windows 7. The older operating system require 3rd party add-ons in order to support bluetooth.
But even though the Microsoft Stack is limited, it comes standard with Windows XP SP2. The programmer needs Visual C++ and the Windows 7 SDK.

Bluetooth applications that are not used on the older operating systems and only require the RFCOMM protocol are ideal candidates for the Microsoft stack and most devices/applications fall into this category. They are easy to create using the MS API.

Bluetooth programming for the Pocket PC and Windows Mobile environment is very similar in nature to its WinXP counterpart. There are two major competing Bluetooth stacks available for PocketPC, the Wincomm stack and the Microsoft stack. But unlike WinXP, the user rarely has the option to change the stack(by installing a different set of drivers). As a result, a PocketPC application developer has to choose one stack over the other or else develop their application in both programming environments.
Surprisingly, the Microsoft Bluetooth stack for PocketPC is more comprehensive than the WinXP stack and provides support for L2CAP and HCI communications.

Java JSR-82
There is a Java API available for Bluetooth programming that is known as JSR82. It is designed so that any Java enabled device will run any Java written application.
Both the RFCOMM and L2CAP transport protocols are supported in JSR82. It also specifies an API for the OBEX protocol. However, many Nokia phones that support JSR82 do not implement OBEX support. Support for L2CAP may also vary, especially on WinXP devices.
JSR82 is a mature and robust API that can be often used to create a large range on Bluetooth applications where other solutions are not available. Applications that require RFCOMM and L2CAP but don't require access to HCI layer are well suited for Java programming.

Objective C
C and Objective C are the languages preferred by Apple for programming Bluetooth applications. The Mac OSX has provided a unified and consistent API for Bluetooth development since OSX 10.1.3. The development kit provides an environment for programming in Objective C for Bluetooth.
The Apple APIs support RFCOMM, L2CAP, SCO and of course HCI(but not directly).
Objective C Bluetooth programming is highly asynchronous and event driven. Graphical user applications almost always use event driven frameworks with a single event loop that waits for user input and dispatches event handlers accordingly. In OSX the Bluetooth API was designed around the event loop.
There is no function that starts a device enquiry and returns when the enquiry is complete. There is no function that listens for an incoming connection and returns when a connection has been established.
Within the iOS framework, the Bluetooth stack is extremely limited and makes bluetooth programming on the iPhone very problematic if the developer wants their program to be distributed on the Apple App Store. Many of the APIs necessary to provide the iPhone with useful bluetooth functionality are banned on the app store.

Android
The Android classes are generally more user friendly than the iOS Objective C classes when it comes to Bluetooth programming.
Android provides a more structured and linear approach to Bluetooth programming.
This is discussed further in the Experimental section of this report. The source code and program flow are listed for the test applications written for each bluetooth experiment.

3.6 Bluetooth Experiments

The following section contains all of the Bluetooth Experiments conducted for this book. The experiments were necessary to find out if bluetooth was a suitable technology to use for indoor location aware applications. Earlier experiments indicated that GPS was ineffective as providing location information in an indoor environment. It was decided that bluetooth was the best candidate for providing the functionality required.

3.6.1 Test the Ability of the Samsung Galaxy S to Discover Bluetooth Devices

Aim/Goals:
To determine the ability of the Samsung Galaxy S running on the Android Operating System to detect multiple bluetooth devices during the Bluetooth Discovery Window.

Data from Previous Experiments:
None.
Follow On Experiments:
There are several more Bluetooth experiments to follow this one.

Methodology/Preparation/Planning:
Sixteen bluetooth enabled devices(mobile/feature/smart phones) were sourced and placed in a large indoor room. An Android software application was written to allow Bluetooth devices to be discovered and counted. A harness was constructed to allow video capture of the results of the testing.

Implementation/Execution:
1. Switch on all bluetooth devices.
2. Give each device a unique human friendly Bluetooth name.
3. Place the Android handset 5 meters away from all the Bluetooth devices.
4. Start the Bluetooth Discovery cycle on the Android handset.
5. Carry out this test 10 times to find the effectiveness of the Android device during the Bluetooth Discovery phase.

Retesting:
The experiment can be retested easily. All phone models were noted, distances measured etc... to allow retesting/recreation.

Hardware Used:
Samsung GalaxyS(GT-I9000)
Panasonic HD Camcorder(DMC-FS30).
16 Bluetooth Enabled mobile/feature/smart phones:

Nokia 2330	SonyEric K610i	Samsung SGHX820
Nokia 6230	SonyEric V630i x 4	Huawei Android
Nokia 6300 x2	SonyEric K770i	Nokia N958Gb
Nokia 6310 x2	SonyEric K800i	

Software Used:
Samsung GalaxyS operating system Android 2.1-update1 used throughout.
A custom Android Application was written to read the Bluetooth information received.
Changes to Plan During Testing:
none.

Validation/Evaluation:
By completing this experiment, we can determine the effectiveness of the modern Android handset in detecting bluetooth devices under ideal conditions.

Calculations and Formulae Used:
None except simple Excel formulae.

Chapter 3

Locations:
A large open plan office in 1st Floor, Block 6, Ballybrit Business Park, Galway.

Results:
The results for each of the 10 discovery cycles are listed here. The smartphone discovery cycle found all 16 devices each time. For example, for Sample 6 (the 6th discovery cycle test), the test began at 94sec on the stopwatch, all 16 devices were found at 99 sec(5 sec) and the discovery cycle ended at 108 sec(14sec total).

	Sample 1	Sample 2	Sample 3	Sample 4	Sample 5	Sample 6	Sample 7	Sample 8	Sample 9	Sample 10
Devices Discovered	16	16	16	16	16	16	16	16	16	16
Start(sec)	15	35	49	65	80	94	109	124	139	153
All devices found	20	39	58	69	84	99	114	128	143	163
End(sec)	29	48	63	78	93	108	122	137	152	166

Analysis:
The smartphone being tested had to read the human friendly NAME of all the Bluetooth devices being scanned and had to accomplish this within the default Bluetooth Discovery window that the OS(in this case Android) allowed.

This was a more difficult test for the smartphone operating system. More classes had to be written to accomplish this task that had to be written for the GPS experiments.

Each Bluetooth discovery window remained active for 13.4sec.
All bluetooth devices were detected in all 10 of the samples taken.

The Samsung GalaxyS maintained consistent reception during the test.
It took an average time of 5.4sec to find all 16 devices during each Discovery cycle.

Conclusion:
The Samsung GalaxyS is capable of finding 16 or more Bluetooth devices during a single Bluetooth Discovery cycle.

In any densely populated urban area either indoors or outdoors, the maximum number of premises within view/reach of a tourist will be less than 16. Therefore, under ideal conditions, the Samsung device is capable of finding enough signals within a Discovery cycle to capture all possible premises within a typical shopping street or indoor/outdoor shopping centre/mall or other tourist area.

3.6.2 Examine the Characteristics of the Bluetooth RSSI Signal in an Open Unobstructed Static Environment

Aim/Goals:
This experiment aims to examine the RSSI signal being received from multiple Bluetooth devices to see if the signal can be used in a meaningful way to enhance the location aware aspects of a modern Bluetooth enabled smartphone.
If the signal remains steady and predictable while the distance and environment remain unchanged, then further testing will be warranted.
[RSSI indicates the power of the radio signal being received by a wireless device... during this experiment the RSSI will be referred to as the 'Signal Strength' or the 'RSSI signal']

Data from Previous Experiments:
None.

Follow On Experiments:
There are several more Bluetooth experiments to follow this one.

Methodology/Preparation/Planning:
Sixteen bluetooth enabled devices(mobile/feature/smart phones) were sourced and placed in a large indoor room. An Android software application was written to allow Bluetooth devices to be discovered and counted. A harness was constructed to allow video capture of the results of the testing.

Implementation/Execution:
1. Switch on all bluetooth devices.
2. Give each device a unique human friendly Bluetooth name.
3. Place the Android handset 5 meters away from all the Bluetooth devices.
4. Start the Bluetooth Discovery cycle on the Android handset.
5. Carry out this test 20 times and record the human friendly NAME and Signal Strength being received during the Bluetooth Discovery phase.

Retesting:
The experiment can be retested easily. All phone models were noted, distances measured etc... to allow retesting/recreation.

Hardware Used:
Samsung GalaxyS(GT-I9000)
Panasonic HD Camcorder(DMC-FS30).
16 Bluetooth Enabled mobile/feature/smart phones:

Nokia 2330	SonyEric K610i	Samsung SGHX820
Nokia 6230	SonyEric V630i x 4	Huawei Android
Nokia 6300 x2	SonyEric K770i	Nokia N958Gb
Nokia 6310 x2	SonyEric K800i	

Software Used:
Samsung GalaxyS operating system Android 2.1-update1 used throughout.
A custom Android Application was written to read the Bluetooth information received.

Changes to Plan During Testing:
none.

Validation/Evaluation:
By completing this experiment, we can determine the effectiveness of the modern Android handset in reading the signal strength of bluetooth devices under ideal conditions..

Calculations and Formulae Used:
None except simple Excel formulae.

Locations:
A large open plan office in 1st Floor, Block 6, Ballybrit Business Park, Galway.

Analysis:
Analysis of the results show that the RSSI
signal remained stable and reasonably even throughout the test. This was to be expected because the bluetooth broadcasting devices and the bluetooth receiver remained in the same positions throughout the test. The results of this test indicate that the RSSI signal can be used to enhance any bluetooth based location aware applications pending the results of more varied experiments.
The average signal from all phones during the tests was 33.78.
The highest average was recorded during Sample 17 at 35.13.
The lowest average was recorded during Sample 18 at 32.00.
The RSSI signal strength varied from phone to phone, but for each specific phone, the RSSI signal remained steady throughout the test.

Conclusion:
The RSSI signal remained steady and predictable during the test.
If the RSSI signal had been erratic and unpredictable under these testing conditions then it would have been pointless to conduct further tests.
Because of the steady behaviour of the RSSI signal it is advisable to design and execute further tests under different conditions to see the effects on the RSSI signal.

Results:

The results for each of the 20 discovery cycles are listed here and on the next page. The smartphone discovery cycle found all 16 devices each time, and recorded their RSSI signals. For example, for Sample 6 (the 6th discovery cycle test), the test began at 94sec on the stopwatch, all 16 devices were found at 99 sec(5 sec) and the discovery cycle ended at 108 sec(14sec total). The RSSI signal strength for each transmitter discovered is listed below the discovery times.

	Sample 1		Sample 2		Sample 3		Sample 4		Sample 5		Sample 6		Sample 7	
Devices Discovered	16		16		16		16		16		16		16	
Start(sec)	15		35		49		65		80		94		109	
All devices found	20		39		58		69		84		99		114	
End(sec)	29		48		63		78		93		108		122	
	Discov Order	RSSI	Discov Order	RSSI	Discov Order	RSSI	Discov Order	RSSI	Discov Order	RSSI	Discov Order	RSSI	Discov Order	RSSI
001Stray-Ref1	13	32	13	37	8	38	16	33	11	38	15	39	9	32
002Stray-Ref2	15	25	8	38	2	33	10	33	13	28	8	30	10	30
01-SonyV630i	5	41	2	38	3	34	12	31	6	35	1	38	5	32
02-SGHX820	1	34	5	25	14	23	5	30	5	30	7	35	6	31
03-N958Gb	12	35	6	37	6	34	4	24	15	28	3	33	11	37
04-Huiwei	2	39	7	29	5	40	9	33	1	29	4	43	8	37
05-Nokia6300	4	33	3	35	10	34	6	34	12	34	14	32	2	36
06-SonyK800I	3	45	14	41	1	45	1	42	3	39	6	43	1	42
07-SonyK770i	7	39	10	35	11	31	13	30	16	29	10	37	13	26
08-Nokia2330	16	17	16	24	15	30	8	23	2	31	16	27	16	30
09-Nokia6310	10	36	11	34	12	38	2	42	8	40	11	38	4	41
10-Nokia6310	14	38	15	27	13	27	7	39	10	33	5	30	15	30
11-Nokia6300	9	31	1	34	16	38	15	37	4	39	13	38	3	34
12-SonyK610i	11	34	12	42	7	39	14	42	9	41	12	35	14	36
13-SonyV630i	6	32	4	28	4	34	3	33	7	32	2	33	7	28
14-Nokia6230	8	33	9	36	9	38	11	31	14	36	9	25	12	24

	Sample 8		Sample 9		Sample 10		Sample 11		Sample 12		Sample 13		Sample 14	
Devices Discovered	16		16		16		16		16		16		16	
Start(sec)	124		139		153		168		182		197		212	
All devices found	128		143		163		178		187		202		216	
End(sec)	137		152		166		181		196		210		225	
	Discov Order	RSSI	Discov Order	RSSI	Discov Order	RSSI	Discov Order	RSSI	Discov Order	RSSI	Discov Order	RSSI	Discov Order	RSSI
001Stray-Ref1	14	36	10	32	13	35	11	37	7	32	6	31	9	32
002Stray-Ref2	16	29	11	32	8	34	13	30	8	22	12	36	11	28
01-SonyV630i	1	35	5	39	3	30	2	35	11	35	5	32	4	33
02-SGHX820	5	25	6	33	2	32	1	33	3	32	1	32	1	35
03-N958Gb	3	35	14	33	7	30	8	37	10	33	9	33	13	30
04-Huiwei	6	42	1	44	5	43	6	44	5	38	4	38	6	44
05-Nokia6300	13	31	13	20	10	29	5	36	13	31	7	33	7	26
06-SonyK800I	4	48	3	48	1	43	7	47	1	47	8	40	2	40
07-SonyK770i	12	32	16	32	14	33	9	30	15	33	10	32	15	33
08-Nokia2330	9	25	7	25	15	20	16	29	14	18	16	21	5	22
09-Nokia6310	10	40	8	40	11	33	15	35	2	42	14	44	3	35
10-Nokia6310	15	39	2	32	16	42	12	32	4	41	15	36	10	27
11-Nokia6300	8	36	4	37	12	35	4	38	6	37	3	32	16	30
12-SonyK610i	2	41	9	35	6	33	10	39	16	41	11	37	8	40
13-SonyV630i	11	25	15	33	4	24	3	18	12	24	2	33	14	34
14-Nokia6230	7	36	12	33	9	33	14	35	9	35	13	33	12	31

The online resource at http://www.irishapps.org/smartlla.html contains all the photo and video files used to capture the above information.

Results:

	Sample 15		Sample 16		Sample 17		Sample 18		Sample 19		Sample 20	
Devices Discovered	16		16		16		16		16		16	
Start(sec)	227		241		256		271		285		300	
All devices found	236		252		260		275		290		306	
End(sec)	240		255		269		284		298		314	
	Discov Order	RSSI	Discov Order	RSSI	Discov Order	RSSI	Discov Order	RSSI	Discov Order	RSSI	Discov Order	RSSI
001Stray-Ref1	11	37	15	33	11	35	16	31	15	37	14	30
002Stray-Ref2	13	32	7	33	12	34	10	34	10	36	8	31
01-SonyV630i	4	14	2	30	4	29	12	27	2	34	3	36
02-SGHX820	2	32	3	33	3	35	7	32	1	19	6	30
03-N958Gb	9	32	4	28	9	35	4	35	6	33	12	29
04-Huiwei	5	44	6	33	1	42	5	37	5	42	7	43
05-Nokia6300	10	35	13	31	16	32	2	32	11	36	2	27
06-SonyK800I	3	44	1	37	2	42	1	44	4	43	1	42
07-SonyK770i	7	34	12	32	7	37	13	31	7	32	10	31
08-Nokia2330	15	23	16	19	8	24	8	14	16	29	16	30
09-Nokia6310	16	39	9	42	5	44	14	39	14	39	11	31
10-Nokia6310	6	33	5	34	13	31	9	17	9	34	15	40
11-Nokia6300	12	38	10	40	14	40	6	34	12	31	5	33
12-SonyK610i	8	37	14	39	10	35	15	37	8	39	13	40
13-SonyV630i	1	34	11	33	6	36	3	37	3	22	4	34
14-Nokia6230	14	29	8	36	15	31	11	31	13	29	9	31

The average RSSI signal strength for each individual transmitter across all 20 tests is listed here:

		Average RSSI
SonyEric V630i	001Stray-Ref1	34.35
SonyEric V630i	002Stray-Ref2	31.4
SonyEric V630i	01-SonyV630i	32.9
Samsung X820	02-SGHX820	30.55
Nokia N958Gb	03-N958Gb	32.55
Huiwei Android	04-Huiwei	39.2
Nokia 6300	05-Nokia6300	31.85
SonyEric K800i	06-SonyK800I	43.1
SonyEric K770i	07-SonyK770i	32.45
Nokia 2330	08-Nokia2330	24.05
Nokia 6310	09-Nokia6310	38.6
Nokia 6310	10-Nokia6310	33.1
Nokia 6300	11-Nokia6300	35.6
SonyEric K610i	12-SonyK610i	38.1
SonyEric V630i	13-SonyV630i	30.35
Nokia 6230	14-Nokia6230	32.3

The average RSSI signal recorded for ALL the transmitters for each individual discovery cycle is listed here:

	Average RSSI
Sample 1	34
Sample 2	33.75
Sample 3	34.75
Sample 4	33.5625
Sample 5	33.875
Sample 6	34.75
Sample 7	32.875
Sample 8	34.6875
Sample 9	34.25
Sample 10	33.0625
Sample 11	34.6875
Sample 12	33.8125
Sample 13	33.9375
Sample 14	32.5
Sample 15	33.5625
Sample 16	33.3125
Sample 17	35.125
Sample 18	32
Sample 19	33.4375
Sample 20	33.625

The online resource at http://www.irishapps.org/smartlla.html contains all the photo and video files used to capture the above information.

3.6.3 Test the Ability of the Samsung Galaxy S to Detect Multiple Bluetooth Signals at Different Distances in an Unobstructed Space

Aim/Goals:
To determine the effect that physical distance has on the effectiveness of a single Bluetooth Discovery cycle.

Data from Previous Experiments:
None.

Follow On Experiments:
There are several more Bluetooth experiments to follow this one.

Methodology/Preparation/Planning:
15 bluetooth enabled devices(mobile/feature/smart phones) were sourced and placed in a large indoor room. One additional bluetooth device was placed beside the Android phone under test to provide a references signal to compare to the other bluetooth devices. An Android software application was written to allow analysis of the Bluetooth signals being received by the Android handset. A harness was constructed to allow video capture of the results of the testing. Distance markers were placed away from the bluetooth devices at distances of 1/5/10/15/20/25/30/35m.

Implementation/Execution:
1. Switch on all bluetooth devices.
2. Give each device a unique human friendly Bluetooth name.
3. Proceed to the first distance marker.
4. Place the Android phone on a harness along with the other 'reference' bluetooth device.
5. Place a video camera onto the harness and record the output from the phone screen.
6. Start the Bluetooth custom reader application.
7. Begin scanning for bluetooth signals.
8. Record the results.
9. Repeat the scanning procedure multiple times at each distance marker.

Retesting:
The experiment can be retested easily. All phone models were noted, distances measured etc... to allow retesting/recreation.

Hardware Used:
Samsung GalaxyS(GT-I9000), Panasonic HD Camcorder(DMC-FS30).
16 Bluetooth Enabled mobile/feature/smart phones:

Nokia 2330	SonyEric K610i	Samsung SGHX820
Nokia 6230	SonyEric V630i x 4	Huawei Android
Nokia 6300 x2	SonyEric K770i	Nokia N958Gb
Nokia 6310 x2	SonyEric K800i	

Software Used:
Samsung GalaxyS operating system Android 2.1-update1 used throughout.
A custom Android Application to read Bluetooth information received.

Changes to Plan During Testing:
none.

Validation/Evaluation:
By completing this experiment, we can determine the maximum number of bluetooth devices a modern smartphone can detect at different distances in an unobstructed environment.

Calculations and Formulae Used:
None except simple Excel formulae.

Locations:
A large open plan office in 1st Floor, Block 6, Ballybrit Business Park, Galway.

Physical Layout:
All readings were taken at the distances shown below...
1m, 5m, 10m, 15m, 20m, 25m, 30m and 35meters.
There were 15 phones placed where the bluetooth logo is shown.
There was an additional phone placed 1m away from the Android phone(receiver) for reference purposes.

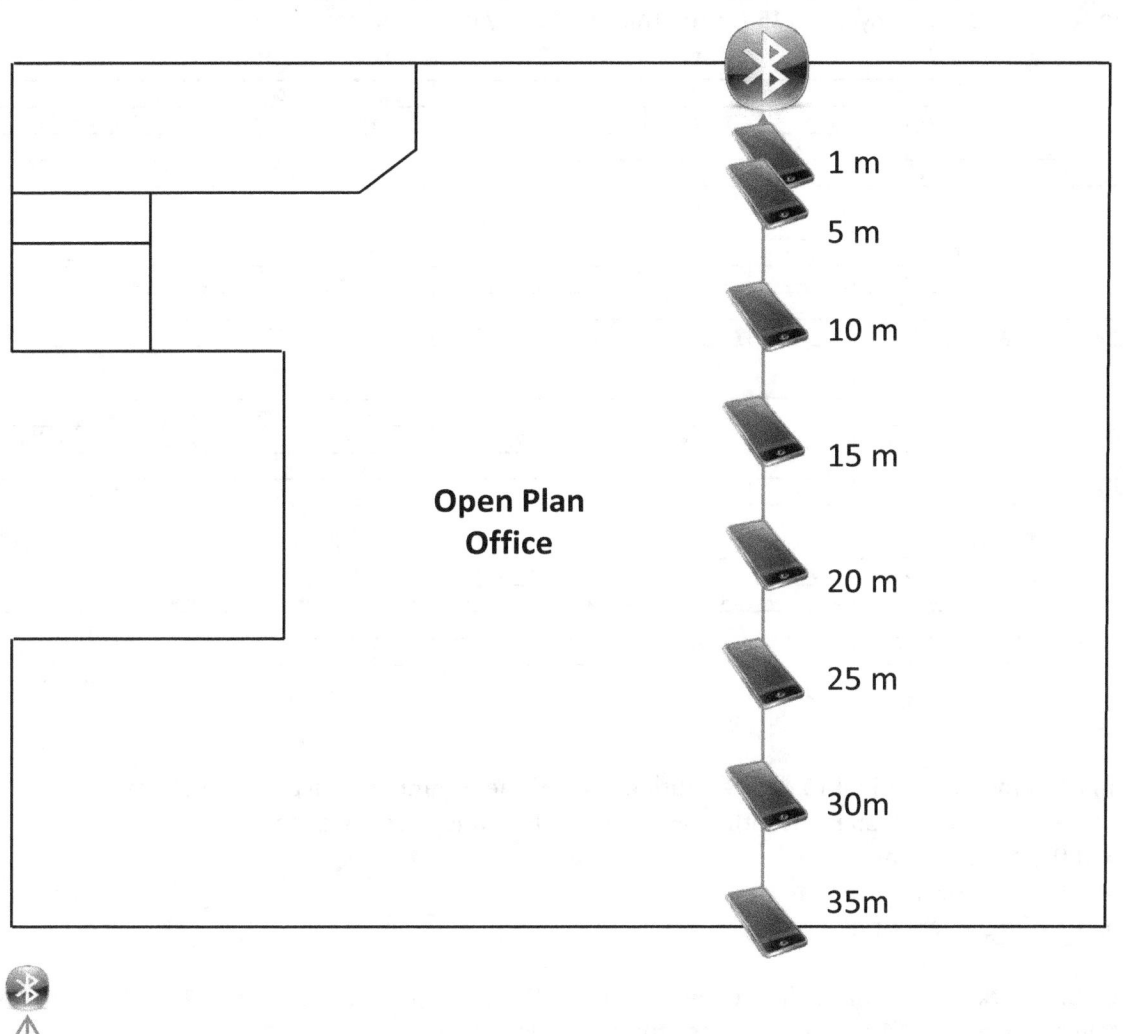

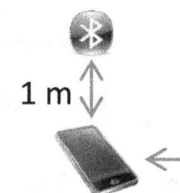

1/5/10/15/20/25/30/35 m

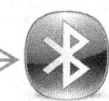

15 bluetooth devices

Results:

The Discovery Cycle took exactly 13.4 seconds for each discovery round.
This table shows the ability of the smartphone to detect bluetooth devices at different distance in open space. For example, at 35m the device detected 12 out of 15 devices during the first discovery cycle, 9/15 for the second discovery cycle, 7/15 for the third discovery cycle and so on.

	1m	1m	1m	1m	1m	5m	5m	5m	5m	5m
	Sample 1	Sample 2	Sample 3	Sample 4	Sample 5	Sample 6	Sample 7	Sample 8	Sample 9	Sample 10
Devices Discovered	15	15	15	15	15	15	15	15	15	15
	10m	10m	10m	10m	10m	15m	15m	15m	15m	15m
	Sample 11	Sample 12	Sample 13	Sample 14	Sample 15	Sample 16	Sample 17	Sample 18	Sample 19	Sample 20
Devices Discovered	15	15	15	15	15	15	15	15	15	15
	20m	20m	20m	20m	20m	25m	25m	25m	25m	25m
	Sample 21	Sample 22	Sample 23	Sample 24	Sample 25	Sample 26	Sample 27	Sample 28	Sample 29	Sample 30
Devices Discovered	15	15	14	15	14	13	15	15	14	14
	30m	30m	30m	30m	30m	35m	35m	35m	35m	35m
	Sample 31	Sample 32	Sample 33	Sample 34	Sample 35	Sample 36	Sample 37	Sample 38	Sample 39	Sample 40
Devices Discovered	14	15	15	15	13	12	9	7	10	9

Analysis:
The smartphone detected all 15 devices during each of the 5 samples at a distance of 1m.
It continued to detect all 15 Bluetooth devices at 5m/10m and 15m distances.
5m >> 100% discovery rate
10m >> 100% discovery rate
15m >>100% discovery rate

At the 20m marker there was a drop in performance. The smartphone detected all 15 of the devices during 3 discovery cycles and 14 out of 15 devices for 2 discovery cycles.
20m >> 97.33% discovery rate

At 25m there was another drop in performance. The smartphone detected all 15 of the devices during 2 discovery cycles, 14 devices during 2 discovery cycles and 13 devices during 1 discovery cycle.
25m >> 94.67% discovery rate

At 30m the device behaved slightly better than at 25m for this set of samples:
30m >> 96.00%

At 35m the performance dropped dramatically to it's worst level:
35m >> 62.67%

Conclusion:
In a situation where the user has line of sight to the premises, a Bluetooth device will be reliably for up to 30m distance. After this distance, Bluetooth performance drops dramatically. It is reasonable to assume that after 35m, the performance will continue to drop just as dramatically.

The online resource at http://www.irishapps.org/smartlla.html
contains all the photo and video files used to capture the above information.

3.6.4 Examine the Characteristics of the Bluetooth RSSI Signal in an Open Unobstructed Space at Different Distances

Aim/Goals:
To analyse the RSSI signal being received from Bluetooth transmitters while changing the distance from the transmitters to the receiver.

Data from Previous Experiments:
None.
Follow On Experiments:
There are several more Bluetooth experiments to follow this one.

Methodology/Preparation/Planning:
15 bluetooth enabled devices(mobile/feature/smart phones) were sourced and placed in a large indoor room. One additional bluetooth device was placed beside the Android phone under test to provide a references signal to compare to the other bluetooth devices. An Android software application was written to allow analysis of the Bluetooth signals being received by the Android handset. A harness was constructed to allow video capture of the results of the testing. Distance markers were placed away from the bluetooth devices at distances of 1/5/10/15/20/25m.

Implementation/Execution:
1. Switch on all bluetooth devices.
2. Give each device a unique human friendly Bluetooth name.
3. Proceed to the first distance marker.
4. Place the Android phone on a harness along with the other 'reference' bluetooth device.
5. Place a video camera onto the harness and record the output from the phone screen.
6. Start the Bluetooth custom reader application.
7. Begin scanning for bluetooth signals.
8. Record the results.
9. Repeat the scanning procedure multiple times at each distance marker.

Retesting:
The experiment can be retested easily.

Hardware Used:
Samsung GalaxyS(GT-I9000)
Panasonic HD Camcorder(DMC-FS30).
16 Bluetooth Enabled mobile/feature/smart phones:

Nokia 2330	SonyEric K610i	Samsung SGHX820
Nokia 6230	SonyEric V630i x 4	Huawei Android
Nokia 6300 x2	SonyEric K770i	Nokia N958Gb
Nokia 6310 x2	SonyEric K800i	

Software Used:
Samsung GalaxyS operating system Android 2.1-update1 used throughout.
A custom Android Application to read Bluetooth information received.

Changes to Plan During Testing:
none.

Validation/Evaluation:
By completing this experiment, we can determine the maximum number of bluetooth devices a modern smartphone can detect at different distances in an unobstructed environment.

Calculations and Formulae Used:
None except simple Excel formulae.

Locations:
A large open plan office in 1st Floor, Block 6, Ballybrit Business Park, Galway.

Physical Layout:
All readings were taken at the distances shown below...
1m, 5m, 10m, 15m, 20m, 25m, 30m and 35meters.
There were 15 phones placed where the bluetooth logo is shown.
There was an additional phone placed 1m away from the Android phone(receiver) for reference purposes.

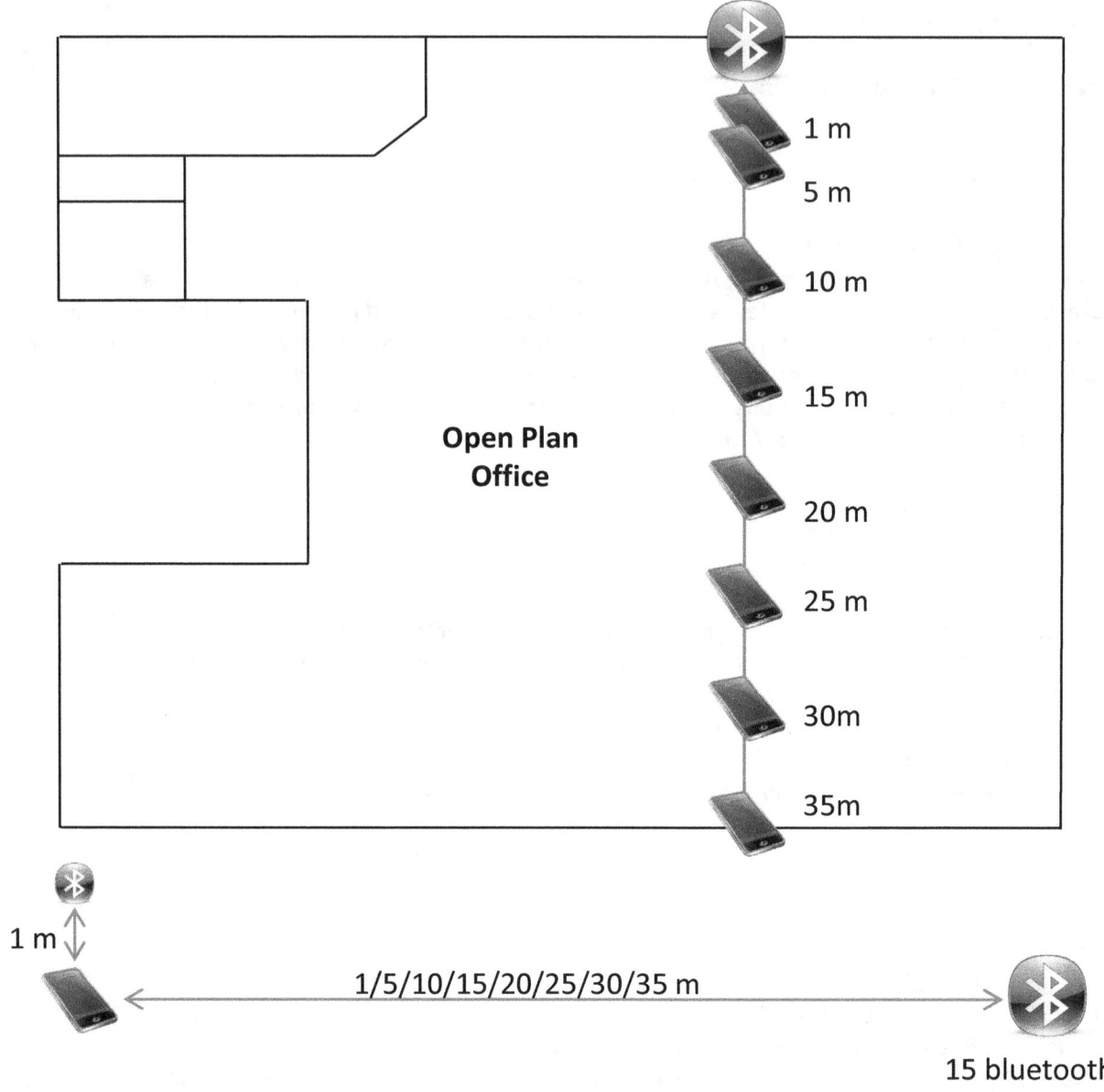

Analysis:
The Android handset(Bluetooth Receiver), showed a steady decline in signal strength reading being picked up as it moved away from the Bluetooth transmitters.

Conclusion:
This test demonstrated that the signal being received from each separate transmitter dropped steadily as the distance increased between transmitter and receiver.

Based on the results of this test, it can be concluded that the RSSI signal can be used as a parameter to estimate which Bluetooth transmitter is closer to the Bluetooth receiver.

In a typical tourism scenario, the transmitters are placed at multiple premises entrances and the receiver is the users smartphone. A Bluetooth enabled device running a sophisticated application, can estimate the relative distances to different premises.

Because the RSSI signal is a unit less, arbitrary measure of the signal strength, it will never be an exact method for finding distances between devices, but this experiment demonstrates that there is a useful, measurable, predictable relationship between signal strength and distance and it should be exploited as a parameter for the developer to use in refining the performance of outdoor and indoor based location aware applications.

Results:
RSSI Signal Strength Tables:
The Discovery Cycle took exactly 13.4 seconds for each discovery round.

This table shows the ability of the smartphone to detect bluetooth RSSI signal strength at different distance in open space. For example, at 5m the device detected all 15 devices during all 5 of the discovery cycles. During each discovery cycle, the RSSI strength recorded from each of the 15 transmitters was recorded. For example during the 2nd discovery cycle at 5m, the RSSI signal strength from each transmitter was 43, 42, 34, 38, 45 as so on.

		1m	1m	1m	1m	1m	5m	5m	5m	5m	5m
		Sample 1	Sample 2	Sample 3	Sample 4	Sample 5	Sample 6	Sample 7	Sample 8	Sample 9	Sample 10
	Devices Discovered	15	15	15	15	15	15	15	15	15	15
SonyEric V630i	001Stray-Ref1	49	40	49	45	38	42	43	52	47	55
SonyEric V630i	01-SonyV630i	46	49	50	54	43	29	42	35	34	40
SonyEric V630i	02-SGHX820	37	38	38	40	36	35	34	32	33	33
Samsung X820	03-N958Gb	42	44	43	41	42	30	38	36	34	36
Nokia N958Gb	04-Huiwei	58	58	58	56	58	40	45	46	43	43
Huiwei Android	05-Nokia6300	39	39	34	32	38	24	22	19	27	31
Nokia 6300	06-SonyK800i	32	45	42	44	43	39	43	39	38	38
SonyEric K800i	07-SonyK770i	40	38	38	41	38	35	37	33	35	30
SonyEric K770i	08-Nokia2330	36	36	34	35	36	23	32	25	28	23
Nokia 2330	09-Nokia6310	39	37	43	43	41	38	40	39	42	44
Nokia 6310	10-Nokia6310	33	35	42	24	33	35	37	35	36	41
Nokia 6310	11-Nokia6300	32	31	31	35	33	29	31	41	34	42
Nokia 6300	12-SonyK610i	39	39	40	38	42	36	26	31	34	31
SonyEric K610i	13-SonyV630i	43	33	44	31	38	35	25	34	38	38
SonyEric V630i	14-Nokia6230	25	32	32	31	27	41	35	31	28	35
Nokia 6230	15-SonyRed	29	36	31	42	38	33	34	38	36	30

		10m	10m	10m	10m	10m	15m	15m	15m	15m	15m
		Sample 11	Sample 12	Sample 13	Sample 14	Sample 15	Sample 16	Sample 17	Sample 18	Sample 19	Sample 20
	Devices Discovered	15	15	15	15	15	15	15	15	15	15
SonyEric V630i	001Stray-Ref1	51	51	52	46	47	29	49	37	47	48
SonyEric V630i	01-SonyV630i	29	31	39	28	25	32	32	32	31	37
SonyEric V630i	02-SGHX820	26	27	29	26	27	17	18	27	29	21
Samsung X820	03-N958Gb	31	33	34	33	33	17	21	28	28	27
Nokia N958Gb	04-Huiwei	46	43	42	45	44	35	40	39	41	41
Huiwei Android	05-Nokia6300	31	37	38	26	37	31	31	22	27	30
Nokia 6300	06-SonyK800i	37	37	37	38	34	38	33	34	33	38
SonyEric K800i	07-SonyK770i	25	30	33	28	32	27	28	27	29	28
SonyEric K770i	08-Nokia2330	23	25	20	29	25	22	21	25	23	25
Nokia 2330	09-Nokia6310	31	30	30	32	34	27	32	23	32	30
Nokia 6310	10-Nokia6310	30	25	31	35	31	24	23	26	21	20
Nokia 6310	11-Nokia6300	33	28	23	32	32	29	19	23	24	16
Nokia 6300	12-SonyK610i	29	28	28	28	27	19	29	30	28	30
SonyEric K610i	13-SonyV630i	35	36	37	32	33	29	32	26	35	33
SonyEric V630i	14-Nokia6230	30	22	24	28	19	27	27	31	26	28
Nokia 6230	15-SonyRed	34	22	32	26	32	28	19	28	23	24

		20m	20m	20m	20m	20m	25m	25m	25m	25m	25m
		Sample 21	Sample 22	Sample 23	Sample 24	Sample 25	Sample 26	Sample 27	Sample 28	Sample 29	Sample 30
	Devices Discovered	15	15	14	15	14	13	15	15	14	14
SonyEric V630i	001Stray-Ref1	47	49	46	54	51	49	56	39	54	48
SonyEric V630i	01-SonyV630i	25	29	32	32	33	24	17	26	22	24
SonyEric V630i	02-SGHX820	21	18	21	22	22	19	21	24	19	19
Samsung X820	03-N958Gb	24	29	24	21	23	27	26	22	19	17
Nokia N958Gb	04-Huiwei	38	37	38	33	36	37	37	28	36	31
Huiwei Android	05-Nokia6300	23	17	16	21	17	17	21	20	16	16
Nokia 6300	06-SonyK800i	34	33	31	31	31	16	29	32	24	29
SonyEric K800i	07-SonyK770i	25	18	23	20	21	23	26	27	26	27
SonyEric K770i	08-Nokia2330	17	21	0	21	0	18	20	18	21	23
Nokia 2330	09-Nokia6310	30	22	20	24	27	21	32	25	32	31
Nokia 6310	10-Nokia6310	24	22	27	21	27	0	25	23	24	25
Nokia 6310	11-Nokia6300	15	20	25	27	30	23	19	16	15	0
Nokia 6300	12-SonyK610i	25	26	24	24	28	0	16	19	0	19
SonyEric K610i	13-SonyV630i	30	33	30	33	29	30	30	32	25	33
SonyEric V630i	14-Nokia6230	32	33	30	25	29	28	28	24	27	27
Nokia 6230	15-SonyRed	29	28	31	24	30	24	25	17	25	21

		30m	30m	30m	30m	30m	35m	35m	35m	35m	35m
		Sample 31	Sample 32	Sample 33	Sample 34	Sample 35	Sample 36	Sample 37	Sample 38	Sample 39	Sample 40
	Devices Discovered	14	15	15	15	13	12	9	7	10	9
SonyEric V630i	001Stray-Ref1	46	45	45	42	41	43	49	48	37	45
SonyEric V630i	01-SonyV630i	28	32	23	33	30	0	0	17	0	14
SonyEric V630i	02-SGHX820	0	16	15	16	13	16	0	0	18	0
Samsung X820	03-N958Gb	22	20	24	24	0	0	15	0	14	0
Nokia N958Gb	04-Huiwei	39	34	31	39	29	22	22	16	25	23
Huiwei Android	05-Nokia6300	23	28	31	23	25	16	21	18	19	11
Nokia 6300	06-SonyK800i	34	22	23	29	25	20	17	21	22	13
SonyEric K800i	07-SonyK770i	23	20	23	17	22	12	0	0	0	0
SonyEric K770i	08-Nokia2330	15	16	18	16	17	14	0	0	0	18
Nokia 2330	09-Nokia6310	30	30	31	30	0	21	0	0	0	21
Nokia 6310	10-Nokia6310	25	26	26	17	27	19	0	0	20	0
Nokia 6310	11-Nokia6300	28	26	28	16	30	20	18	18	18	19
Nokia 6300	12-SonyK610i	25	16	25	20	17	15	16	0	18	0
SonyEric K610i	13-SonyV630i	28	29	30	30	30	22	21	18	22	18
SonyEric V630i	14-Nokia6230	26	27	28	32	28	15	18	15	20	22
Nokia 6230	15-SonyRed	23	22	19	23	27	0	17	0	0	0

Chapter 3

Results:

Average Values for each of the distance markers:

		1m	5m	10m	15m	20m	25m	30m	35m
		Avg over 5 cycles	Avg over 5 cycles	Avg over 5 cycles	Avg over 5 cycles	Avg over 5 cycles	Avg over 5 cycles	Avg over 5 cycles	Avg over 5 cycles
	Devices Discovered	15	15	15	15	14.6	14.2	14.4	9.4
SonyEric V630i	001Stray-Ref1	44.2	47.8	49.4	42	49.4	49.2	43.8	44.4
SonyEric V630i	01-SonyV630i	48.4	36	30.4	32.8	30.2	22.6	29.2	15.5
SonyEric V630i	02-SGHX820	37.8	33.4	27	22.4	20.8	20.4	15	17
Samsung X820	03-N958Gb	42.4	34.8	32.8	24.2	24.2	22.2	22.5	14.5
Nokia N958Gb	04-Huiwei	57.6	43.4	44	39.2	36.4	33.8	34.4	21.6
Huiwei Android	05-Nokia6300	36.4	24.6	33.8	28.2	18.8	18	26	17
Nokia 6300	06-SonyK800I	41.2	39.4	36.6	35.2	32	26	26.6	18.6
SonyEric K800i	07-SonyK770i	39	34	29.6	27.8	21.4	25.8	21	12
SonyEric K770i	08-Nokia2330	35.4	26.2	24.4	23.2	19.67	20	16.4	16
Nokia 2330	09-Nokia6310	40.6	40.6	31.4	28.8	24.6	28.2	30.25	21
Nokia 6310	10-Nokia6310	33.4	36.8	30.4	22.8	24.2	24.25	24.2	19.5
Nokia 6310	11-Nokia6300	32.4	35.4	29.6	22.2	23.4	18.25	25.6	18.6
Nokia 6300	12-SonyK610i	39.6	31.6	28	27.2	25.4	18	20.6	16.33
SonyEric K610i	13-SonyV630i	37.8	34	34.6	31	31	30	29.4	20.2
SonyEric V630i	14-Nokia6230	29.4	34	24.6	27.8	29.8	26.8	28.2	18
Nokia 6230	15-SonyRed	35.2	34.2	29.2	24.4	28.4	22.4	22.8	17

	Percentage Drop from 1m to 35m
001Stray-Ref1	100.45
01-SonyV630i	32.02
02-SGHX820	44.97
03-N958Gb	34.20
04-Huiwei	37.50
05-Nokia6300	46.70
06-SonyK800I	45.15
07-SonyK770i	30.77
08-Nokia2330	45.20
09-Nokia6310	51.72
10-Nokia6310	58.38
11-Nokia6300	57.41
12-SonyK610i	41.24
13-SonyV630i	53.44
14-Nokia6230	61.22
15-SonyRed	48.30

Distance(X) vs RSSI Signal Strength(Y) Graph:

[Note: the '001Stray-Ref1' is a reference signal and it remained 1m away from the Bluetooth receiver at all times… this is why it's signal does not show degradation]

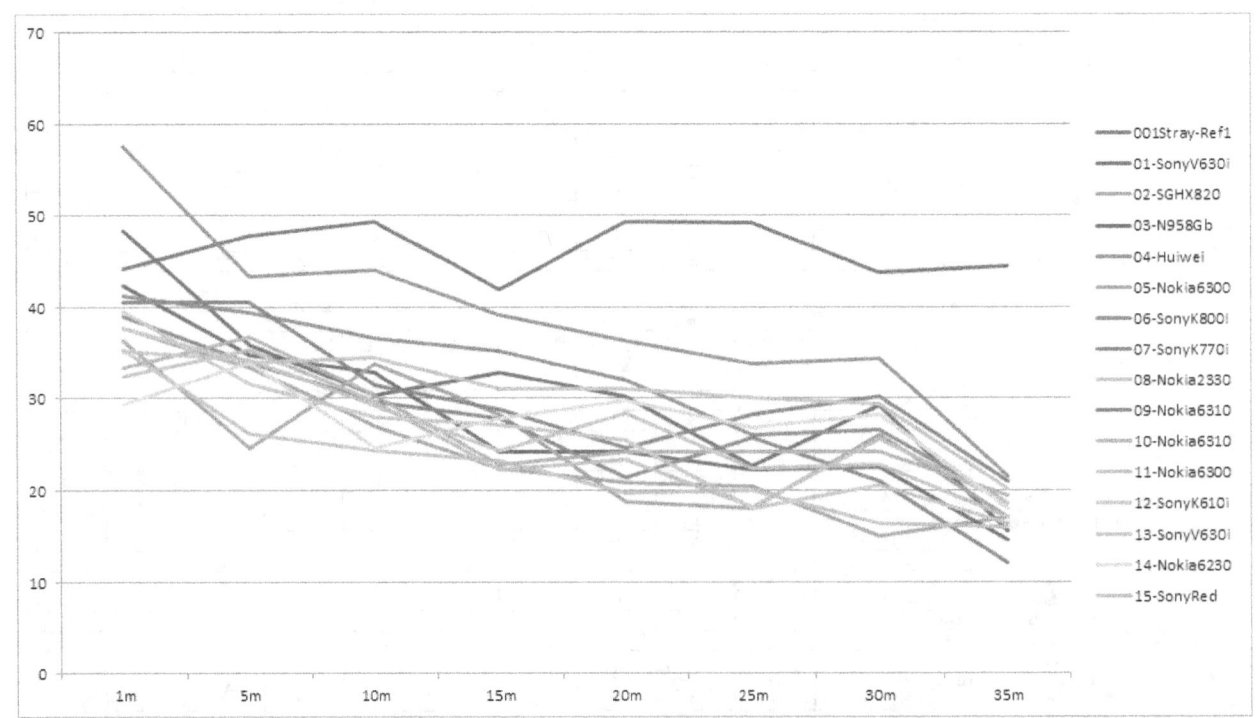

3.6.5 Determine the Drop in Bluetooth Discovery Performance Due to Different Obstructions and Materials

Aim/Goals:
To count the number of Bluetooth devices discovered when the signal has to pass through different materials.

Data from Previous Experiments:
None.

Follow On Experiments:
There are several more Bluetooth experiments to follow this one.

Methodology/Preparation/Planning:
Sixteen bluetooth enabled devices(mobile/feature/smart phones) were sourced and placed in different locations within a building to simulate different operating conditions.
An Android software application was written to allow Bluetooth devices to be discovered and counted. A harness was constructed to allow video capture of the results of the testing.

The following conditions were simulated:
Baseline: No obstruction. The transmitter and receiver are 5m apart in an unobstructed room.
D-Glaze: Transmitter is mounted indoors, and there is a double-glazed window between the transmitter and the outdoor receiver. This simulates a shop owner mounting the device on a window ledge.

Conc-Win: Transmitter is mounted on an internal concrete wall, which is in close proximity to a window(but not within line of sight of the receiver). The receiver is outdoors. This simulates a shop owner mounting the Bluetooth transmitter on a wall close to an external window.

Conc200: There is a 200mm concrete wall between the transmitter and receiver. This simulates a shop owner mounting the transmitter where there is a solid concrete wall between the transmitter and the smartphone user, who is outside the shop(typically in the hallway of a shopping centre or on an outdoor street).

HollowC: There is 300mm concrete hollow code floor between the transmitter and receiver. The simulates the transmitter being in a shop and the smartphone user being directly under or over the shop, in a multi-story shopping centre. Usually in this case the shop owner does not want the signal to be readable to the tourist/end user.

Drywall: There is a 100mm dry wall between the transmitter and receiver. This simulates a shop owner mounting the transmitter where there is a drywall between the transmitter and the smartphone user, who is outside the shop(typically in an adjacent shop).

S-Glaze: Transmitter is mounted indoors, and there is a single-glazed window between the transmitter and the outdoor receiver. This simulates a shop owner mounting the device on a window ledge facing an internal corridor.

Implementation/Execution:
1. Switch on all bluetooth devices.
2. Give each device a unique human friendly Bluetooth name.
3. Place the Android handset 5 meters away from a large wall or barrier constructed from the material being tested and place the transmitters on the other side of the wall/barrier.
4. Start the Bluetooth Discovery cycle on the Android handset.
5. Carry out this test 5 times with and without the barrier to find the difference in Bluetooth performance.

Retesting:
The experiment can be retested easily. All phone models were noted, distances measured etc... to allow retesting/recreation.

Hardware Used:
Samsung GalaxyS(GT-I9000)
Panasonic HD Camcorder(DMC-FS30).
16 Bluetooth Enabled mobile/feature/smart phones:

Nokia 2330	SonyEric K610i	Samsung SGHX820
Nokia 6230	SonyEric V630i x 4	Huawei Android
Nokia 6300 x2	SonyEric K770i	Nokia N958Gb
Nokia 6310 x2	SonyEric K800i	

Software Used:
Samsung GalaxyS operating system Android 2.1-update1 used throughout.
A custom Android Application was written to read Bluetooth information received.

Changes to Plan During Testing:
none.

Validation/Evaluation:
By completing this experiment, we can determine the effectiveness of the modern Android handset in detecting bluetooth devices under different conditions.

Calculations and Formulae Used:
None except simple Excel formulae.

Locations:
A large open plan office in 1st Floor, Block 6, Ballybrit Business Park, Galway.

Analysis:
When the Bluetooth signal had to pass through double-glazing, 200mm internal concrete wall, internal drywall and internal single glazing, there was no loss of devices being discovered by the Bluetooth receiver.
When the signal had to pass through an external concrete wall(200mm concrete and 100mm insulation) there was a very slight loss in one of the Discovery Signals.
When the signal had to pass from one floor to another via 200mm hollow core flooring, then there was significant loss of signal. An average of 8.8 devices out of 15 were detected.

Baseline:	100% discovery rate
Double-glazing:	100% discovery rate
Concrete 200mm:	100% discovery rate
Drywall:	100% discovery rate
Single-glazing:	100% discovery rate
Concrete/Window:	98.67% discovery rate
Hollow Core:	58.67% discovery rate

Conclusion:
There was no significant device discovery drop across any of the materials tested except the hollow core. A further experiment is necessary to measure the exact RSSI signal loss through the materials.

Results:

The tables indicate which transmitters were detected when the bluetooth signal has to pass through different materials. For example, when the bluetooth signal had to pass through hollow core flooring then a significant number of transmitters were not detected. This is why they are marked in yellow.

		Baseline					Double Glazing - Internal to External				
		Cycle 1	Cycle 2	Cycle 3	Cycle 4	Cycle 5	Cycle 1	Cycle 2	Cycle 3	Cycle 4	Cycle 5
	Devices Discovered	15	15	15	15	15	15	15	15	15	15
SonyEric V630i	001Stray-Ref1	✓	✓	✓	✓	✓	✓	✓	✓	✓	✓
SonyEric V630i	01-SonyV630i	✓	✓	✓	✓	✓	✓	✓	✓	✓	✓
SonyEric V630i	02-SGHX820	✓	✓	✓	✓	✓	✓	✓	✓	✓	✓
Samsung X820	03-N958Gb	✓	✓	✓	✓	✓	✓	✓	✓	✓	✓
Nokia N958Gb	04-Huiwei	✓	✓	✓	✓	✓	✓	✓	✓	✓	✓
Huiwei Android	05-Nokia6300	✓	✓	✓	✓	✓	✓	✓	✓	✓	✓
Nokia 6300	06-SonyK800I	✓	✓	✓	✓	✓	✓	✓	✓	✓	✓
SonyEric K800i	07-SonyK770i	✓	✓	✓	✓	✓	✓	✓	✓	✓	✓
SonyEric K770i	08-Nokia2330	✓	✓	✓	✓	✓	✓	✓	✓	✓	✓
Nokia 2330	09-Nokia6310	✓	✓	✓	✓	✓	✓	✓	✓	✓	✓
Nokia 6310	10-Nokia6310	✓	✓	✓	✓	✓	✓	✓	✓	✓	✓
Nokia 6310	11-Nokia6300	✓	✓	✓	✓	✓	✓	✓	✓	✓	✓
Nokia 6300	12-SonyK610i	✓	✓	✓	✓	✓	✓	✓	✓	✓	✓
SonyEric K610i	13-SonyV630i	✓	✓	✓	✓	✓	✓	✓	✓	✓	✓
SonyEric V630i	14-Nokia6230	✓	✓	✓	✓	✓	✓	✓	✓	✓	✓
Nokia 6230	15-SonyRed	✓	✓	✓	✓	✓	✓	✓	✓	✓	✓

		Concrete with nearby window - Internal to External					Concrete 200mm - Internal				
		Cycle 1	Cycle 2	Cycle 3	Cycle 4	Cycle 5	Cycle 1	Cycle 2	Cycle 3	Cycle 4	Cycle 5
	Devices Discovered	15	15	15	14	15	15	15	15	15	15
SonyEric V630i	001Stray-Ref1	✓	✓	✓	✓	✓	✓	✓	✓	✓	✓
SonyEric V630i	01-SonyV630i	✓	✓	✓	✓	✓	✓	✓	✓	✓	✓
SonyEric V630i	02-SGHX820	✓	✓	✓	✓	✓	✓	✓	✓	✓	✓
Samsung X820	03-N958Gb	✓	✓	✓	✓	✓	✓	✓	✓	✓	✓
Nokia N958Gb	04-Huiwei	✓	✓	✓	✓	✓	✓	✓	✓	✓	✓
Huiwei Android	05-Nokia6300	✓	✓	✓	✓	✓	✓	✓	✓	✓	✓
Nokia 6300	06-SonyK800I	✓	✓	✓	✓	✓	✓	✓	✓	✓	✓
SonyEric K800i	07-SonyK770i	✓	✓	✓	✓	✓	✓	✓	✓	✓	✓
SonyEric K770i	08-Nokia2330	✓	✓	✓	✓	✓	✓	✓	✓	✓	✓
Nokia 2330	09-Nokia6310	✓	✓	✓	✓	✓	✓	✓	✓	✓	✓
Nokia 6310	10-Nokia6310	✓	✓	✓	✓	✓	✓	✓	✓	✓	✓
Nokia 6310	11-Nokia6300	✓	✓	✓	✓	✓	✓	✓	✓	✓	✓
Nokia 6300	12-SonyK610i	✓	✓	✓	✓	✓	✓	✓	✓	✓	✓
SonyEric K610i	13-SonyV630i	✓	✓	✓	✓	✓	✓	✓	✓	✓	✓
SonyEric V630i	14-Nokia6230	✓	✓	✓	✗	✓	✓	✓	✓	✓	✓
Nokia 6230	15-SonyRed	✓	✓	✓	✓	✓	✓	✓	✓	✓	✓

		Concrete Hollowcore Floor - 1st floor to gnd floor					Drywall 100mm - Internal				
		Cycle 1	Cycle 2	Cycle 3	Cycle 4	Cycle 5	Cycle 1	Cycle 2	Cycle 3	Cycle 4	Cycle 5
	Devices Discovered	10	9	10	8	7	15	15	15	15	15
SonyEric V630i	001Stray-Ref1	✓	✓	✓	✓	✓	✓	✓	✓	✓	✓
SonyEric V630i	01-SonyV630i	✓	✓	✓	✓	✗	✓	✓	✓	✓	✓
SonyEric V630i	02-SGHX820	✓	✓	✗	✗	✓	✓	✓	✓	✓	✓
Samsung X820	03-N958Gb	✓	✓	✓	✗	✓	✓	✓	✓	✓	✓
Nokia N958Gb	04-Huiwei	✓	✓	✓	✓	✓	✓	✓	✓	✓	✓
Huiwei Android	05-Nokia6300	✓	✓	✓	✓	✓	✓	✓	✓	✓	✓
Nokia 6300	06-SonyK800I	✗	✗	✗	✗	✗	✓	✓	✓	✓	✓
SonyEric K800i	07-SonyK770i	✓	✓	✓	✓	✓	✓	✓	✓	✓	✓
SonyEric K770i	08-Nokia2330	✓	✓	✓	✓	✓	✓	✓	✓	✓	✓
Nokia 2330	09-Nokia6310	✗	✗	✓	✗	✗	✓	✓	✓	✓	✓
Nokia 6310	10-Nokia6310	✓	✓	✓	✓	✓	✓	✓	✓	✓	✓
Nokia 6310	11-Nokia6300	✓	✗	✓	✓	✗	✓	✓	✓	✓	✓
Nokia 6300	12-SonyK610i	✗	✗	✗	✗	✗	✓	✓	✓	✓	✓
SonyEric K610i	13-SonyV630i	✓	✓	✓	✓	✗	✓	✓	✓	✓	✓
SonyEric V630i	14-Nokia6230	✗	✗	✓	✗	✗	✓	✓	✓	✓	✓
Nokia 6230	15-SonyRed	✗	✗	✗	✗	✗	✓	✓	✓	✓	✓

		Glass Laminated - Internal				
		Cycle 1	Cycle 2	Cycle 3	Cycle 4	Cycle 5
	Devices Discovered	15	15	15	15	15
SonyEric V630i	001Stray-Ref1	✓	✓	✓	✓	✓
SonyEric V630i	01-SonyV630i	✓	✓	✓	✓	✓
SonyEric V630i	02-SGHX820	✓	✓	✓	✓	✓
Samsung X820	03-N958Gb	✓	✓	✓	✓	✓
Nokia N958Gb	04-Huiwei	✓	✓	✓	✓	✓
Huiwei Android	05-Nokia6300	✓	✓	✓	✓	✓
Nokia 6300	06-SonyK800I	✓	✓	✓	✓	✓
SonyEric K800i	07-SonyK770i	✓	✓	✓	✓	✓
SonyEric K770i	08-Nokia2330	✓	✓	✓	✓	✓
Nokia 2330	09-Nokia6310	✓	✓	✓	✓	✓
Nokia 6310	10-Nokia6310	✓	✓	✓	✓	✓
Nokia 6310	11-Nokia6300	✓	✓	✓	✓	✓
Nokia 6300	12-SonyK610i	✓	✓	✓	✓	✓
SonyEric K610i	13-SonyV630i	✓	✓	✓	✓	✓
SonyEric V630i	14-Nokia6230	✓	✓	✓	✓	✓
Nokia 6230	15-SonyRed	✓	✓	✓	✓	✓

Results:

		Baseline	D-Glaze	Conc-Win	Conc200	HollowC	Drywall	S-Glaze
SonyEric V630i	001Stray-Ref1	5	5	5	5	5	5	5
SonyEric V630i	01-SonyV630i	5	5	5	5	4	5	5
SonyEric V630i	02-SGHX820	5	5	5	5	3	5	5
Samsung X820	03-N958Gb	5	5	5	5	4	5	5
Nokia N958Gb	04-Huiwei	5	5	5	5	5	5	5
Huiwei Android	05-Nokia6300	5	5	5	5	5	5	5
Nokia 6300	06-SonyK800I	5	5	5	5	0	5	5
SonyEric K800i	07-SonyK770i	5	5	5	5	5	5	5
SonyEric K770i	08-Nokia2330	5	5	5	5	5	5	5
Nokia 2330	09-Nokia6310	5	5	5	5	4	5	5
Nokia 6310	10-Nokia6310	5	5	5	5	5	5	5
Nokia 6310	11-Nokia6300	5	5	5	5	3	5	5
Nokia 6300	12-SonyK610i	5	5	5	5	0	5	5
SonyEric K610i	13-SonyV630i	5	5	5	5	4	5	5
SonyEric V630i	14-Nokia6230	5	5	4	5	0	5	5
Nokia 6230	15-SonyRed	5	5	5	5	0	5	5

Results for 5 Bluetooth Discovery Cycles through each of the 7 different materials.

	Baseline					Double Glazing - Internal to External				
	Cycle 1	Cycle 2	Cycle 3	Cycle 4	Cycle 5	Cycle 1	Cycle 2	Cycle 3	Cycle 4	Cycle 5
Devices Discovered	15	15	15	15	15	15	15	15	15	15

	Concrete with nearby window - Internal to External					Concrete 200mm - Internal				
	Cycle 1	Cycle 2	Cycle 3	Cycle 4	Cycle 5	Cycle 1	Cycle 2	Cycle 3	Cycle 4	Cycle 5
Devices Discovered	15	15	15	14	15	15	15	15	15	15

	Concrete Hollowcore Floor - 1st floor to gnd floor					Drywall 100mm - Internal				
	Cycle 1	Cycle 2	Cycle 3	Cycle 4	Cycle 5	Cycle 1	Cycle 2	Cycle 3	Cycle 4	Cycle 5
Devices Discovered	10	9	10	8	7	15	15	15	15	15

	Glass Laminated - Internal				
	Cycle 1	Cycle 2	Cycle 3	Cycle 4	Cycle 5
Devices Discovered	15	15	15	15	15

Averages over the Five Bluetooth Discovery Cycles:

	Baseline	D-Glaze	Conc-Win	Conc200	HollowC	Drywall	S-Glaze
Devices Discovered	15	15	14.8	15	8.8	15	15

The online resource at http://www.irishapps.org/smartlla.html contains all the photo and video files used to capture the above information and the information on the previous page.

3.6.6 Examine the Drop in Bluetooth RSSI Signal Strength Due to Different Materials Placed Between the Receiver and Transmitter

Aim/Goals:
To ascertain the effect that different materials have in blocking the Bluetooth signal so that transmitters can be strategically placed to allow the desired signal propagation. This will allow Bluetooth users to maximise or limit the Bluetooth signal being received by the smartphone user from their transmitters.

Data from Previous Experiments:
None.
Follow On Experiments:
There are several more Bluetooth experiments to follow this one.

Methodology/Preparation/Planning:
15 bluetooth enabled devices(mobile/feature/smart phones) were sourced and placed in different locations within a large commercial building, to simulate different conditions as listed below and on the next page. One additional bluetooth device was placed beside the Android phone under test to provide a references signal to compare to the other bluetooth devices. An Android software application was written to allow analysis of the Bluetooth signals being received by the Android handset. A harness was constructed to allow video capture of the results of the testing.

The following conditions were simulated:
Baseline: No obstruction. The transmitter and receiver are 5m apart in an unobstructed room.

D-Glaze: Transmitter is mounted indoors, and there is a double-glazed window between the transmitter and the outdoor receiver. This simulates a shop owner mounting the device on a window ledge.

Conc-Win: Transmitter is mounted on an internal concrete wall, which is in close proximity to a window(but not within line of sight of the receiver). The receiver is outdoors. This simulates a shop owner mounting the Bluetooth transmitter on a wall close to an external window.

Conc200: There is a 200mm concrete wall between the transmitter and receiver. This simulates a shop owner mounting the transmitter where there is a solid concrete wall between the transmitter and the smartphone user, who is outside the shop(typically in the hallway of a shopping centre or on an outdoor street).

HollowC: There is 300mm concrete hollow code floor between the transmitter and receiver. The simulates the transmitter being in a shop and the smartphone user being directly under or over the shop, in a multi-story shopping centre. Usually in this case the shop owner does not want the signal to be readable to the tourist/end user.

Drywall: There is a 100mm dry wall between the transmitter and receiver. This simulates a shop owner mounting the transmitter where there is a drywall between the transmitter and the smartphone user, who is outside the shop(typically in an adjacent shop).

S-Glaze: Transmitter is mounted indoors, and there is a single-glazed window between the transmitter and the outdoor receiver. This simulates a shop owner mounting the device on a window ledge facing an internal corridor.

Implementation/Execution:
1. Switch on all bluetooth devices.
2. Give each device a unique human friendly Bluetooth name.
3. Proceed to the first position.
4. Place the Android phone on a harness along with the other 'reference' bluetooth device.
5. Place a video camera onto the harness and record the output from the phone screen.
6. Start the Bluetooth custom reader application.
7. Begin scanning for bluetooth signals.
8. Record the results.
9. Repeat the scanning procedure multiple times at each distance marker.

Retesting:
The experiment can be retested easily. All phone models were noted, distances measured etc... to allow retesting/recreation.

Hardware Used:
Samsung GalaxyS(GT-I9000)
Panasonic HD Camcorder(DMC-FS30).
16 Bluetooth Enabled mobile/feature/smart phones:

Nokia 2330	SonyEric K610i	Samsung SGHX820
Nokia 6230	SonyEric V630i x 4	Huawei Android
Nokia 6300 x2	SonyEric K770i	Nokia N958Gb
Nokia 6310 x2	SonyEric K800i	

Software Used:
Samsung GalaxyS operating system Android 2.1-update1 used throughout.
A custom Android Application to read Bluetooth information received.

Changes to Plan During Testing:
none.

Validation/Evaluation:
By completing this experiment, we can determine the maximum number of bluetooth devices a modern smartphone can detect at different distances in an unobstructed environment.

Calculations and Formulae Used:
None except simple Excel formulae.

Locations:
A large open plan office in 1st Floor, Block 6, Ballybrit Business Park, Galway.

Physical Layout:
All readings were taken at a distance of 5m.
There were 15 phones placed where the bluetooth logo is shown.
There was an additional phone placed 1m away from the Android phone(receiver) for reference purposes.
The Bluetooth devices were shielded behind different materials.

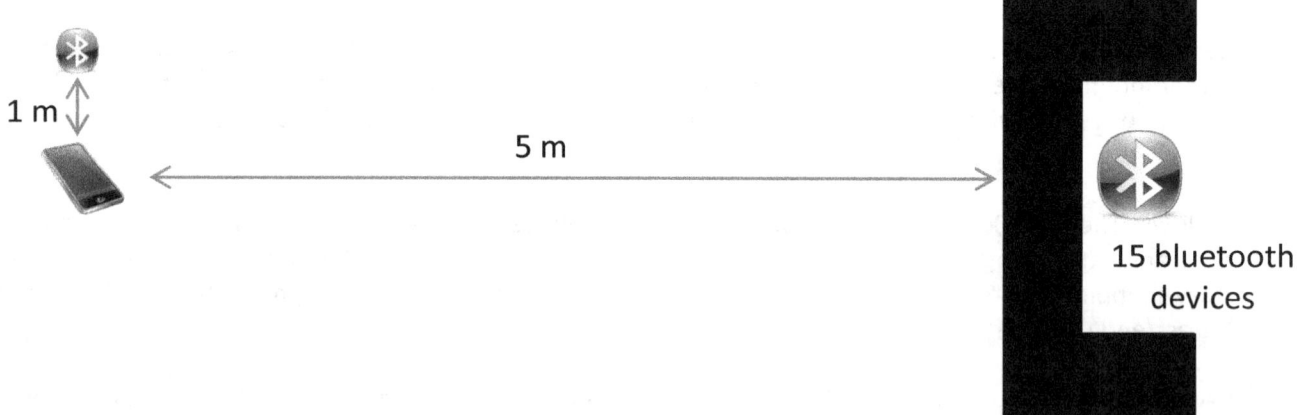

Analysis:
Some of the materials resulted in no significant loss of RSSI signal (above the loss through air) as the microwave Bluetooth signal passed through.
200mm concrete, drywall and laminate single-glazing(6.7mm) showed no loss what so ever, compared to transmission through air.
External double glazing(4mm glass-12mm air-4mm glass) showed a drop in signal strength of 20.5%.
Concrete/double glazing showed a drop of 15.2%.
The biggest drop was for hollow core flooring, which dropped 60.2%

Conclusion:
Some materials have little effect on the bluetooth signal.
This means that the premises owner has considerable latitude in where they wish to place the Bluetooth transmitter.
If the developer of a Bluetooth enabled, location aware application wants to limit the Bluetooth signal from one floor to another then a lower limit will have to be placed on the devices being shown to the user, based on the RSSI signal. To isolate different floors within a multi-storey shopping centre, signals with an RSSI of 20 or below should be ignored.

Chapter 3

Results:

		Baseline					Double Glazing - Internal to External				
		Cycle 1	Cycle 2	Cycle 3	Cycle 4	Cycle 5	Cycle 1	Cycle 2	Cycle 3	Cycle 4	Cycle 5
	Devices Discovered	15	15	15	15	15	15	15	15	15	15
SonyEric V630i	001Stray-Ref1	63	62	60	62	63	55	64	64	66	65
SonyEric V630i	01-SonyV630i	38	36	38	38	37	35	38	29	38	39
SonyEric V630i	02-SGHX820	22	25	28	31	25	20	32	22	17	31
Samsung X820	03-N958Gb	34	33	37	33	32	27	31	30	25	24
Nokia N958Gb	04-Huiwei	46	39	47	42	23	21	36	28	35	35
Huiwei Android	05-Nokia6300	32	37	38	38	40	29	33	32	34	36
Nokia 6300	06-SonyK800I	42	45	42	37	32	22	25	21	34	32
SonyEric K800i	07-SonyK770i	34	33	31	36	36	25	29	28	26	24
SonyEric K770i	08-Nokia2330	25	34	30	30	32	16	27	19	18	22
Nokia 2330	09-Nokia6310	35	33	39	30	37	28	31	31	32	34
Nokia 6310	10-Nokia6310	38	32	34	25	36	27	38	32	30	25
Nokia 6310	11-Nokia6300	32	29	35	33	32	28	27	31	25	32
Nokia 6300	12-SonyK610i	33	23	36	37	36	19	19	26	22	20
SonyEric K610i	13-SonyV630i	41	37	39	37	38	22	36	29	28	32
SonyEric V630i	14-Nokia6230	32	37	34	36	37	20	25	20	25	27
Nokia 6230	15-SonyRed	36	40	41	38	38	26	30	30	17	28

		Concrete with nearby window - Internal to External					Concrete 200mm - Internal				
		Cycle 1	Cycle 2	Cycle 3	Cycle 4	Cycle 5	Cycle 1	Cycle 2	Cycle 3	Cycle 4	Cycle 5
	Devices Discovered	15	15	15	14	15	15	15	15	15	15
SonyEric V630i	001Stray-Ref1	64	64	63	63	66	64	62	67	67	67
SonyEric V630i	01-SonyV630i	37	37	38	38	41	26	31	26	32	33
SonyEric V630i	02-SGHX820	28	29	29	31	30	34	36	35	37	31
Samsung X820	03-N958Gb	28	27	32	32	28	28	35	35	36	34
Nokia N958Gb	04-Huiwei	40	41	41	39	41	43	42	38	46	46
Huiwei Android	05-Nokia6300	29	30	24	22	30	40	25	40	35	27
Nokia 6300	06-SonyK800I	32	23	31	17	21	37	35	20	37	41
SonyEric K800i	07-SonyK770i	34	21	31	36	28	43	37	42	35	41
SonyEric K770i	08-Nokia2330	31	29	29	30	29	31	30	21	29	21
Nokia 2330	09-Nokia6310	25	35	31	29	15	29	35	43	34	36
Nokia 6310	10-Nokia6310	32	33	32	33	33	45	39	37	42	38
Nokia 6310	11-Nokia6300	32	15	30	31	31	39	37	27	35	40
Nokia 6300	12-SonyK610i	28	20	28	25	27	16	32	34	33	17
SonyEric K610i	13-SonyV630i	30	32	31	31	30	31	36	32	24	36
SonyEric V630i	14-Nokia6230	28	16	18	0	21	32	38	34	30	37
Nokia 6230	15-SonyRed	27	33	34	30	26	32	32	29	28	29

		Concrete Hollowcore Floor - 1st floor to gnd floor					Drywall 100mm - Internal				
		Cycle 1	Cycle 2	Cycle 3	Cycle 4	Cycle 5	Cycle 1	Cycle 2	Cycle 3	Cycle 4	Cycle 5
	Devices Discovered	10	9	10	8	7	15	15	15	15	15
SonyEric V630i	001Stray-Ref1	68	68	67	64	69	65	65	65	65	66
SonyEric V630i	01-SonyV630i	16	18	13	16	0	31	39	31	37	38
SonyEric V630i	02-SGHX820	13	13	0	0	13	38	33	33	38	34
Samsung X820	03-N958Gb	15	16	15	0	16	36	33	39	40	35
Nokia N958Gb	04-Huiwei	25	29	24	26	28	45	46	43	42	44
Huiwei Android	05-Nokia6300	20	17	18	20	21	35	24	31	28	25
Nokia 6300	06-SonyK800I	0	0	0	0	0	41	38	32	43	41
SonyEric K800i	07-SonyK770i	20	19	21	17	20	48	37	46	42	49
SonyEric K770i	08-Nokia2330	21	17	22	20	20	30	35	27	35	37
Nokia 2330	09-Nokia6310	0	0	23	0	0	41	37	31	41	33
Nokia 6310	10-Nokia6310	26	26	25	26	26	44	42	32	43	35
Nokia 6310	11-Nokia6300	13	0	14	12	0	35	39	28	37	38
Nokia 6300	12-SonyK610i	0	0	0	0	0	39	36	32	32	24
SonyEric K610i	13-SonyV630i	19	18	14	16	0	36	46	38	39	27
SonyEric V630i	14-Nokia6230	0	0	0	0	0	34	36	37	32	34
Nokia 6230	15-SonyRed	0	0	0	0	0	34	34	36	26	38

		Glass Laminated - Internal				
		Cycle 1	Cycle 2	Cycle 3	Cycle 4	Cycle 5
	Devices Discovered	15	15	15	15	15
SonyEric V630i	001Stray-Ref1	67	68	67	68	67
SonyEric V630i	01-SonyV630i	38	39	37	36	40
SonyEric V630i	02-SGHX820	26	32	38	38	33
Samsung X820	03-N958Gb	32	31	32	24	37
Nokia N958Gb	04-Huiwei	47	41	42	49	37
Huiwei Android	05-Nokia6300	31	43	45	46	42
Nokia 6300	06-SonyK800I	38	37	35	26	39
SonyEric K800i	07-SonyK770i	37	43	45	42	45
SonyEric K770i	08-Nokia2330	29	28	31	30	32
Nokia 2330	09-Nokia6310	43	35	39	49	39
Nokia 6310	10-Nokia6310	32	43	33	35	33
Nokia 6310	11-Nokia6300	34	37	35	38	32
Nokia 6300	12-SonyK610i	27	41	24	27	27
SonyEric K610i	13-SonyV630i	39	28	39	38	27
SonyEric V630i	14-Nokia6230	32	28	37	39	37
Nokia 6230	15-SonyRed	22	43	25	31	33

Chapter 3

Results:

		Concrete Hollowcore Floor - 1st floor to gnd floor					Drywall 100mm - Internal				
		Cycle 1	Cycle 2	Cycle 3	Cycle 4	Cycle 5	Cycle 1	Cycle 2	Cycle 3	Cycle 4	Cycle 5
	Devices Discovered	10	9	10	8	7	15	15	15	15	15
SonyEric V630i	001Stray-Ref1	68	68	67	64	69	65	65	65	65	66
SonyEric V630i	01-SonyV630i	16	18	13	16	0	31	39	31	37	38
SonyEric V630i	02-SGHX820	13	13	0	0	13	38	33	33	38	34
Samsung X820	03-N958Gb	15	16	15	0	16	36	33	39	40	35
Nokia N958Gb	04-Huiwei	25	29	24	26	28	45	46	43	42	44
Huiwei Android	05-Nokia6300	20	17	18	20	21	35	24	31	28	25
Nokia 6300	06-SonyK800I	0	0	0	0	0	41	38	32	43	41
SonyEric K800i	07-SonyK770i	20	19	21	17	20	48	37	46	42	49
SonyEric K770i	08-Nokia2330	21	17	22	20	20	30	35	27	35	37
Nokia 2330	09-Nokia6310	0	0	23	0	0	41	37	31	41	33
Nokia 6310	10-Nokia6310	26	26	25	26	26	44	42	32	43	35
Nokia 6310	11-Nokia6300	13	0	14	12	0	35	39	28	37	38
Nokia 6300	12-SonyK610i	0	0	0	0	0	39	36	32	32	24
SonyEric K610i	13-SonyV630i	19	18	14	16	0	36	46	38	39	27
SonyEric V630i	14-Nokia6230	0	0	0	0	0	34	36	37	32	34
Nokia 6230	15-SonyRed	0	0	0	0	0	34	34	36	26	38

		Glass Laminated - Internal				
		Cycle 1	Cycle 2	Cycle 3	Cycle 4	Cycle 5
	Devices Discovered	15	15	15	15	15
SonyEric V630i	001Stray-Ref1	67	68	67	68	67
SonyEric V630i	01-SonyV630i	38	39	37	36	40
SonyEric V630i	02-SGHX820	26	32	38	38	33
Samsung X820	03-N958Gb	32	31	32	24	37
Nokia N958Gb	04-Huiwei	47	41	42	49	37
Huiwei Android	05-Nokia6300	31	43	45	46	42
Nokia 6300	06-SonyK800I	38	37	35	26	39
SonyEric K800i	07-SonyK770i	37	43	45	42	45
SonyEric K770i	08-Nokia2330	29	28	31	30	32
Nokia 2330	09-Nokia6310	43	35	39	49	39
Nokia 6310	10-Nokia6310	32	43	33	35	33
Nokia 6310	11-Nokia6300	34	37	35	38	32
Nokia 6300	12-SonyK610i	27	41	24	27	27
SonyEric K610i	13-SonyV630i	39	28	39	38	27
SonyEric V630i	14-Nokia6230	32	28	37	39	37
Nokia 6230	15-SonyRed	22	43	25	31	33

Average Values for each of the distance markers:

		Baseline	D-Glaze	Conc-Win	Conc200	HollowC	Drywall	S-Glaze
SonyEric V630i	001Stray-Ref1	62	62.8	64	65.4	67.2	65.2	67.4
SonyEric V630i	01-SonyV630i	37.4	35.8	38.2	29.6	15.75	35.2	38
SonyEric V630i	02-SGHX820	26.2	24.4	29.4	34.6	13	35.2	33.4
Samsung X820	03-N958Gb	33.8	27.4	29.4	33.6	15.5	36.6	31.2
Nokia N958Gb	04-Huiwei	39.4	31	40.4	43	26.4	44	43.2
Huiwei Android	05-Nokia6300	37	32.8	27	33.4	19.2	28.6	41.4
Nokia 6300	06-SonyK800I	39.6	26.8	24.8	34	NA	39	35
SonyEric K800i	07-SonyK770i	34	26.4	30	39.6	19.4	44.4	42.4
SonyEric K770i	08-Nokia2330	30.2	20.4	29.6	26.4	20	32.8	30
Nokia 2330	09-Nokia6310	34.8	31.2	27	35.4	23	36.6	41
Nokia 6310	10-Nokia6310	33	30.4	32.6	40.2	25.8	39.2	35.2
Nokia 6310	11-Nokia6300	32.2	28.6	27.8	35.6	13	35.4	35.2
Nokia 6300	12-SonyK610i	33	21.2	25.6	26.4	NA	32.6	29.2
SonyEric K610i	13-SonyV630i	38.4	29.4	30.8	31.8	16.75	37.2	34.2
SonyEric V630i	14-Nokia6230	35.2	23.4	20.75	34.2	NA	34.6	34.6
Nokia 6230	15-SonyRed	38.6	26.2	30	30	NA	33.6	30.8

The online resource at http://www.irishapps.org/smartlla.html contains all the photo and video files used to capture the above information and the information on the previous page.

Chapter 3

Results:

Avg RSSI Signal Strength per Transmitter(X) vs Material Type(Y) Graph:

[Note: the '001Stray-Ref1' is a reference signal and it remained 1m away from the Bluetooth receiver at all times... this is why it's signal does not show degradation]

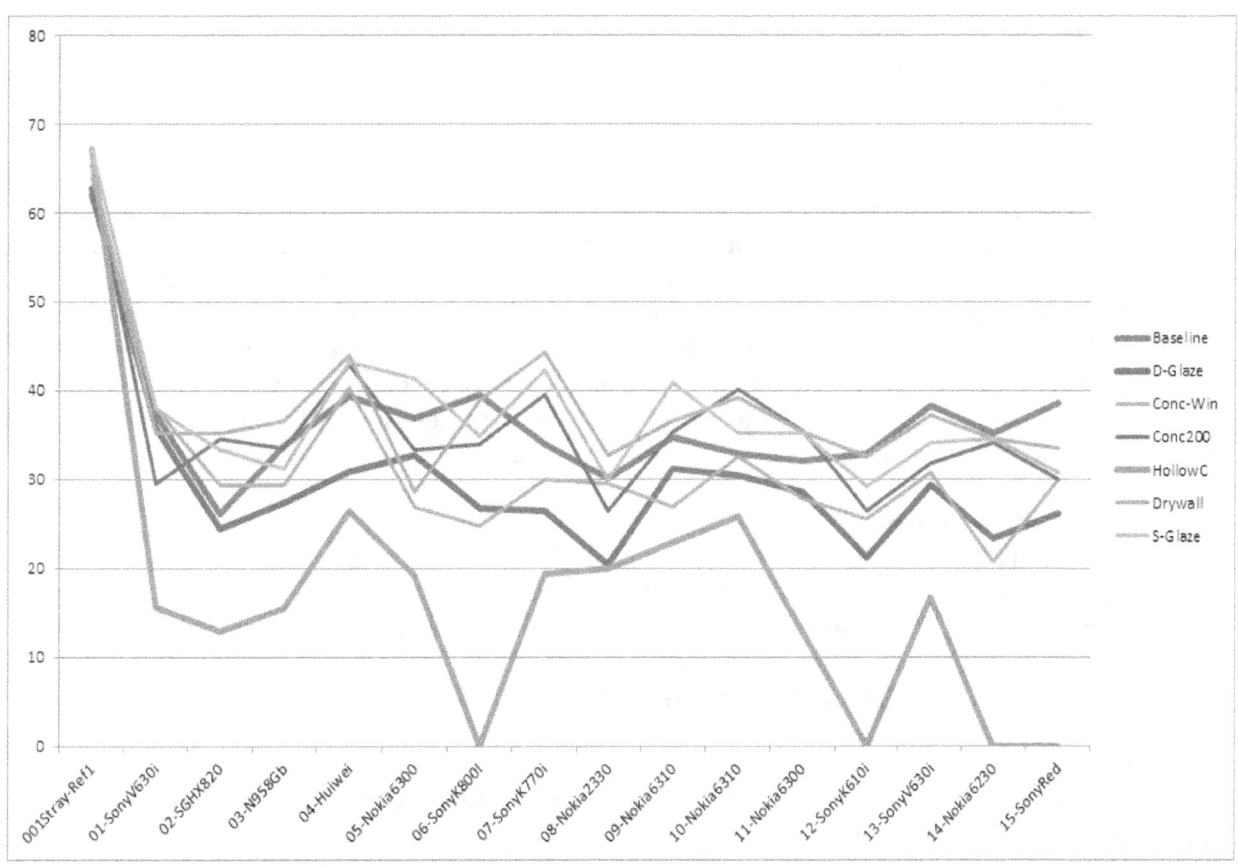

Material Type(X) with RSSI Signal Strength Bar Chart:

[Note: the '001Stray-Ref1' is a reference signal and it remained 1m away from the Bluetooth receiver at all times... this is why it's signal does not show degradation]

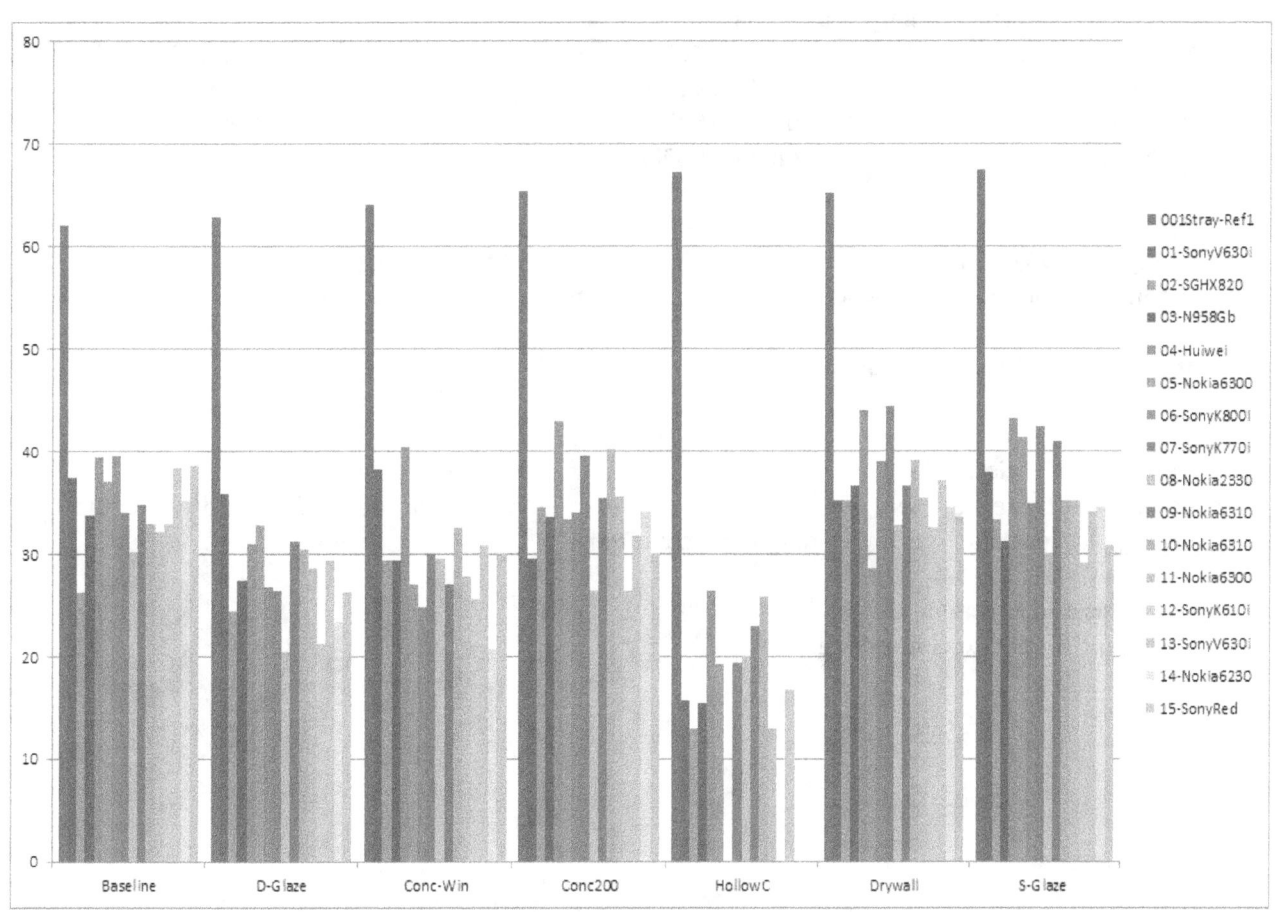

3.6.7 Test Bluetooth Discovery Performance in an Indoor Shopping Centre

Aim/Goals:
To test the usability of Bluetooth as a location beacon in shops within a busy shopping centre.

Data from Previous Experiments:
None.
Follow On Experiments:
None.

Methodology/Preparation/Planning:
An Android software application was written to allow Bluetooth devices to be discovered and counted. A harness was constructed to allow video capture of the results of the testing. 14 bluetooth enabled devices(mobile/feature/smart phones) were sourced and placed in 14 different shops in a busy shopping centre(Galway Shopping Centre, Headford Rd, Galway). Each Bluetooth transmitter(phone) was placed in a secure location close to the cash register in each premises. Each premises name was noted and linked to that specific transmitter. Each transmitter also had a two digit code used in the human friendly name which the application used to recognise the transmitter as being part of the experiment.

Implementation/Execution:
1. Stand outside the first premises, 3m away and at 90deg from the main entrance.
2. Start the Bluetooth Discovery cycle on the Android handset.
3. Record the results of the bluetooth scan and include any stray or 3rd party bluetooth devices which are found during the bluetooth discovery cycle.
4. Move to the next premises and repeat the procedure until all 14 premises are scanned.

Retesting:
The experiment can be retested easily. All phone models were noted, distances measured etc... to allow retesting/recreation.

Hardware Used:
Samsung GalaxyS(GT-I9000)
Panasonic HD Camcorder(DMC-FS30).
16 Bluetooth Enabled mobile/feature/smart phones:

Nokia 2330	SonyEric K610i	Samsung SGHX820
Nokia 6230	SonyEric V630i x 4	Huiwei Android
Nokia 6300 x2	SonyEric K770i	Nokia N958Gb
Nokia 6310 x2	SonyEric K800i	

Software Used:
Samsung GalaxyS operating system Android 2.1-update1 used throughout.
A custom Android Application was written to read Bluetooth information received.

Changes to Plan During Testing:
none.

Validation/Evaluation:
By completing this experiment, we can determine the effectiveness of the modern Android handset in detecting bluetooth devices under real world conditions.

Calculations and Formulae Used:
None except simple Excel formulae.

Locations:
Galway Shopping Centre, Headford Rd., Galway.
Shops participating in the test:
1. O' Briens Off Licence,
2. Car Phone Whouse,
3. Ashford Home Store.
4. Hynes Shoes,
5. Burton,
6. Hanley's Menswear,
7. Center Jewellers,
8. Eason Bookshop,
9. Zhavigo,
10. Sarah's Fashions,
11. Matt O'Flaherty Chemist,
12. Libaas Clothes,
13. CR Tormey Butchers,
14. Cunniffe Elect,

The premises were chosen starting from the north entrance and choosing each shop on the right hand side(southerly) as you entered. If the premises was closed/vacant or the store manager did not want to participate then that store was skipped. Otherwise, all shops were chosen as they were encountered while walking from the North to the South entrance of the shopping centre, until 14 premises had transmitters installed in them.

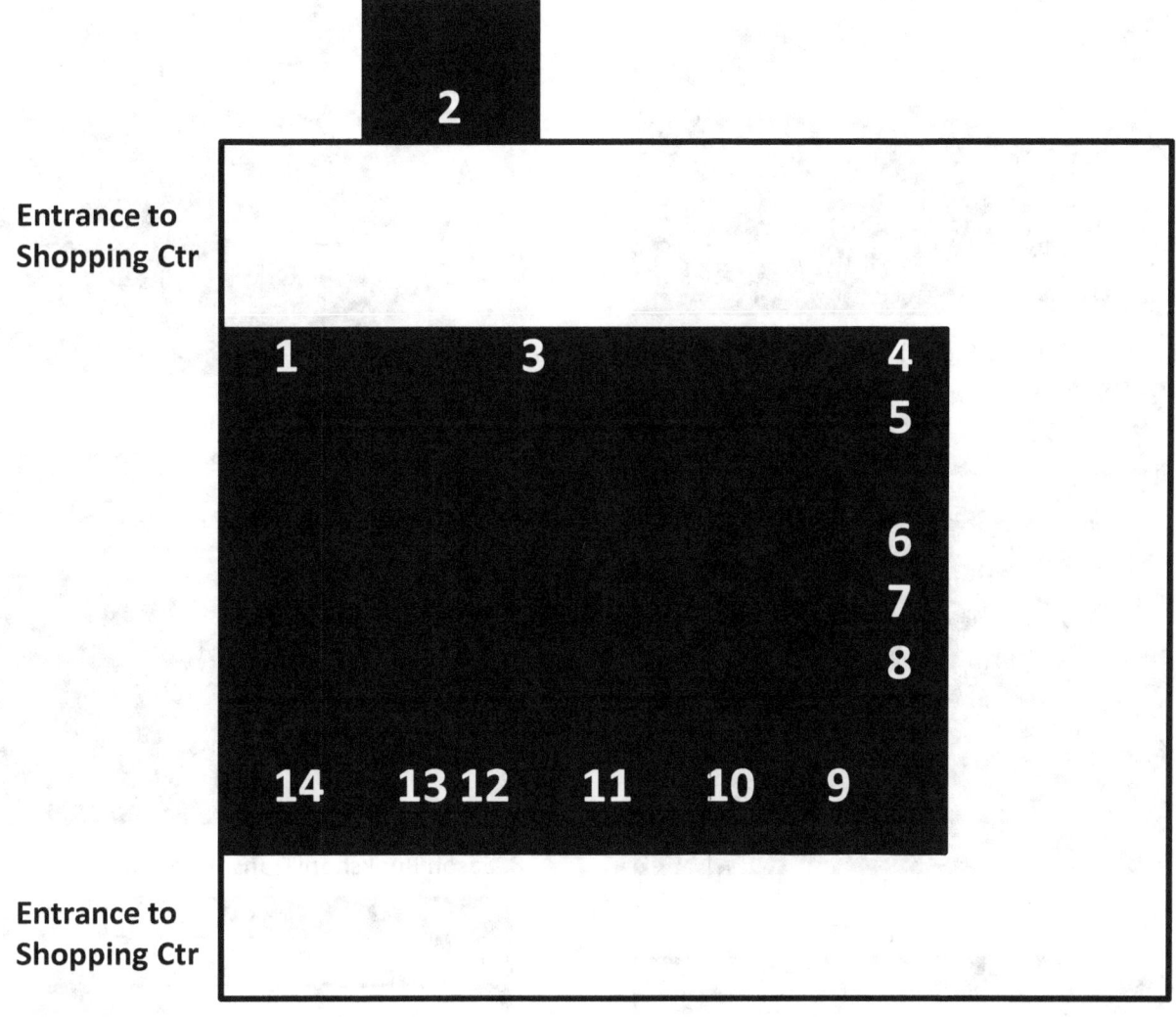

Results:

1. O' Briens Off Licence[Transmitter 06]:

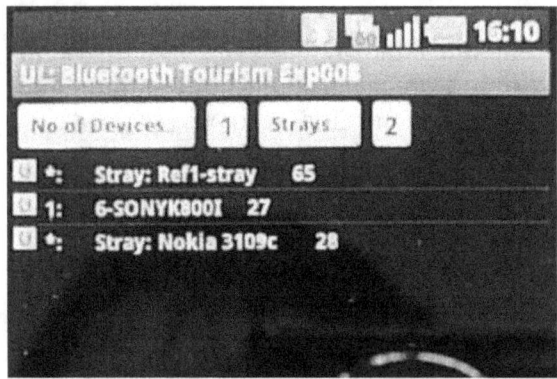

2. Car Phone Whouse[Transmitter 04]:

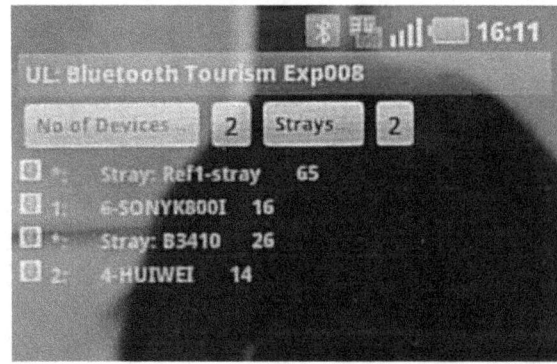

3. Ashford Home Store[Transmitter 15]:

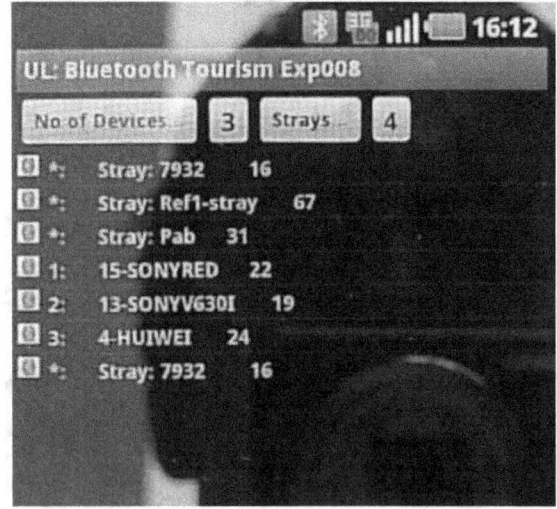

4. Hynes Shoes[Transmitter 13]:

5. Burton[Transmitter 14]:

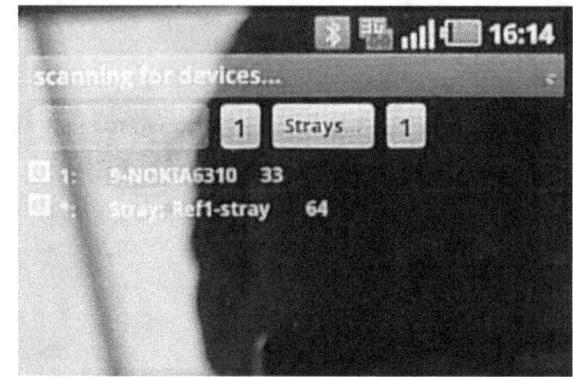

6. Hanley's Menswear[Transmitter 09]:

7. Center Jewellers[Transmitter 07]:

8. Eason Bookshop[Transmitter 10]:

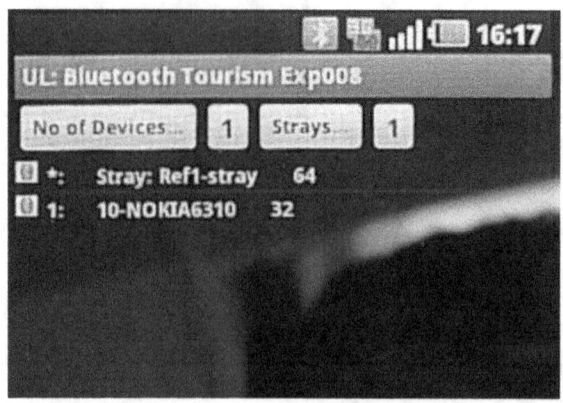

Results:

9. Zhavigo[Transmitter 12]:

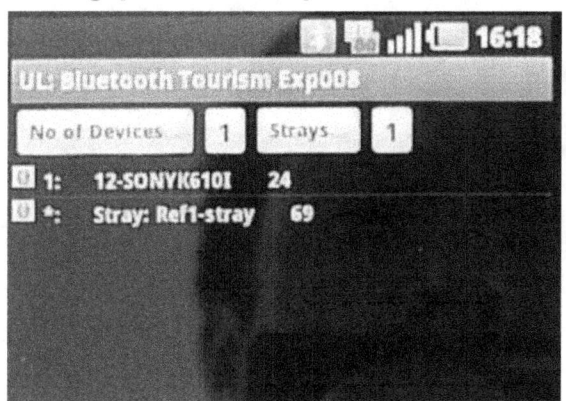

10. Sarah's Fashions[Transmitter 11]:

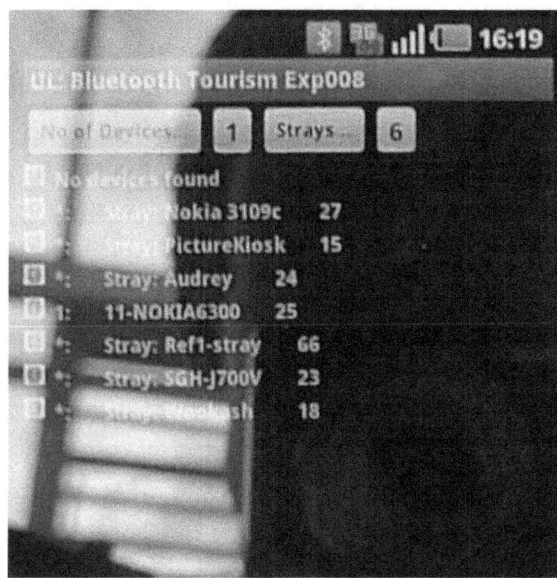

11. Matt O'Flah Chemist[Transmitter 08]:

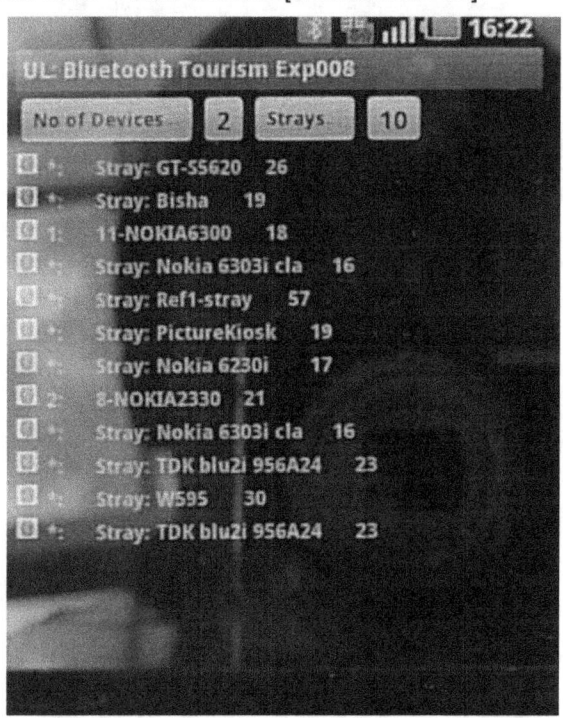

12. Libaas Clothes[Transmitter 02]:

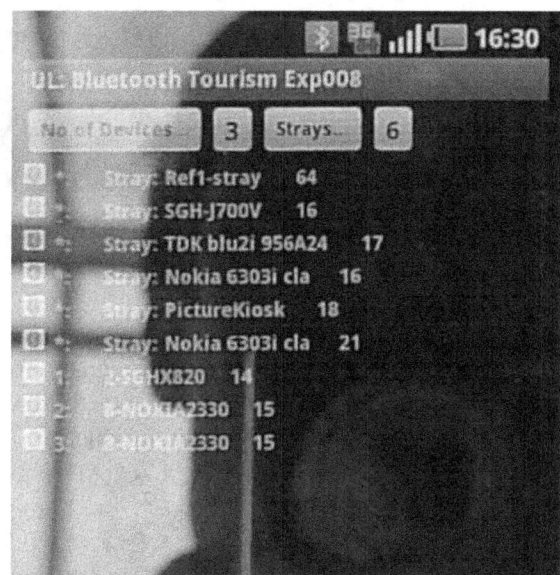

13. CR Tormey Butchers[Transmitter 01]:

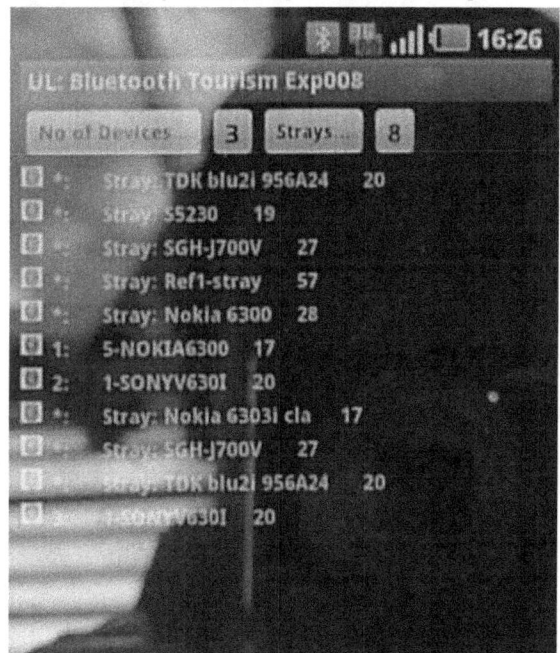

14. Cunniffe Elect[Transmitter 05]:

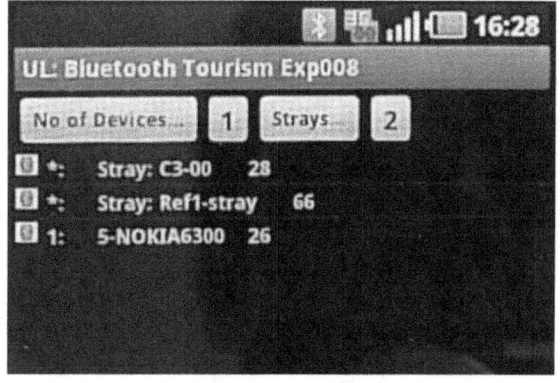

Picture during testing(screen capture from the online video files).

Results:

In the results shown below, the Transmitter model is the model of phone used as the Bluetooth transmitter, the Bluetooth Name is the human friendly name used on the transmitter, the shop location is the shop where the transmitter was placed, the First Location Found column is marked YES if the Bluetooth receiver(the user's phone) picked up this shop when it was directly outside the entrance, the Second Location Found column is marked YES if the receiver failed to recognise that it was outside the shop, but did report it as being the second closest location, the Other Locations Found column indicates how many other shops were found(with lower signal strength) in addition to the target shop, the Strays Found column indicates how many other stray bluetooth signals were found while standing outside the target shop.

Transmitter Model	Bluetooth Name	No	Shop Location	First Location Found	Second Location Found	Other Locations Found	Strays Found
SonyEric V630i	001Stray-Ref1		001Stray-Ref1	NA		NA	NA
Nokia 6300	06-SonyK800i	1	O' Briens Off Licence	YES	n/a	0	2
Nokia N958Gb	04-Huiwei	2	Car Phone Whouse	NO	YES	1	2
Nokia 6230	15-SonyRed	3	Ashford Home Store	NO	YES	2	4
SonyEric K610i	13-SonyV630i	4	Hynes Shoes	YES	n/a	0	3
SonyEric V630i	14-Nokia6230	5	Burton	NO	NO	0	1
Nokia 2330	09-Nokia6310	6	Hanleys Menswear	YES	n/a	0	4
SonyEric K800i	07-SonyK770i	7	Center Jewellers	YES	n/a	0	3
Nokia 6310	10-Nokia6310	8	Eason	YES	n/a	0	1
Nokia 6300	12-SonyK610i	9	Zhavigo	YES	n/a	0	1
Nokia 6310	11-Nokia6300	10	Sarahs Fashions	YES	n/a	0	6
SonyEric K770i	08-Nokia2330	11	Matt O'Flaherty	NO	YES	1	10
SonyEric V630i	02-SGHX820	12	Libaas Clothes	NO	YES	1	6
SonyEric V630i	01-SonyV630i	13	CR Tormey Butchers	YES	n/a	1	8
Huiwei Android	05-Nokia6300	14	Cunniffe Elect	YES	n/a	0	2

Analysis:

On 9 out of 14 occasions, the receiver correctly identified which shop it was closest to.

On 4 out of 14 occasions, the receiver reported that it was the second closest shop when the user was in fact outside the target shop. This is a good result, as the shop is easily within line of sight of the user.

On 1 out of 14 occasions, the receiver completely failed to pick up the Bluetooth signal from that shop. This occurred at the 'Burton' shop. It transpired that that manager of the shop had moved the transmitter, from it's original location and placed it into a strategically poor location. Unfortunately, this was not known during the test and it was assumed that the transmitter was left where it was originally installed(at the cash register).

Conclusion:

These results indicate that the use of Bluetooth tagging is a very successful method of providing location aware functionality in an indoor or outdoor environment.

The online resource at http://www.irishapps.org/smartlla.html contains all the photo and video files used to capture the above information.

3.6.8 Measure the Time Required for Two Android Bluetooth Devices to Establish a Pairing Relationship and then Share Information

Aim/Goals:
To determine the minimum time required for a Bluetooth transmitter to push information such as advertising or marketing data, to a Bluetooth receiver. The transmitter will typically be mounted in a store premises and the receiver will typically be a smartphone running a tourism based Bluetooth application.

Data from Previous Experiments:
None.
Follow On Experiments:
None.

Methodology/Preparation/Planning:
Two Android device were sourced and a suitable Bluetooth application was written and installed on each handset to allow testing of the Bluetooth performance of the devices. A video camera was used to capture the screen images from both phones.

Implementation/Execution:
1. Switch on all bluetooth devices.
2. Give each device a unique human friendly Bluetooth name.
3. Place the Android handsets on the harness.
4. Start the Bluetooth application on both handsets and go through the procedure for establishing a pairing and sending data.
5. Carry out this test 10 times, un-pairing each device before repeating the test.

Retesting:
The experiment can be retested easily by viewing the video of the experiment

Hardware Used:
Samsung GalaxyS(GT-I9000) Premium Android Handset
Huawei Vodafone 845 Budget Android handset
Panasonic HD Camcorder(DMC-FS30).

Software Used:
Samsung GalaxyS operating system Android 2.1-update1 used throughout.
Bluetooth Chat Sample Application from Google.
Changes to Plan During Testing:
none.

Validation/Evaluation:
By completing this experiment, we can determine the effectiveness of the modern Android handset in pushing information over a Bluetooth connection.

Calculations and Formulae Used:
None except simple Excel formulae.

Analysis:
The time required for a smartphone to Discover a Bluetooth transmitter, establish a pairing relationship and transmit a small amount of textual data is consistently under 15 seconds.

This includes the time required by the user to answer the mandatory question during the pairing procedure.

Conclusion:
Devices can discover, pair and transfer data in an acceptably short period of time to make it a viable option for pushing advertising and marketing data to the tourism end user.
Further investigation is required to see if the security questions on the transmitter side can be bypassed. This would possibly involve some operating system modifications/upgrades.

Results:

	Start Discovery Scan (sec)	Find Transmitter and Launch Pairing Procedure (sec)	Receive and Confirm Pairing Security Question (sec)	Accept Security Question at Transmitter (sec)	Receive and Confirm Pairing Security Question (sec)	Accept Security Question at Transmitter (sec)	Receive Data from Transmitter (sec)
Test 01	4	5	9	10	12	13	14
Test 02	4	6	9	10	12	13	13
Test 03	3	6	10	10	13	14	14
Test 04	4	6	10	10	13	13	14
Test 05	4	6	10	10	13	13	14
Test 06	3	5	11	11	13	14	15
Test 07	3	5	10	11	13	13	14
Test 08	4	6	11	11	14	14	15
Test 09	4	6	10	10	13	13	14
Test 10	4	6	10	10	13	13	15
Average	3.7	5.7	10	10.3	12.9	13.3	14.2

The online resource at http://www.irishapps.org/smartlla.html contains all the photo and video files used to capture the above information.

3.7 Hybrid Positioning Systems

With hybrid positioning, we find the location of a handset using a combination of several different positioning technologies. GPS is usually the dominant system used and it is usually backed up by the use of other technologies such as GSM cell tower triangulation, WiFi Skyhook triangulation, bluetooth signals and other positioning system.

Hybrid strategy is usually employed to make up for the failing of satellite technology, especially when the user is operating in an indoor environment or when operating where there are tall buildings or trees causing interference with the satellite signal.
GSM cell towers are not affected to a great extent by these obstructions and work quite well in indoor environments. WiFi skyhook systems are also superior to satellite positioning signals indoors and can give a very precise location fix if the local area supports skyhook WiFi(usually only in US).

Hybrid systems are already being supported by some operating systems such as iOS and Android, and the programmer does not need to be too aware of what's going on in the background in order to take advantage of the technology. You simply state the level of accuracy you desire and whether you want to use a paid or free service, and the OS then looks after the background task of choosing the most appropriate hybrid positioning strategy for your needs.

3.8 Assisted GPS

GPS capable feature phones and smartphones use Assisted GPS extensively. Any modern GPS phone which is operating with an assisted GPS enabled network can usually take advantage of Assisted GPS.
Assisted GPS improves the overall precision of standalone GPS. It often leads to an improvement in the time it takes to first acquire a lock on a GPS location. This is referred to as the 'time to first fix' TTFF of a GPS based positioning system.
Autonomous GPS operates by reading signals from four or more GPS signals(see start of this chapter). Assisted GPS uses information provided from a ground station, that has accurate location information about it's own location, in order to improve the accuracy and responsiveness of the GPS signal it is receiving from the in-orbit satellites.
In a city environment, where the GPS signal is somewhat compromised because of the signal bouncing off buildings and trees, the handset may not be able to establish an accurate position within a reasonable timeframe. It can sometimes take up to 10 minutes to establish a good location fix. Assisted GPS can alleviate this lag and this inaccuracy by using information which will allow quicker acquisition of in-orbit satellites and better calculation of the position of the handset.

Orbital data is supplied to the handset on a regular basis from the ground station. This data is calculated by the ground station using it's own special GPS equipment.

Like Hybrid Positioning Systems, most of the work is done by the OS and all the programmer/user has to do is to enable Assisted GPS within the settings of the phone. Assisted GPS can have an additional cost and can be hard on the battery of the device, so this must be considered when using A-GPS.

3.9 2D Codes

There are hundreds of 1D and 2D code formats available.
The two most popular 2D formats are QR Codes and DataMatrix codes. Both of these codes are widely used and it is difficult to argue in a general sense that one is better than the other. For the purposes of this book, the QR code is used to test the usability and practicality of using a 2D Code to provide tourists with information about shops, historical monuments, and other items of interest to tourists.

The following pages describe the technical details of the QR Code. However, much of the detail can be applied to the DataMatrix format also.

Chapter 3

Any tourist application should support both of these formats. Some areas to consider when comparing both of these formats are listed below and on the next page…. but to summarize, the main difference between the two code formats are that:

The DataMatrix format can display the same information in a smaller area. However, for tourism apps, the tourist must be able to locate the 2d code before they can use it so it must be quite large(eg. greater than 3cm sq.) in order to be visible. Therefore, this efficiency advantage is nullified for the purposes of this book.

The QRCode format has the ability to use Asian 'kana' character sets, something the DataMatrix format is not designed to do(although there are workarounds). This is a stumbling block for the DataMatrix format from a tourism perspective.

Considering that the size factor doesn't really matter for tourism apps, it is better to concentrate on QR Codes for the experimental phase of this book.

3.9.1 2D Code Reader Providers

The following table lists the major 1D and 2D code readers available to mobile users.

	Name	Description
1	2D Sense Platform	Formerly iMatrix, www.2dsense.com is a user-oriented reader that handles QR, Datamatrix and Shotcode
2	3GVision	A player in the mobile barcode industry in Japan, provides access to QR codes over a variety of platforms.
3	BeeTagg	Multi-code reader which also supports it's own proprietary code, the BeeTagg System.
4	Bems	Spanish company uses Datamatrix and QR codes to web enable advertising campaigns, SMS.
5	Camclic	Reads all major 1d and 2d codes, and adds web content to existing physical codes
6	GS1	www.gs1.org, the global standards organisation, also provides barcodes and solutions for barcode marketing
7	i-nigma	Originally developed by 3GVision, reads and creates QR codes.
8	insqribe	Provides QR Code campaign creation, management and tracking facilities
9	Kaywa	Offers a QRcode reader and campaign creator.
10	Masabi	Concentrates on using open barcodes to provide payment and paperless ticketing.
11	Mbarc	Specialising in airline travel, offers mobile ticketing, ID and coupon offers through barcodes
12	Microsoft Tag	Microsofts proprietary HCCB tag uses a high data-storage format for normal barcoding purposes.
13	Mobile Data Systems	Concentrates on Social netowrking, providing both reader apps and personal codes for Facebook / MySpace / etc.
14	Mobile Discovery	Provides a mobile advertising network geared towards barcodes with their Connected Media Platform
15	Mobile Tag	French based company that provides a Datamatrix reader and commercial card code creator
16	Mobiqa	Specialising in mobile ticketing and coupons
17	NeoMedia	concentrates on effective mobile ticketing, two-way transactions and embedded advertising campaigns
18	Nextcode	Barcode decoding software for mobile.
19	Nokia	Available out-of-the-box on most Nokia handsets, their software allows you to read standard barcodes and create your own
20	NTT DoCoMo	Provides software for creating and reading QR code over its family of products.
21	Qipit	Their software enables easy reading of any 1d barcodes.
22	QMCODES	Specialises in 2Dcode campaigns for print media publishers.
23	Quickmark	Focusing mostly on eCommerce and business cards.
24	RapidID	Concentrate on mobile assets tracking and location.
25	Scanbuy	Supports QR and Datamatrix and EZcode.
26	Scanlife	Provides an EZcode reader and creator for personal and commercial use
27	Semacode	The creators of the open-source Datamatrix code
28	ShotCode	Issues the proprietary Shotcode 2d barcode, and provide readers, creators and campaigns around it.
30	Snappr	User friendly 2d and 1d barcode reader, and QR code generator.
31	Tagnition	Specialise in solutions for publishers and agencies.
32	Upcode	Uses Datamatrix codes and covers a wide number of applications for consumers, providers and clients
33	Windows Office Marke	Reading and creating 2d barcodes
34	ZXing	Used for this project. http://code.google.com/p/zxing/ is an open-source Java programme that focuses on decoding 1D/2D barcodes on the device, without communicating with a server.

BeeTagg was used for both the Samsung and the iPhone during testing.

3.9.2 QR Codes

A QR code is a two dimensional matrix code which can be read by dedicated QR scanners and by smartphones with an on-board camera. There are small black squares which are arranged on a white background. The pattern of these squares arranged in a certain fashion, contain the coded information. This information can be in the form of plain Unicode text, a URL or other kinds of data.

QR codes and other codes such as data matrix codes, are often used for commercial tracking of packages, advertising on almost any scale, from the centimetre, to the 100s of meter scale. They are used to hold business card information, to hold URI information and to hold metadata of all kinds. Emails and text messages can also be encoded into QR code format.

Magazines and billboards, business cards and letterheads are increasingly using QR codes to provide a convenient and catchy way to present a URL to a consumer. Camera equipped smartphones are often used to scan the codes and display the information to the used directly on the screen of the phone. URLs can instantly be used with the on-board browser to view the desired content, or the content can come directly from the QR code itself.

2D Codes progressed from the stacked barcode method to the increased information density matrix format.

Multiple Barcode Layout

2D code with stacked barcodes

2D code matrix type

History - Bar code to 2D Code
Barcodes have been in widespread use since the early 1970s. They are easy to read, very accurate and provide a convenient way to embed data and metadata into a product. Because of the popularity of 1D barcodes, there was a demand for smaller, and more densely packed codes which can be more easily read, can contain much more information within the same real-estate, and can be read more quickly and more reliably than traditional 1D codes. Two dimensional codes emerged in order to fill this demand.

The company that developed the QR Code was Denso Wave (a division of Denso Corporation at the time). It was released in 1994 with the aim of producing a code that was information dense and easily interpreted by simple scanner equipment.

As the name implies, two dimensional codes contain information stored in both the X and the Y direction. Traditional barcodes, only contain information stored in one direction.

QR Codes provide the following features compared with conventional bar codes:

High Capacity Encoding of Data
The traditional barcode can contain about twenty digits in a one dimensional direction. The two dimensional QR code can contain hundreds of times the information of the 1D code.
They can handle a diverse range of data types including numeric and alpha characters, oriental scripts, binary and control codes(eg. return, char space). Just over seven thousand characters can be encoded into a single QR code.

Small Printout Size
The same payload of data can be compressed into an area approximately one tenth the size of a traditional one dimensional code.
(For a smaller printout size, Micro QR Codes are available).

Dirt and Damage Resistant
QR Coding has error correction capability. Duplication of data is build into the QR code specification. If some of the QR code is obscured, dirty or damaged then the full content of the code can often be retrieved.

Readable from any direction in 360°
QR Codes are capable of 360 degree (omni-directional) high speed reading.

Structured Append Feature
QR Codes can be divided into multiple data areas.

QR Code Outline Specification
(from www.denso-wave.com)

Symbol size	21 × 21 - 177 × 177 modules (size grows by 4 modules/side)	
Type & Amount of Data (Mixed use is possible.)	Numeric	Max. 7,089 characters
	Alphanumeric	Max. 4,296 characters
	8-bit bytes (binary)	Max. 2,953 characters
	Kanji	Max. 1,817 characters
Error correction (data restoration)	Level L	Approx. 7% of codewords can be restored.
	Level M	Approx. 15% of codewords can be restored.
	Level Q	Approx. 25% of codewords can be restored.
	Level H	Approx. 30% of codewords can be restored.
Structured append	Max. 16 symbols (printing in a narrow area etc.)	

QR Codes are established as ISO (ISO/IEC18004) standard.
http://www.iso.ch/

QR Code System Configuration
QR Code creation software is used in combination with a QR Code printer and a QR Code scanner.
The primary factor to consider when generating a readable QR code is the area in which the QR code had to reside. The smaller the area the better the resolution must be for both the printer and scanner.

QR Code Size Decision Factor

The diagram below illustrates the decisions that have to be made and the factors to consider when determining the size that the QR code will be.

For tourism retail use, the printer is assumed to be a regular inkjet or laser printer, and the scanner a smartphone equipped with a camera.

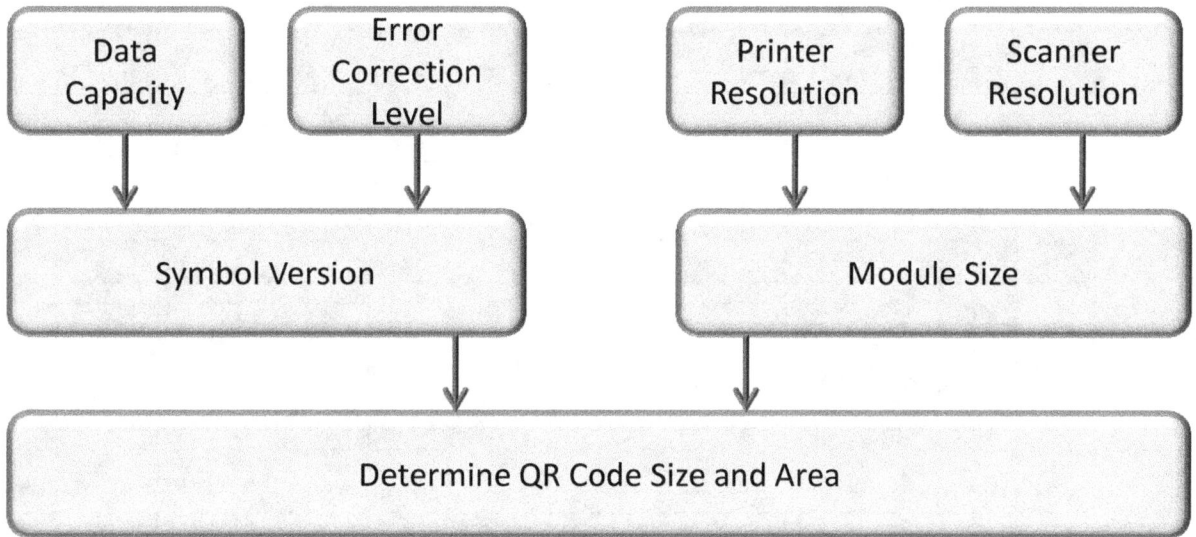

Symbol Version
The symbol versions of QR Codes range from Version 1 to Version 40.
There is a different configuration and layout of the black squares depending on the version in use. The number of black squares are also different for each version.
Version one contains 21 x 21 modules and is the most basic version of QR code. Each subsequent increase in version number, represents an increase of four black dots in the X and Y planes.
The largest version contains 177 black dots in the X and Y axis.
Each incremental version contains more and more data capacity. The capacity of each version is limited my the character types used, and by the level of error correction employed.

Error Correction
As mentioned earlier, QR codes have a sophisticated error correction and recovery mechanism. Data can be easily restored if part of the code becomes unreadable for whatever reason. There are four different error detection levels that can be chosen. The higher the detection level, the less original data can be stored in the code itself. These levels are listed in the box below. Again, the factors to consider when choosing an error correction level include the size of

QR Code Error Correction Capability	
Level L	Approx 7%
Level M	Approx 15%
Level Q	Approx 25%
Level H	Approx 30%

(from www.denso-wave.com)

the code, the real-estate it will possess, the harshness of the operating environment and the degree to which the environment can be controlled.
Level M was used for all the QR codes used during the experimentation phase.

Error Correction Feature - Reed-Solomon Code
Reed-Solomon Code will be familiar to anyone involved in the production of music CDs. This error correction algorithm was first developed for use in the space and aeronautic industries to measure communications noise from probes and satellites.
QR codes take the original data and pass it through a Reed-Solomon filter in order to encode it will error correction redundancy.
For example, if there are 100 QR code words to be encoded, 50 will need to be corrected, 100 code words of Reed-Solomon Code are required(Reed-Solomon Code requires twice the amount of code words to be corrected).
In this case, the total code words are 200, 50 of which can be corrected. This leads to an error correction level of twenty five percent. Referencing the table above shows this to be a Q level correction.

QR Code Table

The following table lists all of the QR Code versions available for use. This is a useful resource when deciding on the level of error correction, the amount of data to be stored in the code and the physical size of the code.

Version	Modules	ECC	Data bits	Numeric	A-num	Binary	Kanji	Version	Modules	ECC	Data bits	Numeric	A-num	Binary	Kanji
1	21x21	L	152	41	25	17	10	21	101x101	L	7456	2232	1352	929	572
		M	128	34	20	14	8			M	5712	1708	1035	711	438
		Q	104	27	16	11	7			Q	4096	1224	742	509	314
		H	72	17	10	7	4			H	3248	969	587	403	248
2	25x25	L	272	77	47	32	20	22	105x105	L	8048	2409	1460	1003	618
		M	224	63	38	26	16			M	6256	1872	1134	779	480
		Q	176	48	29	20	12			Q	4544	1358	823	565	348
		H	128	34	20	14	8			H	3536	1056	640	439	270
3	29x29	L	440	127	77	53	32	23	109x109	L	8752	2620	1588	1091	672
		M	352	101	61	42	26			M	6880	2059	1248	857	528
		Q	272	77	47	32	20			Q	4912	1468	890	611	376
		H	208	58	35	24	15			H	3712	1108	672	461	284
4	33x33	L	640	187	114	78	48	24	113x113	L	9392	2812	1704	1171	721
		M	512	149	90	62	38			M	7312	2188	1326	911	561
		Q	384	111	67	46	28			Q	5312	1588	963	661	407
		H	288	82	50	34	21			H	4112	1228	744	511	315
5	37x37	L	864	255	154	106	65	25	117x117	L	10208	3057	1853	1273	784
		M	688	202	122	84	52			M	8000	2395	1451	997	614
		Q	496	144	87	60	37			Q	5744	1718	1041	715	440
		H	368	106	64	44	27			H	4304	1286	779	535	330
6	41x41	L	1,088	322	195	134	82	26	121x121	L	10,960	3283	1990	1367	842
		M	864	255	154	106	65			M	8496	2544	1542	1059	652
		Q	608	178	108	74	45			Q	6032	1804	1094	751	462
		H	480	139	84	58	36			H	4768	1425	864	593	365
7	45x45	L	1,248	370	224	154	95	27	125x125	L	11,744	3514	2132	1465	902
		M	992	293	178	122	75			M	9024	2701	1637	1125	692
		Q	704	207	125	86	53			Q	6464	1933	1172	805	496
		H	528	154	93	64	39			H	5024	1501	910	625	385
8	49x49	L	1,552	461	279	192	118	28	129x129	L	12,248	3669	2223	1528	940
		M	1,232	365	221	152	93			M	9,544	2857	1732	1190	732
		Q	880	259	157	108	66			Q	6968	2085	1263	868	534
		H	688	202	122	84	52			H	5288	1581	958	658	405
9	53x53	L	1,856	552	335	230	141	29	133x133	L	13,048	3909	2369	1628	1002
		M	1,456	432	262	180	111			M	10,136	3035	1839	1264	778
		Q	1,056	312	189	130	80			Q	7,288	2181	1322	908	559
		H	800	235	143	98	60			H	5608	1677	1016	698	430
10	57x57	L	2,192	652	395	271	167	30	137x137	L	13,880	4158	2520	1732	1066
		M	1,728	513	311	213	131			M	10,984	3289	1994	1370	843
		Q	1,232	364	221	151	93			Q	7,880	2358	1429	982	604
		H	976	288	174	119	74			H	5960	1782	1080	742	457
11	61x61	L	2592	772	468	321	198	31	141x141	L	14744	4417	2677	1840	1132
		M	2032	604	366	251	155			M	11640	3486	2113	1452	894
		Q	1440	427	259	177	109			Q	8264	2473	1499	1030	634
		H	1120	331	200	137	85			H	6344	1897	1150	790	486
12	65x65	L	2960	883	535	367	226	32	145x145	L	15640	4686	2840	1952	1201
		M	2320	691	419	287	177			M	12328	3693	2238	1538	947
		Q	1648	489	296	203	125			Q	8920	2670	1618	1112	684
		H	1264	374	227	155	96			H	6760	2022	1226	842	518
13	69x69	L	3424	1022	619	425	262	33	149x149	L	16568	4965	3009	2068	1273
		M	2672	796	483	331	204			M	13048	3909	2369	1628	1002
		Q	1952	580	352	241	149			Q	9368	2805	1700	1168	719
		H	1440	427	259	177	109			H	7208	2157	1307	898	553
14	73x73	L	3688	1101	667	458	282	34	153x153	L	17528	5253	3183	2188	1347
		M	2920	871	528	362	223			M	13800	4134	2506	1722	1060
		Q	2088	621	376	258	159			Q	9848	2949	1787	1228	756
		H	1576	468	283	194	120			H	7688	2301	1394	958	590
15	77x77	L	4184	1250	758	520	320	35	157x157	L	18448	5529	3351	2303	1417
		M	3320	991	600	412	254			M	14496	4343	2632	1809	1113
		Q	2360	703	426	292	180			Q	10288	3081	1867	1283	790
		H	1784	530	321	220	136			H	7888	2361	1431	983	605
16	81x81	L	4,712	1408	854	586	361	36	161x161	L	19,472	5836	3537	2431	1496
		M	3624	1082	656	450	277			M	15312	4588	2780	1911	1176
		Q	2600	775	470	322	198			Q	10832	3244	1966	1351	832
		H	2024	602	365	250	154			H	8432	2524	1530	1051	647
17	85x85	L	5,176	1548	938	644	397	37	165x165	L	20,528	6153	3729	2563	1577
		M	4056	1212	734	504	310			M	15936	4775	2894	1989	1224
		Q	2936	876	531	364	224			Q	11408	3417	2071	1423	876
		H	2264	674	408	280	173			H	8768	2625	1591	1093	673
18	89x89	L	5,768	1725	1046	718	442	38	169x169	L	21,616	6479	3927	2699	1661
		M	4,504	1346	816	560	345			M	16,816	5039	3054	2099	1292
		Q	3176	948	574	394	243			Q	12016	3599	2181	1499	923
		H	2504	746	452	310	191			H	9136	2735	1658	1139	701
19	93x93	L	6,360	1903	1153	792	488	39	173x173	L	22,496	6743	4087	2809	1729
		M	5,016	1500	909	624	384			M	17,728	5313	3220	2213	1362
		Q	3,560	1063	644	442	272			Q	12,656	3791	2298	1579	972
		H	2728	813	493	338	208			H	9776	2927	1774	1219	750
20	97x97	L	6,888	2061	1249	858	528	40	177x177	L	23,648	7089	4296	2953	1817
		M	5,352	1600	970	666	410			M	18,672	5596	3391	2331	1435
		Q	3,880	1159	702	482	297			Q	13,328	3993	2420	1663	1024
		H	3080	919	557	382	235			H	10208	3057	1852	1273	784

from www.denso-wave.com

Setting Module Size

Setting the QR code size depends on the size of the individual black dots to be printed(this is after the version number is established). The larger the black dots are, the easier the code is to read and the more stable the code is. On the other hand, as the QR Code symbol size gets larger, a larger printing area is required. It is, therefore, necessary to determine the module size of each application after considering all the relevant factors. Of course, all QR codes should be printer in the largest possible area available so that it will be easiest to read.

Version 1 QR Code (21x21 modules)

0.5 mm module size   1.0 mm module size

Printer Head Density and Module Size

The density of the dots in the printer head – number of dots per sq inch – will determine the module size. For example, if the head density is 300dpi and each module is made up of 5 dots, the module size is 0.42 mm2. Increasing the number of dots improves printing quality, eliminates printing width or paper feed speed fluctuations, distortion of axis, blurring, etc, and enables more stable operations. It is recommended for stable operations that each module is made up of 4 or more dots.

Printer and Module Size				
Printer	Head Density	4-dot config	5-dot config	6-dot config
Laser	600dpi 24dot/mm	0.17mm	0.21mm	0.25mm
	360dpi 14dot/mm	0.28mm	0.35mm	0.42mm
Thermal	300dpi 12dot/mm	0.33mm	0.42mm	0.50mm
	200dpi 08dot/mm	0.50mm	0.63mm	0.75mm

(from www.denso-wave.com)

Scanner Factors

Each scanner has its own readable module size limit. The scanner resolution represents this limit.

For example, if a data code symbol is printed with a 300 dpi, 4-dot printer, the module size is 0.34mm. A scanner resolution of less than 0.34mm is required to read the symbol.

There is no point in increasing the resolution of the printer if the scanner is incapable of reading to that resolution.

For modern smartphones, the scanning resolution is not a problem, as the camera has a resolution exceeding most high end QR scanners.

Module

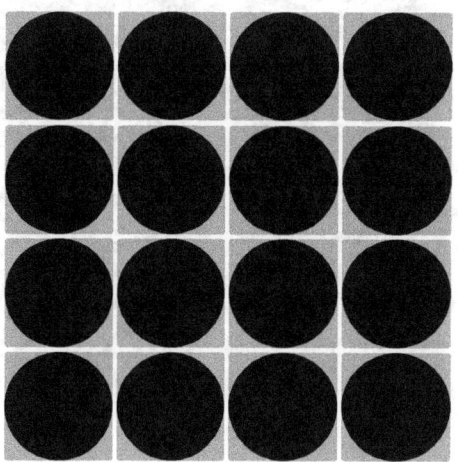

Dots

Chapter 3

Securing Margin

Another factor to consider at this stage is the size of the margin that is required around the 2d code. After the version and black dot size has been determined, the quiet zone around the QR code or the white margin area must be set.

Most QR codes require at least a distance of four black dots or modules between it and the next QR code or text on the same page or canvas.

Margin:
4 or more screen dots.

Calculating a QR Code Area

The following example shows how to calculate the overall size of the QR code including the quiet zone.
Example of a 50 alphanumeric characters large QR Code:
We use the standard tourism level of M. Use the maximum capacity table and version table listed earlier in this chapter to find the appropriate version number to use. Based on the table, we choose version three which can store over fifty characters with level M.
Version3 has 29 screen dots at 0.254mm/dot each which gives us 7.366mm.
With a minimum of 4 screen dots quiet zone gives 9.398mm
In other words, the required QR Code area is 9.398mm2.

3.9.3 Other 2D Code Types

QR codes aren't the only ones available, there are dozens of standards and formats, used for a variety of specialist situations. Below is a table of typical 2D Codes and their features.

QR Code and Data Matrix Example Contains Text:
"Smartphones and Location Aware Applications for the Tourism Sector. Chapter: Technology Available for Building Tourism & Location Aware Applications."

PDF417 and Maxi Cube Example Contains Text:
"Smartphones and Location Aware Applications for the Tourism Sector."

Different Formats				
	QR Code	PDF417	DataMatrix	MaxiCode
Developer	Denso	Symbol Tech	RVSI Acuity	UPS
Country	Japan	USA	USA	USA
Type	Matrix	Stacked Bar Code	Matrix	Matrix
Numeric	7089	2710	3116	138
Alphanumeric	4296	1850	2355	93
Binary	2953	1018	1556	
Main Features	Large capacity, small size	Large capacity	Small printout size	High speed scan
Main Uses	All categories	All categories	All categories	Logistics
Standardization	AIM, ISO	AIM, ISO	AIM, ISO	AIM, ISO

(from www.denso-wave.com)

MaxiCode

Like PDF417, maxi code is open source and free to use.
It was released by UPS in the early 1990s.
It is traditionally used in the logistics, inventory and courier businesses. It uses dots rather than squares to encode its information. These dots are arranged hexagonally. It is very standardised and is therefore, not very suitable to be used in the wild!! The tourism sector is not a suitable arena for MaxiCodes.

Each one is usually 1in square and contains a circular pattern in the middle. Eight maxi codes can be chained to produce a single set of data. They can be read very quickly by dedicated maxicode scanners.

Portable Data File 417

PDF417 is not as popular as QR code but is used extensively in the transport, ID card and logistics industries. It is a stacked barcode system. Like all 2D coding systems, information is stored in the X and Y axis.

Some of the more interesting features of PDF417 are:
Linking. you can have a number of 2d codes which are linked to one another and which form a master code when they are scanned together... the codes do not have to be scanned in a linear fashion.
Public domain format. It is an open source format... anyone can use it royalty free.
Format
It contains many rows stacked on top of one another. There can be a maximum of 90 rows per code and a minimum of 3 rows. Each row contains the following features from left to righ.
Quiet Buffer. Like the QR code, you have to have a white space which contains no information and acts as a buffer between each code. The PDF417 scanner requires this to recognise the code.
Start/Stop Info. This tells the code scanner what type of code it is dealing with. PDF417 has is own unique start and stop code.
Left/Right Side Codeword. This contains information about each row. It tells the scanner which row it is in the sequence(max of 90 rows), it also tells the scanner what error correction scheme is in use.
The US postal service uses PDF417 codes and will accept any mail using them. They are also used by the airlines on their boarding passes.

DataMatrix

Data Matrix is the main competitor to the QR code for consumers/tourists and the general public. All popular smartphone applications that use 2d codes, generally support both the data matrix and the QR code formats.
It is another 2dim code format, and was developed around the same time as the QR code. It holds black square cells against a white background.
There are many small differences between the QR code and the data matrix codes, but for the purposes of this report it is not worth discussing them as they are largely irrelevant to

our needs, and either code could have been chosen over the other. Information to be encoded is similar to the QR information allowed, except that the QR code framework has better support for oriental character sets. This is because the QR code specification was developed by Denso in Japan.
Data Matrix is rectangular in shape, and each black square represent bits of information. Error correction is used and a finder and timing pattern are used to allow the scanner to interpret the code. The finder information is used for orientation(to allow 360deg scanning) and the timing pattern gives a count of the bits in the symbol.
Applications include all the uses of QR codes. Traditional uses of Data Matrix codes include the marking of electronic components because of the matrix effectiveness at encoding information in small spaces. It is superior to most other codes in this regard.

3.9.4 SPARQ Codes

SPARQCodes are like normal QR codes. They are simply a QR code with URI information embedded in them rather than the usual plain text information. Most code readers will recognise that the QR code is a SparQCode and will automatically open a browser after the code has been scanned.

Most applications that use SPARQCodes usually use the URL to jump to the link using the smartphones embedded Web Browser.

3.10 2D Code Experiment

There was one 2D code experiment conducted.

3.10.1 Using 2D Codes to Provide Tourist Information

Aim/Goals:
To test the viability of using 2D codes to provide tourists with information on shops, venues and other tourist attractions.

Data from Previous Experiments:
This experiment used the location data from Exp001.

Follow On Experiments:
None.

Methodology/Preparation/Planning:
5 locations were chosen from a busy shopping district in Galway city.

An aluminium harness was constructed to house both smartphones and to allow the use of the camera on both phones.

This ensured that both phones were tested under similar conditions.

Implementation/Execution:
1. Proceed to the first location.
2. Hold a specially constructed clipboard and place both phones on the clipboard.
3. Place a video camera onto the clipboard and record the output from each phone simultaneously.
4. Start the QR code readers on each phone.
5. Begin scanning the text and URI QR codes at each of the five locations.
7. Allow the camera to record the screen output from both phones.
8. Shut down both QRCode applications and stop and save the recorded video(s).

Retesting:
The experiment can be retested easily, as only one street is being used.

Hardware Used:
Apple iPhone 3GS
Samsung GalaxyS(GT-I9000)
Panasonic HD Camcorder(DMC-FS30).

Software Used:
iPhone operating system iOS 4.2.1 used throughout.
Samsung GalaxyS operating system Android 2.1-update1 used throughout.
A 3rd party Android(java) application to read 2D codes.
A 3rd party Apple(objective-C) application to read 2D codes.

Weather(observed 2011-03-01 14:20):
Weather during this experiment was generally, dry and sunny. Temperature of 9degC.

Changes to Plan During Testing:
none.

Validation/Evaluation:
By completing this experiment, it can be determined if using 2D codes is an effective way of providing information to tourists.

Calculations and Formulae Used:
None except simple Excel formulae.

Locations:
All locations were on Williamsgate St. and Shop St., Galway(city centre)..

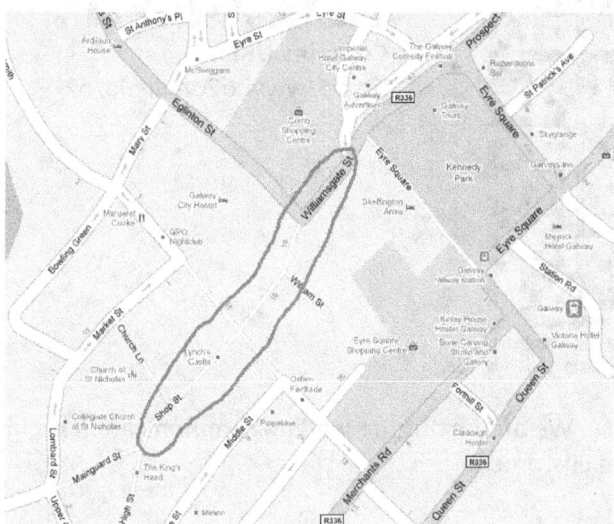

No	Name	Latitude	Longitude
1	O2 Shop	53.274350	-9.050687
2	Logues	53.274197	-9.050716
3	GBC	53.274182	-9.050888
4	EyreSq SC	53.274072	-9.051042
5	Monsoon	53.273994	-9.051117

There were 5 locations in all.

Analysis:
The smartphones being tested had to read and interpret each QR Code in a short enough time so as to keep a typical tourist interested. If the phones managed to read the barcodes in an average time of 10 seconds or less, then this is considered adequate for tourism use.

Chapter 3

Location 01 - outdoor:

(Actual size of QR Codes during the test)

O2 Shop

The following two QR Codes were used to test this location.
The information contained in the QR Codes are listed below the graphic.

Text QR Code

URL QR Code

Contains URL:
http://www.o2online.ie/o2

Contains Text:
Welcome to the O2 Shop on Eyre Square Galway. We are one of the leading communication providers in Ireland. We offer solutions to over 1.7 million customers.

Location 02 - outdoor:

Logues

The following two QR Codes were used to test this location.
The information contained in the QR Codes are listed below the graphic.

Text QR Code

URL QR Code

Contains URL:
http://www.logues.ie

Contains Text:
Logues footwear: We stock such well known brands as Clarks, K , Ecco, Grenson, Loake to mention but a few. We also specialize in Irish dancing shoes.

Location 03 - outdoor:

GBC

(Actual size of QR Codes during the test)

The following two QR Codes were used to test this location.
The information contained in the QR Codes are listed below the graphic.

Text QR Code

URL QR Code

Contains URL:
http://www.gbcgalway.com/

Contains Text:
Galway Bakery Company est. in 1936 have earned a reputation as a Galway Restaurant and Coffee shop for cuisine excellence. We provide two floors of fabulous cuisine catering for everyone's need at all times of the day.

Location 04 - outdoor:

Eyre Sq Shopping Ctr

The following two QR Codes were used to test this location.
The information contained in the QR Codes are listed below the graphic.

Text QR Code

URL QR Code

Contains URL:
http://www.eyresquarecentre.com/

Contains Text:
Eyre Square Centre is Galway City's liveliest and attractive meeting place incorporating over 60 local and national stores including Penneys, New Look, Champion Sports, Dunnes Stores, Burger King, Vero Moda & Mothercare.

Location 05 - outdoor:

Monsoon North

The following two QR Codes were used to test this location.
The information contained in the QR Codes are listed below the graphic.

(Actual size of QR Codes during the test)

Text QR Code

URL QR Code

Contains URL:
http://www.monsoon.co.uk/
fusion/ galway-monsoon-and-
accessorize/stry/galway/

Contains Text:
Monsoon has developed a strong brand with a highly distinctive identity. The intrinsic beauty of fabric, colour and technique so evident in the early sourcing of Monsoon's products from the Far East continues to exercise a strong influence.

Analysis of Results:
Total across all four tests conducted.

	No of Tests	Avg Char per Test	Avg Time to Recognise Code	Avg time per character
Android Plain Text	15	196.6	2.63	0.016
Android URL	16	40.67	0.97	0.027
iPhone Plain Text	15	196.6	3.9	0.024
iPhone URL	16	40.67	1.83	0.038

Analysis of all four tests carried out:
Samsung GalaxyS vs iPhone:
The Samsung detected ALL full text QR codes successfully producing a hit rate of 100%
The iPhone detected ALL full text QR codes successfully producing a hit rate of 100%
The Samsung required an average of 2.63 sec to detect full text QR codes.
The iPhone required an average of 3.90 sec to detect full text QR codes.
[The Samsung outperformed the iPhone by 1.27sec per code read]
The Samsung detected ALL URI QR codes successfully producing a hit rate of 100%
The iPhone detected ALL URI QR codes successfully producing a hit rate of 100%
The Samsung required an average of 0.97sec to detect URI QR codes.
The iPhone required an average of 1.83sec to detect URI QR codes.
[The Samsung outperformed the iPhone by 0.86sec per code read]

Conclusion:
During the four test where both phones were put head to head, the Samsung produced consistently better results.
However, both phones showed their ability to perform excellently.
Either phone is suitable for QR code reading for the tourism industry.

Results:

There were 62 QR codes scanned in total. 30 plain text QR Codes and 32 URI QR Codes.
The number of characters contained in each code was recorded.
The time was noted when each QR code was fully inside the scanning window and the time was noted when the phone fully recognised the QR code. In this way, the amount of time that the phone required to read the code was determined.

Test No	Location Name	QRCode Type	No of Characters	In Frame mm:ss	Recognised mm:ss	OS Type	Time to Recognise sec	Time to Recognise per character - sec
1	O2 Shop	Plain Text	156	00:25	00:41	Android	16	0.102564103
2	O2 Shop	Plain Text	156	00:43	00:54	iPhone	9	0.057692308
3	O2 Shop	Plain Text	156	01:32	01:33	Android	1	0.006410256
4	O2 Shop	Plain Text	156	01:35	01:45	iPhone	10	0.064102564
5	O2 Shop	URL	25	02:01	02:01	Android	0.5	0.02
6	O2 Shop	URL	25	02:01	02:01	iPhone	0.5	0.02
7	O2 Shop	URL	25	02:16	02:17	Android	1	0.04
8	O2 Shop	URL	25	02:16	02:17	iPhone	1	0.04
9	O2 Shop	Plain Text	156	02:56	03:02	Android	6	0.038461538
10	O2 Shop	Plain Text	156	03:03	03:18	iPhone	15	0.096153846
11	O2 Shop	URL	25	03:28	03:28	Android	0.5	0.02
12	O2 Shop	URL	25	03:28	03:28	iPhone	0.5	0.02
13	Logues	Plain Text	149	04:03	04:04	Android	1	0.006711409
14	Logues	Plain Text	149	04:03	04:03	iPhone	0.5	0.003355705
15	Logues	Plain Text	149	04:35	04:37	Android	2	0.013422819
16	Logues	Plain Text	149	04:38	04:53	iPhone	15	0.100671141
17	Logues	Plain Text	149	05:27	05:33	Android	6	0.040268456
18	Logues	Plain Text	149	05:24	05:25	iPhone	1	0.006711409
19	Logues	URL	20	05:47	05:47	Android	0.5	0.025
20	Logues	URL	20	05:46	05:46	iPhone	0.5	0.025
21	Logues	URL	20	05:58	05:58	Android	0.5	0.025
22	Logues	URL	20	05:58	05:58	iPhone	0.5	0.025
23	Logues	URL	20	06:09	06:10	Android	1	0.05
24	Logues	URL	20	06:09	06:10	iPhone	1	0.05
25	GBC	Plain Text	218	07:21	07:21	Android	0.5	0.002293578
26	GBC	Plain Text	218	07:22	07:22	iPhone	0.5	0.002293578
27	GBC	Plain Text	218	07:33	07:33	Android	0.5	0.002293578
28	GBC	Plain Text	218	07:35	07:35	iPhone	0.5	0.002293578
29	GBC	Plain Text	218	00:18	00:20	Android	2	0.009174312
30	GBC	Plain Text	218	00:20	00:21	iPhone	1	0.004587156
31	GBC	URL	25	00:35	00:35	Android	0.5	0.02
32	GBC	URL	25	00:35	00:35	iPhone	0.5	0.02
33	GBC	URL	25	01:22	01:22	Android	0.5	0.02
34	GBC	URL	25	01:21	01:21	iPhone	0.5	0.02
35	GBC	URL	25	01:33	01:33	Android	0.5	0.02
36	GBC	URL	25	01:32	01:32	iPhone	0.5	0.02
37	EyreSqSC	Plain Text	220	02:10	02:11	Android	1	0.004545455
38	EyreSqSC	Plain Text	220	02:12	02:13	iPhone	1	0.004545455
39	EyreSqSC	Plain Text	220	02:20	02:20	Android	0.5	0.002272727
40	EyreSqSC	Plain Text	220	02:22	02:22	iPhone	0.5	0.002272727
41	EyreSqSC	Plain Text	220	02:32	02:33	Android	1	0.004545455
42	EyreSqSC	Plain Text	220	02:34	02:34	iPhone	0.5	0.002272727
43	EyreSqSC	URL	32	02:42	02:42	Android	0.5	0.015625
44	EyreSqSC	URL	32	02:42	02:42	iPhone	0.5	0.015625
45	EyreSqSC	URL	32	02:51	02:52	Android	1	0.03125
46	EyreSqSC	URL	32	02:51	02:51	iPhone	0.5	0.015625
47	EyreSqSC	URL	32	02:59	03:00	Android	1	0.03125
48	EyreSqSC	URL	32	02:59	03:00	iPhone	1	0.03125
49	Monsoon	Plain Text	240	03:51	03:51	Android	0.5	0.002083333
50	Monsoon	Plain Text	240	03:53	03:56	iPhone	3	0.0125
51	Monsoon	Plain Text	240	04:04	04:05	Android	1	0.004166667
52	Monsoon	Plain Text	240	04:06	04:06	iPhone	0.5	0.002083333
53	Monsoon	Plain Text	240	04:17	04:17	Android	0.5	0.002083333
54	Monsoon	Plain Text	240	04:14	04:14	iPhone	0.5	0.002083333
55	Monsoon	URL	76	04:26	04:26	Android	0.5	0.006578947
56	Monsoon	URL	76	04:28	04:32	iPhone	4	0.052631579
57	Monsoon	URL	76	04:44	04:46	Android	2	0.026315789
58	Monsoon	URL	76	04:40	04:43	iPhone	3	0.039473684
59	Monsoon	URL	76	04:52	04:54	Android	2	0.026315789
60	Monsoon	URL	76	04:52	05:01	iPhone	9	0.118421053
61	Monsoon	URL	76	05:09	05:11	Android	2	0.026315789
62	Monsoon	URL	76	05:12	05:16	iPhone	4	0.052631579

Results:

Both the Samsung GalaxyS and the iPhone scanned a total of 15 plain text QR codes.
The smallest QR code contained 149 alpha-numeric characters and the largest contained 240.
The average size of QR code was 196.6 characters.

The Samsung GalaxyS(Android) device recorded a fastest time of 0.5seconds to read the QR codes and a slowest time of 16seconds.
The average time for the Android device was 2.63seconds.

The iPhone 3GS(iOS) device recorded a fastest time of 0.5seconds to read the QR codes and a slowest time of 15seconds.
The average time for the iOS device was 3.90seconds.

	Test No	Location Name	QRCode Type	No of Characters	In Frame mm:ss	Recognised mm:ss	OS Type	Time to Recognise sec	Time to Recognise per character - sec
1	1	O2 Shop	Plain Text	156	00:25	00:41	Android	16	0.102564103
2	3	O2 Shop	Plain Text	156	01:32	01:33	Android	1	0.006410256
3	9	O2 Shop	Plain Text	156	02:56	03:02	Android	6	0.038461538
4	13	Logues	Plain Text	149	04:03	04:04	Android	1	0.006711409
5	15	Logues	Plain Text	149	04:35	04:37	Android	2	0.013422819
6	17	Logues	Plain Text	149	05:27	05:33	Android	6	0.040268456
7	25	GBC	Plain Text	218	07:21	07:21	Android	0.5	0.002293578
8	27	GBC	Plain Text	218	07:33	07:33	Android	0.5	0.002293578
9	29	GBC	Plain Text	218	00:18	00:20	Android	2	0.009174312
10	37	EyreSqSC	Plain Text	220	02:10	02:11	Android	1	0.004545455
11	39	EyreSqSC	Plain Text	220	02:20	02:20	Android	0.5	0.002272727
12	41	EyreSqSC	Plain Text	220	02:32	02:33	Android	1	0.004545455
13	49	Monsoon	Plain Text	240	03:51	03:51	Android	0.5	0.002083333
14	51	Monsoon	Plain Text	240	04:04	04:05	Android	1	0.004166667
15	53	Monsoon	Plain Text	240	04:17	04:17	Android	0.5	0.002083333

	Test No	Location Name	QRCode Type	No of Characters	In Frame mm:ss	Recognised mm:ss	OS Type	Time to Recognise sec	Time to Recognise per character - sec
1	2	O2 Shop	Plain Text	156	00:43	00:54	iPhone	9	0.057692308
2	4	O2 Shop	Plain Text	156	01:35	01:45	iPhone	10	0.064102564
3	10	O2 Shop	Plain Text	156	03:03	03:18	iPhone	15	0.096153846
4	14	Logues	Plain Text	149	04:03	04:03	iPhone	0.5	0.003355705
5	16	Logues	Plain Text	149	04:38	04:53	iPhone	15	0.100671141
6	18	Logues	Plain Text	149	05:24	05:25	iPhone	1	0.006711409
7	26	GBC	Plain Text	218	07:22	07:22	iPhone	0.5	0.002293578
8	28	GBC	Plain Text	218	07:35	07:35	iPhone	0.5	0.002293578
9	30	GBC	Plain Text	218	00:20	00:21	iPhone	1	0.004587156
10	38	EyreSqSC	Plain Text	220	02:12	02:13	iPhone	1	0.004545455
11	40	EyreSqSC	Plain Text	220	02:22	02:22	iPhone	0.5	0.002272727
12	42	EyreSqSC	Plain Text	220	02:34	02:34	iPhone	0.5	0.002272727
13	50	Monsoon	Plain Text	240	03:53	03:56	iPhone	3	0.0125
14	52	Monsoon	Plain Text	240	04:06	04:06	iPhone	0.5	0.002083333
15	54	Monsoon	Plain Text	240	04:14	04:14	iPhone	0.5	0.002083333

Both devices performed excellently at reading full text QR Codes and are very capable for performing 2D code reading for the tourism market.

The Android device marginally out performed the iOS device by an average of 1.27 sec per code read.

The online resource at http://www.irishapps.org/smartlla.html
contains all the photo and video files used to capture the above information and the information on the previous page.

Results:

Both the Samsung GalaxyS and the iPhone scanned a total of 16 URI QR codes.
The smallest QR code contained 20 alpha-numeric characters and the largest contained 76.
The average size of QR code was 40.67 characters.

The Samsung GalaxyS(Android) device recorded a fastest time of 0.5seconds to read the QR codes and a slowest time of 2seconds.
The average time for the Android device was 0.97seconds.

The iPhone 3GS(iOS) device recorded a fastest time of 0.5seconds to read the QR codes and a slowest time of 9seconds.
The average time for the iOS device was 1.83seconds.

Test No		Location Name	QRCode Type	No of Characters	In Frame mm:ss	Recognised mm:ss	OS Type	Time to Recognise sec	Time to Recognise per character - sec
1	5	O2 Shop	URL	25	02:01	02:01	Android	0.5	0.02
2	7	O2 Shop	URL	25	02:16	02:17	Android	1	0.04
3	11	O2 Shop	URL	25	03:28	03:28	Android	0.5	0.02
4	19	Logues	URL	20	05:47	05:47	Android	0.5	0.025
5	21	Logues	URL	20	05:58	05:58	Android	0.5	0.025
6	23	Logues	URL	20	06:09	06:10	Android	1	0.05
7	31	GBC	URL	25	00:35	00:35	Android	0.5	0.02
8	33	GBC	URL	25	01:22	01:22	Android	0.5	0.02
9	35	GBC	URL	25	01:33	01:33	Android	0.5	0.02
10	43	EyreSqSC	URL	32	02:42	02:42	Android	0.5	0.015625
11	45	EyreSqSC	URL	32	02:51	02:52	Android	1	0.03125
12	47	EyreSqSC	URL	32	02:59	03:00	Android	1	0.03125
13	55	Monsoon	URL	76	04:26	04:26	Android	0.5	0.006578947
14	57	Monsoon	URL	76	04:44	04:46	Android	2	0.026315789
15	59	Monsoon	URL	76	04:52	04:54	Android	2	0.026315789
16	61	Monsoon	URL	76	05:09	05:11	Android	2	0.026315789

Test No		Location Name	QRCode Type	No of Characters	In Frame mm:ss	Recognised mm:ss	OS Type	Time to Recognise sec	Time to Recognise per character - sec
1	6	O2 Shop	URL	25	02:01	02:01	iPhone	0.5	0.02
2	8	O2 Shop	URL	25	02:16	02:17	iPhone	1	0.04
3	12	O2 Shop	URL	25	03:28	03:28	iPhone	0.5	0.02
4	20	Logues	URL	20	05:46	05:46	iPhone	0.5	0.025
5	22	Logues	URL	20	05:58	05:58	iPhone	0.5	0.025
6	24	Logues	URL	20	06:09	06:10	iPhone	1	0.05
7	32	GBC	URL	25	00:35	00:35	iPhone	0.5	0.02
8	34	GBC	URL	25	01:21	01:21	iPhone	0.5	0.02
9	36	GBC	URL	25	01:32	01:32	iPhone	0.5	0.02
10	44	EyreSqSC	URL	32	02:42	02:42	iPhone	0.5	0.015625
11	46	EyreSqSC	URL	32	02:51	02:51	iPhone	0.5	0.015625
12	48	EyreSqSC	URL	32	02:59	03:00	iPhone	1	0.03125
13	56	Monsoon	URL	76	04:28	04:32	iPhone	4	0.052631579
14	58	Monsoon	URL	76	04:40	04:43	iPhone	3	0.039473684
15	60	Monsoon	URL	76	04:52	05:01	iPhone	9	0.118421053
16	62	Monsoon	URL	76	05:12	05:16	iPhone	4	0.052631579

Both devices performed excellently at reading URI QR Codes and are very capable for performing 2D code reading for the tourism market.

The Android device again marginally out performed the iOS device by an average of 0.86sec per code read.

The online resource at http://www.irishapps.org/smartlla.html
contains all the photo and video files used to capture the above information.

3.11 Near Field Communications[NFC]

Near field communication, or NFC, is currently(March 2011) available on the newest smartphones. It is available on the Nexus S and will be available on the iPhone5. See Appendix D1 for a full listing. It is an exciting new development in the close range communications field. It's primary use will be as a replacement to credit cards if the necessary technology and technical hurdles can be overcome.
It operates in a range of 3cm or less and at a frequency of 13.56 MHz at data rates from 100 to 850 kilobits per sec. NFC is similar to Bluetooth and can be considered to be an extension of bluetooth technology. With NFC there is always a target which is often not powered directly and an initiator which actively seeks out the target or multiple targets. The master generates an RF field which powers the target and allows collection of electronic data from the target. Communication between two powered devices is also possible.

NFC can be considered a good alternative(or update) of RFID tagging.

NFC can also be used to setup connections between phones. For example, it can be used to initiate bluetooth communication between devices and pair them without going through the laborious procedure of authorizing two bluetooth devices.

NFC can be considered a good alternative or complement to using 2D codes.
Instead of having a QR code containing the required information, the user could touch his NFC enabled smartphone off a NFC tag and get the information that way, making it slightly quicker than pointing the camera and scanning a QR code or other 2d code.

3.12 Augmented Reality

Augmented reality is a very exciting and eye catching way to present data about a users surroundings, by superimposing images, text and sounds over the physical space that the user is occupying or surveying.

With augmented-reality smartphone apps, informative graphics appear on the screen as you point your camera at different items. For example, when you move your camera to display a city street, the phone will overlay a description of each shop onto the cameras screen display as it moves over the shop.

Examples of Augmented Reality Apps are:

Layar:
Layar is a mobile app for discovering information about the world around you. Layar displays digital information called "layers" into your smartphone's field of vision.

WikiTube:
Wikitude will overlay the camera's display and the objects you look at with additional interactive content and information

The camera view is overlaid with data or links that contain the location metadata relating to that attraction or premises.

4. Localisation and Internationalisation for Tourism

For the purposes of this chapter only, when reference is made to a 'language' it refers to a human spoken/written language and not to a software programming language.

Localisation refers to the actions that must be undertaken to ensure that a smartphone application is suitable for each region in which it will be distributed and that it is suitable for end users from different regions and cultures.

The area of localisation is a complex one and an entire book could be devoted to discussing the various methods and technical hurdles associated with this area, such as computer encoded text and alphabets, numerals, writing direction, number formats, date formats, time zones, regulatory compliance etc..
There are many different levels of localisation with different titles. For example, the following titles all refer to localisation in different ways and with different meanings: Localised(L10n), Multilingualised(m17n), Internationalized(i18n) etc.

For the purposes of this book we will focus on the written and spoken language differences from region to region. We will discuss in detail how to prepare n tourist application so that it displays the correct language for the user.
As a case study in localisation and language translation, the tourism centre in Bunratty Castle was used. During the sections that follow, references are made to the Bunratty Tourism Centre in Co. Clare. See section 1.3.3 for details.

4.1 Manual Language Translation

The historical method, and still the most popular amongst traditional software applications is manual language translation.
During this localisation approach, the entire contents of the software application are manually translated using language experts and then this translated content is substituted for the original content of the application.
This substitution is done in various ways.

The simplest method is to create and maintain a separate version of the software application for each region. For example, if your application was provided in English, Italian, Chinese, Spanish and Polish, then you would create five distinct applications.
Although this is the most straight forward method, it is also the least desirable from the point of view of application maintenance, upgrading and bug fixing. It is impractical to maintain multiple versions of the same software application project, as any change to one version means the same change would have to be made to all language versions of the same application.

To avoid this situation, most smartphone operating systems provide a mechanism to allow the developer to create one version of the software that will allow substitution of the manually translated content in an automatic manner. It is beyond the scope of this book to discuss all the methods in use, however, we will discuss the method used my the main two operating systems, iOS and Android.

To generalise, the following practice is used by most operating systems/development languages:
The original text of the application and all the translated text(s) are placed into resource strings which are accessed by the program during runtime. All of these libraries are shipped with the application(or optionally downloaded from a server) and the appropriate library is accessed depending on which language the end user chooses in the Settings section of the application.
This approach works well in minimising the changes that have to be made to an application during bug-fixing and upgrading. For example, if there is a problem with a calculation algorithm or the colour of the UI needs to be changed, then only one change needs to be made to the source code. Of course, if a user message needs to be altered, then ALL the language resource files will have to be modified.

4.2 Automatic Language Translation

Automatic language translation is a newer approach to localisation.
This involves the 'on-the-fly' automatic translation of the native text of an application into a different language. This translation is managed by internal classes or by using 3rd party APIs such as Google's Translate set of APIs.
During the Bunratty case study, a test application was written in Android to test out the effectiveness of this approach. This application is discussed later in this chapter.
In order to use most 3rd party APIs, the smartphone must maintain a constant connection to the internet, in order to submit the text for translation and to receive the translated text back from the 3rd party server.

This approach has it advantages and disadvantages over traditional Manual translation methods.
The big advantage is that the developer does not have to employ an army of expert linguists in order to translate all the text of an application. This is a big cost saving for the developer. Another advantage is that the developer does not have to maintain a large set of language resource files in order to cater for each language. A third advantage is that the developer can cater for almost every common language spoken(depending on the API used of course). The Google API caters for 50 languages including Irish.

The big disadvantage is that the automatic APIs will never produce a perfect translation, and sometimes will return nothing but gibberish. Again, this is totally dependent of the quality of the API used. However, Google's API must be considered one of the best available, and even at it's best, it is always obvious that the translated text was not translated by a native speaker.
There are numerous examples of this provided later during the discussion of the Bunratty site.

Another disadvantage, is that the developer must allow for a slight lag during the translation process. The speed of the translation is dependent on the amount of text being translated, the speed of the internet connection and the speed of the 3rd party server that is carrying out the translation.
Also, the developer must add additional functionality to their software to incorporate the API, and to carry out translations for every string on the user interface and for every text file and piece of information presented to the end user.

4.3 Manual Translation using AndroidOS

Android makes things very easy for the developer when designing an application to operate in multiple regions or for end users with different spoken languages.

Provided the developer follows standard Android procedures when writing an application, it can very easily be converted into a multi-lingual application, even if it was not originally designed to do so.

Usually when multiple languages are not an issue and the developer doesn't envision having to internationalize the application, then you would place the files in the `res/values/strings.xml` location.
To support both English and other languages, you would create multiple folders, `res/values-en` and `res/values-XX`, where the value after the hyphen is the ISO 639-13 two-letter code for the language you want. Your English-language strings would go in **res/values-en/strings.xml** and the foreign language ones in **res/values-XX/strings.xml**. Android will choose the proper file based on the user's device settings.

For example, if you plan to use five languages(as we have done later in this chapter) then you would have the following resource files:
Replace the default `res/values/strings.xml` with:

`res/values-en/strings.xml`	English
`res/values-lt/strings.xml`	Lithuanian
`res/values-ga/strings.xml`	Irish
`res/values-pl/strings.xml`	Polish
`res/values-es/strings.xml`	Spanish
`res/values-sv/strings.xml`	Swedish

The software developer does not need to provide a special settings screen and does not need to build any additional logic into the application.

The same routine is followed for all the different resources used by your application within the Android development environment. For different Menus for different countries, use the same convention…
Replace the `res/menu/abcde.xml` with:

`res/menu-en/abcde.xml`	English
`res/menu-lt/abcde.xml`	Lithuanian
`res/menu-ga/abcde.xml`	Irish
`res/menu-pl/abcde.xml`	Polish
`res/menu-es/abcde.xml`	Spanish
`res/menu-sv/abcde.xml`	Swedish

4.4 Manual Translation using iOS

Apple also provide a mechanism for localising applications written in iOS.
The same technique is used in the sense that there are separate files for each spoken language. However, the iOS approach is more complicated and laborious than the Android approach.

Nib files(the GUI), icons and images, and static text can all be localised(same as Android).

In a non-localised application, all the Resources reside in the `.app` directory.
In a localised application, Xcode moves all relevant resources into a separate new directory for each new language supported by your application.
In our example we would have:

`en.lproj`	English
`lt.lproj`	Lithuanian
`ga.lproj`	Irish
`pl.lproj`	Polish
`es.lproj`	Spanish
`sv.lproj`	Swedish

You must inform Xcode that you wish to localise the application. It will not automatically use the localised directories.
To do this you must go into the Properties section of each file that you wish to localise and choose 'Make File Localizable' and follow some additional minor steps for each language you wish to use.

The procedure for localising the strings in an application is more cumbersome. You need to run a macro on the original string file in order to generate the new translated string file… you then take this new string file, do the translation on it and copy it back into the application.

Like the Android system, the iPhone will choose the correct languages and settings, based on the Spoken language and locale settings that are on the iPhone OS. No additional coding or setup is required in order to ascertain what language the end user wishes to use.

4.5 Bunratty Case Study

The following 18 pages contain a case study to demonstrate the differences between automatic and manual translation for the purposes of localising a tourism based smartphone application.

The study involved taking an existing native English online mobile tourist guide and then translating it into a number of languages using Manual and Automatic methods.
A comparison was then made of the results of both translation methods.

The content for translation was taken from an existing Symbian/HTML tourist guide written several years ago for the Bunratty Castle Folk Park in Co. Clare. The tourist guide was written by MobiNode in Limerick and at the time targeted the Nokia N95 and other similar mobile phones.

A custom Android based translation application was written for the Samsung GalaxyS smartphone and this was used to automatically translate the native English content using the Google Translation API.
(see Appendix A5 for the complete source code).

The details of the Android application are discussed on the following page.
The pages that follow that, demonstrate the results of doing a Manual translation using a number of expert translators and the results of doing the same translations using the Google Translation API.

The results of both methods are then compared, in order to ascertain the effectiveness and accuracy of using the Automatic method of language translation.

4.5.1 The 'Bunratty Translate' Software App

In order to test the effectiveness of the Google Translate API, a software application was written for the Samsung GalaxyS device(Android) which took some of the text from the Bunratty example and translated it into the following languages: Lithuanian, Irish, Polish, Spanish and Swedish. This translation was then examined and then translated back to english to see if the API had done a good job.

The following steps had to be taken within Android, to allow the use of the Google API.
1. Permission had to be granted to establish an internet connection
```
<uses-perm android:name="android.permission.INTERNET"/>
```
2. A spinner class was used to allow the user to choose which language to pick(via on array).
```xml
<?xml version="1.0" encoding="utf-8"?>
    <resources>
        <array name="languages">
            <item>Lithuanian (lt)</item>
            <item>Irish (ie)</item>
            <item>Polish (pl)</item>
            <item>Spanish (es)</item>
            <item>Swedish (sv)</item>
        </array>
    </resources>
```
3. Call the Google API
```
String q = URLEncoder.encode(original, "UTF-8" );
URL url = new URL("http://ajax.googleapis.com/
    ajax/services/language/translate"+"?v=1.0"+"&q=
    "+ques+"&langpair=" + to-from+"%7C"+rom-to);
con = (HttpURLConnection) url.openConnection();
```

The following results were returned for a sample of each language:

(See following six pages for the breakdown).

	% Error Words	% Error Sentences
Lithuanian	9.52	22.22
Irish	6.35	11.11
Polish	6.35	11.11
Spanish	1.59	0
Swedish	2.38	0

From the results, we can conclude that the automatic translation is not good enough in any language, to equal the effect of getting a human(native speaker) to translate the same material.
Spanish came very close to achieving this, and definitely matched what non-native human speaking translators could achieve.

However, there are an increasing number of native english websites, that use Google APIs or similar APIs to carry out their translation and localisation so it is becoming much more acceptable to have less than perfect translations in applications in general.

Using APIs instead of human translators is definitely a viable option for smaller budget tourism applications.

4.5.2 Translate Software App Results
Overall Results:

Lithuanian	No of words	Words Translated InCorrectly	Grammer mistakes	Unintelligible
Sentence 1	8	1	0	No
Sentence 2	13	1	1	No
Sentence 3	17	2	1	No
Sentence 4	8	0	1	No
Sentence 5	13	3	2	Yes
Sentence 6	14	0	0	No
Sentence 7	28	1	2	No
Sentence 8	12	2	1	No
Sentence 9	13	2	2	Yes

Results	
No of words	126
Words Translated InCorrectly	12
% Error Words	9.52
No of Sentences	9
Grammer Mistakes	10
Unintelligible Sentences	2
% Error Sentences	22.22

Irish	No of words	Words Translated InCorrectly	Grammer mistakes	Unintelligible
Sentence 1	8	2	2	Yes
Sentence 2	13	1	1	No
Sentence 3	17	1	0	No
Sentence 4	8	0	1	No
Sentence 5	13	0	0	No
Sentence 6	14	0	0	No
Sentence 7	28	3	1	No
Sentence 8	12	1	0	No
Sentence 9	13	0	1	No

Results	
No of words	126
Words Translated InCorrectly	8
% Error Words	6.35
No of Sentences	9
Grammer Mistakes	6
Unintelligible Sentences	1
% Error Sentences	11.11

Polish	No of words	Words Translated InCorrectly	Grammer mistakes	Unintelligible
Sentence 1	8	3	1	Yes
Sentence 2	13	1	1	No
Sentence 3	17	0	0	No
Sentence 4	8	0	0	No
Sentence 5	13	1	0	No
Sentence 6	14	0	0	No
Sentence 7	28	0	0	No
Sentence 8	12	2	1	No
Sentence 9	13	1	1	No

Results	
No of words	126
Words Translated InCorrectly	8
% Error Words	6.35
No of Sentences	9
Grammer Mistakes	4
Unintelligible Sentences	1
% Error Sentences	11.11

Spanish	No of words	Words Translated InCorrectly	Grammer mistakes	Unintelligible
Sentence 1	8	1	0	No
Sentence 2	13	0	1	No
Sentence 3	17	0	0	No
Sentence 4	8	0	0	No
Sentence 5	13	0	0	No
Sentence 6	14	0	0	No
Sentence 7	28	0	0	No
Sentence 8	12	0	1	No
Sentence 9	13	1	0	No

Results	
No of words	126
Words Translated InCorrectly	2
% Error Words	1.59
No of Sentences	9
Grammer Mistakes	2
Unintelligible Sentences	0
% Error Sentences	0.00

Swedish	No of words	Words Translated InCorrectly	Grammer mistakes	Unintelligible
Sentence 1	8	0	0	No
Sentence 2	13	1	0	No
Sentence 3	17	1	0	No
Sentence 4	8	0	0	No
Sentence 5	13	0	0	No
Sentence 6	14	0	0	No
Sentence 7	28	1	1	No
Sentence 8	12	0	0	No
Sentence 9	13	0	0	No

Results	
No of words	126
Words Translated InCorrectly	3
% Error Words	2.38
No of Sentences	9
Grammer Mistakes	1
Unintelligible Sentences	0
% Error Sentences	0.00

4.5.3 Manual vs Auto Translation Results
Lithuanian

	Lithuanian	Sentence from User Interface
1	Original English	Bunratty is one of Ireland's premier visitor attractions.
	Expert Translation	Bunratty yra viena iš labiausiai lankomų turistų vietų.
	API Translation	Bunratty yra vienas iš Airijos premjeras turistų lankomų vietų.
	API Translated Back	Bunratty is one of Ireland's premier tourist attractions.
2	Original English	Let us help you explore the historic Castle and the vibrant Folk Park.
	Expert Translation	Mes norime Jums padėti geriau pažinti šią istorinę pilį ir gyvybingą folklorinį parką.
	API Translation	Leiskite mums padėti Jums ištirti istorinę pilį ir energingas liaudies parke.
	API Translated Back	Let us help you explore the historic Castle and Folk Park, energetic.
3	Original English	May we suggest that you first visit Belvoir School House on Main Street in the Folk Park.
	Expert Translation	Pirmiausia mes siūlome aplankyti Belvoiro Mokyklą, esančią Pagrindinėje Folkloro parko gatvėje
	API Translation	Gegužės mes rekomenduojame, kad jūs pirmojo vizito Belvoir School House on Main Street liaudies parke.
	API Translated Back	May we suggest that you first visit Belvoir School House on Main Street People's Park.
4	Original English	The School House is on the Main Street. As you enter the park, turn right, head up hill and keep left. The School is the first building on your left as you enter Main Street.
	Expert Translation	Mokyklą rasite Pagrindinėje gatvėje (Main street). Atvykę į parką, pasukite į dešinę ir pakilkite į kalną, laikydamiesi kairiosios pusės. Mokykla bus pirmasis pastatas kairėje pusėje, kai tik atsidursite Pagrindinėje gatvėje.
	API Translation	School House yra pagrindinėje gatvėje. Kaip įvesti parkas, pasukite į dešinę, galva ant kalno ir laikykitės kairės. Mokykla yra pirmasis pastatas kairėje pusėje, kaip įvesti Main Street.
	API Translated Back	School House is on the main street. How to enter the park, turn right and head onto the hill and keep left. The school is the first building on the left hand side as you enter Main Street.
5	Original English	The school, built originally at Belvoir in East Clare in the early 19th century, is typical of many to be found all over the country at this time.
	Expert Translation	Ši mokykla buvo pastatyta Belvoiro miestelyje, Rytinėje Clare apskrities pusėje, XIX amžiaus pradžioje ir yra labai panaši į daugelį to laikmečio šalies mokyklų.
	API Translation	mokyklos, pastatytas iš pradžių ne Belvoir Rytų Clare 19 amžiaus pradžioje, yra būdingas daugeliui galima rasti visame šiuo metu šalyje.
	API Translated Back	School, originally built at Belvoir in East Clare in the early 19th century, is typical of many can be found all over the country at present.
6	Original English	Typically 30-40 children would have studied in each of the two classrooms. They would have copied out their lessons on slate using sticks of chalk.
	Expert Translation	Kiekvienoje iš dviejų mokyklos klasių mokėsi vidutiniškai apie 30-40 mokinių. Užrašams buvo naudojama lenta ir kreida.
	API Translation	Paprastai 30-40 vaikų būtų tiriamas kiekvienos iš dviejų kabinetų. Jie būtų nukopijuoti iš jų pamokos šiferis naudojant lazdelės kreida.
	API Translated Back	Usually 30 to 40 children will be studied in each of the two classrooms. They are copied from the lessons of their slate with chalk sticks.

Irish

	Irish	Sentence from User Interface
1	Original English	Bunratty is one of Ireland's premier visitor attractions.
	Expert Translation	Ta Bunratty ar cheann dena h-aiteanna turasoireachta is iomraiti cailiula in Eirinn.
	API Translation	Tá Bun Raite ar cheann de na nithe na hÉireann do chuairteoirí premier.
	API Translated Back	Bunratty is one of the objects of Ireland's premier visitor.
2	Original English	Let us help you explore the historic Castle and the vibrant Folk Park.
	Expert Translation	Cabhraimis leat aithne a chur ar an chaislean stairiuil agus ar an sraidbhaile beomhar.
	API Translation	Lig linn cabhrú leat iniúchadh a dhéanamh ar an gCaisleán stairiúil agus Daonpháirc bríomhar.
	API Translated Back	Let us help you explore the historic Castle and Folk lively.
3	Original English	May we suggest that you first visit Belvoir School House on Main Street in the Folk Park.
	Expert Translation	Molaimis cuairt ar Theach Scoil Bhelvoir ar an bpriomhshraid mar thus.
	API Translation	Bealtaine molaimid duit chéad chuairt Belvoir Theach na Scoile ar an bPríomhshráid sa Daonpháirc.
	API Translated Back	May we suggest you first visit Belvoir School House on Main Street in Folk.
4	Original English	The School House is on the Main Street. As you enter the park, turn right, head up hill and keep left. The School is the first building on your left as you enter Main Street.
	Expert Translation	Ta Teach Scoil Bhelvoir suite ar an bpriomhshraid.ar shroichint an ionaid teigh ar dheis,suas an mhallaigh agus ta an Scoil ar chle agus tu tagtha go dti an Priomhshraid.
	API Translation	Is é an Teach Scoile ar an tSráid Mhór. Réir mar a théann tú isteach ar an pháirc, cas ar dheis, cnoc ceann suas agus a choinneáil ar chlé. Is é an Scoil an chéad fhoirgneamh ar do chlé mar a théann tú isteach tSráid Mhór.
	API Translated Back	The School House on Main Street. As you enter the park, turn right, head up hill and keep left. School is the first building on your left as you enter Main Street.
5	Original English	The school, built originally at Belvoir in East Clare in the early 19th century, is typical of many to be found all over the country at this time.
	Expert Translation	Togadh an Scoil seo ag tus an naou cead deag i mBelvoir,in Oirthear Contae an Chlair.Togadh macasamhail na scoile seo ag an am sin ar fud na tire.
	API Translation	Tá an scoil, a tógadh ar dtús ag Belvoir in Oirthear an Chláir sa 19ú céad, is gnách go leor le fáil ar fud na tíre ag an am seo.
	API Translated Back	The school, originally built at Belvoir in East Clare in the 19th century, many commonly available throughout the country at this time.
6	Original English	Typically 30-40 children would have studied in each of the two classrooms. They would have copied out their lessons on slate using sticks of chalk.
	Expert Translation	Ba ghnath go mbiodh idir 30 agus 40 scolaire ag foghlaim I ngach seomra den da sheomra.Scriobhaidis a gcuid ceachtanna ar shlata ag baint usaide as cailc.
	API Translation	De ghnáth, bheadh 30-40 leanaí a bhfuil staidéar déanta i ngach ceann den dá sheomra ranga. Bheadh siad a gcuid ceachtanna a chóipeáil ar slinn ag baint úsáide as na maidí cailce.
	API Translated Back	Typically, 30-40 children would have studied in each of their classrooms. They would be copying their lessons on slate by using sticks of chalk.

Chapter 4

Polish

	Polish	Sentence from User Interface
1	Original English	**Bunratty is one of Ireland's premier visitor attractions.**
	Expert Translation	Bunratty jest jedną z głównych Irlandzkich atrakcji turystycznych
	API Translation	Bunratty jest jedną z atrakcji premier Irlandii gości.
	API Translated Back	Bunratty is one of the attractions of Ireland's premier hotel.
2	Original English	**Let us help you explore the historic Castle and the vibrant Folk Park.**
	Expert Translation	Odkryjmy razem historyczny zamek oraz park ludowy
	API Translation	Pozwól nam pomóc zbadać historycznym Zamku oraz tętniącej życiem Folk Park.
	API Translated Back	Let us help you explore the historic Castle and Folk Park lively.
3	Original English	**May we suggest that you first visit Belvoir School House on Main Street in the Folk Park.**
	Expert Translation	Proponujemy Państwu zwiedzenie budynku szkoły „Belvior", mieszczącego się przy głównej ulicy w parku ludowym.
	API Translation	Maja sugerujemy pierwsza wizyta Belvoir School House na Main Street w Folk Park.
	API Translated Back	May we suggest you first visit Belvoir School House on Main Street in the Folk Park.
4	Original English	**The School House is on the Main Street. As you enter the park, turn right, head up hill and keep left. The School is the first building on your left as you enter Main Street.**
	Expert Translation	Szkoła znajduje się przy głównej drodze kiedy dojadą państwo do parku ludowego, należy skręcić w prawo a następnie na górce kierować się w lewo. Szkoła mieści się po lewej stronie przy głównej drodze.
	API Translation	House School znajduje się na Main Street. Jak wejść do parku, skręcić w prawo, pod górę głowy i trzymać się lewej strony. Szkoła to pierwszy budynek po lewej stronie jak wchodzisz Main Street.
	API Translated Back	School House is located on Main Street. As you enter the park, turn right at the top of the head and keep left. The school is the first building on the left as you enter Main Street.
5	Original English	**The school, built originally at Belvoir in East Clare in the early 19th century, is typical of many to be found all over the country at this time.**
	Expert Translation	Szkoła ta, wybudowana pierwotnie w zachodniej części hrabstwa clare na początku XIX wieku. Jest jednym z wielu odkryć typowych dla tejże epoki.
	API Translation	W szkole, zbudowany pierwotnie w Belvoir w East Clare w początku 19 wieku, jest typowa dla wielu można znaleźć w całym kraju w tym czasie.
	API Translated Back	The school was originally built in Belvoir in East Clare in the early 19th century, is typical of many can be found throughout the country at that time.
6	Original English	**Typically 30-40 children would have studied in each of the two classrooms. They would have copied out their lessons on slate using sticks of chalk.**
	Expert Translation	Do każdej z dwóch salek szkolnych uczęszczało zazwyczaj od 30 do 40 uczniów. Wszelkie notatki były sporządzane przez uczniów na tabliczkach za pomocą kredy
	API Translation	Zwykle 30-40 dzieci będą musiały studiował w każdej z dwóch klas. Będą musieli kopiować swoje lekcje na łupku za pomocą laski kredy.
	API Translated Back	Usually 1930 to 1940 children will have studied in each of the two classes. They will have to copy their lessons on slate with chalk sticks.

Spanish

	Spanish	Sentence from User Interface
1	Original English	**Bunratty is one of Ireland's premier visitor attractions.**
	Expert Translation	Bunratty is una de las primeras Atracciones turisticas en Irlanda.
	API Translation	Bunratty es una de las atracciones turísticas de Irlanda.
	API Translated Back	Bunratty is one of the attractions of Ireland.
2	Original English	**Let us help you explore the historic Castle and the vibrant Folk Park.**
	Expert Translation	Permitanos ayudarlo a explorar El Castillo Historico y el vibrante Parque del Pueblo
	API Translation	Vamos a ayudarle a explorar el histórico Castillo y la vibrante Folk Park.
	API Translated Back	Let us help you explore the historic Castle and Folk Park's vibrant.
3	Original English	**May we suggest that you first visit Belvoir School House on Main Street in the Folk Park.**
	Expert Translation	Nos permite sugerirle que su primera visita sea A la casa escuela Belvoir en la Calle principal del Parque del Pueblo
	API Translation	Le sugerimos que primero visite Belvoir School House en Main Street, en el Parque del Pueblo.
	API Translated Back	We suggest you first visit Belvoir School House on Main Street in the Village Park.
4	Original English	**The School House is on the Main Street. As you enter the park, turn right, head up hill and keep left. The School is the first building on your left as you enter Main Street.**
	Expert Translation	La Casa Escuela esta en la Calle principal. Al entrar al parque, gire a la derecha, siga por la colina y mantenga la izquierda. La escuela es el primer edificio a su izquierda al entrar a la calle principal.
	API Translation	La Casa de la escuela está en la calle principal. Al entrar en el parque, girar a la derecha, la cabeza encima de la colina y manténgase a la izquierda. La escuela es el primer edificio a su izquierda al entrar en la calle principal.
	API Translated Back	The School House is on Main Street. Upon entering the park, turn right, head up the hill and keep left. The school is the first building on your left as you enter the main street.
5	Original English	**The school, built originally at Belvoir in East Clare in the early 19th century, is typical of many to be found all over the country at this time.**
	Expert Translation	Esta escuela, originalmente construida en East Clare a inicios del siglo 19, es comun para muchos ser encontrada en todo el país en este tiempo.
	API Translation	La escuela, construida originalmente en Belvoir en el este de Clara en el siglo 19, es típico de muchos que se encuentran en todo el país en este momento.
	API Translated Back	The school, originally built in Belvoir in East Clare in the 19 th century, is typical of many found throughout the country at this time.
6	Original English	**Typically 30-40 children would have studied in each of the two classrooms. They would have copied out their lessons on slate using sticks of chalk.**
	Expert Translation	Comunmente de 30 a 40 ninos han Estudiado en cada una de las dos Aulas de clase. Ellos habran Copiado sus lecciones en pizarra Usando pedazos de tizza.
	API Translation	Por lo general 30 a 40 niños que han estudiado en cada uno de los dos salones de clase. Ellos han copiado sus lecciones en la pizarra utilizando palos de tiza.
	API Translated Back	Usually 30 to 40 children who have studied in each of the two classrooms. They have copied their lessons on the blackboard using chalk sticks.

Swedish

	Swedish	Sentence from User Interface
1	Original English	Bunratty is one of Ireland's premier visitor attractions.
	Expert Translation	Bunratty är en av Irlands främsta besöksattraktioner.
	API Translation	Bunratty är en av Irlands främsta sevärdheter.
	API Translated Back	Bunratty is one of Ireland's premier attractions.
2	Original English	Let us help you explore the historic Castle and the vibrant Folk Park.
	Expert Translation	Låt oss hjälpa Dig utforska det historiska slottet och folkpark.
	API Translation	Låt oss hjälpa dig att utforska det historiska slott och den livliga Folk Park.
	API Translated Back	Let us help you explore the historic castles and the lively People's Park.
3	Original English	May we suggest that you first visit Belvoir School House on Main Street in the Folk Park.
	Expert Translation	Får vi föreslå att du först besöker Belvoir skolhus på Main street
	API Translation	Får vi föreslå att du första besök Belvoir School House på Main Street i Folk Park.
	API Translated Back	May we suggest that you first visit Belvoir School House on Main Street in the People's Park.
4	Original English	The School House is on the Main Street. As you enter the park, turn right, head up hill and keep left. The School is the first building on your left as you enter Main Street.
	Expert Translation	Skolhuset ligger på Main street. När du går in i parken så svänger Du till höger. Gå upp för backen och Håll till vänster. Skolan är första Byggnaden på vänster sida när du Kommer in på Main street.
	API Translation	Skolan House ligger på Main Street. När du matar in i parken, sväng höger, huvudet upp backen och håll vänster. Skolan är den första byggnaden på vänster sida när du kommer in Main Street.
	API Translated Back	School House located on Main Street. As you enter the park, turn right, head up the hill and keep left. The school is the first building on your left as you enter Main Street.
5	Original English	The school, built originally at Belvoir in East Clare in the early 19th century, is typical of many to be found all over the country at this time.
	Expert Translation	Skolan som byggdes under tidigt 1800-tal vid Belvoir i östra Clare är ett typiskt exempel på skolor som än idag finns spridda runt hela landet.
	API Translation	Skolan, byggd ursprungligen på Belvoir i East Clare i början av 19-talet, är typisk för många som finns över hela landet just nu.
	API Translated Back	The school, built originally at Belvoir in East Clare in the early 19th century, is typical of many that exist across the country right now.
6	Original English	Typically 30-40 children would have studied in each of the two classrooms. They would have copied out their lessons on slate using sticks of chalk.
	Expert Translation	Normalt sett studerade 30-40 elever I vardera klassrum. riffeltavlor Användes för att skriva ned sina Uppgifter
	API Translation	Typiskt 30-40 barn skulle ha studerat i vardera av de två klassrummen. De skulle ha kopierat sina lektioner på skiffer med pinnar av krita.
	API Translated Back	Typically, 30-40 children would be studied in each of the two classrooms. They would have copied their lessons on slates with sticks of chalk.

4.5.4 Manually Translated Files

The following ten pages contain screenshots from an application, written for the Bunratty Castle Folk Park in Co. Clare(written by MobaNode Ltd in 2007).

The manual translation was carried out by a number of language experts.

Lithuanian Translation:
Bunratty
Pradžia

Bunratty yra viena iš labiausiai lankomų turistų vietų.
Mes norime Jums padėti geriau pažinti šią istorinę pilį ir gyvybingą folklorinį parką.
- Siūlomi maršrutai
- Bunratty folklorinis parkas
- Bunratty pilis
- Kavinės, restoranai
- Renginiai
- Kaip atvykti
- Kontaktai

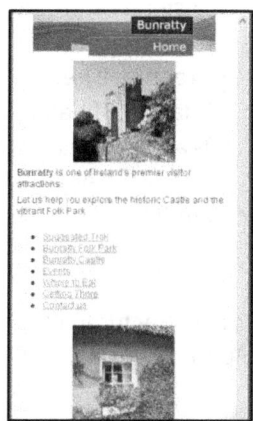

Bunratty
Papildoma Informacija
Pirmiausia mes siūlome aplankyti Belvoiro Mokyklą, esančią
Pagrindinėje Folkloro parko gatvėje (Main street)
Kaip atvykti
Ne ačiū. Kiti maršrutai

Plačiau apie Mokyklą
Atgal
Į pradžią

Bunratty
Kaip atvykti
Belvoiro Mokykla
Mokyklą rasite Pagrindinėje gatvėje (Main street). Atvykę į parką, pasukite į dešinę ir pakilkite į kalną, laikydamiesi kairiosios pusės. Mokykla bus pirmasis pastatas kairėje pusėje, kai tik atsidursite Pagrindinėje gatvėje.

Plačiau apie mokyklą
Atgal į maršrutus
Atgal į renginius
Į pradžią

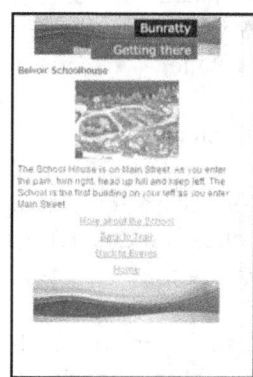

Bunratty
Pastatai

Mokyklos pastatas
Ši mokykla buvo pastatyta Belvoiro miestelyje, Rytinėje Clare apskrities pusėje, XIX amžiaus pradžioje ir yra labai panaši į daugelį to laikmečio šalies mokyklų.

Mokyklos istorija
Mokyklos renginiai
Tęsti maršrutą
Kiti pastatai
Į pradžią

Chapter 4

Irish Translation:

Bunraite
Home
Ta Bunratty ar cheann dena h-aiteanna turasoireachta is iomraiti cailiula in Eirinn.

Cabhraimis leat aithne a chur ar an chaislean stairiuil agus ar an sraidbhaile beomhar.

- Siuloidi gur fiu tabhairt futhu..
- Sraidbhaile traidisiunta Bhunraite.
- Caislean Bhunraite.
- Imeachtai .
- Aiteanna ithe.
- Eolas an Bhealai.
- Dean teagmhail linn.

Molaimis cuairt ar Theach Scoil Bhelvoir ar an bpriomhshraid mar thus.

Conas teacht ar Theach Scoil Bhelvoir.
Mo bhuichas ach ni mian liom cuairt a thabhairt ar an ait sin.

Eolas breise faoi Scoil Bhelvoir.
Ar ais.
Ag Baile.

Teach Scoil Bhelvoir.

Ta Teach Scoil Bhelvoir suite ar an bpriomhshraid.ar shroichint an ionaid teigh ar dheis,suas an mhallaigh agus ta an Scoil ar chle agus tu tagtha go dti an Priomhshraid.

Eolas breise faoin Scoil.
Ar filleadh ar ais.
Ar filleadh ar Imeachtai.
Ag Baile.

Teach na Scoile.

Togadh an Scoil seo ag tus an naou cead deag i mBelvoir,in Oirthear Contae an Chlair.Togadh macasamhail na scoile seo ag an am sin ar fud na tire.

Stair Theach na Scoile.
Imeachtai Theach na Scoile.
An turas ar lean.
Foirgnimh stairiula eile.
Ag Baile.

Stair Theach na Scoile.

Ba ghnath go mbiodh idir 30 agus 40 scolaire ag foghlaim I ngach seomra den da sheomra.Scriobhaidis a gcuid ceachtanna ar shlata ag baint usaide as cailc.

Ar ais.
Ag baile.

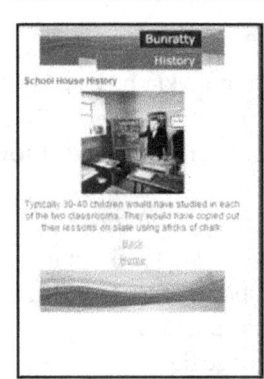

Polish Translation:

Bunratty jest jedną z głównych Irlandzkich atrakcji turystycznych

Odkryjmy razem historyczny zamek oraz park ludowy

- Proponowany szlak
- Park Ludowy "Bunratty"
- Zamek "Brunatty"
- Wydarzenia historyczne
- Gdzie spożywać posiłki
- Dojazd
- Kontakt

Więcej (informacji)

Proponujemy Państwu zwiedzenie budynku szkoły „Belvior", mieszczącego się przy głównej ulicy w parku ludowym.
Dojazd
Powrót – Dalsze szlaki
Więcej informacji na temat szkoły
Powrót
Strona główna

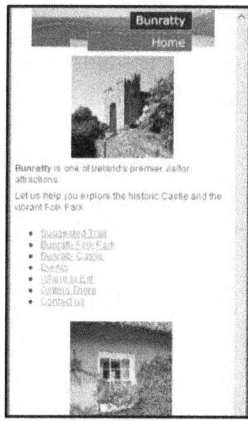

Dojazd

Szkoła znajduje się przy głównej drodze kiedy dojadą państwo do parku ludowego, należy skręcić w prawo a następnie na górce kierować się w lewo. Szkoła mieści się po lewej stronie przy głównej drodze.
Więcej informacji dotyczących szkoły
Powrót do szlaków
Powrót do wydarzeń historycznych
Strona główna

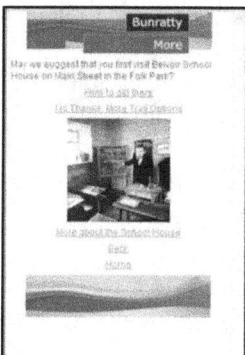

Budynki
Szkoła

Szkoła ta, wybudowana pierwotnie w zachodniej części hrabstwa clare na początku XIX wieku. Jest jednym z wielu odkryć typowych dla tejże epoki.

Historja szkołyi
Wydarzenia historyczne dotyczące szkoły
Kontynuacja trasy
Inne budynki
Strona główna

Historia
Historia szkoły
Do każdej z dwóch salek szkolnych uczęszczało zazwyczaj od 30 do 40 uczniów. Wszelkie notatki były sporządzane przez uczniów na tabliczkach za pomocą kredy
Powrót
Strona główna

Spanish Translation:

Bunratty is una de las primeras Atracciones turisticas en Irlanda.

Permitanos ayudarlo a explorar El Castillo Historico y el vibrante Parque del Pueblo

- Sendero sugerido
- Parque del Pueblo Bunratty
- Castillo Bunratty
- Donde comer?
- Entrando alli
- Contactenos

Nos permite sugerirle que su primera visita sea A la casa escuela Belvoir en la Calle principal del Parque del Pueblo?

Como llegar alli?
No gracias, Mas opciones de Senderos

Mas acerca de la Casa Escuela
Regresar
Home (Index is how you translate Home when is a site)

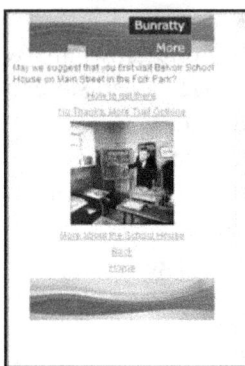

Entrando alli

Casa Escuela Belvoir

La Casa Escuela esta en la Calle principal. Al entrar al parque, gire a la derecha, siga por la colina y mantenga la izquierda. La escuela es el primer edificio a su izquierda al entrar a la calle principal.

Mas acerca de la escuela
Regresando al sendero
Regresar a eventos
Home (index)

Edificios

Casa Escuela

Esta escuela, originalmente construida en East Clare a inicios del siglo 19, es comun para muchos ser encontrada en todo el pais en este tiempo.

Historia de la casa escuela
Eventos de la casa escuela
Continuar con el sendero
Otros edificios
Home (index)

Historia
Historia de la Casa Escuela
Comunmente de 30 a 40 ninos han Estudiado en cada una de las dos Aulas de clase. Ellos habran Copiado sus lecciones en pizarra Usando pedazos de tizza.

Regresar
Home

Chapter 4

Swedish Translation:

Bunratty är en av Irlands främsta besöksattraktioner.

Låt oss hjälpa Dig utforska det historiska slottet och folkpark.

- Rekommenderat spår
- Bunratty folkpark
- Bunratty slott
- Evenemang
- Matställen
- Hitta dit
- Kontakta oss

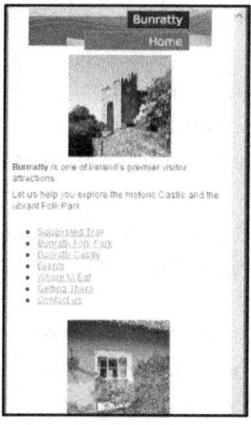

Får vi föreslå att du först besöker Belvoir skolhus på Main street?

Hur du hittar dit
Nej tack, fler spårval.

Mer om skolhuset
Tillbaka
Hem

Belvoir skolhus

Skolhuset ligger på Main street. När du går in i parken så svänger Du till höger. Gå upp för backen och Håll till vänster. Skolan är första Byggnaden på vänster sida när du Kommer in på Main street.

Mer om skolan
Tillbaka till spåret
Tillbaka till evenemang
Hem

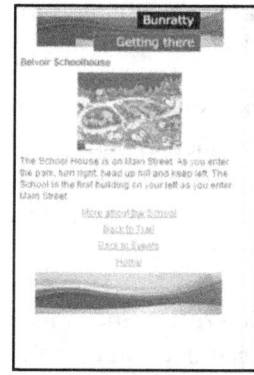

Skolhuset

Skolan som byggdes under tidigt 1800-tal vid Belvoir i östra Clare är ett typiskt exempel på skolor som än idag finns spridda runt hela landet.

Skolhusets historia
Evenemang i skolhuset
Fortsätt på spåret
Andra byggnader
Hem

Normalt sett studerade 30-40 elever I vardera klassrum. riffeltavlor Användes för att skriva ned sina Uppgifter

Tillbaka
Hem

---

5. Discussion and Conclusions

5.1 Global Navigation Satellite Systems

This report has looked in detail at the two operational satellite systems, GPS and Glonass and at the soon to be launched Galileo satellite system. The US GPS system is the dominant GNSS and is the only one currently supported by todays smartphones.

The most modern smartphones available as of March 2011 were tested extensively for GPS accuracy and responsiveness. The most downloaded tourism applications were also reviewed during this book.

Based on the research conducted while preparing this book, it must be concluded that the current range of location aware tourism applications do not exploit the full potential of GPS for providing useful functionality to the tourism user.

The GPS accuracy and responsiveness displayed, while operating in the harshest of urban environments, shows that GPS is an excellent tool for providing accurate location aware information to the smartphone user.

With the anticipated introduction of the European Galileo system in early 2012 and with the anticipated inclusion of Galileo receivers in the newest smartphones to be released after Galileo goes live, we can expect the accuracy of satellite based navigation systems to increase dramatically. Resolution of hybrid GPS/Galileo equipped smartphones will increase from 3m radius to 30cm radius.

Bearing this in mind, it is essential that todays Irish tourism operators incorporate satellite based location aware technologies into their marketing and advertising strategies in order to attract the maximum number of tourists to businesses.

The objectives of this book have been met with respect to GNSS.
Detailed experimentation has demonstrated that global navigation satellite systems are capable of providing smartphone users with the necessary information to pinpoint their location relative to the premises or tourism attraction that they are interested in or that a tourism operator wants their attention drawn to.

The results indicate that as of March 2011, the latest release of smartphones have achieved the necessary accuracy and responsiveness to avoid providing false positives to the user when they are searching out specific premises and when they are trying to distinguish one premises from another.

5.2 Bluetooth

It became obvious from an early stage of testing that global navigation satellite systems were ineffective in an indoor environment and that other options would have to be explored.

GSM Triangulation was investigated along with Skyhook WiFi Triangulation. Lack of coverage of both of these technologies in Ireland meant that they were ineffective in providing the quality of service required to provide indoor location aware functionality.

Bluetooth had been used previously to provide location based information to feature phone users, so it was decided to focus on this area in detail, to investigate it's potential for providing location aware functionality to the tourism user when they were operating in areas of poor GPS reception, such as indoor environments.

The theoretical aspects and limitations of Bluetooth were investigated and a series of tests were designed and implemented in order to find out the effectiveness of the Bluetooth signal as a means of tagging premises with location information so that tourism users of smartphones could be targeted.

These tests proved that Bluetooth tagging of premises in indoor and outdoor environments was effective in providing location aware information to the tourist.

(Unfortunately, the Apple iOS severely limits the Bluetooth functionality available to the 3rd party developer of smartphone applications, so implementation of any kind of useful Bluetooth functionality is currently limited to the non Apple smartphones).

The final Bluetooth test conducted for this book concentrated on the area of 'push' advertising and marketing, where information is pushed from the transmitter to the Bluetooth enabled smartphone user rather than being embedded in the application. These tests showed the potential of this dynamic approach in capturing the roving tourist's attention.

In conclusion, Bluetooth is excellent at providing the tourist with relevant information about the shops and attractions that they are in proximity to. Further research in the areas of 'push' advertising and marketing is recommended.

5.3 2D Codes

2D coding is growing in popularity and the use of QR Codes and DataMatrix codes has become mainstream in the past six months in particular. They are now used by all the major supermarkets and restaurant chains on their promotional materials.

An investigation into using 2D Codes to provide information to the smartphone equipped tourist was conducted. An analysis of the different formats of 2D Codes was conducted and a test was carried out using the most widespread code in use today, the QR Code.

This test showed that the modern smartphone could easily read a QR Code and display the information encoded in the QR Code, or use it as a URI to point to information on the web or to information embedded in a smartphone application.

2D Codes can be used to provide information at a premises entrance, or inside a premises to show information about specific attractions.

In conclusion, 2D Codes are already mainstream and they will soon be a requirement for any tourism attraction that wishes to remain relevant to the evolving tourism demography.

5.4 Smartphones and Operating Systems

There are currently a large range of operating systems on the market which cater specifically for smartphones and there are an even greater array of smartphone handsets available, each running various iterations of the leading operating systems.

Future trends in the smartphone world are hard to predict. There is competition amongst the leading manufacturers and smartphone operating system providers for domination of the market.

In Feb 2011, Nokia and Microsoft announced an alliance which should place the Microsoft operating system within a challenging position in the smartphone market and they may soon occupy the number 3 position behind iOS and Android.

In conclusion, it is recommended that tourism operators and developers concentrate on the Android operating system first, followed by the iOS operating system and if resources allow, then the Microsoft Phone 7 operating system should be catered for.

5.5 Objectives

Objective 1 was achieved in section 2, where a detailed analysis was carried out into the market leaders in the smartphone industry.

Objective 2 was achieved in sections 2.2.3, 2.3,3, 2.5.4, 2.6.3 and 2.8.3 where an account was given of the smartphone handsets in widespread use.

Objective 3 was achieved in section 1.4 where a listing and description was given for the most popular tourism applications.

Objective 4 was achieved in sections 3.1, 3.3, 3.4, 3.5, 3.7 – 3.11 where a thorough analysis of the hardware technologies necessary for location based functionality were covered.

The first part of objective 5 was achieved in sections 2.2.1, 2.3.1, 2.5.1, 2.6.1 and 2.7.1 where research was carried out on the best software options for different smartphones. The second part of objective 5 was achieved in sections 2.4.3, 2.4.4 and 2.4.5 where experimentation was carried out on the different coding techniques across the different smartphones for providing GPS, bluetooth and database functionality.

Objective 6 was achieved in sections 2.2 to 2.8 where the operating systems of each of the leading smartphone manufacturers was discussed.

Objective 7 was achieved in sections 2.2.1 and 2.3.1 and in section 2.9 and in other sections in chapter 2 where the different programming languages available to smartphone developers was discussed.

Objective 8 was achieved in sections 3.2, 3.6, 4.5.1 where several custom software applications were written using Android Java and iOS Objective-C to find the possibilities and limits of smartphone programming on the leading two smartphones.

Objective 9 was achieved in sections 3.2, 3.6, 3.10 and 4.5 where experiments were carried out in the areas of GNSS, Bluetooth, QR coding and localisation in order to establish the abilities of modern smartphones to cater to the tourism sector in the provision of location aware applications.

Objective 10 was achieved in section 4, where analysis and experimentation occurred into the area of internationalization of smartphone applications for the tourism sector.

5.6 Recommendations for Future Work

Future research and testing is advised in the GNSS area, especially when the new European Galileo system is officially launched.

Further research in the area of push notifications using Bluetooth technology is advisable, particularly in the area of automation of the security notifications during the pairing procedure between Bluetooth devices. Further research is also recommended in the integration of Bluetooth tagging into GPS based applications, so that the Bluetooth tagged locations can be used in a seamless manner to extend the functionality of an application in the indoor environment. The human friendly name could contain the GPS coordinates of the indoor premises and relay this information to a smartphone GPS application via the Bluetooth Discovery cycle, so that the app could continue to work in areas of poor GPS coverage.
Near Field Communications will likely be an area for future investigation when the technology becomes widespread. It has great potential to be used in conjunction with Bluetooth as a solution to the security pairing issue and to be used as a possible alternative or enhancement to 2D Codes.
As mentioned in section 3, the area of social media and the use of ever increasing personal information makes it viable to consider individual targeting of tourists when presenting them with marketing and other information. This is an area worthy of consideration for further study.
The demographics associated with smartphone usage amongst tourists in Ireland is worthy of further study. It is likely that most tourists in 5-10 years time will be using smartphones, but in the meantime, it will be of vital interest to the tourism operator to know which demographics are using smartphones.

5.7 Future Trends

As pointed out at the beginning of this report, this is a snapshot in time of the smartphone technology available as of March 2011. The industry is evolving at a fast rate and it is difficult to predict what the next trend or technology will be in the smartphone arena. In 2010 there were 8.2 billion mobile apps downloaded. In 2011 it is predicted that 17.7 billion apps will be downloaded[Gartner 2011]. This represents a growth of 117%. If this kind of growth continues and the major manufacturers continue to put their considerable resources into research and development of smartphones, then we can expect major innovations to occur in the next 5 to 10 years.

It is very likely that the European Galileo system will be fully operational in less than 5 years time and will be installed on almost all smartphones. This should increase the GNSS accuracy of smartphones from the current 3m radius to less than a 30cm radius. This will enable tourism operators to target their customers with much greater location accuracy.

Smartphones are becoming increasingly more powerful. It is reasonable to assume that smartphones will replace a users desktop or laptop altogether with the next 5 to 10 years. There will be docking stations at the home or office, rather than dedicated home or office computers. The smartphone user will have all the information and functionality that they currently have in their office on their mobile device even when they are on holidays as a tourist.
This means that all interaction with social media and other cloud services will occur on the users smartphone, even when they are at home or in the office which means that much more information about the user can be ascertained through automated interaction with their smartphone after user consent is granted(possibly similar to the permissions in place for bluetooth). Again, this will lead to more personalised targeting of individuals and a more tailored user experience when they enter a tourism zone.

Increases in web access speeds will continue to occur. In 5 to 10 years time the download times on smartphones will have surpassed the quickest existing landline broadband speeds. It is likely that almost all applications will be cloud based allowing for instant upgrading and updating of information contained within an application. This will allow for extremely dynamic applications that update in real time. It will be feasible to upload from the premises computer to the cloud and then download this information to the tourists smartphone quicker and more seamlessly that the current method of pushing information in a local manner. This will eliminate the need for local connections between the smartphone and the tourism premises or shop.

Gaming is already a major industry within the smartphone world and it is likely that many of the tourism based applications will be packaged as interactive games rather than the current trend of creating a semi-interactive tourist guide. As processors become more powerful and social media becomes more integrated into the smartphone experience, we can expect augmented reality, group based gaming to become a regular part of the attraction for tourists visiting tourism sites. Applications such as Scavenger(sec 1.4.1) are already beginning to go down this route.

5.8 Final Comments

It is clear from the research and testing carried out, that smartphones and location aware applications will have a central role to play in the attraction of future tourists to any region.
It will be essential for the tourism operators in Ireland to embrace these technologies and exploit them in order to remain competitive in the global tourism market.

Bibliography

Nirav Mehta
ISBN 978-1-847193-43-8

Mobile Web Development

Reto Meier
ISBN: 978-0-470-56552-0

Professional Android 2 Application Development

Jaizki Mendizabal Samper, Roc Berenguer Pérez, Juan Meléndez Lagunilla

GPS & Galileo: Dual RF Front-end Receiver and Design, Fabrication, and Test.

ISBN: 978-0-07-159869-9, MHID: 0-07-159869-3.

Rob Miles

Windows Phone Programming in C#

Mark L. Murphy
ISBN-13: 978-1-4302-2419-8

Beginning Android

Fritz Anderson
Sept 2008
Sams
ISBN-13: 978-0-321-55263-1

Xcode 3 Unleashed

W. Frank Ableson, Charlie Collins, and Robi Sen
April 2009
Manning
ISBN: 1933988673

Unlocking Android

Christopher Allen Shannon Applecline
Dec 2008
Manning
ISBN 193398886X

iPhone in Action

Toby Boudreaux
Aug 2009
O'Reilly
ISBN: 978-0-596-15546-9

Programming the iPhone User Experience

James A. Brannan
Aug 2009
McGraw Hill
ISBN: 9780071626491

iPhone SDK Programming

Ed Burnette
Jan 2009
Pragmatic
ISBN-13: 978-1-934356-56-2

Hello, Android

Yu-Chung Cheng
January 2005

University of California, San Diego.
Yatin Chawathe, Anthony LaMarca,
Intel Research Seattle. John Krumm,
Microsoft Corporation.
IRS-TR-05-003

Accuracy Characterization for
Metropolitan-scale Wi-Fi Localization.

Andrew M. Duncan
Dec 2002
O'Reilly
ISBN: 0-596-00423-0

Objective-C Pocket Reference

Steve Holzner
June 2004
O'Reilly
ISBN : 0-596-00710-8

Eclipse Cookbook

Sayed Y. Hashimi and Satya Komatineni
May 2010
Apress
ISBN-13: 978-1-4302-1596-7

Pro Android

Len Jacobson
May 2007
Artech House Publishers;
ISBN-10: 159693042X

GNSS Markets and Applications

Michael Juntao Yuan
July 2005
O'Reilly
ISBN: 0-596-00961-5

Nokia Smartphone Hacks

Chris King
Dec 2009
Apress
ISBN-13: 978-1-4302-2656-7

Advanced BlackBerry Development

H. Labiod, H. Afifi, C de Santis
Nov 2010
Springer
ISBN 978-1-4020-5396-2

WiFi, Bluetooth, Zigbee and WiMax

Dave Mabe
Oct 2005
O'Reilly
ISBN: 0-596-10115-5

BlackBerry Hacks

Mallick
March 2003
Wiley
ISBN 0-47121419-1

Mobile and Wireless Design Essentials

Dave Mark
Nov 2009
Apress
ISBN-13: 978-1-4302-2403-7

iPhone Advanced Projects

Dan Pilone, Tracey Pilone
Oct 2009
O'Reilly
ISBN: 978-0-596-80354-4

Head First iPhone Development

Dr. Prasad, Vikas Gupta, Avnish Dass
Nov 2001
Wiley
ISBN: 0-7645-4905-7

WAP, Bluetooth and 3G Programming

Rick Rogers, John Lombardo,
Zigurd Mednieks, and Blake Meike
May 2009
O'Reilly
ISBN: 978-0-596-52147-9

Android Application Development

Huang, Rudolph
Sept 2007
Cambridge University Press
ISBN 978-052170375-8

Bluetooth Essentials for Programmers

Erica Sadun
Jan 2010
Addison-Wesley
ISBN-10: 0-321-55545-7

The iPhone developer's cookbook

Lee, Schneider, Schell
Apr 2004
Prentice Hall
ISBN 0131172638

Mobile Applications

James Steele, Nelson To
Oct 2010
Addison-Wesley
ISBN-13: 978-0-321-74123-3

The Android Developer's Cookbook

Timothy J. Thompson, Paul J. Kline, and
C Bala Kumar
Feb 2008

Bluetooth Application Programming
with the Java APIs, Essentials Edition

Morgan Kaufmann
ISBN-13: 978-0-12-374342-8

Paul Thurrott
Nov 2010
Wiley
ISBN: 978-0-470-88659-5

Windows Phone 7 Secrets

Jonathan A. Zdziarski
Oct 2008 iPhone Open Application Development
O'Reilly
ISBN-13: 978-0-59-651855-4

Jonathan Zdziarski
Jan 2009 iPhone SDK Application Development
O'Reilly
ISBN-13: 978-0-596-15405-9

Papers/Market Research:
Gartner Inc 2010-11-10:
Worldwide Mobile Phone Sales Grew 35 Percent in Third Quarter 2010;
Smartphone Sales Increased 96 Percent
Gartner Inc. (NYSE: IT) Information technology research and advisory company.
http://www.gartner.com/it/
10 November 2010

Canalys Report 2011-02-01
Smart phone market exceeded 100 million units in Q4 2010
Palo Alto, Singapore and Reading(UK) - Monday, 31 January 2011
http://www.canalys.com/pr/2011/r2011013.html
31 January 2011

Markets and Markets
World Mobile Applications Market - Advanced Technologies, Global Forecast (2010 - 2015)
http://www.marketsandmarkets.com
Publishing Date: August 2010
Report Code: TC 1304

Websites:
http://www.dragonfiresdk.com/
http://www.anscamobile.com/corona/
http://www.appcelerator.com/
http://www.openhandsetalliance.com/android_overview.html
http://maemo.org/
http://qt.nokia.com/downloads/
http://us.blackberry.com/developers/
http://create.msdn.com/en-US/
http://www.silverlight.net/
http://en.wikipedia.org/wiki/Windows_Mobile/
http://developer.palm.com/
http://developer.android.com/
http://www.brighthub.com/
http://pa.rezendi.com/
http://wiki.forum.nokia.com
http://www.skyhookwireless.com/
http://gps.about.com/od/glossary/g/wifi_position.htm
http://gps.about.com/od/beforeyoubuy/a/howgpsworks.htm
http://www.denso-wave.com/qrcode/index-e.html
http://www.iso.ch/
http://en.wikipedia.org/wiki/PDF417
http://www.sqlite.org/
http://www.microsoft.com/sqlserver/2005/en/us/
http://www.oracle.com/technetwork/database/database-lite/
http://www.sybase.com/products/databasemanagement/sqlanywhere

A1. Visual Basic Source Code for Experiment 2.2.1

Visual Basic Functions Used to Analyse the Calibrated GPS Data.

```
Sub EditPositions_forRawData()
Dim cgID As String
Dim title As String
Dim descr As String
Dim latitude As String
Dim longitude As String
Dim altitude As String
Dim accuracy As String
Dim time As String
Dim counter1 As Integer
Dim counter2 As Integer
Dim counter0 As Integer
    counter1 = 1
    counter2 = 1

    'Eliminate Duplicates
    For counter0 = 1 To 1500
        Range("A" & counter0 + 3).Select
        If Range("K" & counter0 + 1).Value <> "" Then
            If Range("K" & counter0 + 1).Value = Range("K" & counter0).Value Then
                Rows(counter0 + 1 & ":" & counter0 + 1).Delete Shift:=xlUp
                counter0 = counter0 - 1
            End If
        End If
    Next
    'END Eliminate Duplicates
    For counter1 = 1 To 1500
        '*****
        cgID = Range("A" & counter1).Value
        title = Range("B" & counter1).Value
        descr = Range("C" & counter1).Value
        latitude = Range("D" & counter1).Value
        longitude = Range("E" & counter1).Value
        altitude = Range("F" & counter1).Value
        accuracy = Range("G" & counter1).Value
        time = Range("K" & counter1).Value

        Range("M" & counter2).Value = title
        Range("M" & counter2 + 1).Value = descr
        Range("M" & counter2 + 2).Value = "(" & cgID & ")"
        Range("M" & counter2 + 3).Value = ""
        Range("M" & counter2 + 4).Value = ""
        Range("M" & counter2 + 5).Value = ""

        Range("O" & counter2).Value = latitude
        Range("O" & counter2 + 1).Value = longitude
        Range("O" & counter2 + 2).Value = altitude
        Range("O" & counter2 + 3).Value = accuracy
        Range("O" & counter2 + 4).Value = time
        Range("O" & counter2 + 5).Value = ""
        Range("O" & counter2 + 6).Value = ""
        counter2 = counter2 + 7
    Next

Dim colCount, rowCount As Integer
Dim colArray(50) As String

    colArray(1) = "P"
    colArray(2) = "Q"

    colArray(48) = "BK"
    colArray(49) = "BL"
    colArray(50) = "BM"

    colCount = 1
    rowCount = 1
```

Appendix A

```vba
Do While rowCount > 0
    If Range("M" & rowCount).Value = Range("M" & rowCount + 7).Value Then
        If colCount >= 1 And colCount <= 50 Then
            Range(colArray(colCount) & rowCount).Value = Range("O" & rowCount + 7).Value
            Range(colArray(colCount) & rowCount + 1).Value = Range("O" & rowCount + 8).Value
            Range(colArray(colCount) & rowCount + 2).Value = Range("O" & rowCount + 9).Value
            Range(colArray(colCount) & rowCount + 3).Value = Range("O" & rowCount + 10).Value
            Range(colArray(colCount) & rowCount + 4).Value = Range("O" & rowCount + 11).Value
            Range(colArray(colCount) & rowCount + 5).Value = Range("O" & rowCount + 12).Value

            Range("M" & rowCount + 7 & ":O" & rowCount + 13).Delete Shift:=xlUp
            colCount = colCount + 1
        ElseIf colCount > 50 Then
            rowCount = -1
            MsgBox "ERROR: The number of records per location has
                    exceeded 50... close without saving and redo"
        End If
    Else
        rowCount = rowCount + 7
        colCount = 1
        If Range("M" & rowCount + 7).Value = "" Then
            rowCount = -1
        End If
    End If

  End If
Loop

End Sub

Sub Gen_LAT_LONGCombo_gen_CheckLoopCounts()
Dim counter As Integer
Dim counter2 As Integer
Dim cgString As String

    counter2 = 12
    For counter = 1 To 50
        Range("D" & counter2).Value = "Lat/Long"
        Range("F" & counter2).Value = Str(Range("F" & counter2 - 4).Value)
            + ", " + Str(Range("F" & counter2 - 3).Value)
        Range("G" & counter2).Value = Str(Range("G" & counter2 - 4).Value)
            + ", " + Str(Range("G" & counter2 - 3).Value)
        Range("H" & counter2).Value = Str(Range("H" & counter2 - 4).Value)
            + ", " + Str(Range("H" & counter2 - 3).Value)
        Range("I" & counter2).Value = Str(Range("I" & counter2 - 4).Value)
            + ", " + Str(Range("I" & counter2 - 3).Value)
        Range("J" & counter2).Value = Str(Range("J" & counter2 - 4).Value)
            + ", " + Str(Range("J" & counter2 - 3).Value)
        Range("K" & counter2).Value = Str(Range("K" & counter2 - 4).Value)
            + ", " + Str(Range("K" & counter2 - 3).Value)
        Range("L" & counter2).Value = Str(Range("L" & counter2 - 4).Value)
            + ", " + Str(Range("L" & counter2 - 3).Value)
        Range("M" & counter2).Value = Str(Range("M" & counter2 - 4).Value)
            + ", " + Str(Range("M" & counter2 - 3).Value)
        Range("N" & counter2).Value = Str(Range("N" & counter2 - 4).Value)
            + ", " + Str(Range("N" & counter2 - 3).Value)
        Range("O" & counter2).Value = Str(Range("O" & counter2 - 4).Value)
            + ", " + Str(Range("O" & counter2 - 3).Value)
        Range("P" & counter2).Value = Str(Range("P" & counter2 - 4).Value)
            + ", " + Str(Range("P" & counter2 - 3).Value)
        Range("Q" & counter2).Value = Str(Range("Q" & counter2 - 4).Value)
            + ", " + Str(Range("Q" & counter2 - 3).Value)
        Range("R" & counter2).Value = Str(Range("R" & counter2 - 4).Value)
            + ", " + Str(Range("R" & counter2 - 3).Value)
        counter2 = counter2 + 7
    Next

    Range("A1").Select
End Sub
```

Appendix A

```vb
Sub XML_Edit()
Dim masterCount As Integer
Dim counter, counter2, counter3 As Integer
Dim cgFilename As String
Dim totalLat, totalLong, totalAlt As Double
Dim avgLat, avgLong, avgAlt As Double
Dim cgDirectory As String
    cgDirectory = "K:\UL Masters Project\Experiments\
    VBOX Results\2010-10-31 Galway(all static)\"
    MsgBox "Remember to answer NO when asked DO YOU WANT TO SAVE XxxxxxxxX.csv"
    For masterCount = 1 To 150
        Workbooks.OpenXML Filename:="" & cgDirectory & "a" & masterCount & ".kml", _
            LoadOption:=xlXmlLoadImportToList
        cgFilename = Range("E1").Value
        Columns("A:U").Select
        Selection.Delete Shift:=xlToLeft
        Range("A1").Select
        Range("A1").Select
        Selection.TextToColumns Destination:=Range("A1"), DataType:=xlDelimited, _
            TextQualifier:=xlDoubleQuote, ConsecutiveDelimiter:=True, Tab:=False, _
            Semicolon:=False, Comma:=False, Space:=True, Other:=False, FieldInfo _
            :=Array(Array(1, 1), Array(2, 1), Array(3, 1), Array(4, 1), Array(134, 1)) _
            , TrailingMinusNumbers:=True
        Cells.Select
        Cells.EntireColumn.AutoFit
        Range("A1").Select
    For counter = 2 To 301
        Range("B1").Select
        Selection.Cut
        Range("A" & counter).Select
        ActiveSheet.Paste
        Columns("B:B").Select
        Selection.Delete Shift:=xlToLeft
    Next
    Rows("1:1").Select
    Selection.Delete Shift:=xlUp
    Range("A1").Select
    Columns("A:A").Select
    Selection.TextToColumns Destination:=Range("A1"), DataType:=xlDelimited, _
            TextQualifier:=xlDoubleQuote, ConsecutiveDelimiter:=False, Tab:=False, _
            Semicolon:=False, Comma:=True, Space:=False, Other:=False, FieldInfo _
            :=Array(Array(1, 1), Array(2, 1), Array(3, 1)), TrailingMinusNumbers:=True
    Columns("A:A").Select
    Selection.Cut
    Columns("C:C").Select
    Selection.Insert Shift:=xlToRight
    Range("A1").Select
    For counter3 = 1 To 310
        If Range("A" & counter3).Value = "" Then
            If counter2 = 0 Then
                counter2 = counter3
            End If
        End If
    Next
        counter2 = counter2 - 1
        Range("A302").Value = "=SUM(A1:A300)"
        Range("B302").Value = "=SUM(B1:B300)"
        Range("C302").Value = "=SUM(C1:C300)"
        totalLat = Range("A302").Value
        totalLong = Range("B302").Value
        totalAlt = Range("C302").Value
        avgLat = totalLat / counter2
        avgLong = totalLong / counter2
        avgAlt = totalAlt / counter2
        Range("A304").Value = avgLat
        Range("B304").Value = avgLong
        Range("C304").Value = avgAlt
        Range("E1").Value = avgLat
        Range("F1").Value = avgLong
        Range("G1").Value = avgAlt
        ActiveWorkbook.SaveAs Filename:="" & cgDirectory & cgFilename & ".csv", _
            FileFormat:=xlCSV, CreateBackup:=False

        ActiveWorkbook.Close
    Next
End Sub
```

A2. Java Source Code for 'GPS AutoLog' Android Application for Experiment 2.2.2

Constants.java

```java
package ie.cathalgreaney.gpsautolog;
import android.provider.BaseColumns;
import android.net.Uri;
public interface Constants extends BaseColumns {
public static final String TABLE_NAME = "gpsautolog";

//Columns in the GPS Auto Log Table
public static final String TITLE = "title";
public static final String DESCRIPTION =
"description";
public static final String LATITUDE = "latitude";
public static final String LONGITUDE = "longitude";
public static final String ALTITUDE = "altitude";
public static final String ACCURACY = "accuracy";
public static final String BEARING = "bearing";
public static final String PROVIDER = "provider";
public static final String SPEED = "speed";
public static final String TIME = "time";

public static final String AUTHORITY =
"ie.cathalgreaney.gpsautolog";
public static final Uri CONTENT_URI =
Uri.parse("content://" + AUTHORITY +
"/" + TABLE_NAME);
}
```

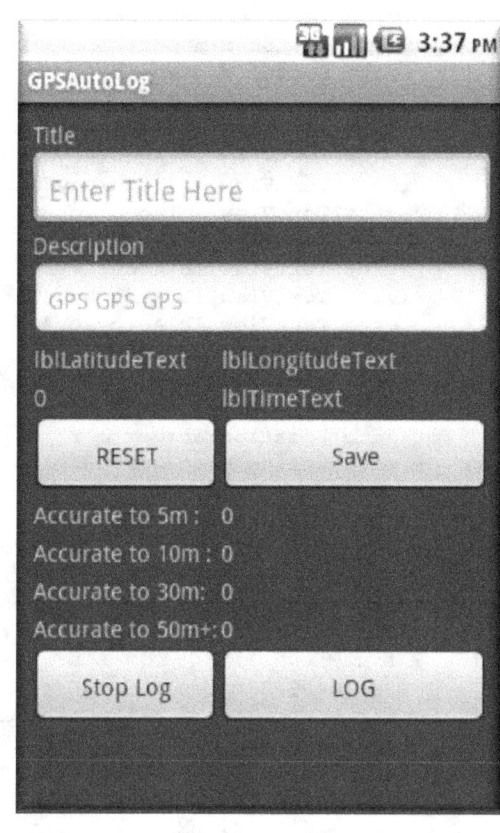

GPSAutolog.java

```java
package ie.cathalgreaney.gpsautolog;
import static android.provider.BaseColumns._ID;
import static ie.cathalgreaney.gpsautolog.Constants.ACCURACY;
import static ie.cathalgreaney.gpsautolog.Constants.ALTITUDE;
import static ie.cathalgreaney.gpsautolog.Constants.BEARING;
import static ie.cathalgreaney.gpsautolog.Constants.CONTENT_URI;
import static ie.cathalgreaney.gpsautolog.Constants.DESCRIPTION;
import static ie.cathalgreaney.gpsautolog.Constants.LATITUDE;
import static ie.cathalgreaney.gpsautolog.Constants.LONGITUDE;
import static ie.cathalgreaney.gpsautolog.Constants.PROVIDER;
import static ie.cathalgreaney.gpsautolog.Constants.SPEED;
import static ie.cathalgreaney.gpsautolog.Constants.TIME;
import static ie.cathalgreaney.gpsautolog.Constants.TITLE;
import android.app.ListActivity;
import android.content.ContentValues;
import android.database.Cursor;
import android.os.Bundle;
import android.view.View;
import android.widget.Button;
import android.widget.EditText;
import android.widget.SimpleCursorAdapter;
import android.widget.TextView;

import java.util.List; // Location
import android.location.Criteria; // Location
import android.location.Location; // Location
import android.location.LocationListener; // Location
import android.location.LocationManager; // Location
import android.location.LocationProvider; // Location

public class GPSAutoLog extends ListActivity implements LocationListener {
private TextView lblTitle;
private TextView lblDescription;
private EditText txtTitle;
private EditText txtDescription;
private TextView lblLatitude;
```

Appendix A

```java
    private TextView lblLongitude;
    private TextView lblAltitude;
    private TextView lblAccuracy;
    private TextView lblBearing;
    private TextView lblProvider;
    private TextView lblSpeed;
    private TextView lblTime;
    private Button btnUpdate;
    private Button btnSave;

    private TextView lblAccuracy1Label;
    private TextView lblAccuracy1;
    private TextView lblAccuracy2Label;
    private TextView lblAccuracy2;
    private TextView lblAccuracy3Label;
    private TextView lblAccuracy3;
    private TextView lblAccuracy4Label;
    private TextView lblAccuracy4;
    private Button btnStop;
    private Button btnLog;

    private LocationManager mgr; // Location
    private String best; // Location

    @Override
    public void onCreate(Bundle savedInstanceState) {

        super.onCreate(savedInstanceState);
        setContentView(R.layout.main);
        findViews(); // Initialize the controls
        refreshGPSScreen(); // Show the existing DB entries
        saveButton(); //GUI initialization
        updateButton(); //GUI initialization
        stopButton(); //GUI initialization
        logButton(); //GUI initialization
        mgr = (LocationManager) getSystemService(LOCATION_SERVICE);
        Criteria criteria = new Criteria();
        best = mgr.getBestProvider(criteria, true);
        Location location = mgr.getLastKnownLocation(best);
    }//end public void onCreate

    @Override
    protected void onResume() {
        super.onResume();
        mgr.requestLocationUpdates("gps", 500, 1, this);
    }
    @Override
    protected void onPause() {
        super.onPause();
        mgr.removeUpdates(this);
    }
    public void onLocationChanged(Location location) {
        String cgDescription;
        String cgPreviousAccuracy;
        String cgPreviousTime;
        String cgPreviousCount5;
        String cgPreviousCount10;
        String cgPreviousCount30;
        String cgPreviousCount50;
        String cgNewAccuracy;
        String cgNewTime;
        String cgNewCount5;
        String cgNewCount10;
        String cgNewCount30;
        String cgNewCount50;
        float cgFloatAcc;
        int cgAccuracy = 0;
        int cgCount5 = 0;
        int cgCount10 = 0;
        int cgCount30 = 0;
        int cgCount50 = 0;

        cgDescription = lblDescription.getText().toString().trim();
```

```java
        cgPreviousAccuracy = lblAccuracy.getText().toString().trim();
        cgPreviousTime = lblTime.getText().toString().trim();
        cgPreviousCount5 = lblAccuracy1.getText().toString().trim();
        cgPreviousCount10 = lblAccuracy2.getText().toString().trim();
        cgPreviousCount30 = lblAccuracy3.getText().toString().trim();
        cgPreviousCount50 = lblAccuracy4.getText().toString().trim();
        dumpLocation(location);

    @Override
    if (cgDescription == "LOGGING") {
        addGPSAutoLogFromScreen();
    }

    cgNewAccuracy = lblAccuracy.getText().toString().trim();
    cgFloatAcc = Float.parseFloat(cgNewAccuracy);
    cgNewTime = lblTime.getText().toString().trim();
    cgAccuracy = (int) (cgFloatAcc);
    cgCount5 = Integer.parseInt(cgPreviousCount5);
    cgCount10 = Integer.parseInt(cgPreviousCount10);
    cgCount30 = Integer.parseInt(cgPreviousCount30);
    cgCount50 = Integer.parseInt(cgPreviousCount50);

    if (cgAccuracy <= 5) {
        cgCount5++;
    } else if ((cgAccuracy > 5) && (cgAccuracy <= 10)) {
        cgCount10++;
    } else if ((cgAccuracy > 10) && (cgAccuracy <= 30)) {
        cgCount30++;
    } else {
        cgCount50++;
    }

        cgNewCount5 = "" + cgCount5;
        cgNewCount10 = "" + cgCount10;
        cgNewCount30 = "" + cgCount30;
        cgNewCount50 = "" + cgCount50;

        lblAccuracy1.setText(cgNewCount5);
        lblAccuracy2.setText(cgNewCount10);
        lblAccuracy3.setText(cgNewCount30);
        lblAccuracy4.setText(cgNewCount50);
    }
    public void onProviderDisabled(String provider) {
        lblTitle.setText("Provider disabled: " + provider);
    }
    public void onProviderEnabled(String provider) {
        lblTitle.setText("Provider enabled: " + provider);
    }
    public void onStatusChanged(String provider, int status, Bundle extras) {
        lblTitle.setText("Provider status changed: " + provider + ", " +
            "status=" + S[status] + ", extras=" + extras);
    }
    //THE REMAINING CODE for LocationTest/Log/dumpLocation/dumpProviders
    private static final String[] A = {"invalid", "n/a", "fine", "coarse" };
    private static final String[] P = {"invalid", "n/a", "low", "medium", "high" };
    private static final String[] S = {"out of service", "temp unavailable", "available" };

    private void dumpLocation(Location location) {
        if (location == null) {
            lblLatitude.setText("no info");
            lblLongitude.setText("no info");
            lblAltitude.setText("no info");
            lblAccuracy.setText("0");
            lblBearing.setText("no info");
            lblProvider.setText("no info");
            lblSpeed.setText("no info");
            lblTime.setText("no info");
        } else {
            lblLatitude.setText("" + location.getLatitude());
            lblLongitude.setText("" + location.getLongitude());
            lblAltitude.setText("" + location.getAltitude());
            lblAccuracy.setText("" + location.getAccuracy());
```

```java
        lblBearing.setText("" + location.getBearing());
        lblProvider.setText("" + location.getProvider());
        lblSpeed.setText("" + location.getSpeed());
        lblTime.setText("" + location.getTime());
        }//end if-else
    }

    private void findViews() {
        lblTitle = (TextView) findViewById(R.id.lblTitle);
        lblDescription = (TextView) findViewById(R.id.lblDescription);
        txtTitle = (EditText) findViewById(R.id.txtTitle);
        txtDescription = (EditText) findViewById(R.id.txtDescription);
        lblLatitude = (TextView) findViewById(R.id.lblLatitude);
        lblLongitude = (TextView) findViewById(R.id.lblLongitude);
        lblAltitude = (TextView) findViewById(R.id.lblAltitude);
        lblAccuracy = (TextView) findViewById(R.id.lblAccuracy);
        lblBearing = (TextView) findViewById(R.id.lblBearing);
        lblProvider = (TextView) findViewById(R.id.lblProvider);
        lblSpeed = (TextView) findViewById(R.id.lblSpeed);
        lblTime = (TextView) findViewById(R.id.lblTime);
        btnUpdate = (Button) findViewById(R.id.btnUpdate);
        btnSave = (Button) findViewById(R.id.btnSave);

        lblAccuracy1Label = (TextView) findViewById(R.id.lblAccuracy1Label);
        lblAccuracy1 = (TextView) findViewById(R.id.lblAccuracy1);
        lblAccuracy2Label = (TextView) findViewById(R.id.lblAccuracy2Label);
        lblAccuracy2 = (TextView) findViewById(R.id.lblAccuracy2);
        lblAccuracy3Label = (TextView) findViewById(R.id.lblAccuracy3Label);
        lblAccuracy3 = (TextView) findViewById(R.id.lblAccuracy3);
        lblAccuracy4Label = (TextView) findViewById(R.id.lblAccuracy4Label);
        lblAccuracy4 = (TextView) findViewById(R.id.lblAccuracy4);

        btnStop = (Button) findViewById(R.id.btnStop);
        btnLog = (Button) findViewById(R.id.btnLog);

    }
    private void refreshGPSScreen() {
        Cursor cursor = getGPSAutoLog();
        showGPSAutoLog(cursor);
    }
    private void addGPSAutoLogFromScreen() {
        String cgTitle = txtTitle.getText().toString().trim();
        String cgDescription = txtDescription.getText().toString().trim();
        String cgLatitude = lblLatitude.getText().toString().trim();
        String cgLongitude = lblLongitude.getText().toString().trim();
        String cgAltitude = lblAltitude.getText().toString().trim();
        String cgAccuracy = lblAccuracy.getText().toString().trim();
        String cgBearing = lblBearing.getText().toString().trim();
        String cgProvider = lblProvider.getText().toString().trim();
        String cgSpeed = lblSpeed.getText().toString().trim();
        String cgTime = lblTime.getText().toString().trim();
        addGPSAutoLog(cgTitle, cgDescription, cgLatitude,
        cgLongitude, cgAltitude, cgAccuracy,
        cgBearing, cgProvider, cgSpeed, cgTime);
        refreshGPSScreen();
    }
    private void setGPSAutoLogToScreen() {
        //basically this is a reset...

        lblTitle.setText("Title");
        lblLatitude.setText("Latitude");
        lblLongitude.setText("Longitude");
        lblAltitude.setText("Altitude");
        lblAccuracy.setText("0");
        lblBearing.setText("Bearing");
        lblProvider.setText("Provider");
        lblSpeed.setText("Speed");
        lblTime.setText("Time");
        lblAccuracy1.setText("0");
        lblAccuracy2.setText("0");
        lblAccuracy3.setText("0");
        lblAccuracy4.setText("0");
    }
```

```java
//Listeners*************************************************************
private void saveButton() {
   btnSave.setOnClickListener(new Button.OnClickListener() {
   public void onClick(View v)
   {
      addGPSAutoLogFromScreen();
   }
});}
private void updateButton() {
   btnUpdate.setOnClickListener(new Button.OnClickListener() {
   public void onClick(View v) {
   setGPSAutoLogToScreen();
   }
});}

private void stopButton() {
   btnStop.setOnClickListener(new Button.OnClickListener() {
   public void onClick(View v) {
      // action here
      lblDescription.setText("Stopped Logging");
   }
});}
private void logButton() {
   btnLog.setOnClickListener(new Button.OnClickListener() {
   public void onClick(View v) {
      // action here
      lblDescription.setText("LOGGING");
   }
});}
   //END Listeners*******************************************************

   //Database Methods****************************************************
private void addGPSAutoLog(String string1, String string2, String string3,
   String string4, String string5, String string6,
   String string7, String string8, String string9, String string10) {
   ContentValues values = new ContentValues();
   values.put(TITLE, string1);
   values.put(DESCRIPTION, string2);
   values.put(LATITUDE, string3);
   values.put(LONGITUDE, string4);
   values.put(ALTITUDE, string5);
   values.put(ACCURACY, string6);
   values.put(BEARING, string7);
   values.put(PROVIDER, string8);
   values.put(SPEED, string9);
   values.put(TIME, string10);
   getContentResolver().insert(CONTENT_URI, values);
}

private static String[] FROM = { _ID, TITLE, DESCRIPTION, LATITUDE,
                                 LONGITUDE, ALTITUDE, ACCURACY,
                                 BEARING, PROVIDER, SPEED, TIME, };
   private static String ORDER_BY = _ID + " DESC";
   private Cursor getGPSAutoLog() {
   return managedQuery(CONTENT_URI, FROM, null, null, ORDER_BY);
}

//Takes a cursor as input and spits out info
private static int[] TO = { R.id.item1, R.id.item2, R.id.item3,
                            R.id.item4, R.id.item5, R.id.item6,
                            R.id.item7, R.id.item8, R.id.item9, R.id.item10, R.id.item11, };
   private void showGPSAutoLog(Cursor cursor) {
   SimpleCursorAdapter adapter = new SimpleCursorAdapter(this,
                                 R.layout.item, cursor, FROM, TO);
   setListAdapter(adapter);
}
   //END Database Methods************************************************
}//END CLASS
```

Appendix A   Appendix p9

GPSAutologData.java

```java
package ie.cathalgreaney.gpsautolog;
import static android.provider.BaseColumns._ID;
import static ie.cathalgreaney.gpsautolog.Constants.TABLE_NAME;
import static ie.cathalgreaney.gpsautolog.Constants.TITLE;
import static ie.cathalgreaney.gpsautolog.Constants.DESCRIPTION;
import static ie.cathalgreaney.gpsautolog.Constants.LATITUDE;
import static ie.cathalgreaney.gpsautolog.Constants.LONGITUDE;
import static ie.cathalgreaney.gpsautolog.Constants.ALTITUDE;
import static ie.cathalgreaney.gpsautolog.Constants.ACCURACY;
import static ie.cathalgreaney.gpsautolog.Constants.BEARING;
import static ie.cathalgreaney.gpsautolog.Constants.PROVIDER;
import static ie.cathalgreaney.gpsautolog.Constants.SPEED;
import static ie.cathalgreaney.gpsautolog.Constants.TIME;
import android.content.Context;
import android.database.sqlite.SQLiteDatabase;
import android.database.sqlite.SQLiteOpenHelper;
public class GPSAutoLogData extends SQLiteOpenHelper {
    private static final String DATABASE_NAME = "gpsautolog.db";
    private static final int DATABASE_VERSION = 2;
    public GPSAutoLogData(Context ctx) {
        super(ctx, DATABASE_NAME, null, DATABASE_VERSION);
    }
    @Override
    public void onCreate(SQLiteDatabase db) {
        db.execSQL("CREATE TABLE " + TABLE_NAME + " (" + _ID + " INTEGER PRIMARY
                            KEY AUTOINCREMENT, " +
                            TITLE + " TEXT NOT NULL, " +
                            DESCRIPTION + " TEXT NOT NULL, " +
                            LATITUDE + " TEXT NOT NULL, " +
                            LONGITUDE + " TEXT NOT NULL, " +
                            ALTITUDE + " TEXT NOT NULL, " +
                            ACCURACY + " TEXT NOT NULL, " +
                            BEARING + " TEXT NOT NULL, " +
                            PROVIDER + " TEXT NOT NULL, " +
                            SPEED + " TEXT NOT NULL, " +
                            TIME + " TEXT NOT NULL);");
    }
    @Override
    public void onUpgrade(SQLiteDatabase db, int oldVersion, int newVersion) {
        db.execSQL("DROP TABLE IF EXISTS " + TABLE_NAME);
        onCreate(db);
    }
}//END CLASS
```

GPSAutologProvider.java

```java
package ie.cathalgreaney.gpsautolog;
import static android.provider.BaseColumns._ID;
import static ie.cathalgreaney.gpsautolog.Constants.AUTHORITY;
import static ie.cathalgreaney.gpsautolog.Constants.CONTENT_URI;
import static ie.cathalgreaney.gpsautolog.Constants.TABLE_NAME;
import android.content.UriMatcher;
import android.database.Cursor;
import android.database.sqlite.SQLiteDatabase;
import android.net.Uri;
import android.text.TextUtils;
public class GPSAutoLogProvider extends ContentProvider {
    private static final int GPSAUTOLOG = 1;
    private static final int GPSAUTOLOG_ID = 2;
    private static final String CONTENT_TYPE
        = "vnd.android.cursor.dir/vnd.cathalgreaney.gpsautolog";
    private static final String CONTENT_ITEM_TYPE
        = "vnd.android.cursor.item/vnd.cathalgreaney.gpsautolog";
    private GPSAutoLogData gpsautolog;
    private UriMatcher uriMatcher;
    @Override
    public boolean onCreate() {
        uriMatcher = new UriMatcher(UriMatcher.NO_MATCH);
        uriMatcher.addURI(AUTHORITY, "gpsautolog", GPSAUTOLOG);
        uriMatcher.addURI(AUTHORITY, "gpsautolog/#", GPSAUTOLOG_ID);
        gpsautolog = new GPSAutoLogData(getContext());
        return true;
    }
```

```java
@Override
public Cursor query(Uri uri, String[] projection, String selection,
    String[] selectionArgs, String orderBy) {
    if (uriMatcher.match(uri) == GPSAUTOLOG_ID) {
        long id = Long.parseLong(uri.getPathSegments().get(1));
        selection = appendRowId(selection, id);
    }
    SQLiteDatabase db = gpsautolog.getReadableDatabase();
    Cursor cursor = db.query(TABLE_NAME, projection, selection,
        selectionArgs, null, null, orderBy);
    cursor.setNotificationUri(getContext().getContentResolver(), uri);
    return cursor;
}
@Override
public String getType(Uri uri) {
    switch (uriMatcher.match(uri)) {
    case GPSAUTOLOG:
        return CONTENT_TYPE;
    case GPSAUTOLOG_ID:
        return CONTENT_ITEM_TYPE;
    default:
        throw new IllegalArgumentException("Unknown URI " + uri);
    }
}
@Override
public Uri insert(Uri uri, ContentValues values) {
    SQLiteDatabase db = gpsautolog.getWritableDatabase();
    if (uriMatcher.match(uri) != GPSAUTOLOG) {
        throw new IllegalArgumentException("Unknown URI " + uri);
    }
    long id = db.insertOrThrow(TABLE_NAME, null, values);
    Uri newUri = ContentUris.withAppendedId(CONTENT_URI, id);
    getContext().getContentResolver().notifyChange(newUri, null);
    return newUri;
}
@Override
public int delete(Uri uri, String selection,
    String[] selectionArgs) {
    SQLiteDatabase db = gpsautolog.getWritableDatabase();
    int count;
    switch (uriMatcher.match(uri)) {
    case GPSAUTOLOG:
        count = db.delete(TABLE_NAME, selection, selectionArgs);
        break;
    case GPSAUTOLOG_ID:
        long id = Long.parseLong(uri.getPathSegments().get(1));
        count = db.delete(TABLE_NAME, appendRowId(selection, id),
            selectionArgs);
        break;
    default:
        throw new IllegalArgumentException("Unknown URI " + uri);
    }
    // Notify any watchers of the change
    getContext().getContentResolver().notifyChange(uri, null);
    return count;
}
@Override
public int update(Uri uri, ContentValues values,
    String selection, String[] selectionArgs) {
    SQLiteDatabase db = gpsautolog.getWritableDatabase();
    int count;
    switch (uriMatcher.match(uri)) {
    case GPSAUTOLOG:
        count = db.update(TABLE_NAME, values, selection,
            selectionArgs);
        break;
    case GPSAUTOLOG_ID:
        long id = Long.parseLong(uri.getPathSegments().get(1));
        count = db.update(TABLE_NAME, values, appendRowId(
            selection, id), selectionArgs);
        break;
    default:
        throw new IllegalArgumentException("Unknown URI " + uri);
    }
```

```java
        // Notify any watchers of the change
        getContext().getContentResolver().notifyChange(uri, null);
        return count;
    }
    /** Append an id test to a SQL selection expression */
    private String appendRowId(String selection, long id) {
        return _ID + "=" + id
                + (!TextUtils.isEmpty(selection)
                    ? " AND (" + selection + ')'
                    : "");
    }
}

    @Override
    public int delete(Uri uri, String selection,
            String[] selectionArgs) {
        SQLiteDatabase db = gpsautolog.getWritableDatabase();
        int count;
        switch (uriMatcher.match(uri)) {
        case GPSAUTOLOG:
            count = db.delete(TABLE_NAME, selection, selectionArgs);
            break;
        case GPSAUTOLOG_ID:
            long id = Long.parseLong(uri.getPathSegments().get(1));
            count = db.delete(TABLE_NAME, appendRowId(selection, id),
                    selectionArgs);
            break;
        default:
            throw new IllegalArgumentException("Unknown URI " + uri);
        }

        // Notify any watchers of the change
        getContext().getContentResolver().notifyChange(uri, null);
        return count;
    }

    @Override
    public int update(Uri uri, ContentValues values,
            String selection, String[] selectionArgs) {
        SQLiteDatabase db = gpsautolog.getWritableDatabase();
        int count;
        switch (uriMatcher.match(uri)) {
        case GPSAUTOLOG:
            count = db.update(TABLE_NAME, values, selection,
                    selectionArgs);
            break;
        case GPSAUTOLOG_ID:
            long id = Long.parseLong(uri.getPathSegments().get(1));
            count = db.update(TABLE_NAME, values, appendRowId(
                    selection, id), selectionArgs);
            break;
        default:
            throw new IllegalArgumentException("Unknown URI " + uri);
        }

        // Notify any watchers of the change
        getContext().getContentResolver().notifyChange(uri, null);
        return count;
    }
    /** Append an id test to a SQL selection expression */
    private String appendRowId(String selection, long id) {
        return _ID + "=" + id
                + (!TextUtils.isEmpty(selection)
                    ? " AND (" + selection + ')'
                    : "");
    }
}
```

Main.xml

```xml
<?xml version="1.0" encoding="utf-8"?>
<LinearLayout xmlns:android="http://schemas.android.com/apk/res/android"
    android:orientation="vertical"
    android:layout_width="fill_parent"
    android:layout_height="fill_parent"
    android:background="#0000aa"
    >
    <TableLayout
        android:layout_width="fill_parent"
        android:layout_height="fill_parent"
        android:stretchColumns="1"
        android:padding="10dip"
        android:visibility="visible">
        <TextView
            android:id="@+id/lblTitle"
            android:text="@string/lblTitleText"
            android:visibility="visible">
        </TextView>
        <EditText
            android:id="@+id/txtTitle"
            android:text="@string/txtTitleText"
            android:hint="@string/txtTitleHint"
            android:padding="10dip"
            android:textSize="18sp">
        </EditText>
        <TextView
            android:id="@+id/lblDescription"
            android:text="@string/lblDescriptionText"
            android:visibility="visible">
        </TextView>
        <EditText
            android:id="@+id/txtDescription"
            android:text="@string/txtDescriptionText"
            android:hint="@string/txtDescriptionHint"
            android:padding="10dip"
            android:textSize="15sp">
        </EditText>
        <TableRow>
        <TextView
            android:id="@+id/lblLatitude"
            android:text="@string/lblLatitudeText"
            android:visibility="visible"
            android:padding="1dip"
            android:textSize="15sp">
        </TextView>
         <TextView
            android:id="@+id/lblLongitude"
            android:text="@string/lblLongitudeText"
            android:visibility="visible"
            android:padding="1dip"
            android:textSize="15sp">
        </TextView>
        </TableRow>
        <TableRow>
         <TextView
            android:id="@+id/lblAccuracy"
            android:text="@string/lblAccuracyText"
            android:visibility="visible"
            android:padding="1dip"
            android:textSize="15sp">
        </TextView>
         <TextView
            android:id="@+id/lblTime"
            android:text="@string/lblTimeText"
            android:visibility="visible"
            android:padding="1dip"
            android:textSize="15sp">
        </TextView>

        </TableRow>
        <TableRow>
        <TextView
            android:id="@+id/lblBearing"
            android:text="@string/lblBearingText"
            android:visibility="gone"
            android:padding="1dip"
            android:textSize="15sp">
        </TextView>
         <TextView
            android:id="@+id/lblProvider"
            android:text="@string/lblProviderText"
            android:visibility="gone"
            android:padding="1dip"
            android:textSize="15sp">
        </TextView>
        </TableRow>
        <TableRow>
        <TextView
            android:id="@+id/lblSpeed"
            android:text="@string/lblSpeedText"
            android:visibility="gone"
            android:padding="1dip"
            android:textSize="15sp">
        </TextView>
         <TextView
            android:id="@+id/lblAltitude"
            android:text="@string/lblAltitudeText"
            android:visibility="gone"
            android:padding="1dip"
            android:textSize="15sp">

        </TextView>
        </TableRow>
            <TableRow>
        <Button
            android:id="@+id/btnUpdate"
            android:text="@string/btnUpdateText"
            android:visibility="visible"
            android:padding="10dip"
            android:textSize="15sp">
        </Button>
        <Button
            android:id="@+id/btnSave"
            android:text="@string/btnSaveText"
            android:visibility="visible"
            android:padding="10dip"
            android:textSize="15sp"
            >
        </Button>
</TableRow>
```

Appendix A

Main.xml

```xml
<TableRow>
    <TextView
    android:id="@+id/lblAccuracy1Label"
    android:text="@string/lblAccuracy1LabelText"
    android:visibility="visible"
    android:padding="1dip"
    android:textSize="15sp">
    </TextView>
    <TextView
    android:id="@+id/lblAccuracy1"
    android:text="@string/lblAccuracy1Text"
    android:visibility="visible"
    android:padding="1dip"
    android:textSize="15sp">

    </TextView>
</TableRow>
    <TableRow>
    <TextView
    android:id="@+id/lblAccuracy2Label"
    android:text="@string/lblAccuracy2LabelText"
    android:visibility="visible"
    android:padding="1dip"
    android:textSize="15sp">
    </TextView>
    <TextView
    android:id="@+id/lblAccuracy2"
    android:text="@string/lblAccuracy2Text"
    android:visibility="visible"
    android:padding="1dip"
    android:textSize="15sp">

    </TextView>
</TableRow>
    <TableRow>
    <TextView
    android:id="@+id/lblAccuracy3Label"
    android:text="@string/lblAccuracy3LabelText"
    android:visibility="visible"
    android:padding="1dip"
    android:textSize="15sp">
    </TextView>
    <TextView
    android:id="@+id/lblAccuracy3"
    android:text="@string/lblAccuracy3Text"
    android:visibility="visible"
    android:padding="1dip"
    android:textSize="15sp">

    </TextView>
</TableRow>
    <TableRow>
    <TextView
    android:id="@+id/lblAccuracy4Label"
    android:text="@string/lblAccuracy4LabelText"
    android:visibility="visible"
    android:padding="1dip"
    android:textSize="15sp">
    </TextView>
    <TextView
    android:id="@+id/lblAccuracy4Label"
    android:text="@string/lblAccuracy4LabelText"
    android:visibility="visible"
    android:padding="1dip"
    android:textSize="15sp">
    </TextView>
    <TextView
    android:id="@+id/lblAccuracy4"
    android:text="@string/lblAccuracy4Text"
    android:visibility="visible"
    android:padding="1dip"
    android:textSize="15sp">

    </TextView>
</TableRow>
    <TableRow>
<Button
android:id="@+id/btnStop"
android:text="@string/btnStopText"
android:visibility="visible"
android:padding="10dip"
android:textSize="15sp">
</Button>
<Button
android:id="@+id/btnLog"
android:text="@string/btnLogText"
android:visibility="visible"
android:padding="10dip"
android:textSize="15sp"
>
</Button>
</TableRow>


<ListView
android:id="@android:id/list"
android:layout_width="wrap_content"
    android:layout_height="wrap_content"
    android:visibility="visible">
</ListView>

</TableLayout>

</LinearLayout>
```

Manifest.xml

```xml
<?xml version="1.0" encoding="utf-8"?>
<manifest
        xmlns:android="http://schemas.android.com/apk/res/android"
        package="ie.cathalgreaney.gpsautolog"
        android:versionCode="1"
        android:versionName="1.0">
    <uses-permission
            android:name="android.permission.ACCESS_COARSE_LOCATION">
    </uses-permission>
    <uses-permission
            android:name="android.permission.ACCESS_FINE_LOCATION">
    </uses-permission>
    <application
            android:icon="@drawable/icon" android:label="@string/app_name">
            <provider
                    android:name=".GPSAutoLogProvider"
                    android:authorities="ie.cathalgreaney.gpsautolog">
            </provider>
            <activity
                    android:name=".GPSAutoLog"
                    android:label="@string/app_name">
                <intent-filter>
                <action
                        android:name="android.intent.action.MAIN" />
                <category
                        android:name="android.intent.category.LAUNCHER" />
                </intent-filter>
            </activity>
    </application>
    <uses-sdk android:minSdkVersion="7" />
</manifest>
```

A3. Java Source Code for 'GPS Galway' Android Application for Experiment 2.2.5 and 2.2.6

GPSGalway.java

```java
package ie.cathalgreaney.GPSGalway;
import android.app.Activity;
import android.app.Application;
import android.app.ProgressDialog;
import android.app.Service;
import android.content.Context;
import android.content.Intent;
import android.database.Cursor;
import android.location.Criteria;
import android.location.GpsStatus;
import android.location.Location;
import android.location.LocationListener;
import android.location.LocationManager;
import android.opengl.Visibility;
import android.os.Bundle;
import android.os.IBinder;
import android.util.FloatMath;
import android.widget.Button;
import android.widget.EditText;
import android.widget.TextView;
import android.widget.Toast;

public class GPSGalway extends Activity {
    private LocationManager cglocationManager;
    private LocationListener locationListener;
    Cursor cursor;
    String cgCurrLongitude;
    String cgCurrLatitude;
    String cgAccuracy, cgTime;
    String cgDistValues[];
    double cgDistance;
    boolean cgGPSEnabled = false;
    TextView lblHeading;
    TextView lblCurrLatitude, lblCurrLongitude;
    TextView lblNo1, lblName1, lblLatitude1,
    lblLongitude1, lblDistance1;
    @Override
    public void onCreate(Bundle savedInstanceState) {
        super.onCreate(savedInstanceState);
        setContentView(R.layout.main);
        findViews(); // Initialize the controls
        DBAdapter db = new DBAdapter(getBaseContext());
        db.open();
        db.deleteAllLocations();
        db.close();
        BindLocationInfo1();
        //BindLocationInfo2();
        try{
            cgGPSEnabled=cglocationManager.isProviderEnabled(LocationManager.GPS_PROVIDER);
        } catch(Exception ex){}
        if(!cgGPSEnabled ){
            //TextView txt = (TextView)findViewById(R.id.text1);
            //txt.setText("  ");
        }
        try{
            //TextView txt = (TextView)findViewById(R.id.text1);
            //txt.setText("You are Now at Location :");
            locationListener = new GPSLocationListener();
            Criteria criteria = new Criteria();
            criteria.setAccuracy(Criteria.ACCURACY_FINE);
            cglocationManager = (LocationManager)
            getBaseContext().getSystemService(Context.LOCATION_SERVICE);
            String bestProvider = cglocationManager.getBestProvider(criteria, true);
            cglocationManager.requestLocationUpdates(bestProvider,
            1000, 0, locationListener);
```

```java
            //        cgLocationManager.requestLocationUpdates(
            //        LocationManager.GPS_PROVIDER, 0, 0,locationListener);

            BindLocationInfo1();
            //BindLocationInfo2();
        }catch(Exception e){
            //Toast.makeText(getBaseContext(),e.toString(), Toast.LENGTH_LONG).show();
            //TextView txt = (TextView)findViewById(R.id.text1);
            //txt.setText("");
            //TextView cgLongitude = (TextView)findViewById(R.id.latitud);
            //cgLongitude.setText("No Location Found, Please Turn GPS ON");
        }
    }//end void onCreate
    public class GPSLocationListener implements LocationListener {
        public void onLocationChanged(Location location) {
            if (location != null) {
                cgCurrLatitude = String.valueOf(roundNumber(location.getLatitude(),6));
                cgCurrLongitude = String.valueOf(roundNumber(location.getLongitude(),6));
                lblCurrLatitude.setText(cgCurrLatitude);
                lblCurrLongitude.setText(cgCurrLongitude);
                BindLocationInfo2();
                //location.distanceBetween(startLatitude,
                    startLongitude, endLatitude, endLongitude, results)
            }//end if
        }//end onLocationChanged

        public void onProviderDisabled(String arg0) {
            Toast.makeText(getBaseContext(), "Gps Provider disabled",
            Toast.LENGTH_SHORT).show();
            // TODO Auto-generated method stub
        }

        public void onProviderEnabled(String arg0) {
            // TODO Auto-generated method stub
            Toast.makeText(getBaseContext(), "Gps Provider ENABLED",
            Toast.LENGTH_SHORT).show();
        }

        public void onStatusChanged(String arg0, int arg1, Bundle arg2) {
            // TODO Auto-generated method stub
            //Toast.makeText(getBaseContext(), "Status Changed", Toast.LENGTH_SHORT).show();
        }
    }//end class GPSLocationListener

    public static double roundNumber(double num, int dec) {
        return Math.round(num * Math.pow(10, dec))/Math.pow(10, dec);
    }
    public double calculateDistance(String current_latitud,
        String current_longitud, String dest_latitud, String dest_longitude) {

        if (current_latitud == null || current_longitud == null ){
            double value = 0.000;
            return value;
        }
        /**float pk = (float) (180/3.14169);
        float a1 = Float.valueOf(current_latitud) / pk;
        float a2 = Float.valueOf(current_longitud) / pk;
        float b1 = Float.valueOf(dest_latitud) / pk;
        float b2 = Float.valueOf(dest_longitude) / pk;
        float t1 = FloatMath.cos(a1) * FloatMath.cos(a2) *
        FloatMath.cos(b1) * FloatMath.cos(b2);
        float t2 = FloatMath.cos(a1) * FloatMath.sin(a2) *
        FloatMath.cos(b1) * FloatMath.sin(b2);
        float t3 = FloatMath.sin(a1) * FloatMath.sin(b1);
        double tt = Math.acos(t1 + t2 + t3);
        double value = roundNumber(6366000*tt,3);
        */
        double cgLat1 = Double.valueOf(current_latitud);
        //lblHeading.setText(String.valueOf(cgLat1));
        double cgLon1 = Double.valueOf(current_longitud);
        //lblHeading.setText(String.valueOf(cgLon1));
        double cgLat2 = Double.valueOf(dest_latitud);
        //lblHeading.setText(String.valueOf(cgLat2));
        double cgLon2 = Double.valueOf(dest_longitude);
```

```java
        double cgX = 69.1 * (cgLat2 - cgLat1);
        double cgY = 69.1 * -(cgLon2 - cgLon1) * Math.cos(cgLat1/57.3);

        double cgDist = 1603.9 * Math.sqrt(cgX * cgX + cgY * cgY);

        double cgFinal = 1609.3 * (Math.sqrt(((69.1 * (cgLat1 - cgLat2)) *
        (69.1 * (cgLat1 - cgLat2))) + ((69.1 * (cgLon1 - cgLon2) *
        Math.cos(cgLat2/57.3)) * (69.1 * (cgLon1 - cgLon2) * Math.cos(cgLat2/57.3)))));
        //cgFinal = 0;

        return cgFinal;
    }//end double calculateDistance

    public void BindLocationInfo1() {

        try {

            DBAdapter db = new DBAdapter(getBaseContext());
            db.open();
            db.addLocation("01-O2Shop", "53.274350", "-9.050687", " ");

            cursor = db.getAllLocations();
            cursor.moveToFirst();

            //cgHeadings.setText("TITLE"+ "
            "+ "LATTITUDE"+ "         "+"LONGITUDE"+ "         " + "DIST(m)");

            lblNo1.setText(cursor.getString(0));
            lblName1.setText(cursor.getString(1));
            lblLatitude1.setText(cursor.getString(2));
            lblLongitude1.setText(cursor.getString(3));
            lblDistance1.setText("xxx.xxx");
            cursor.moveToNext();

            db.close();
        } catch (Exception ex) {
            Toast.makeText(getBaseContext(), ex.toString(), Toast.LENGTH_LONG).show();
        }
    }//end BindLocationInfo1


    public void BindLocationInfo2() {
        String tempLatitude;
        String tempLongitude;
        String tempDistance;
        Double tempDoubleDistance;
        try {
            tempLatitude = lblLatitude1.getText().toString().trim();
            tempLongitude = lblLongitude1.getText().toString().trim();
            //tempDoubleDistance = calculateDistance(cgCurrLatitude,
            cgCurrLongitude, tempLatitude , tempLongitude);
            //tempDistance = String.valueOf(tempDoubleDistance);

            tempDistance = String.valueOf(roundNumber(calculateDistance
            (cgCurrLatitude, cgCurrLongitude, tempLatitude , tempLongitude),3));
            lblDistance1.setText(tempDistance);


        } catch (Exception ex) {
            Toast.makeText(getBaseContext(), ex.toString(), Toast.LENGTH_LONG).show();
        }
    }//end BindLocationInfo2

    private void findViews() {
        lblHeading  = (TextView)findViewById(R.id.lblHeading);
        lblCurrLatitude = (TextView)findViewById(R.id.lblCurrLatitude);
        lblCurrLongitude = (TextView)findViewById(R.id.lblCurrLongitude);

        lblNo1  = (TextView)findViewById(R.id.lblNo1);
        lblName1  = (TextView)findViewById(R.id.lblName1);
        lblLatitude1  = (TextView)findViewById(R.id.lblLatitude1);
        lblLongitude1  = (TextView)findViewById(R.id.lblLongitude1);
        lblDistance1  = (TextView)findViewById(R.id.lblDistance1);
    }
```

DBAdapter.java

```java
package ie.cathalgreaney.GPSGalway;
import android.content.ContentValues;
import android.content.Context;
import android.database.Cursor;
import android.database.SQLException;
import android.database.sqlite.SQLiteDatabase;
import android.database.sqlite.SQLiteOpenHelper;
import android.util.Log;
import android.widget.Toast;
public class DBAdapter {
public static final String ID = "_id";
public static String TITLE = "title";
public static String DESCRIPTION = "description";
public static String LATTITUDE = "lattitude";
public static String LONGITUDE = "longitude";
public static String ALTITUDE = "altitude";
public static String ACCURACY = "accuracy";
public static String TIME = "time";
public static String DISTANCE = "distance";
private static final String TAG = "GPSLocation";
private static final String DATABASE_NAME = "GPSGalway.db";
private static final String DATABASE_TABLE = "MyLocations";
private static final int DATABASE_VERSION = 2;
private static final String DATABASE_CREATE =
    "create table MyLocations (_id integer primary key autoincrement, "
    + "title text not null , description text  , lattitude text  ,
    longitude text , altitude text , accuracy text , time text ,distance text );";

private final Context context;
private DatabaseHelper DBHelper;
private SQLiteDatabase db;

public DBAdapter(Context ctx) {
    this.context = ctx;
    DBHelper = new DatabaseHelper(context);
}

private static class DatabaseHelper extends SQLiteOpenHelper {
    DatabaseHelper(Context context) {
        super(context, DATABASE_NAME, null, DATABASE_VERSION);
}
@Override
public void onCreate(SQLiteDatabase db) {
    db.execSQL(DATABASE_CREATE);
    // db.execSQL(DATABASE_CREATE_Status);
}
@Override
public void onUpgrade(SQLiteDatabase db, int oldVersion, int newVersion) {
    Log.w(TAG, "Upgrading database from version " + oldVersion + " to "
    + newVersion + ", which will destroy all old data");
    db.execSQL("DROP TABLE IF EXISTS MyLocations");
    onCreate(db);
}

// ---opens the database---
public DBAdapter open() throws SQLException {
    db = DBHelper.getWritableDatabase();
    return this;
}
// ---closes the database---
public void close() {
    DBHelper.close();
}
public boolean deleteAllLocations() {
    // db.rawQuery("DELETE FROM MySpamContacts ", null);
    return db.delete(DATABASE_TABLE, "1=1", null) > 0;
}
```

```java
public void refreshContent()
{
    db.execSQL("DROP TABLE IF EXISTS MyLocations");
    db.execSQL(DATABASE_CREATE);
}
// ---insert a User into the database---
public long addLocation(String title, String latitud, String longitud, String distance) {
            ContentValues initialValues = new ContentValues();
            initialValues.put(TITLE, title);
            initialValues.put(LATTITUDE, latitud);
            initialValues.put(LONGITUDE, longitud);
            initialValues.put(DISTANCE, distance);


            return db.insert(DATABASE_TABLE, null, initialValues);
}
public Cursor getAllLocations() {
            return db.query(DATABASE_TABLE, new String[]
                    { ID, TITLE, LATTITUDE, LONGITUDE,
                    ALTITUDE, ACCURACY, TIME ,DISTANCE},
                    null, null, null, null, null);
}

public boolean updateLocation(String title, String distance) {
            ContentValues args = new ContentValues();
            args.put(TITLE, title);
            args.put(DISTANCE, distance);
            //Toast.makeText(context, "old : " + oldName + " New : " + name1 + " ",
            //Toast.LENGTH_SHORT).show();
            return db.update(DATABASE_TABLE, args, "title='" + title +
            "'",null) > 0;
}
```

Appendix A

Main.xml

```xml
<?xml version="1.0" encoding="utf-8"?>
<ScrollView
xmlns:android="http://schemas.android.com/apk/res/android"
android:layout_width="fill_parent"
android:layout_height="fill_parent">
<LinearLayout
xmlns:android="http://schemas.android.com/apk/res/android"
    android:orientation="vertical"
    android:layout_width="fill_parent"
    android:layout_height="fill_parent">

<TextView
    android:id ="@+id/lblHeading"
    android:text="@string/lblHeadingText"
    android:layout_width="fill_parent"
    android:layout_height="wrap_content">
    </TextView>
 <LinearLayout
 android:layout_width="wrap_content"
 android:layout_height="wrap_content"
 android:orientation="horizontal">
  <TextView
    android:id = "@+id/lblLatitude"
    android:text="@string/lblLatitudeText"
    android:layout_width="wrap_content"
    android:layout_height="wrap_content">
  </TextView>
  <TextView
    android:id = "@+id/lblCurrLatitude"
android:text="@string/lblCurrLatitudeText"
    android:layout_width="wrap_content"
    android:layout_height="wrap_content">
  </TextView>
  <TextView
    android:layout_width="10dip"
    android:layout_height="wrap_content"
    android:visibility="invisible">
  </TextView>
  <TextView
    android:id = "@+id/lblLongitude"
    android:text="@string/lblLongitudeText"
    android:layout_width="wrap_content"
    android:layout_height="wrap_content">
  </TextView>
  <TextView
    android:id = "@+id/lblCurrLongitude"
android:text="@string/lblCurrLongitudeText"
    android:layout_width="wrap_content"
    android:layout_height="wrap_content">
  </TextView>
</LinearLayout>
 <TableLayout
xmlns:android="http://schemas.android.com/apk/res/android"
    android:orientation="vertical"
    android:layout_width="fill_parent"
    android:layout_height="fill_parent">
<TableRow>
 <TextView
    android:id="@+id/lblTitleNo"
    android:text="@string/lblTitleNoText"
    android:visibility="gone">
    </TextView>
 <TextView
    android:id="@+id/lblTitleName"
    android:text="@string/lblTitleNameText"
    android:paddingLeft="10dip">
    </TextView>
 <TextView
    android:id="@+id/lblTitleLatitude"
android:text="@string/lblTitleLatitudeText"
    android:paddingLeft="10dip">
    </TextView>
 <TextView
    android:id="@+id/lblTitleLongitude"
android:text="@string/lblTitleLongitudeText"
    android:paddingLeft="10dip">
    </TextView>
 <TextView
    android:id="@+id/lblTitleDistance"
android:text="@string/lblTitleDistanceText"
    android:paddingLeft="10dip">
    </TextView>
 </TableRow>
  <TableRow>
 <TextView
    android:id="@+id/lblNo1"
    android:text="@string/lblNo1Text"
    android:visibility="gone">
    </TextView>
 <TextView
    android:id="@+id/lblName1"
    android:text="@string/lblName1Text">
    </TextView>
 <TextView
    android:id="@+id/lblLatitude1"
    android:text="@string/lblLatitude1Text"
    android:paddingLeft="10dip">
    </TextView>
 <TextView
    android:id="@+id/lblLongitude1"
    android:text="@string/lblLongitude1Text"
    android:paddingLeft="10dip">
    </TextView>
 <TextView
    android:id="@+id/lblDistance1"
    android:text="@string/lblDistance1Text"
    android:paddingLeft="10dip">
    </TextView>
 </TableRow>
 </TableLayout>
</LinearLayout>
</ScrollView>
```

Appendix A

Strings.xml

```xml
<?xml version="1.0" encoding="utf-8"?>
<resources>
<string name="hello">Hello World, GPSGalway!</string>
<string name="app_name">GPSGalway</string>

<string name="lblHeadingText">You are now at Location:</string>

<string name="lblLatitudeText">Latitude:</string>
<string name="lblCurrLatitudeText">xx.xxxxxx</string>
<string name="lblLongitudeText">Longitude:</string>
<string name="lblCurrLongitudeText">xx.xxxxxx</string>


<string name="lblTitleNoText">No</string>
<string name="lblTitleNameText">Name</string>
<string name="lblTitleLatitudeText">Latitude</string>
<string name="lblTitleLongitudeText">Longitude</string>
<string name="lblTitleDistanceText">Distance</string>

<string name="lblNo1Text">lblNo1Text</string>
<string name="lblName1Text">lblName1Text</string>
<string name="lblLatitude1Text">lblLatitude1Text</string>
<string name="lblLongitude1Text">lblLongitude1Text</string>
<string name="lblDistance1Text">lblDistance1Text</string>
</resources>
```

Manifest.xml

```xml
<?xml version="1.0" encoding="utf-8"?>
<manifest xmlns:android="http://schemas.android.com/apk/res/android"
    package="ie.cathalgreaney.GPSGalway"
    android:versionCode="1"
    android:versionName="1.0">
    <uses-permission
    android:name="android.permission.ACCESS_COARSE_LOCATION">
    </uses-permission>
    <uses-permission
    android:name="android.permission.ACCESS_FINE_LOCATION">
    </uses-permission>
    <application android:icon="@drawable/icon" android:label="@string/app_name">
        <activity android:name=".GPSGalway"
                  android:label="@string/app_name">
            <intent-filter>
                <action android:name="android.intent.action.MAIN" />
                <category android:name="android.intent.category.LAUNCHER" />
            </intent-filter>
        </activity>

    </application>
    <uses-sdk android:minSdkVersion="7" />
</manifest>
```

A4. Objective-C Source Code for 'GPS Galway' iOS Application for Experiment 2.2.5 and 2.2.6

GPSGalwayAppDelegate.h

```objectivec
#import <UIKit/UIKit.h>
#import <sqlite3.h>

@class GPSGalwayViewController;

@interface GPSGalwayAppDelegate : NSObject
   <UIApplicationDelegate> {
     UIWindow *window;
     GPSGalwayViewController   *viewController;
}
@property (nonatomic, retain) IBOutlet UIWindow *window;
@property (nonatomic, retain) IBOutlet GPSGalwayViewController
    *viewController;
+(sqlite3 *) getNewDBConnection;
@end
```

GPSGalwayAppDelegate.m

```objectivec
#import "GPSGalwayAppDelegate.h"
#import "GPSGalwayViewController.h"
@implementation GPSGalwayAppDelegate
@synthesize window;
@synthesize viewController;

- (void)createCopyOfDatabase{
    BOOL success;
    NSError *error;

    NSFileManager *fileManager = [NSFileManager defaultManager];
    NSArray *paths = NSSearchPathForDirectoriesInDomains
    (NSDocumentDirectory, NSUserDomainMask, YES);
    NSString *documentsDirectory = [paths objectAtIndex:0];
    NSString *writableDBPath = [documentsDirectory
    stringByAppendingPathComponent:@"proximity.sqlite"];
    success = [fileManager   fileExistsAtPath:writableDBPath];

    if (success)   return;
    NSString   *defaultDBPath = [[[NSBundle mainBundle] resourcePath]
                    stringByAppendingPathComponent:@"proximity.sqlite"];
    success = [fileManager copyItemAtPath:defaultDBPath toPath:writableDBPath error:&error];
    if (!success) {
       NSAssert1(0, @"Failed to create writable database file with message '%@'.",
       [error localizedDescription]);
    }
}
+(sqlite3 *) getNewDBConnection{
   sqlite3 *newDBconnection;
   NSArray *paths = NSSearchPathForDirectoriesInDomains
   (NSDocumentDirectory, NSUserDomainMask, YES);
   NSString *documentsDirectory = [paths objectAtIndex:0];
   NSString *path = [documentsDirectory
   stringByAppendingPathComponent:@"proximity.sqlite"];

   if (sqlite3_open([path UTF8String], &newDBconnection) == SQLITE_OK) {
       NSLog(@"Database successfully opened");
   }
   else {
      NSLog(@"Error in opening database");
      [paths release];
      [path release];
      [documentsDirectory   release];
   }
   return newDBconnection;
}
```

```objc
#pragma mark -
#pragma mark Application lifecycle

- (BOOL)application:(UIApplication *)application
  didFinishLaunchingWithOptions:(NSDictionary *)launchOptions {

    [self createCopyOfDatabase];
    [window addSubview:viewController.view];
    [window makeKeyAndVisible];
    return YES;
}

#pragma mark -
#pragma mark Memory management

- (void)dealloc {
    [viewController release];
    [window release];
    [super dealloc];
}

@end
```

GPSGalwayViewController.h

```objc
@class LocationsTableCell;
#import <UIKit/UIKit.h>
#import <sqlite3.h>
#import <math.h>
#import <CoreLocation/CoreLocation.h>
#import "GPSGalwayAppDelegate.h"
@interface GPSGalwayViewController : UIViewController
<CLLocationManagerDelegate, UIScrollViewDelegate>
{
    CLLocationManager *locationManager;
    CLLocationDegrees userLat, userLongi;
    CLLocationDegrees locationLat, locationLongi;
    NSMutableArray *locationsArray;
    NSString *latiStr, *longiStr;
    NSString *_userlatitude, *_userlongitude;
    double   distance;
    UINavigationBar   *navigationBar;
    UILabel *nameTitle, *LATTitle;
    UILabel *LONGTitle, *DISTTitle;
    UIView *scrollSubview;
    IBOutlet UILabel *gpsLatitude;
    IBOutlet UILabel *gpsLongitude;
    IBOutlet UIToolbar  *toolbar;
    IBOutlet UIScrollView  *scrollbarView;
    IBOutlet UILabel *loc1,*loc30;
    IBOutlet UILabel *lati1,*lati30;
    IBOutlet UILabel *longi1,*longi30;
    IBOutlet UILabel *dist1,*dist30;
}
@property(nonatomic,retain) NSString   *userlatitude;
@property(nonatomic,retain) NSString   *userlongitude;
@property(nonatomic,retain) CLLocationManager *locationManager;
@property(nonatomic,assign) CLLocationDegrees   userLat;
@property(nonatomic,assign) CLLocationDegrees   userLongi;
@property(nonatomic,assign) CLLocationDegrees   locationLat;
@property(nonatomic,assign) CLLocationDegrees   locationLongi;
@property(nonatomic, retain) NSMutableArray  *locationsArray;
@property (nonatomic, retain) UIScrollView  *scrollbarView;
@property(nonatomic, retain) IBOutlet UINavigationBar  *navigationBar;
@property(nonatomic, retain) UIView *scrollSubview;
-(void) initializeTableData;
-(void)displayExistingLocationsData;
-(void) pingUserLocation:(NSTimer *)aTimer;
-(void)locationManager:(CLLocationManager *)manager
@end
```

Appendix A

GPSGalwayViewController.m

```objc
#import "GPSGalwayViewController.h"
#import "GPSGalwayAppDelegate.h"
@implementation GPSGalwayViewController
@synthesize locationsArray;
@synthesize navigationBar;
@synthesize locationManager;
@synthesize userLat, userLongi;
@synthesize locationLat,locationLongi;
@synthesize userlatitude = _userlatitude;
@synthesize userlongitude = _userlongitude;
@synthesize scrollbarView;
@synthesize scrollSubview;
#pragma mark -
#pragma mark UIViewController methods
- (void)loadView {
    [super loadView];
    [self.view addSubview:scrollbarView];
    [scrollbarView setContentSize:CGSizeMake(320, 300)];
    [scrollbarView setScrollEnabled:YES];
    [scrollbarView setClipsToBounds:YES];
    [NSTimer scheduledTimerWithTimeInterval:1.0 target:self
     selector:@selector(pingUserLocation:) userInfo:nil  repeats:YES];
}
- (void)viewDidLoad
    [super viewDidLoad];
    locationsArray =[ [NSMutableArray alloc] init];
    [self   initializeTableData];         //Making Database connection
}
-  (BOOL)shouldAutorotateToInterfaceOrientation:
    (UIInterfaceOrientation)interfaceOrientation {
        return (interfaceOrientation == UIInterfaceOrientationPortrait);
    }
- (void)didReceiveMemoryWarning  {
   [super  didReceiveMemoryWarning];
}
- (void)viewDidUnload
{
    self.scrollbarView = nil;
    scrollSubview = nil;
    self.view = nil;
}
#pragma mark -
#pragma mark CLLocationManager delegate methods

-(void)locationManager:(CLLocationManager *)manager
        didUpdateToLocation:(CLLocation *)newLocation
                    fromLocation:(CLLocation *)oldLocation
{
    CLLocationCoordinate2D  location =  newLocation.coordinate;
    userLat = location.latitude;
    userLongi = location.longitude;
    _userlatitude = [NSString   stringWithFormat:@"%f", userLat];
    gpsLatitude.text = _userlatitude;
    _userlongitude = [NSString   stringWithFormat:@"%f", userLongi];
    gpsLongitude.text = _userlongitude;
    NSLog(@"locationManager time:%@:", [NSDate  date]);

    NSString *lat1 = [NSString   stringWithFormat:@"%@", lati1.text];
    NSString *lon1 = [NSString  stringWithFormat:@"%@",longi1.text];
    distance = [self  calculateDistance:_userlatitude :_userlongitude :lat1 :lon1];
    dist1.text = [[NSString  alloc]  initWithFormat:@"%.3f", distance];
    NSString *lat30 = [NSString   stringWithFormat:@"%@", lati30.text];
    NSString *lon30 = [NSString   stringWithFormat:@"%@",longi30.text];
    distance = [self  calculateDistance:_userlatitude :_userlongitude :lat30 :lon30];
    dist30.text = [[NSString   alloc] initWithFormat:@"%.3f", distance];

    if (self.scrollbarView.dragging)
    {
        [self.scrollbarView  touchesEnded:UITouchPhaseBegan
```

```objc
                    withEvent:UIControlEventTouchDragInside];
    }
    [manager stopUpdatingLocation];
}
- (void)locationManager: (CLLocationManager *)manager
        didFailWithError: (NSError *)error
{
    NSLog(@"Root location Error:%@", error);
    [manager stopUpdatingLocation];
}
#pragma mark -
#pragma mark private methods
-(void)pingUserLocation:(NSTimer *)aTimer
{
    NSLog(@"ping Userlocation");
    locationManager = [[CLLocationManager alloc] init];
    locationManager.delegate = self;
    locationManager.desiredAccuracy = kCLLocationAccuracyBest;
    [locationManager startUpdatingLocation];
}
-(void) initializeTableData
{
    sqlite3 *db = [GPSGalwayAppDelegate getNewDBConnection];
    sqlite3_stmt *statement = nil;
    const char *sql = "select * from location";
    if(sqlite3_prepare_v2(db,sql, -1, &statement, NULL)!=SQLITE_OK)
    {
        NSAssert1(0,@"Error preparing statement", sqlite3_errmsg(db));
    }
    else {
        while(sqlite3_step(statement) == SQLITE_ROW)
        {
            [locationsArray addObject:[NSString
            stringWithFormat:@"%s| %s| %s",(char*)sqlite3_column_text(statement,1),

            (char*)sqlite3_column_text(statement,3),
            (char*)sqlite3_column_text(statement,4)]];
        }
    }
    sqlite3_finalize(statement);
    [self displayExistingLocationsData];
}
- (void) displayExistingLocationsData
{
    NSString *str1 = [[NSString alloc] initWithString:[locationsArray objectAtIndex:0]];
    NSArray *array1 = [[[NSArray alloc] initWithArray:
                [str1 componentsSeparatedByString:@"|"]] autorelease];
    loc1.text = [array1 objectAtIndex:0];
    lati1.text = [array1 objectAtIndex:1];
    longi1.text = [array1 objectAtIndex:2];
    NSString *str30 = [[NSString alloc] initWithString:[locationsArray
objectAtIndex:29]];
    NSArray *array30 = [[[NSArray alloc] initWithArray:
                [str30 componentsSeparatedByString:@"|"]] autorelease];
    loc30.text = [array30 objectAtIndex:0];
    lati30.text = [array30 objectAtIndex:1];
    longi30.text = [array30 objectAtIndex:2];
}
-(double) calculateDistance:(NSString*)
                    current_latitud:(NSString*)
                    current_longitud:(NSString*)
                    dest_latitud:(NSString*)
                    dest_longitude
{
    if (current_latitud == @"" || current_longitud == @"")
    {
        double value = 0.000;
        return value;
    }

    double cgLat1 = [current_latitud doubleValue];
    double cgLon1 = [current_longitud doubleValue];
    double cgLat2 = [dest_latitud doubleValue];
    double cgLon2 = [dest_longitude doubleValue];
```

```objc
        double cgX = 69.1 * (cgLat2 - cgLat1);
        double cgY = 69.1 * -(cgLon2 - cgLon1) * cos(cgLat1/57.3);
        double cgDist = 1603.9 * sqrt(cgX * cgX + cgY * cgY);
        NSLog(@"Calculate distance: %.6f", cgDist);
        double cgFinal = 1609.3 * (sqrt(((69.1 * (cgLat1 - cgLat2)) *
                    (69.1 * (cgLat1 - cgLat2))) + ((69.1 * (cgLon1 - cgLon2) *
                    cos(cgLat2/57.3)) * (69.1 * (cgLon1 - cgLon2) * cos(cgLat2/57.3)))));
        return (cgFinal);
}       //end  of calculateDistance

#pragma mark dealloc methods
- (void)dealloc {
        [locationsArray release];
        [latiStr  release];
        [longiStr release];
        [_userlatitude  release];
        [_userlongitude release];
        [loc1, loc30   release];
        [lati1, lati30  release];
        [longi1, longi30  release];
        [dist1, dist30  release];
        [toolbar release];
        [scrollbarView  release];
        [navigationBar release];
        [nameTitle, DISTTitle release];
        [LATTitle, LONGTitle   release];
        [gpsLatitude, gpsLongitude release];
        [super   dealloc];
}
@end
```

A5. Java Source Code for 'Translate' Android Application for Chapter 4

Translate.java
```java
package ie.cathalgreaney.translate;
import java.util.concurrent.ExecutorService;
import java.util.concurrent.Executors;
import java.util.concurrent.Future;
import java.util.concurrent.RejectedExecutionException;
import android.app.Activity;
import android.os.Bundle;
import android.os.Handler;
import android.text.Editable;
import android.text.TextWatcher;
import android.view.View;
import android.widget.AdapterView;
import android.widget.ArrayAdapter;
import android.widget.EditText;
import android.widget.Spinner;
import android.widget.TextView;
import android.widget.AdapterView.OnItemSelectedListener;

public class Translate extends Activity {
    private Spinner fromSpinner;
    private Spinner toSpinner;
    private EditText origText;
    private TextView transText;
    private TextView retransText;
    private TextWatcher textWatcher;
    private OnItemSelectedListener itemListener;
    private Handler guiThread;
    private ExecutorService transThread;
    private Runnable updateTask;
    private Future transPending;

    @Override
    public void onCreate(Bundle savedInstanceState) {
        super.onCreate(savedInstanceState);
        setContentView(R.layout.main);
        initThreading();
        findViews();
        setAdapters();
        setListeners();
    }
    @Override
    protected void onDestroy() {
        transThread.shutdownNow();
        super.onDestroy();
    }
    private void findViews() {
        fromSpinner = (Spinner) findViewById(R.id.from_language);
        toSpinner = (Spinner) findViewById(R.id.to_language);
        origText = (EditText) findViewById(R.id.original_text);
        transText = (TextView) findViewById(R.id.translated_text);
        retransText = (TextView) findViewById(R.id.retranslated_text);
    }
    private void setAdapters() {
        ArrayAdapter<CharSequence> adapter = ArrayAdapter.createFromResource(
                this, R.array.languages, android.R.layout.simple_spinner_item);
        adapter.setDropDownViewResource(android.R.layout.simple_spinner_dropdown_item);
        fromSpinner.setAdapter(adapter);
        toSpinner.setAdapter(adapter);
        fromSpinner.setSelection(8); // English (en)
        toSpinner.setSelection(21); // French (fr)
    }
    private void setListeners() {
        textWatcher = new TextWatcher() {
            public void beforeTextChanged(CharSequence s, int start,
                    int count, int after) {
            }
```

```java
        public void onTextChanged(CharSequence s, int start,
                int before, int count) {queueUpdate(1000);
        }
        public void afterTextChanged(Editable s) {
        }
    };
    itemListener = new OnItemSelectedListener() {
        public void onItemSelected(AdapterView parent, View v, int position, long id) {
            queueUpdate(200);
        }
        public void onNothingSelected(AdapterView parent) {
        }
    };
    origText.addTextChangedListener(textWatcher);
    fromSpinner.setOnItemSelectedListener(itemListener);
    toSpinner.setOnItemSelectedListener(itemListener);
}
private void initThreading() {
    guiThread = new Handler();
    transThread = Executors.newSingleThreadExecutor();
    updateTask = new Runnable() {
        public void run() {
            String original = origText.getText().toString().trim();
            if (transPending != null) transPending.cancel(true);
            if (original.length() == 0) {
                transText.setText(R.string.empty);
                retransText.setText(R.string.empty);
            } else {
                transText.setText(R.string.translating);
                retransText.setText(R.string.translating);
                try {
                    TranslateTask translateTask = new TranslateTask(
                            Translate.this, original, getLang(fromSpinner), getLang(toSpinner));
                    transPending = transThread.submit(translateTask);
                } catch (RejectedExecutionException e) {
                    transText.setText(R.string.translation_error);
                    retransText.setText(R.string.translation_error);
                }
            }
        }
    };
}
private String getLang(Spinner spinner) {
    String result = spinner.getSelectedItem().toString();
    int lparen = result.indexOf('(');
    int rparen = result.indexOf(')');
    result = result.substring(lparen + 1, rparen);
    return result;
}
private void queueUpdate(long delayMillis) {
    guiThread.removeCallbacks(updateTask);
    guiThread.postDelayed(updateTask, delayMillis);
}
public void setTranslated(String text) {
    guiSetText(transText, text);
}
public void setRetranslated(String text) {
    guiSetText(retransText, text);
}
private void guiSetText(final TextView view, final String text) {
    guiThread.post(new Runnable() {
        public void run() {
            view.setText(text);
        }
    });
}
}
```

Appendix A

TranslateTask.java

```java
package ie.cathalgreaney.translate;
import java.io.BufferedReader;
import java.io.IOException;
import java.io.InputStreamReader;
import java.net.HttpURLConnection;
import java.net.URL;
import java.net.URLEncoder;
import org.json.JSONException;
import org.json.JSONObject;
import android.util.Log;

public class TranslateTask implements Runnable {
    private static final String TAG = "TranslateTask";
    private final Translate translate;
    private final String original, from, to;
    TranslateTask(Translate translate, String original, String from, String to) {
        this.translate = translate;
        this.original = original;
        this.from = from;
        this.to = to;}
    public void run() {
        String trans = doTranslate(original, from, to);
        translate.setTranslated(trans);
        String retrans = doTranslate(trans, to, from);
        translate.setRetranslated(retrans);}
    private String doTranslate(String original, String from, String to) {
        String result = translate.getResources().getString(R.string.translation_error);
        HttpURLConnection con = null;
        try {
            if (Thread.interrupted())
                throw new InterruptedException();
            String q = URLEncoder.encode(original, "UTF-8");
            URL url = new URL(
                    "http://ajax.googleapis.com/ajax/services/language/translate"
                        + "?v=1.0" + "&q=" + q + "&langpair=" + from
                        + "%7C" + to);
            con = (HttpURLConnection) url.openConnection();
            con.setReadTimeout(10000);
            con.setConnectTimeout(15000);
            con.setRequestMethod("GET");
            con.addRequestProperty("Referer",
                    "http://www.pragprog.com/titles/eband3/hello-android");
            con.setDoInput(true);
            con.connect();
            if (Thread.interrupted())
                throw new InterruptedException();
                BufferedReader reader = new BufferedReader(
                    new InputStreamReader(con.getInputStream(), "UTF-8"));
            String payload = reader.readLine();
            reader.close();
            JSONObject jsonObject = new JSONObject(payload);
            result = jsonObject.getJSONObject("responseData")
                    .getString("translatedText")
                    .replace("&#39;", "'")
                    .replace("&amp;", "&");
        if (Thread.interrupted()) throw new InterruptedException();
        } catch (IOException e) {
            Log.e(TAG, "IOException", e);
        } catch (JSONException e) {
            Log.e(TAG, "JSONException", e);
        } catch (InterruptedException e) {
            Log.d(TAG, "InterruptedException", e);
            result = translate.getResources().getString(
                    R.string.translation_interrupted);
        } finally {
            if (con != null) {
                con.disconnect();}}
        return result;}}
```

Appendix A

Main.xml

```xml
<?xml version="1.0" encoding="utf-8"?>
<ScrollView
xmlns:android="http://schemas.android.com/apk/res/android"
    android:layout_width="fill_parent"
    android:layout_height="fill_parent">
    <TableLayout
    android:layout_width="fill_parent"
    android:layout_height="fill_parent"
    android:stretchColumns="1"
    android:padding="10dip">
    <TableRow>
    <TextView
    android:text="@string/from_text"
    android:visibility="visible">
    </TextView>
    <Spinner
    android:id="@+id/from_language"
    android:visibility="visible">
    </Spinner>
    </TableRow>
    <EditText
    android:id="@+id/original_text"
    android:hint="@string/original_hint"
    android:padding="10dip"
    android:textSize="18sp">
    </EditText>
    <TableRow>
     <TextView
    android:text="@string/to_text"
    android:visibility="visible">
    </TextView>
    <Spinner
    android:id="@+id/to_language"
    android:visibility="visible">
    </Spinner>
    </TableRow>
    <TextView
    android:id="@+id/translated_text"
    android:padding="10dip"
    android:textSize="18sp">
    </TextView>
    <TextView
    android:text="@string/back_text">
    </TextView>
    <TextView
    android:id="@+id/retranslated_text"
    android:padding="10dip"
    android:textSize="18sp">
    </TextView>
    </TableLayout>
</ScrollView>
```

Arrays.xml

```xml
<?xml version="1.0" encoding="utf-8"?>
<resources>
<array name="languages">
<item>English (en)</item>
<item>Irish (ie)</item>
<item>Latvian (lv)</item>
<item>Lithuanian (lt)</item>
<item>Polish (pl)</item>
<item>Spanish (es)</item>
<item>Swedish (sv)</item>
</array>
</resources>
```

Strings.xml

```xml
<?xml version="1.0" encoding="utf-8"?>

<resources>
<string name="app_name">Translate</string>
<string name="from_text">Cathals Translator:</string>
<string name="to_text">To:</string>
<string name="back_text">And back again:</string>
<string name="original_hint">Enter text to translate</string>
<string name="empty"></string>
<string name="translating">Translating...</string>
<string name="translation_error">(Translation error)</string>
<string name="translation_interrupted">(Translation interrupted)</string>
</resources>
```

Manifest.xml

```xml
?xml version="1.0" encoding="utf-8"?>
<manifest xmlns:android="http://schemas.android.com/apk/res/android"
      package="ie.cathalgreaney.translate"
      android:versionCode="1"
      android:versionName="1.0">
    <uses-permission android:name="android.permission.INTERNET" />
    <application android:icon="@drawable/icon" android:label="@string/app_name">
        <activity android:name=".Translate"
                  android:label="@string/app_name">
            <intent-filter>
                <action android:name="android.intent.action.MAIN" />
                <category android:name="android.intent.category.LAUNCHER" />
            </intent-filter>
        </activity>
    </application>
    <uses-sdk android:minSdkVersion="7" />
</manifest>
```

B1. Calibrated GPS Readings for Experiment 2.2.1 and 2.2.3

The calibrated GPS files are a set of text based data files containing the information obtained from the calibrated GPS device used to gather baseline location coordinates for this book. Each file contains roughly 8 pages of raw GPS data and there is between one and three files for each of the 70 locations used in Experiment 2.2.1. It is impractical to list all the data in hardcopy.
This section lists all the files for experiment 2.2.1 and 2.2.3 and there is a printout of the first page of one of these files to show the format of the information.

To view any of these files in full go to the online resource for this book at:
http://www.irishapps.org/appendixb1.html

```
S_VBOX_010 Block6.VBO
S_VBOX_014 Monaghans.VBO
S_VBOX_017 Liosban.VBO
S_VBOX_019 Townhall.VBO
S_VBOX_020 Courthouse.VBO
S_VBOX_032 Monsoon South.VBO
S_VBOX_042 Vision Express.VBO
S_VBOX_046 Dubrey.VBO
S_VBOX_049 McCarthys.VBO
S_VBOX_054 Tommy Hilfiger.VBO
S_VBOX_055 River Island.VBO
S_VBOX_058 Unknown StNicks.VBO
S_VBOX_070 AIB.VBO
S_VBOX_074 Hearts.VBO
S_VBOX_092 Unknown Salthill Hotel.VBO
S_VBOX_094 Joyces SC.VBO

3Store - cat2.VBO
AIB-1 - cat3.VBO
AIB-2 - cat3.VBO
Anthony Ryans - cat2.VBO
Block6-1 - cat4.VBO
Block6-2 - cat4.VBO
Body Shop - cat3.VBO
BOI - cat3.VBO
Brennans - cat2.VBO
Brennans2 - cat2.VBO
Brown Thomas - cat3.VBO
Butlers - cat2.VBO
Cafe Express - cat2.VBO
Camera Shop - cat3.VBO
Carpenters - cat2.VBO
Carphone Whouse - cat2.VBO
Cathedral - cat3.VBO
Corner Shop - cat3.VBO
Courthouse-1 - cat2.VBO
Courthouse-2 - cat2.VBO

Dubrey-1 - cat2.VBO
Dunnes - cat4.VBO
Eason1 - cat2.VBO
Eason2 - cat2.VBO
Elles Cafe - cat2.VBO
Eyre House - cat3.VBO
EyreSq SC - cat2.VBO
EyreSq SC - cat3.VBO
EyreSq SC - cat4.VBO
EyreSq SC.VBO
Fallers - cat3.VBO
Flanagans - cat2.VBO
Flanagans2 - cat2.VBO
Foot Locker - cat3.VBO
Galway GC - cat4.VBO
Galway GC-2 - cat4.VBO
Garavans - cat3.VBO
GBC - cat2.VBO
GBC - cat3.VBO
GBC.VBO
Hanleys - cat2.VBO
Hartmanns - cat3.VBO
Hearts-1 - all.VBO
Hearts-1 - cat3.VBO
Hearts-1 - cat4.VBO
Hearts-2 - cat3.VBO
Hollands - cat3.VBO
HSamuel - all.VBO
HSamuel - cat2.VBO
HSamuel - cat3.VBO
HSamuel2 - cat3.VBO
Joyces SC - all.VBO
Joyces SC - cat4.VBO
Joyces SC - cat5.VBO
Joyces SC-1 - cat4.VBO
Lazlo - cat3.VBO
Lifestyle - cat2.VBO
```

```
Liosban-1 - cat4.VBO
Liosban-2 - cat4.VBO
Logues.VBO
Maxwells - cat3.VBO
McCambridges - cat3.VBO
McCarthys-1 - cat2.VBO
McCarthys-2 - cat2.VBO
McDonalds - cat3.VBO
Meteor - cat2.VBO
Monaghans-1 - cat3.VBO
Monsoon North - cat3.VBO
Monsoon South-1 - cat2.VBO
Monsoon South-2 - cat2.VBO
O2 ShopSt - cat2.VBO
O2 Williamsgate - cat3.VBO
O2 Williamsgate - cat4.VBO
O2 Williamsgate.VBO
Omniplex - cat2.VBO
Powells - all.VBO
Powells - cat3.VBO
Powells - cat4.VBO
River Island-1 - cat2.VBO
River Island-2 - cat2.VBO
Sailin - cat4.VBO
Salthill Hotel - cat2.VBO
Sasha - cat3.VBO
Schuh - cat2.VBO
Seapoint - cat3.VBO
StNicks-1 - cat4.VBO
Supermacs - all.VBO
Supermacs - cat2.VBO
Supermacs - cat3.VBO
Taaffes1 - cat2.VBO
Taaffes2 - cat2.VBO
Tommy Hil - cat2.VBO
Townhall-1 - cat2.VBO
Townhall-2 - cat3.VBO
Treasure Chest - cat2.VBO
Tribes - cat3.VBO
Vision Express-1 - cat2.VBO
Vision Express-2 - all.VBO
Vision Express-2 - cat2.VBO
Vision Express-2 - cat3.VBO
Vodafone - cat3.VBO
Webworks - all.VBO
Webworks - cat2.VBO
Webworks - cat3.VBO
Whelans Chemist - cat3.VBO

Zatzuma1 - all.VBO
Zatzuma1 - cat3.VBO
Zatzuma1 - cat4.VBO
Zatzuma2 - cat2.VBO
Zerep - cat3.VBO
Zhavigo - cat2.VBO
Zhavigo2 - cat2.VBO
Ballybane-TuamRd-2.VBO
Barefield Bypass1.VBO
Barefield Bypass2.VBO
Crusheen-Barefield Bypass1.VBO
Crusheen-Barefield Bypass2.VBO
Dooradoyle-Tunnel.VBO
Ennis-Limerick.VBO
filelist.txt
Gort North-South.VBO
Gort-Galway.VBO
kml
Limerick Tunnel-Castletroy.VBO
Limerick Tunnel-Dooradoyle.VBO
Limerick-Bunratty.VBO
Parkway-Limerick.VBO
Roscam-Clarinbridge.VBO
UL-Plassey Park.VBO
VBOX_101.VBO
VBOX_102.VBO
VBOX_103.VBO
VBOX_105.VBO
VBOX_111.VBO
VBOX_112.VBO
VBOX_113.VBO
VBOX_114.VBO
VBOX_115.VBO
VBOX_116.VBO
VBOX_118 UL Public Carpark.VBO
VBOX_119 UL Stables Arch Paddock.VBO
VBOX_139 UL Eng Research.VBO
VBOX_145.VBO
VBOX_146.VBO
VBOX_147.VBO
```

```
File created on 29/10/2010 @ 12:35

[header]
satellites
time
latitude
longitude
velocity kmh
heading
height
Event 1 time

[channel units]

[comments]
(c)2001 - 2007 Racelogic
VBII SX10 V01.06 B. 0001
Firmware Revision : 033
GPS : S-SX2g

Serial Number : 00014436
Log Rate (Hz) : 10.00
Kalman Filter - Pos : 0  Vel : 0
Gps Optimisation : High Dynamics

[module Information]

[column names]
sats time lat long velocity heading height event-1

[data]
008 123523.60 +3197.443481 +00540.190925 000.159 177.75 +0103.11 0.00000
008 123527.60 +3197.443411 +00540.190933 000.125 177.75 +0103.12 0.00000
008 123527.70 +3197.443412 +00540.190934 000.435 177.75 +0103.11 0.00000
008 123527.80 +3197.443414 +00540.190936 000.545 177.75 +0103.11 0.00000
008 123527.90 +3197.443406 +00540.190935 000.021 177.75 +0103.11 0.00000
008 123528.00 +3197.443406 +00540.190934 000.198 177.75 +0103.11 0.00000
008 123528.10 +3197.443405 +00540.190936 000.052 177.75 +0103.11 0.00000
008 123528.20 +3197.443403 +00540.190936 000.131 177.75 +0103.11 0.00000
008 123528.30 +3197.443405 +00540.190937 000.058 177.75 +0103.11 0.00000
008 123528.40 +3197.443407 +00540.190938 000.394 177.75 +0103.11 0.00000
008 123528.50 +3197.443402 +00540.190939 000.110 177.75 +0103.11 0.00000
008 123528.60 +3197.443399 +00540.190937 000.117 177.75 +0103.11 0.00000
008 123528.70 +3197.443400 +00540.190937 000.235 177.75 +0103.11 0.00000
008 123528.80 +3197.443397 +00540.190939 000.137 177.75 +0103.11 0.00000
                             -
                             -
                             -
   <There are 420 lines removed... see online resources for the complete file
          and all other 159 files relating to the 70 locations>
                             -
                             -
                             -
008 123610.10 +3197.443252 +00540.191143 000.192 177.75 +0102.57 0.00000
008 123610.20 +3197.443254 +00540.191143 000.149 177.75 +0102.56 0.00000
008 123610.30 +3197.443252 +00540.191143 000.230 177.75 +0102.57 0.00000
008 123610.40 +3197.443250 +00540.191143 000.105 177.75 +0102.56 0.00000
008 123610.50 +3197.443249 +00540.191141 000.173 177.75 +0102.57 0.00000
END
```

B2. Location Analysis for Experiment 2.2.1
Location 001: O2 Shop, Williamsgate St., Eyre Sq., Galway.

Results:
Results File: O2 Williamsgate.VBO
Recorded on: 31/10/2010 @ 20:50
Contains: 140 category 3 locations - USABLE
                         65 category 4 locations - USABLE

Category 3 samples produced an average location of:
53.27434317, -9.050454331, 70.33933824
Latitude: 53.27434317
Longitude: -9.050454331
Altitude: 70.33933824

Category 4 samples produced an average location of:
53.27434487, -9.050452733, 68.72
Latitude: 53.27434487
Longitude: -9.050452733
Altitude: 68.72

All samples produced an average location of:
53.2743437, -9.050453838, 69.84005076
Latitude: 53.2743437
Longitude: -9.050453838
Altitude: 69.84005076

Exact Location

Analysis:
Distance from Category 4 to Category 3 result:
$1603.9 * \sqrt{x*x + y*y}$
$x = 69.1 * (53.27434487 - 53.27434317)$
$y = 69.1 * -(9.050452733 - 9.050454331) * \cos(53.27434317/57.3)$

Distance(calculated):   0.216867885 m

There are less that 100 category 4 GPS points, but they are verified by the category 3 information. However, all the mapping tools show this location to be over 15m ESE from it's expected position on the maps. Therefore, the Google maps location was used rather than the Vbox location.
Maps: 53.274350,-9.050687

Yahoo Maps

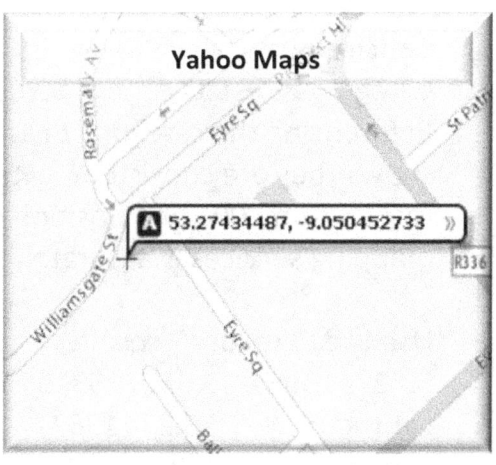
Yahoo Maps

Conclusion:
There are not enough category 4 samples to Google, Bing and Yahoo Maps, they are also verified by Google Street View photos.

Use the Maps result.
53.274350, - 9.050687
Latitude: 53.274350
Longitude: - 9.050687

Google Street View

Location 002: Logues Shoes, Williamsgate St., Eyre Sq., Galway.

Results:
Results File: VBOX_005 Logues .VBO
Recorded on: 31/10/2010 @ 20:50
Contains: 250 category 2 locations - USABLE
Category 2 samples produced an average location of:
53.27419677, -9.0507163, 65.73536667
Latitude: 53.27419677
Longitude: -9.0507163
Altitude: 65.73536667

Exact Location

Analysis:
Distance from Location 001(Category 4 location):
Location 001: 53.27434487, -9.050452733, 68.72
Category 2:   53.27419677, -9.0507163, 65.73536667

$1603.9 * sqrt(x*x + y*y)$
$x = 69.1 * (53.27419677 - 53.27434487)$
$y = 69.1 * -(9.0507163 - 9.050452733) * cos(53.27434487/57.3)$

Distance(calculated):   24.05138337 m
Bearing(calculated):   226.785deg
Distance(measured):   24 m
Bearing(observed):   225 deg

Distance calculated and distance measured are consistent.
Bearing calculated and bearing observed are consistent.

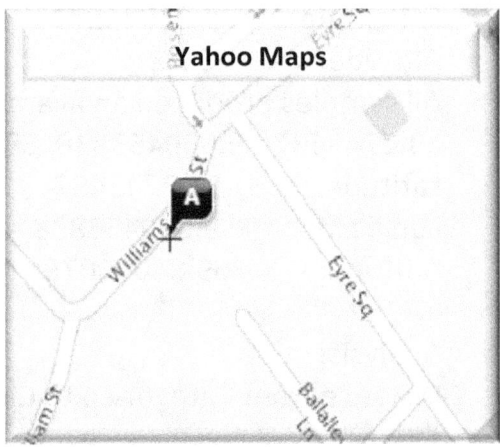
Yahoo Maps

Conclusion:
Category 2 results cannot be used on their own. Referencing the category 2 results to Location 001 shows they are consistent with the category 4 results from 001 and position on the online mapping services is accurate.

Use the Category 2 result.
53.27419677, -9.0507163, 65.73536667
Latitude: 53.27419677
Longitude: -9.0507163
Verified using Google Street View.
Verified using Google, Yahoo and Bing Maps.

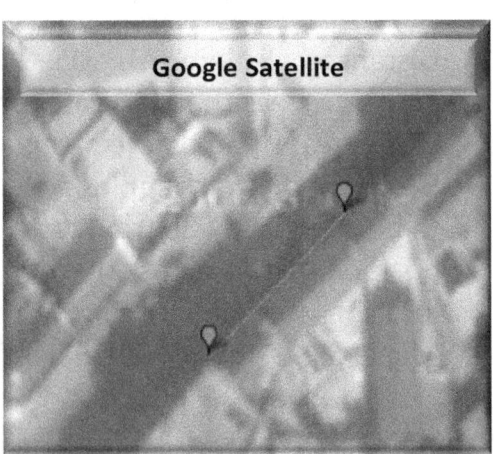
Google Satellite

Google Street View

Appendix B

Location 003: GBC Restaurant, Williamsgate St., Galway.

Results:
Results File: VBOX_006 GBC.VBO
Recorded on: 31/10/2010 @ 20:51
Contains: 300 category 2 locations - USABLE
                          24 category 3 locations - USABLE

Category 2 samples produced an average location of:
53.27420875, -9.050817943, 77.105
Latitude: 53.27420875
Longitude: -9.050817943, Altitude: 77.105
Category 3 samples produced an average location of:
53.27423787, -9.050819957, 81.49
Latitude: 53.27423787
Longitude: -9.050819957, Altitude: 81.49
All samples produced an average location of:
53.27420498, -9.05081806, 72.79243333
Latitude: 53.27420498
Longitude: -9.05081806, Altitude: 72.79243333

Analysis:

Distance from Category 3 to Category 2 result:
1603.9 * sqrt(x * x + y * y)
x = 69.1 * (53.27423787 - 53.27420875)
y = 69.1 * -(9.050819957 - 9.050817943) * cos(53.27420875 /57.3)

Distance(calculated):   3.240989368 m

Inconsistent result... Requires further attention. There are less than 100 samples of category 3 information, so it must be verified.

Distance from Location 004(Category 4 location):
Location 004:
53.27407154, -9.051042107, 77.38713115
Category 3:   53.27423787, -9.050819957, 81.49
1603.9 * sqrt(x * x + y * y)
x = 69.1 * (53.27423787 - 53.27407154)
y = 69.1 * -(53.27407154 - 9.051042107) * cos(53.27407154 /57.3)

Distance(calculated):   23.67233111 m
Bearing(calculated):   38.595 deg
Distance(measured):   16 m
Bearing(observed):   40 deg

Conclusion:
Calculated and measured distance from Location 004 is inconsistent. Calculated result is:
53.2741815, -9.0508877
Latitude: 53.2741815
Longitude: - 9.0508877
Verified using Google Street View.
Verified using Google, Yahoo and Bing Maps.

Exact Location

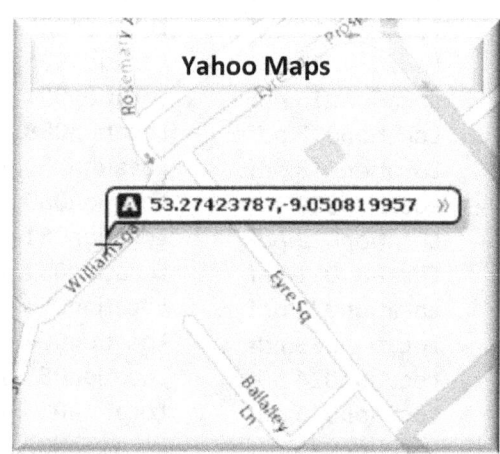
Yahoo Maps

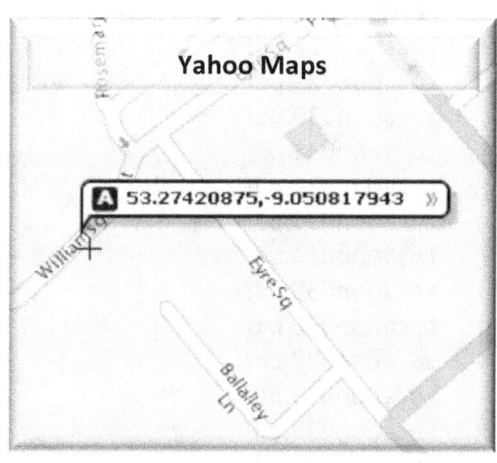
Yahoo Maps

Google Street View

There are 70 locations in all and each one has a single page in the same format as the three previous pages. To view any of these files in full go to the online resource for this book at:
http://www.irishapps.org/appendixb2.html

Online Files:

Location001.pdf
Location002.pdf
Location003.pdf
Location004.pdf
Location005.pdf
Location006.pdf
Location007.pdf
Location008.pdf
Location009.pdf
Location010.pdf
Location011.pdf
Location012.pdf
Location013.pdf
Location014.pdf
Location015.pdf
Location016.pdf
Location017.pdf
Location018.pdf
Location019.pdf
Location020.pdf
Location021.pdf
Location022.pdf
Location023.pdf
Location024.pdf
Location025.pdf
Location026.pdf
Location027.pdf
Location028.pdf
Location029.pdf
Location030.pdf
Location031.pdf
Location032.pdf
Location033.pdf
Location034.pdf
Location035.pdf
Location036.pdf
Location037.pdf
Location038.pdf
Location039.pdf
Location040.pdf
Location041.pdf
Location042.pdf
Location043.pdf
Location044.pdf
Location045.pdf
Location046.pdf
Location047.pdf
Location048.pdf
Location049.pdf
Location050.pdf
Location051.pdf
Location052.pdf
Location053.pdf
Location054.pdf
Location055.pdf
Location056.pdf
Location057.pdf
Location058.pdf
Location059.pdf
Location060.pdf
Location061.pdf
Location062.pdf
Location063.pdf
Location064.pdf
Location065.pdf
Location066.pdf
Location067.pdf
Location068.pdf
Location069.pdf
Location070.pdf

B3. Raw GPS Data Overlaid onto Google/Yahoo Maps for Experiment 2.2.3

Route 001: Galway: Ballybrit – Briarhill - Carnmore.
Results:
Log Files: Ballybrit–Briarhill-Carnmore-1.VBO
               Ballybrit–Briarhill-Carnmore-2.VBO
Date Created: 2010-10-29
Analysis/Conclusion:
Google and Yahoo are accurate.
One Yahoo location needs to be updated.

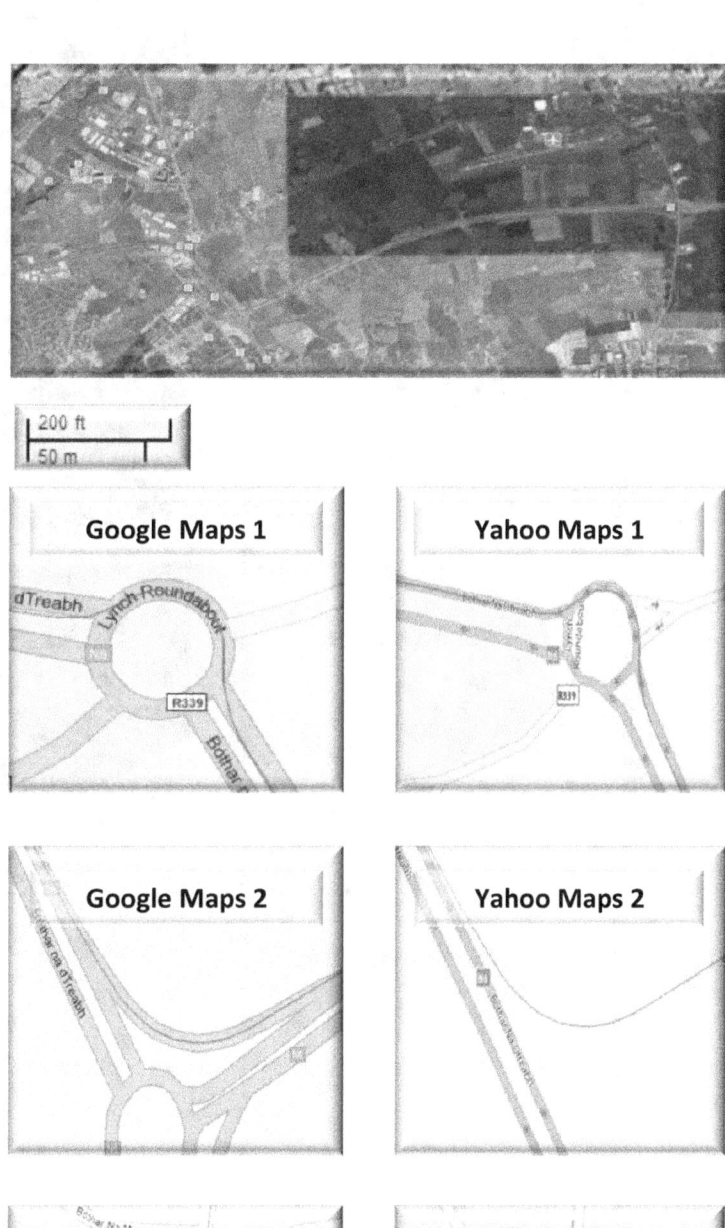

Route 002: Galway: Ballybrit – Tuam Rd - Mervue.

Results:
Log Files: Ballybane-TuamRd-1/2.VBO
TuamRd-Mervue-1.VBO
Date Created: 2010-10-29/30
Analysis/Conclusion:
Google and Yahoo are accurate.

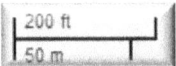

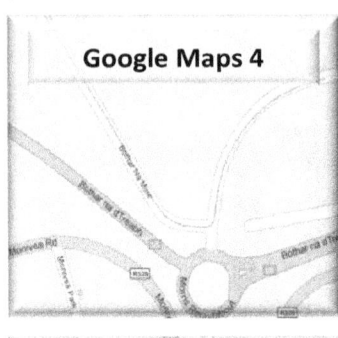
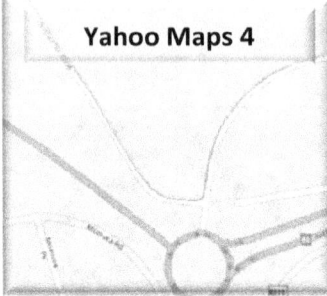

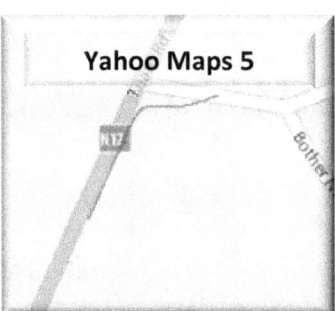

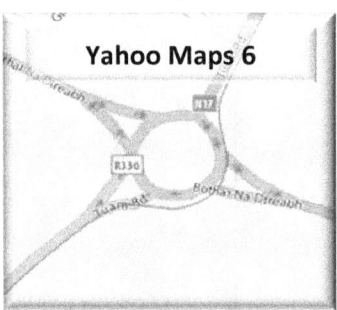

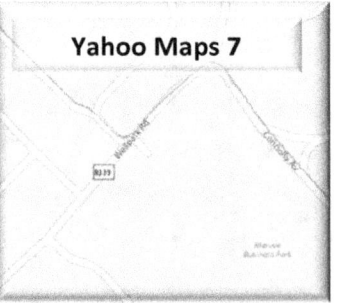

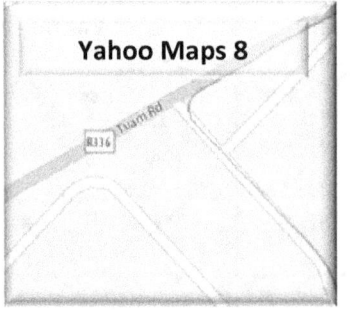

Route 003:   Galway: Kingston – Headford Rd.

Results:
Log Files: JoycesSC-GalwatSC-1.VBO
Date Created: 2010-10-30
Analysis/Conclusion:
Google and Yahoo are accurate.

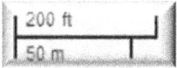

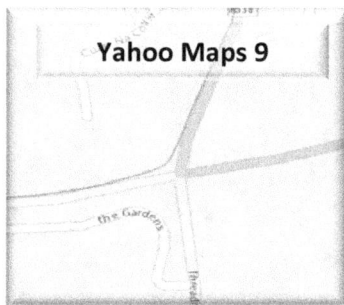

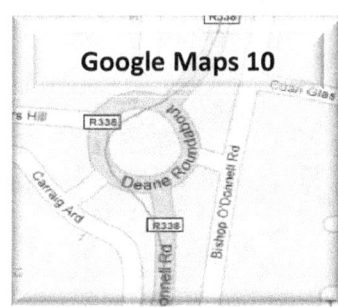
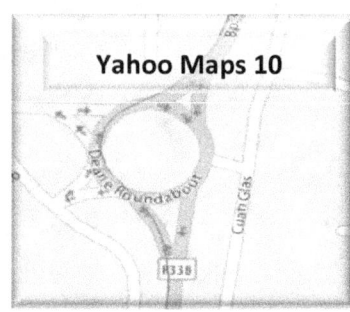

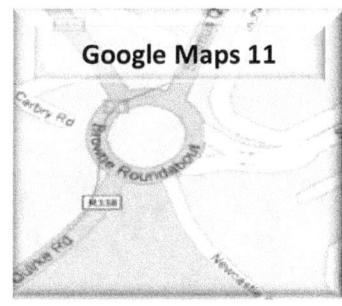
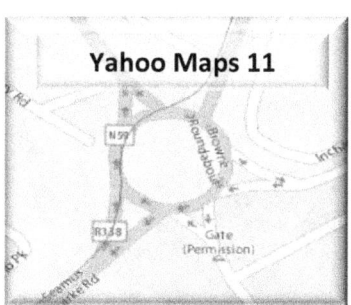

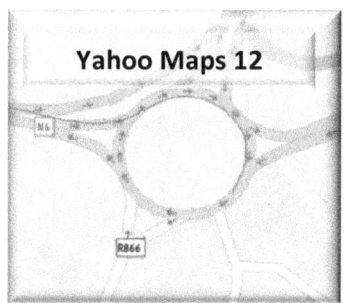

There are 16 pages in all and each one has a single page in the same format as the three previous pages.
To view any of these files in full go to the online resource for this book at:
http://www.irishapps.org/appendixb3.html

Online files:
Route001.pdf
Route002.pdf
Route003.pdf
Route004.pdf
Route005.pdf
Route006.pdf
Route007.pdf
Route008.pdf
Route009.pdf
Route010.pdf
Route011.pdf
Route012.pdf
Route013.pdf
Route014.pdf
Route015.pdf
Route016.pdf

C1. Photos and Videos from the GNSS Experiments

All photos and videos are available from the online resource at:
http://www.irishapps.org/appendixc1.html

Videos from Experiments 2.2.1 to 2.2.6:
2011-01-03 iPhone v Samsung GPS-Exp5.MOV
2011-01-05 iPhone v Samsung Google Maps-Exp5.MOV
2011-01-05 iPhone v Samsung GPS-Exp5.MOV
2011-01-20 iPhone v Samsung GPS1-Exp5.MOV
2011-01-20 iPhone v Samsung GPS2-Exp5.MOV
2011-01-25 iPhone v Samsung GPS1-Exp5.MOV
2011-01-25 iPhone v Samsung GPS2-Exp5.MOV
2011-01-25 iPhone v Samsung GPS3-Exp5.MOV
2011-01-25 iPhone v Samsung GPS4-Exp5.MOV
2011-03-07 iPh3v4vGalSvNexus GPS1-Exp7.MOV
2011-03-07 iPh3v4vGalSvNexus GPS2-Exp7.MOV
2011-03-07 iPh3v4vGalSvNexus GPS3-Exp7.MOV
2011-03-07 iPh3v4vGalSvNexus GPS4-Exp7.MOV
2011-03-07 iPh3v4vGalSvNexus GPS5-1-Exp7.MOV
2011-03-07 iPh3v4vGalSvNexus GPS5-2-Exp7.MOV
2011-03-07 iPh3v4vGalSvNexus GPS6-Exp7.MOV

C2. Photos and Videos from the 2D Code Experiments

All photos and videos are available from the online resource at:
http://www.irishapps.org/appendixc2.html

Videos from Experiments 2.10.1:
2011-03-01 iPhone and Samsung QRCode Exp6-1.MOV
2011-03-01 iPhone and Samsung QRCode Exp6-2.MOV

C3. Photos and Videos from the Bluetooth Experiments

All photos and videos are available from the online resource at:
http://www.irishapps.org/appendixc3.html

Photos from Experiments 2.6.1 to 2.6.6:
2011-03-18 Bluetooth 10m Mark.JPG
2011-03-18 Bluetooth 15m Mark.JPG
2011-03-18 Bluetooth 15m Mark2.JPG
2011-03-18 Bluetooth 1m Mark.JPG
2011-03-18 Bluetooth 20m Mark.JPG
2011-03-18 Bluetooth 25m Mark.JPG
2011-03-18 Bluetooth 30m Mark.JPG
2011-03-18 Bluetooth 5m Mark.JPG
2011-03-18 Bluetooth 5m Mark2.JPG
2011-03-18 Bluetooth 5m Mark3.JPG
2011-03-18 Bluetooth All Transmitters.JPG
2011-03-18 Bluetooth All Transmitters2.JPG
2011-03-18 Bluetooth Harness and Video.JPG
2011-03-18 Bluetooth Harness and Video2.JPG
2011-03-18 Bluetooth Stray Ref.JPG
2011-03-18 Bluetooth Transmitters 1-6.JPG
2011-03-18 Bluetooth Transmitters 12-16.JPG
2011-03-18 Bluetooth Transmitters 7-11.JPG

Videos from Experiments 2.6.1 to 2.6.6:
011-03-18 Bluetooth001.MOV
2011-03-18 Bluetooth002 1of2.MOV
2011-03-18 Bluetooth002 2of2.MOV
2011-03-19 Bluetooth Baseline 5m.MOV
2011-03-19 Bluetooth Double Glazing.MOV
2011-03-19 Bluetooth ExtWall and Window.MOV
2011-03-19 Bluetooth IntConc200mm.MOV
2011-03-19 Bluetooth IntDryWall 100mm.MOV
2011-03-19 Bluetooth IntGlass Laminated.MOV
2011-03-19 Bluetooth IntHollowcore.MOV

Photos from Experiment 2.6.7(Galway Shopping Ctr):
2011-03-21 Bluetooth Ashford.JPG
2011-03-21 Bluetooth Burton.JPG
2011-03-21 Bluetooth CarphoneWhouse.JPG
2011-03-21 Bluetooth Center.JPG
2011-03-21 Bluetooth CRTormey.JPG
2011-03-21 Bluetooth Cunniffe.JPG
2011-03-21 Bluetooth Eason.JPG
2011-03-21 Bluetooth Hallway1.JPG
2011-03-21 Bluetooth Hallway2.JPG
2011-03-21 Bluetooth Hallway3.JPG
2011-03-21 Bluetooth Hanley.JPG
2011-03-21 Bluetooth Hynes.JPG
2011-03-21 Bluetooth Libaas.JPG
2011-03-21 Bluetooth MattOFlaherty.JPG
2011-03-21 Bluetooth Scanning1.JPG
2011-03-21 Bluetooth Scanning2.JPG
2011-03-21 Bluetooth Scanning3.JPG
2011-03-21 Bluetooth Scanning4.JPG
2011-03-21 Bluetooth Zhavigo.JPG

Videos from Experiment 2.6.7(Galway Shopping Ctr):
2011-03-21 Bluetooth Ashford.MOV
2011-03-21 Bluetooth Burtons.MOV
2011-03-21 Bluetooth Car Phone Warehouse.MOV
2011-03-21 Bluetooth Center Jeweller.MOV
2011-03-21 Bluetooth CR Tormey.MOV
2011-03-21 Bluetooth Cunniffe Elect.MOV
2011-03-21 Bluetooth Eason.MOV
2011-03-21 Bluetooth Hanleys.MOV
2011-03-21 Bluetooth Hynes Shoes.MOV
2011-03-21 Bluetooth Libaas.MOV
2011-03-21 Bluetooth Matt OFlaherty.MOV
2011-03-21 Bluetooth OBriens.MOV
2011-03-21 Bluetooth Sarahs.MOV
2011-03-21 Bluetooth Zhavigo.MOV

Videos from Experiment 2.6.8(Pair and Share Data):
2011-03-22 Bluetooth Pairing Test01.MOV
2011-03-22 Bluetooth Pairing Test02.MOV
2011-03-22 Bluetooth Pairing Test03.MOV
2011-03-22 Bluetooth Pairing Test04.MOV
2011-03-22 Bluetooth Pairing Test05.MOV
2011-03-22 Bluetooth Pairing Test06.MOV
2011-03-22 Bluetooth Pairing Test07.MOV
2011-03-22 Bluetooth Pairing Test08.MOV
2011-03-22 Bluetooth Pairing Test09.MOV
2011-03-22 Bluetooth Pairing Test10.MOV

D1. NFC Enabled Mobile Phones

NFC Enabled Mobile Phones - March 2011
Nokia C7-00
Nokia 6212 Classic
Nokia 6131 NFC
Nokia 6680
Nokia 3220 + NFC Shell
Samsung S5230 Tocco Lite/Star/Player One/Avila
Samsung SGH-X700 NFC
Samsung D500E
SAGEM my700X Contactless
LG 600V
Motorola L7 (SLVR)
Benq T80
Sagem Cosyphone
Google Nexus S
Samsung Galaxy S II
Samsung Wave 578

www.ingramcontent.com/pod-product-compliance
Lightning Source LLC
Chambersburg PA
CBHW081045170526
45158CB00006B/1866